THE CHARLTON
STANDARD CATALOGUE OF

BESWICK
POTTERY

First Edition

By
Diana and John Callow

Publisher
W.K. Cross

The Charlton Press

Toronto, Ontario • Birmingham, Michigan

Canadian Cataloguing In Publication Data

Callow, Diana
    The Charlton standard catalogue of Beswick pottery

Includes index.
ISBN 0-88968-192-9

1. Beswick (Firm) - Catalogs. 2. Pottery figures - Collectors and collecting - England - Catalogs.
I. Callow, John, 1923 or 4-   II. Title

NK4210.B44C34 1997   738.8'2'029442   C97-931525-5

EDITORIAL

Editor	Jean Dale
Assistant Editor	Maria Angelica Villalba
Assistant Editor	Nicola Leedham
Graphic Technician	Davina Rowan
Photography	John Callow

ACKNOWLEDGMENTS

The Charlton Press wishes to thank those who have helped and assisted with the first edition of *The Charlton Standard Catalogue of Beswick Pottery*.

CONTRIBUTORS

The Publisher would like to thank the following individuals or companies who graciously supplied photographs or allowed us access to their collections for photographic purposes. We offer sincere thanks to:
Linda Brown, Glostershire, **Pamela Colclough** (deceased), Staffordshire, **Joyce Garrad**, Glostershire, **Linda Isgrove,** West Midlands, **Mavis and Peter Whitelock**, Buckinghamshire, the staff at **John Beswick** and the staff of **Royal Doulton**.

A SPECIAL NOTE TO COLLECTORS

We welcome and appreciate any comments or suggestions in regard to *The Charlton Standard Catalogue of Beswick Pottery*. As you proceed through the book you will find many illustration squares which contain only a line drawing from the Beswick shape book. It is our goal to replace these line drawings over time with actual photographs. We would greatly appreciate your help in this endeavour. If you would like to participate in pricing or supply previously unavailable data or information, please contact Jean Dale at (416) 488-1418.

**Printed in Canada
in the Province of Ontario**

Editorial Offices:
2040 Yonge Street, Suite 208
Toronto, Ontario M4S 1Z9

HOW TO USE THIS CATALOGUE

THE LISTINGS

This book has been designed to serve two specific purposes. First, to furnish the Beswick enthusiast with accurate listings containing vital information and photographs to aid in the building of a rewarding collection. Secondly, this publication provides Beswick collectors and dealers with current market prices for the complete line of Beswick pottery.

Within the individual listings, the pieces are listed in order of their shape number. After this number comes the item's name or description. Next comes Designer, the date of Issue and withdrawal (if exact date of withdrawal is not known we indicate the last time the piece was seen advertised through the designation "by"), Size (either height or diameter depending on the shape), and Colour(s). The Series to which the piece belongs (if applicable) is listed next. Lastly, the suggested retail price is given in American, Canadian and British funds.

A NOTE ON PRICING

In addition to providing accurate information, this catalogue gives readers the most up-to-date retail prices for Beswick pottery in American, Canadian and British currencies.

To accomplish this, The Charlton Press continues to access an international pricing panel of Beswick experts that submits prices based on both dealer and collector retail price activity. These market prices are carefully analysed and adjusted to reflect accurate valuations in each of these three markets.

Please be aware that all prices given in a particular currency are for figures within that particular country. The prices published herein have not been calculated using exchange rates exclusively. They have been determined solely by supply and demand within the country in question.

A necessary word of caution. No pricing catalogue can be, or should be, a fixed price list. This catalogue, therefore, should be considered as a pricing guide only - showing the most current retail prices based on market demand within a particular region for the various items.

Prices published herein are for pieces in mint condition. Collectors are cautioned that a repaired or restored piece may be worth as little as 50 per cent of the value of the same piece in mint condition.

A NOTE ON THE PHOTOGRAPHS

In some cases, drawings of models have been used to represent unobtainable pieces. The reader is cautioned that all photographs so utilized are to be used for model characteristics only. More specific details concerning a piece (i.e. size) should be determined from the information listed below the photograph.

CONTENTS

INTRODUCTION

We have been collecting Beswick Ware for many many years, drawn into the hobby when we first realized the quality of the Beswick products. We soon developed into Beswick addicts. At that time we pursued our hobby in isolation, visiting Collectors Fairs trying to add to our increasing family of "Beswicks." As we progressed along the way we thirsted for information. We had acquired Collectors Book No. 4 and a few odd bits and pieces - really only scraps of information - and thought it was time to make a real effort to gather the knowledge we were seeking. We therefore wrote to Royal Doulton asking for information about specific models.

Subsequently it was suggested that we should visit the Beswick factory at Gold Street, Longton, Stoke-on-Trent and on the first of several visits we discovered that little direct information on early production was available. Fortunately, there we met and were greatly assisted by the late Pamela Colclough, who had accumulated a small archive of early price lists etc. In addition we were able to study and make notes from the "Shape Book," a record started at the factory in the early nineteen thirties, containing sketches of most of the pieces, together with entries which gave the designer's names and the modelling dates.

We learnt that only from the 1930s had any form of backstamp been used, and that most of these had been in use for many years and were then still current. Therefore, backstamps cannot generally be used as a means of dating.

We quickly realized that we needed to locate other collectors, who like ourselves, were interested in finding out more about the Beswick models. This we thought hopefully would in turn lead to discovering additional information.

Based on our previous experience as members of a collecting society, we decided to take the plunge and start a collector's club of our own for Beswick enthusiasts. The Beswick Collectors Circle, as it was named, was started during 1985 and continued until our retirement as Co-ordinators at the end of 1995.

The aim of this present book, written by Collectors for Collectors, is to provide a guide to Beswick decorative and other ware covering the period from the foundation of the company in 1894 to 1973. By 1973 the take-over by Royal Doulton had taken place and all production of this type of ware had ceased.

We hope that this book will serve as a useful guide and as a means by which you will be able to identify the models quickly. The arrangement of the chapters has been chosen with this object in mind and to make this process as easy as possible. Many of the models have been illustrated by using photographs and where this has not been possible we have done our best to show you what these shapes would have looked like by a variety of other means.

History of the Company

The following short history of the company is based on contemporary articles from *The Pottery Gazette*.

The earliest reference to the company we have found is the advertisement illustrated below, which is from the January 1st, 1894 issue of *The Pottery Gazette*.

This is the year now accepted for the start of the company, although Beswick catalogues of the 1960s give 1896 as the year of its foundation. The content of the advertisement however leads one to suppose that the firm of J. W. BESWICK was already well established as a manufacturer of pottery, so great is the variety of articles on offer.

Success must have followed on very quickly for James Wright Beswick. His company rapidly grew as a manufacturer of earthenware and majolica with a reputation for quality at a competitive price. By August, 1896 we read that "owing to increase of business" a second premises had been taken, the Britannia Works in High Street, Longton, where china was produced. Only two years later at the beginning of 1898 the Gold Street works, still the home of Beswick today, had been acquired and by 1899 was in full operation.

J. W. BESWICK,

BALTIMORE WORKS, ALBION STREET, LONGTON,

MANUFACTURER OF

Majolica and Earthenware Specialities.   **Leading Lines in Majolica Jugs.**
Gilt Jugs in all Decorations. Figures of all descriptions. Flower Pots and Pedestals in all Colours. Hanging Pots with or without Chains. Cheese Stands, Bread Trays, Spittoons, Green Glaze Plates and Comports, Hand-painted Vases in Newest Styles of Decoration, &c. &c.

SPECIAL LINES IN CHINA, JET, AND ROCKINGHAM,
SUITABLE FOR HOME AND EXPORT.

PRICES SENT ON APPLICATION.

Advertisement from the Pottery Gazette January 1894

The year 1899 also marked the end of production at the Baltimore Works. Production of china was restarted in 1908 at the King Street Works, formerly of Bridgett & Bates, and continued for a while under the old name. From 1915 china was produced at the Warwick Works, Chadwick Street until 1930, when production of all china ceased. (Note this guide does not deal with any of the china, such as "Warwick" china, marketed with a backstamp of Beswick & Sons and a crown).

By 1905 the Britannia Works had also been given up and production concentrated at Gold Street where additions and alterations had been made to the premises.

When James Wright Beswick died in 1920, at the age of seventy-five, the firm was taken over by his son John, whose name lives on today. John died in 1934 and was succeeded by his son, John Ewart Beswick, who became Chairman and Managing Director.

"Mr. Ewart," as he was always known, had worked in the business since leaving school, as also had Mr. Ewart's uncle, Mr. Gilbert Beswick who was half-brother to John. "Mr. Gilbert" also joined in the management of the company at that time and was later appointed Sales Director about 1960. When in the late 1960s, Ewart Beswick was ready to retire, no member of the immediate family was available to carry on the business, and the company was incorporated into the Royal Doulton Group.

Initially a private company, Beswick became a private limited company in 1938. It was converted to a public limited company in 1957 and became part of the Royal Doulton Group in 1969.

The Early Years - 1894 to 1934

A description of the exhibit at "The Furnishing Trades Exhibition and Market" at the Agricultural Hall, Islington, London, in March, 1898, at which about twenty exhibits only, were devoted to pottery, reads as follows:

"Mr. J.W. Beswick, of Albion Street and High Street, Longton, made a good display with his majolica ware. Flower pots, suspension pots, jugs, spittoons, baskets, pedestals and pots, umbrella stands and bread trays showed the variety of his manufactures. His earthenware exhibits comprised samples of toilet ware — many shapes and decorations — dinner and tea ware and a good assortment of jugs. His other exhibits comprised C.C ware, china tea ware and jet and Rockingham ware. In these were shown some nicely-shaped teapots. Fancy goods included vases, pots, figures, cheese stands and covers and bread trays. Altogether it was a very good and nicely-assorted exhibit."

The figures mentioned above were probably the Staffordshire type mantle-piece ornaments in the shape of generals, gardeners, milkmaids, dogs etc., which had been popular fifty years before, and surprisingly for which there was still a demand. A special line were the "Staffordshire dogs," made in nine sizes. These were facing left and right in pairs, in white and gold or red and black, and were very similar in shape to those in production today.

The following illustrations from *The Pottery Gazette* for February 1901 and March 1905 show some of the products listed above.

An assortment of Beswick Ware including Flown Blue

Left to right: Spiral shaped teacup and saucer, "Queen" teapot, "Britannia" flower pot, "Roseberry" flower pot, "Durban" flower pot, "Paris" cup and saucer. Bottom (left to right): Staffordshire dog, "Jap" vase, "Alexandra" vase, umbrella stand, "York" vase, "Victoria" vase and Swan flower pot

Left to right - "Trent" Jug, "Princess" Flower Pot and "Acme" Jug

"Acme" shaped Toilet Set - Jug and Ewer

By 1908 we read that " Mr. J. W. Beswick is a manufacturer of useful domestic ware in great variety. He makes goods of the popular class, both as to appearance and price. He aims at giving good value, and, though he does not manufacture the highest grades, he has some very good lines. He is well known for his jugs, and produces many excellent patterns on good useful shapes."

J. W. Beswick was known principally as a manufacturer of earthenware, and in the illustration, shown below, from *The Pottery Gazette* for April, 1913 everything, with the exception of the ewer and basin, was entirely new for that year.

Production of such items would have spanned a number of years and therefore it is not possible to know exactly in which year any particular piece would have been made.

Unfortunately, these items of early manufacture do not carry a backstamp or any marking by which they can be easily recognized. One needs to have some knowledge of the shapes produced (see page xvi to xx) and the decorations employed, before early pieces can be identified.

On later pieces shape names and/or numbers may be impressed or a decoration number may be present, as an aid to identification. The various patterns used were interchangeable with the various shapes, and vice versa.

The clock set is described as having a blue ground with painted game figures, stippled in gold, and four sizes were available. The vase on the left is in the "Aden" shape and the one on the right "Alexandra". The flowerpots are "Douglas" and "Fulham" shapes. An example of the "Douglas" shape in a decoration typical of the mid-1920s can be seen on page 440. It was available in five sizes ranging from 6 ½" to 10 ½"

Below may be seen a variety of shapes:

Two shapes of toilet ware dating from 1925 are shown above, the "York" and "Victory,"
the latter may also be seen in a different decoration in the colour plate No 4/4

A selection of items dating from June 1928. Left to Right - "Rita" Vase (7" tall), "Regent" Bowl
(8 ½" diameter), "Len" Vase (8 ½" tall) and "Rena" Vase (7" tall)

A selection of Vases dating from September 1929. Left to Right - "Lille" (10 ½" tall), "Rhos" (9" tall),
"Stafford" (6" tall), "Regal" (6" tall) and "Roslin (10 ½" tall)

Also we have the coloured plates which show more of the shapes available. The vase 9" tall with the shape name "Blythe" (see plate 2/4) must have been popular, as many examples have been seen in various decorations. The pair of vases shape name "Albany," 11 ½" tall, decorated with a pattern of carmine roses picked out in gilt on a jet-black background carry a much earlier decoration number, 3072. This decoration was evidently a success when introduced, for it continued to be available until 1930, which probably explains why so many pieces decorated with this design have survived to turn up relatively often at fairs.

The "Bluebird" pattern (decoration number 6155) is shown on another pair of vases in the "Sale" shape (see plate 3/2). This decoration is a lithographed design in attractive colours, and is also fairly common today. As well as being employed on vases, as in this illustration, it was used on teapots, candlesticks and pieces for a dressing table or trinket set. This style of decoration must have been well-liked, because we have noticed its use on a number of pieces, which have not been made at the Beswick factory. The Beswick decoration number should remove all doubt as to origin.

At the time the Shape Book was started, in the early 1930s, shape names were being replaced by shape numbers, although there was a period of overlap.

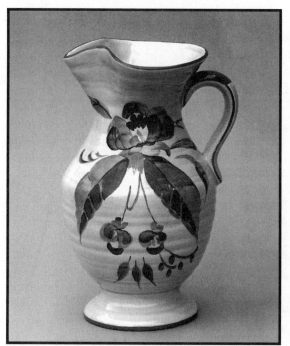

For example the jug, shown here, with the name "Ruth" and the backstamp "Beswick Handcraft," later carried the impressed number "72," alone or together with the name "Ruth."
This jug, in a satin matt finish, has a cream background with orange trim on the base, rim and handle. The decoration is in blue, brown, orange and green.

Fashions change, in pottery as in all things, and whereas in the early days, a pronounced demand was encountered for pottery of the more highly coloured type, as the 1930s approached, a softer, less flamboyant style of decoration was being demanded.

The vase shown below reflects this change. It is impressed with the shape name "Rhos" and is beautifully decorated with hand-painted blue, white, yellow and black flowers. On a mottled grey background it is finished in a matt glaze. Surprisingly the flowers, the rim and the base are still picked out in gilt.

This style of decoration marked the transition between the earlier more ornate products and the large number of jugs, vases etc. decorated with matt glazes, in well over two hundred shapes, which followed.

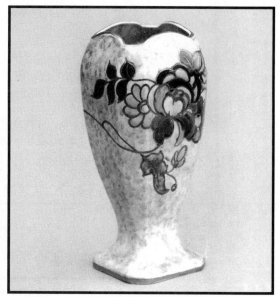

Rhos Vase

Prices continued to be aimed at a level to sell readily in the popular markets, while at the same time the quality of the products was maintained or even improved, with new designs and decorations being shown at the British Industries Fairs. These new shapes continued to be modelled at a rapidly increasing rate, and employed lithographed designs which were inexpensive, or were decorated in hand-painted styles in underglaze or enamel colours, which reflected a tendency to move towards a superior product.

The advertisement from *The Pottery Gazette* dated May 1st, 1930, shown on the following page, marks the introduction of the "Beswick Ware" logo. This logo was also used for many years as a backstamp.

Beswick Ware.

What about it?

A sound body with a brilliant, non-absorbent, non-crazing glaze fashioned in hundreds of shapes in fancy and useful earthenware.

Beautifully decorated quick-selling lines

VASES, POTS, ROSE BOWLS, FLOATING BOWLS, CLOCK SETS, BISCUITS, TOILETS & TRINKETS, JUGS, TEAPOTS, Etc.   Everything the householder needs in earthenware.

Send for price lists and illustrations or visit our showrooms either at the factory or at Buchanan Buildings, Holborn, London.

JOHN BESWICK, GOLD STREET, LONGTON

This advertisement from The Pottery Gazette (May 1, 1930) marks the introduction of the "Beswick Ware" logo. This logo was also used for many years as a backstamp.

The arrangement of the pieces in this illustration probably accounts for the use of the name "Cosy" which is impressed on the base, because the individual items nestle together in depressions in the tray. The decoration is in a strong orange typical of the period with white, black and gold.

At the same time, as the above advertisement suggests, due to the less prosperous nature of the times, there was a move away from purely ornamental wares to those of greater utility. We find that as the demand for ornamental wares declined, John Beswick turned his attention increasingly to tableware, with the single exception of dinner sets, and as had always been his custom, to novelties in a large variety of styles.

The Pottery Gazette for October 1931 reported an increasing business in such lines as "cosy" sets (teapot, hot-water jug and cream on a tray), egg sets, cruet sets, triple trays and the like.

By 1932, all sorts of new and attractive lines were much in evidence — lines which were both useful and ornamental. For example the "Wild Rose" design finished off in silver, which can be seen in the photograph for the Preserve (Shape 53, Miscellaneous Chapter). Also there was a hollyhock decoration in a similar finish and a marigold design with an orange edge.

In place of the grounded and panelled, stippled and gilt vases and clock sets, the new shapes had pleasing lines and simple decorations.

The Salad Ware series was prominent among the new creations and a range known as "Gardena" Ware, modelled in the form of flowers embossed and tinted in pastel shades was also introduced at this time. Items in this series are shown here and in the coloured plate 4/1.

New jug-vases in six different styles of decoration were launched to compete with Conintental designs.

Displayed on the John Beswick stand at the British Industries Fair in 1933, a newly modelled series of tableware known as "Flowerkist" (see plate 4/2) attracted the attention of Queen Mary, who purchased a quantity of this pattern. One can see that it was a most appealing design of sweetpeas on a background resembling wickerwork. (The royal patronage was later recognized by the use of a backstamp stating "As purchased by Her Majesty The Queen").

Both the Queen and the Duchess of York (the present Queen Mother) also purchased items of Salad Ware, some with a green ground and some with primrose.

Also featured on the stand were pieces of a range of table sundries modelled to depict a thatched cottages. The forerunner for the Cottage Ware series is shown here.

"Gardena" Ware

'Thatched Cottage' - a forerunner to the Cottage Ware Series

Beswick shapes shown in an advertisement in 1934

1933 also saw the introduction of a number of jugs and vases decorated with a matt glaze. So successful were they, that a firm of pottery distributors, G. Hardy & Co., of Nottingham, negotiated with John Beswick to have a number of these ornamental lines and other novelties produced to their own shapes and designs. These were originally sold under the name of "Trentham Art Ware," but when the arrangement ended, about seven years later, many pieces remained in production to be sold under the Beswick name.

Sadly John Beswick did not live to see the great growth in these and similar lines and in the new novelties that were introduced as, after a long illness, he died in October 1934.

In the years that followed there was great activity and each year that passed saw the introduction of an increasing number of new shapes in ornamental ware and novelties. These new shapes were mostly the work of modellers working on a freelance basis. Production was supervised by James Hayward the Decorating Manager, who was responsible for the continued development of the matt glazes, which had proved so successful. Examples of these can be found in a great variety of mostly soft colours, in browns, blues, greens and yellows, to name but a few.

The War Years 1939-1945

Restrictions on the home front and the need to export as much as possible, resulted in many changes of emphasis in production. Fortunately the company continued to operate successfully during these very difficult times.

The outbreak of war in 1939 coincided with what, at first sight, would seem to be a surprising and dramatic expansion in, and a change in the nature of, the products from the Beswick factory. The stimulus for all this activity was the need for Britain at that time to export in order to survive, and in the period to the end of 1945, around three hundred new shapes were added. With the European companies being prevented from exporting, Beswick seized their chance to expand their markets overseas, and particularly into the then Dominions.

War time controls imposed on the home market by the Board of Trade, restricted domestic sales to everyday articles. Beswick was no exception and even their breakfast and tea-ware with a minimum decoration of three gold lines, was later reduced to one gold line! Production of vases, jugs and bowls in a great variety of shapes and decorations in the plain, embossed and incised styles for which Beswick had been noted for a number of years continued and eighty per cent of their output was accounted for by export.

On a personal note

In 1985 when we founded The Beswick Collectors Circle we had no idea of the impact which would result from our actions. We soon found out that the world was full of Beswick Collectors and the interest in Beswick Ware was greater that we could have ever foreseen.

Little notices, on the factory's products, soon turned up at Collectors Fairs - a new innovation for Beswick pieces in those days - and the word was spreading rapidly that Beswick was ready to take its place in the collecting world. This happened almost overnight.

The Circle was the first club to be formed for collectors of Beswick, and in the ten years during which we were the Co-ordinators, we saw the introduction of special Auctions for Beswick Ware, Collectors Fairs with dealers specialising in Beswick, books written especially for Beswick collectors, special Beswick models being commissioned, and the House of Beswick established in the world of collecting for all time.

Our aim was to get the products of Beswick appreciated for their quality, both in the modelling and in the decorations applied to the great variety of shapes - something for everyone to enjoy.

When we retired from The Circle in 1995 a new Beswick Club was formed and the interest in Beswick goes from "strength to strength". We hope that for years to come many people will enjoy the hobby as much as we have done and still do, especially the search for that elusive piece.

We wish you all, as we used to say, "Happy Beswicking."

Diana and John Callow

A Guide to Identification

For pieces produced prior to 1930, after which time the script "Beswick Ware" backstamp is likely to be present, only a hand-painted decoration number or an impressed shape name may be found. By 1900, the decoration numbering had already reached around the 1000 mark, by 1914 around 2500, and by 1932 was approaching 7000!

To assist in identification we have included:

Shape Names: An alphabetical listing of a selection of shape names, together with the corresponding shape numbers where known.

Shape names or numbers may be impressed on the underside of a piece. In some instances the shape number may be stamped.

Shape Illustrations: Illustrations of a variety of early shapes. Many of these shapes continued in production after the introduction of the shape book and were allocated shape numbers.

Backstamps: Illustrations of the variety of backstamps, in rough chronological order, used by Beswick.

SHAPE NAMES AND NUMBERS

Shape Name	Shape Number	Item	Shape Name	Shape Number	Item	Shape Name	Shape Number	Item
Acme		Toilet set	Eric		Flower holder	Regent		Plant pot
Aden		Vase	Eric		Clock case	Rena		Vase
Albany		Handled vase	Eton		Flower holder	Rheims		Plant pot
Alexandra		Vase	Eton		Vase	Rhos	57	Vase
Alpha	64	Vase	Exeter		Vase	Rita		Covered jar
Arran	68	Vase	Flora	58	Vase	Rome	53	Preserve
Arras		Vase	Fulham		Plant pot	Rose	56	Vase
Athens		Vase	Hague		Vase	Roslin	54	Vase
Avon			Holborn		Handled vase	Rouen		Handled vase
Baltic		Plant Pot	Iris	104		Royal	63	
Bell	110	Vase	Italian		Handled vase	Ruby	115	Vase
Blythe	106	Vase	Kelt	67		Ruth	72	Jug
Bow		Vase	Kew	113		Ryde	55	Vase
Bude	52	Vase	Laurie		Covered vase	Rye		Vase
Castle Brush			Leeds		Vase	Sale		Handled vase
Ciro	70	Vase	Len	59	Vase	Sandon		Flower holder
Cleo	65	Vase	Leyden	50	Vase	Sparta	107	Vase
Clyde			Lille	105	Vase	Stafford		Flower holder
Crete	66	Vase	Lily	109	Vase	Sudan		Flower holder
Cuba		Covered Vase	Looe	49	Vase	Toy		Clock case
Deal		Vase	Louvain		Covered jar	Toy		Flower holder
Delhi		Vase	Lynn		Handled vase	Trent		Shallow bowl
Delta	71	Vase	Lynton	111	Vase	Troy		Vase
Doris		Flower Holder	Malta		Vase	Tyne	103	
Dresden	122	Vase	Mona	112	Ash tray	Vera		Flower holder
Douglas		Plant pot	Monmouth		Flower holder	Victoria		Covered vase
Durbar		Covered vase	Nankin		Covered vase	Victory		Toilet set
Dutch			Octagon			Warwick		Clock case
Edam		Vase	Opal	51	Vase	Windsor		Plant pot
Egypt		Covered vase	Oxford		Flower holder	Windsor	60	Vase
Eler	69	Vase	Pearl		Vase	Wye		Vase
Elite	73	Vase	Pekin		Covered vase	York		Toilet set
Ena		Flower holder	Princess		Plant pot	York	108	Vase
Ena		Plant pot	Regal	61	Vase			

SHAPES

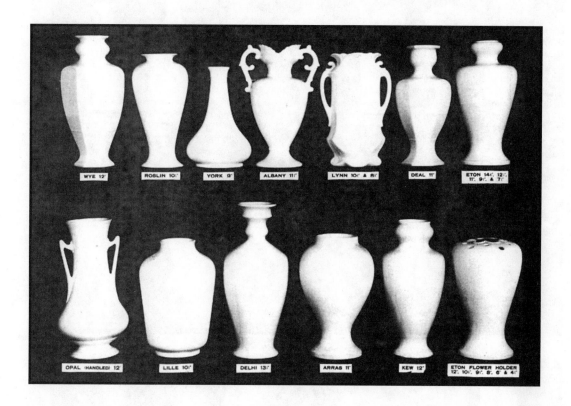

RYDE 10½"   RHOS 9"   FLORA 8½", 7½" & 6½"   BOW 11"   RUBY 9"   SPARTA 9½"   TROY 9"

HOLBORN 13½"   ATHENS (HANDLED) 13"   DURBAR 17" & 20"   EXETER 13"   SALE (HANDLED) 13½"

ROSE 8½", 7½" & 6½"   LYNTON 7½"   BLYTHE 9"   LILY 5½"   LEEDS 9"   RENA 7½"   WINDSOR 9"

ROUEN 16" & 15"   VICTORIA 20", 18" & 16"   NANKIN 20", 18" & 16"   PEKIN 19", 18" & 17"

ENA DIAM 9"

WINDSOR 7½", 5½", 4½", 4" & 3½" DIAM

BALTIC 9½", 8½", 7½" & 6½" DIAM

DOUGLAS 10½", 9½", 8½", 7½" & 6½" DIAM

PRINCESS 9½" DIAM

RHEIMS 11½", 10" & 8½" DIAM

REGENT 9½", 8½" & 7½" DIAM

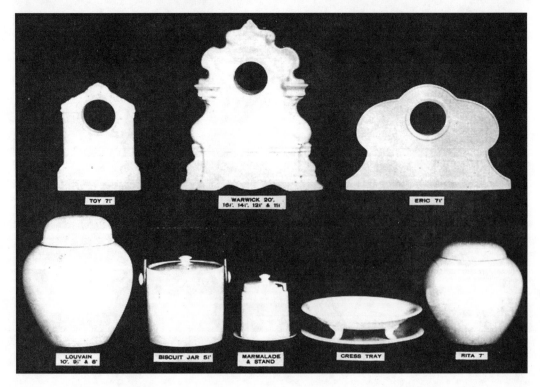

TOY 7½"

WARWICK 20", 16½", 14½", 12½" & 11½"

ERIC 7½"

LOUVAIN 10", 9½" & 8"

BISCUIT JAR 5½"

MARMALADE & STAND

CRESS TRAY

RITA 7"

BACKSTAMPS

Backstamp 1 — Beswick Ware ENGLAND

Backstamp 1 is of the earliest printed backstamp. It may also be found with "ENGLAND" replaced by "MADE IN ENGLAND" and with the addition of "MADE IN ENGLAND" impressed in the base.

Backstamp 2 — Beswick Handcraft
ENGLAND

Backstamp 2 shows a version used on more highly decorated pieces, in this case on a jug, "Ruth", the colours are strong and the decoration is of deco style flowers and leaves.

Backstamp 3 — Impressed name and
MADE IN ENGLAND

Backstamp 3 illustrates a style which gave the name of the decoration as well as the decoration number. The shape name, in this case "ROME" is impressed, together with "MADE IN ENGLAND."

Backstamp 4 — "H. M. THE QUEEN"

Backstamp 4 shows a backstamp announcing royal patronage, The Queen mentioned here is Queen Mary, the wife of King George V.

Backstamp 5 — "H.M. QUEEN MARY"

Backstamp 5 is the backstamp which can be found on items of the "Sundial" pattern. The form of words was necessary because after the death of King George V, Queen Mary became the Queen Mother. The registration number corresponds with the year 1938.

Backstamp 6 — TRENTHAM ART WARE

Backstamp 6 is the backstamp used for the Trentham Art Wares. A gummed label with similar wording was also used.

Widely used backstamps, many of them still current, are illustrated below.

In addition to the first small gummed seal, green with gold lettering, an alternative larger oval style with gold lettering on a black or red ground was used. The small green seal was replaced by the small oval style.

Backstamp 7 — Small gummed seal (first style) green with gold lettering

Backstamp 10 — Circular BESWICK ENGLAND

Backstamp 8 — Small gummed label (second style) green with gold lettering

Backstamp 11 — Oval BESWICK ENGLAND

Backstamp 9 — Large gummed seal

Backstamp 12 — BESWICK ENGLAND

Backstamp 13 — BESWICK 'B' ENGLAND

SECTION ONE
SERIES WARE

Victoria No. 1 Deco 3013

CM SERIES

In addition to the "contemporary" models of animals and birds (see *The Charlton Standard Catalogue of Beswick Animals*) which formed part of this series, Colin Melbourne also modelled a collection of nineteen ornamental pieces, mainly bowls and vases.

These items, as with the animals and birds, represented a break with the Beswick tradition and ventured into an area where there were unsatisfied demands. It was an attempt to produce commercially, wares which had before that time been the province of the studio potter.

Their appeal relied on their shape, enhanced by the texture of the glaze and the decoration, for which James Hayward, the Decorating Manager at that time, was responsible. The colours were subdued and subtle with glazes combining the use of gloss and matt finishes, in a variety of colours. Examples are also known decorated in copper lustre. The shapes were intended to match the contemporary scene of the time, and an advertisement in January, 1957 proclaimed "Modern in Conception - High Aesthetic Merit and Workmanship."

Today these shapes are either very much admired or thoroughly disliked, there does not seem to be room for half measures! Following their introduction their popularity proved to be relatively short-lived, as most had been withdrawn by 1963.

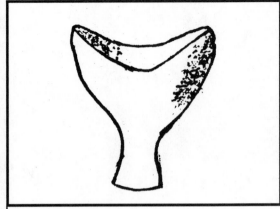

Shape 1392 Vase

Designer:	Colin Melbourne in 1956
Issued:	1957 - by 1963
Height:	9 ½", 24.0 cm
Colour:	Assorted colours, including copper lustre

Market	Range
U.S.A.	$20.00 - 60.00
Canada	$30.00 - 90.00
U.K.	£10.00 - 30.00

Shape 1393 Vase

Designer:	Colin Melbourne in 1956
Issued:	1957 - by 1963
Height:	5 ¾", 14.6 cm
Colour:	Assorted colours, including copper lustre

Market	Range
U.S.A.	$20.00 - 60.00
Canada	$30.00 - 90.00
U.K.	£10.00 - 30.00

Shape 1394 Vase

Designer:	Colin Melbourne in 1956
Issued:	1957 - by 1963
Height:	7", 17.8 cm
Colour:	Assorted colours, including copper lustre

Market	Range
U.S.A.	$20.00 - 60.00
Canada	$30.00 - 90.00
U.K.	£10.00 - 30.00

Shape 1395 Vase

Designer:	Colin Melbourne in 1956
Issued:	1957 - by 1962
Height :	11 ¾", 29.8 cm
Colour:	Assorted colours, including copper lustre

Market	Range
U.S.A.	$20.00 - 60.00
Canada	$30.00 - 90.00
U.K.	£10.00 - 30.00

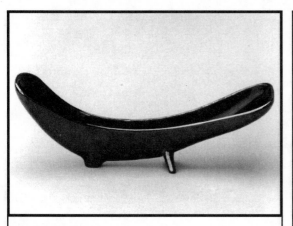

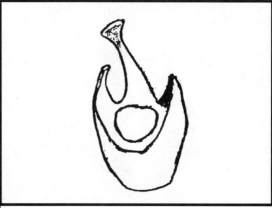

Shape 1396 Bowl

Designer:	Colin Melbourne in 1956
Issued:	1957 - by 1963
Length:	10 ½″, 26.7 cm
Colour:	Assorted colours, including copper lustre

Market	Range
U.S.A.	$20.00 - 60.00
Canada	$30.00 - 90.00
U.K.	£10.00 - 30.00

Shape 1397 Vase

Designer:	Colin Melbourne in 1956
Issued:	1957 - by 1963
Height :	7 ¾″, 19.7 cm
Colour:	Assorted colours, including copper lustre

Market	Range
U.S.A.	$20.00 - 60.00
Canada	$30.00 - 90.00
U.K.	£10.00 - 30.00

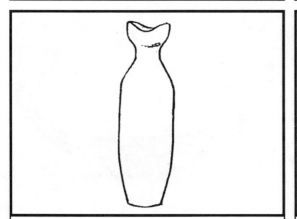

Shape 1398 Vase

Designer:	Colin Melbourne in 1956
Issued:	1957 - by 1963
Height:	11 ½″, 29.2 cm
Colour:	Assorted colours, including copper lustre

Market	Range
U.S.A.	$20.00 - 60.00
Canada	$30.00 - 90.00
U.K.	£10.00 - 30.00

Shape 1399 Vase

Designer:	Colin Melbourne in 1956
Issued:	1957 - by 1963
Height :	6″, 15.0 cm
Colour:	Assorted colours, including copper lustre

Market	Range
U.S.A.	$20.00 - 60.00
Canada	$30.00 - 90.00
U.K.	£10.00 - 30.00

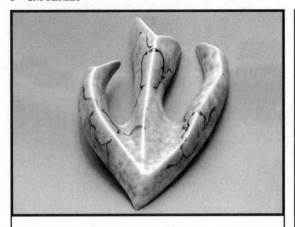

Photograph not
available
at press time

Shape 1400 Wall vase

Designer: Colin Melbourne in 1956
Issued: 1957 - by 1963
Height: 7 ½", 19.1 cm
Colour: Assorted colours, including copper lustre

Market	Range
U.S.A.	$20.00 - 60.00
Canada	$30.00 - 90.00
U.K.	£10.00 - 30.00

Shape 1401 Vase

Designer: Colin Melbourne in 1956
Issued: 1957 - by 1963
Size: Unknown
Colour: Assorted colours, including copper lustre

Market	Range
U.S.A.	$20.00 - 60.00
Canada	$30.00 - 90.00
U.K.	£10.00 - 30.00

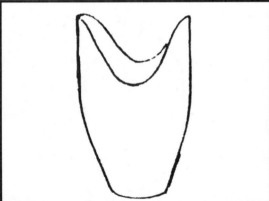

Shape 1402 Vase

Designer: Colin Melbourne in 1956
Issued: 1957 - by 1963
Height: 7 ½", 19.1 cm
Colour: Assorted colours, including copper lustre

Market	Range
U.S.A.	$20.00 - 60.00
Canada	$30.00 - 90.00
U.K.	£10.00 - 30.00

Shape 1403 Bowl

Designer: Colin Melbourne in 1956
Issued: 1957 - by 1969
Length: 14 ½", 36.8 cm
Colour: Assorted colours, including copper lustre

Market	Range
U.S.A.	$20.00 - 60.00
Canada	$30.00 - 90.00
U.K.	£10.00 - 30.00

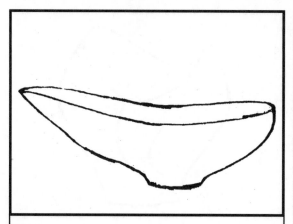

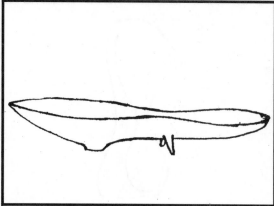

Shape 1404 Bowl

Designer:	Colin Melbourne in 1956
Issued:	1957 - by 1966
Length:	9 ¾", 24.7 cm
Colour:	Assorted colours, including copper lustre

Market	Range
U.S.A.	$20.00 - 60.00
Canada	$30.00 - 90.00
U.K.	£10.00 - 30.00

Shape 1405 Bowl

Designer:	Colin Melbourne in 1956
Issued:	1957 - by 1963
Length:	14", 35.5 cm
Colour:	Assorted colours, including copper lustre

Market	Range
U.S.A.	$20.00 - 60.00
Canada	$30.00 - 90.00
U.K.	£10.00 - 30.00

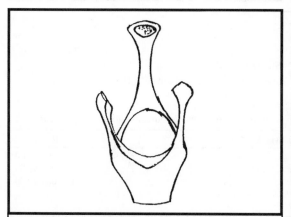

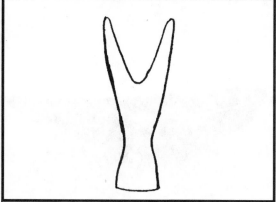

Shape 1408 Pot holder

Designer:	Colin Melbourne in 1956
Issued:	1957 - by 1963
Height:	14", 35.5 cm
Colour:	Assorted colours, including copper lustre

Market	Range
U.S.A.	$20.00 - 60.00
Canada	$30.00 - 90.00
U.K.	£10.00 - 30.00

Shape 1466 Vase

Designer:	Colin Melbourne in 1956
Issued:	1957 - by 1963
Height :	8 ¾", 22.2 cm
Colour:	Assorted colours, including copper lustre

Market	Range
U.S.A.	$20.00 - 60.00
Canada	$30.00 - 90.00
U.K.	£10.00 - 30.00

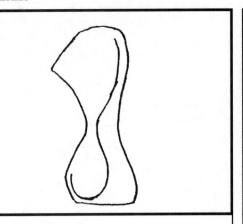

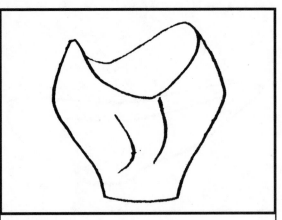

Shape 1477 Lamp base

Designer: Colin Melbourne in 1957
Issued: 1957 - by 1963
Size: Unknown
Colour: Assorted colours, including copper lustre

Market	Range
U.S.A.	$20.00 - 60.00
Canada	$30.00 - 90.00
U.K.	£10.00 - 30.00

Shape 1478 Pot vase

Designer: Colin Melbourne in 1957
Issued: 1957 - by 1963
Height: 6 ½", 16.5 cm
Colour: Assorted colours, including copper lustre

Market	Range
U.S.A.	$20.00 - 60.00
Canada	$30.00 - 90.00
U.K.	£10.00 - 30.00

Shape 1479 Bowl

Designer: Colin Melbourne in 1957
Issued: 1957 - by 1966
Length: 8 ½", 21.6 cm
Colour: Assorted colours, including copper lustre

Market	Range
U.S.A.	$20.00 - 60.00
Canada	$30.00 - 90.00
U.K.	£10.00 - 30.00

COTTAGE WARE

Items of tableware modelled to depict thatched cottages were first introduced at the British Industries Fair in April, 1933, and were an immediate success. Their popularity is obvious by the fact that most items continued to be available until they were all withdrawn at the beginning of 1971. Examples of another item, modelled as a cottage with a removable roof, have also been found. This is an earlier piece, as it does not carry a shape number it is illustrated on page xiii of the introduction.

The "Cottage Ware" series had an embossed and hand-painted decoration with trees and flowers. The thatch was usually light brown, with the tops of the chimneys painted in dark brown. Shape numbers 243, 247, 248 and 1128 however, have been found with grey chimney tops.

Some shapes were produced during the 1930s only, with the thatch in "helio-blue." These items have a more detailed and colourful decoration, and in our experience are very rare.

The numbered series consisted of 23 items, all in a gloss finish and included a cheese dish in the shape of Log Cabin and a cruet of "Tudor" houses.

Shape 239   Teapot, large

Designer: Mr. White in 1932
Issued: 1933 - 1970
Height: 6", 15.0 cm
Colour: Cream, light and dark brown

Description	U.S. $	Can. $	U.K. £
Teapot, large	110.00	150.00	55.00

Shape 240   Teapot, small

Designer: Mr. White in 1932
Issued: 1933 - 1970
Height :   5 ¼", 13.3 cm
Colour: Cream, light and dark brown

Description	U.S. $	Can. $	U.K. £
Teapot, small	90.00	125.00	45.00

Shape 241   Hot water jug

Designer: Mr. White in 1932
Issued: 1933 - 1970
Height: 6 ¾", 17.2 cm
Colour: Cream, light and dark brown

Description	U.S. $	Can. $	U.K. £
Hot water jug	100.00	150.00	50.00

Shape 242   Milk jug

Designer: Mr. White in 1932
Issued: 1933 - 1970
Height: 4 ½", 11.9 cm
Colour: Cream, light and dark brown

Description	U.S. $	Can. $	U.K. £
Milk jug	60.00	90.00	30.00

Shape 243   Covered sugar, round

Designer:	Mr. White in 1932
Issued:	1933 - 1970
Height:	4 ¾", 12.1 cm
Colour:	Cream, light and dark brown

Description	U.S. $	Can. $	U.K. £
Covered sugar round	60.00	90.00	30.00

Note: Also known with grey chimney top.

Shape 244   Covered preserve, rectangular

Designer:	Mr. White in 1932
Issued:	1. 1933 - 1970
	2. 1930s only
Height :	3 ¾", 9.5 cm
Colour:	1. Cream, light and dark brown
	2. Helio-blue

Colour	U.S. $	Can. $	U.K. £
1. Cream and browns	70.00	100.00	35.00
2. Helio-blue		Rare	

Shape 245   Open Sugar

Designer:	Mr. White in 1932
Issued:	1. 1933 - 1970
	2. 1930s only
Height:	2 ¾", 7.0 cm
Colour:	1. Cream, light and dark brown
	2. Helio-blue

Colour	U.S. $	Can. $	U.K. £
1. Cream and browns	50.00	75.00	25 .00
2. Helio-blue		Rare	

Shape 246   Cream jug

Designer:	Mr. White in 1932
Issued:	1933 - 1970
Height :	2 ½", 6.4 cm
Colour:	Cream, light and dark brown

Description	U.S. $	Can. $	U.K. £
Cream jug	40.00	60.00	20.00

Shape 247   Covered butter, round

Designer: Mr. White in 1932
Issued: 1933 - 1970
Height: 4 ¾", 12.1 cm
Colour: Cream, light and dark brown, and green

Description	U.S. $	Can. $	U.K. £
Covered butter, round	110.00	150.00	55.00

Note: Also known with grey chimney top.

Shape 248   Covered muffin, round

Designer: Mr. White in 1932
Issued: 1933 - 1969
Height :   5 ½", 14.0 cm
Colour: Cream, light and dark brown, and green

Description	U.S. $	Can. $	U.K. £
Covered muffin, round	150.00	225.00	75.00

Note: Also known with grey chimney top.

Shape 249   Biscuit barrel, square

Designer: Mr. White in 1932
Issued: 1933 - 1970
Height: 7", 17.8 cm
Colour: Cream, light and dark brown, and green

Description	U.S. $	Can. $	U.K. £
Chrome handle	125.00	175.00	60.00
Rafia handle	125.00	175.00	65.00
Without handle	100.00	150.00	55.00

Note: This biscuit barrel came with either a chrome or
raffia handle, or without a handle.

Shape 250   Cheese dish, large

Designer: Mr. White in 1932
Issued: 1. 1933 - 1970
             2. 1930s only
Height :   6 ¼", 15.9 cm
Colour: 1. Cream, light and dark brown, and green
             2. Helio-blue

Colour	U.S. $	Can. $	U.K. £
1. Cream and browns	90.00	125.00	45.00
2. Helio-blue		Rare	

Shape 251   Cheese dish, medium

Designer:	Mr. White in 1932
Issued:	1933 - 1970
Height:	5 ¼", 13.3 cm
Colour:	Cream, light and dark brown, and green

Description	U.S. $	Can. $	U.K. £
Cheese dish, medium	75.00	125.00	40.00

Shape 252   Log cabin cheese dish

Designer:	Mr. White in 1932
Issued:	1. 1933 - 1970
	2. 1930s only
Height :	5", 12.7 cm
Colour:	1. Cream, light and dark brown, and green
	2. Helio-blue

Colour	U.S. $	Can. $	U.K. £
1. Cream, brown, green	75.00	125.00	35.00
2. Helio-blue		Rare	

Shape 253   Shakespeare cruet set
(three pieces on a base)

Designer:	Mr. White in 1932
Issued:	1933 - 1970
Height:	3 ¼", 8.3 cm
Colour:	Cream, light and dark brown, and green

Description	U.S. $	Can. $	U.K. £
Shakespeare cruet set	75.00	100.00	35.00

Shape 254   Tobacco jar with lid, round

Designer:	Albert Hallam in 1932
Issued:	1933 - by 1954
Height :	5", 12.7 cm
Colour:	Cream, light and dark brown, and green

Description	U.S. $	Can. $	U.K. £
Tobacco jar with lid		Rare	

Photograph not
available
at press time

Shape 255   Tobacco jar

Designer:	Albert Hallam in 1932
Issued:	1933 - by 1954
Size:	Unknown
Colour:	Cream, light and dark brown, and green

Description	U.S. $	Can. $	U.K. £
Tobacco jar		Rare	

Shape 273   Cheese dish, small

Designer:	Mr. Symcox in 1932
Issued:	1933 - 1970
Height :	4 ½", 11.9 cm
Colour:	Cream, light and dark brown, and green

Description	U.S. $	Can. $	U.K. £
Cheese dish, small	75.00	110.00	40.00

Shape 1115   Cream jug

Designer:	Arthur Gredington in 1948
Issued:	1948 - 1970
Height:	3 ½", 8.9 cm
Colour:	Cream, light and dark brown, and green

Description	U.S. $	Can. $	U.K. £
Cream jug	40.00	60.00	20.00

Shape 1128   Covered sugar

Designer:	Unknown
Issued:	1948 - 1970
Height :	3 ¾", 9.5 cm
Colour:	Cream, light and dark brown, and green

Description	U.S. $	Can. $	U.K. £
Covered sugar	60.00	90.00	30.00

Note: Based on shape 245, and the lid from shape 243.
Also known with grey chimney top.

Shape 1149 Cup and saucer

Designer: Albert Hallam in 1949
Issued: 1949 - 1962
Height: Cup — 2 ¾", 7.0 cm
Diameter: Saucer — 5 ¾", 14.6 cm
Colour: Cream, light and dark brown, and green

Description	U.S. $	Can. $	U.K. £
Cup and saucer	125.00	175.00	65.00

Shape 1196 Plate, small house

Designer: Unknown
Issued: c.1951 - 1962
Diameter: 6 ½", 16.5 cm
Colour: Cream, light and dark brown, and green

Description	U.S. $	Can. $	U.K. £
Plate	100.00	125.00	50.00

Shape 1211 Plate, large house

Designer: Albert Hallam in 1951
Issued: 1951 - 1962
Diameter: 8", 20.3 cm
Colour: Cream, light and dark brown, and green

Description	U.S. $	Can. $	U.K. £
Plate	125.00	150.00	55.00

Stand for Teapot

Designer: Unknown
Issued: Unknown
Diameter: 6 ¼", 15.9 cm
Colour: Green

Description	U.S. $	Can. $	U.K. £
Stand for teapot	35.00	50.00	20.00

Shape 247 Covered Butter

Cottage Ware Series Ware
Shape 244 Covered Preserve

Shape 250 Cheese dish, large

GEORGE SMITH'S
FLOWER CONTAINERS

George Smith was the design consultant for a series of pottery containers produced especially for use in flower arranging. The collection included classical shapes for traditional arrangements, as well as unusual shapes intended to complement the more abstract style of presentation popular in the late 1960s. The colours of the containers were carefully chosen to enhance both floral and foliage displays and a brochure was issued in 1968 illustrating some of the containers with examples of their use.

There were twenty designs in total, the last four being added only a short while before they were all withdrawn.

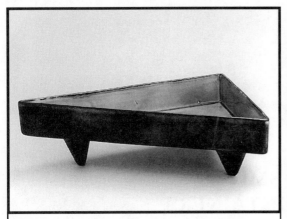

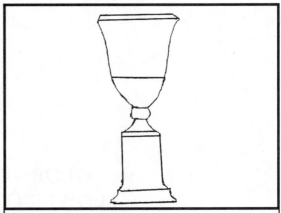

**Shape 1985 Flower container, triangular in shape
with three feet**

Modeller: Albert Hallam in 1964
Issued: 1965 - 1972
Size: 14" x 8" x 4", 35.5 x 20.3 x 10.1 cm
Colour: 1. Metallic blue   2. Metallic black/blue
              3. Metallic black/mustard
              4. White - matt

Market	Range
U.S.A.	$30.00 - 75.00
Canada	$45.00 - 100.00
U.K.	£15.00 - 35.00

Shape 1986 Chalice vase

Modeller: Albert Hallam in 1964
Issued: 1965 - by 1972
Height :   12 ½", 31.7 cm
Colour: White - matt

Description	U.S. $	Can. $	U.K. £
Chalise vase	50.00	75.00	30.00

Shape 1987 Bowl on pedestal

Modeller: Albert Hallam in 1964
Issued: 1965 - by 1972
Size: 10" x 10 ½", 25.4 x 26.7 cm
Colour: White - matt

Description	U.S. $	Can. $	U.K. £
Pedestal bowl	50.00	75.00	30.00

Shape 1988 Melon bowl

Modeller: Albert Hallam in 1964
Issued: 1965 - by 1972
Size: 10" x 5 ½", 25.4 x 14 cm
Colour: 1. Matt green/glossy mustard
              2. Matt grey/glossy blue
              3. White - matt

Market	Range
U.S.A.	$30.00 - 75.00
Canada	$45.00 - 100.00
U.K.	£15.00 - 35.00

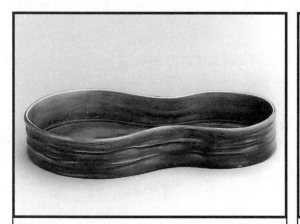

Shape 1989 Lake bowl

Modeller:	Albert Hallam in 1964
Issued:	1965 - 1972
Size:	12 ¼" x 7 ½" x 2", 31.1 x 19.1 x 5 cm
Colour:	1. Matt green/glossy mustard
	2. Matt grey/glossy blue
	3. Metallic black 4. White - matt

Market	Range
U.S.A.	$30.00 - 75.00
Canada	$45.00 - 100.00
U.K.	£15.00 - 35.00

Shape 2005 Cherub/Cupid vase

Modeller:	Albert Hallam, Mr. Murphy in 1965
Issued:	1965 - by 1972
Height :	12 ½", 31.7 cm
Colour:	1. Metallic black
	2. Opaque white

Market	Range
U.S.A.	$50.00 - 75.00
Canada	$75.00 - 100.00
U.K.	£20.00 - 40.00

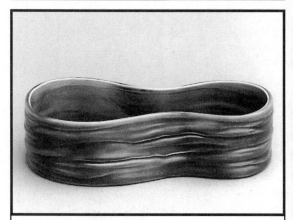

Shape 2068 Lake bowl

Modeller:	Albert Hallam in 1966
Issued:	1967 - 1972
Size:	8 ¼" x 2", 21 x 5 cm
Colour:	1. Matt green/glossy mustard
	2. Matt grey/glossy blue
	3. White - matt

Market	Range
U.S.A.	$20.00 - 50.00
Canada	$30.00 - 75.00
U.K.	£10.00 - 25.00

Shape 2069 Bowl

Modeller:	Albert Hallam in 1966
Issued:	1967 - by 1972
Size:	8" x 3 ½", 20.3 x 8.9 cm
Colour:	1. Matt green/glossy mustard
	2. Matt grey/glossy blue

Market	Range
U.S.A.	$30.00 - 50.00
Canada	$45.00 - 75.00
U.K.	£15.00 - 25.00

Shape 2081 Round vase

Modeller:	Graham Tongue in 1967
Issued:	1968 - by 1972
Height:	4″, 10.1 cm
Colour:	1. Matt green/glossy mustard
	2. Matt grey/glossy blue

Market	Range
U.S.A.	$20.00 - 35.00
Canada	$25.00 - 50.00
U.K.	£10.00 - 20.00

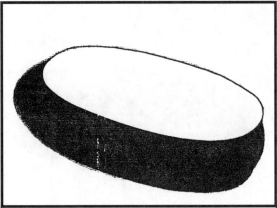

Shape 2153 Oval bowl

Modeller:	Graham Tongue in 1967
Issued:	1968 - 1972
Size :	12″ x 3 ½″, 30.5 x 8.9 cm
Colour:	1. Golden green/lime green
	2. White - matt

Market	Range
U.S.A.	$30.00 - 50.00
Canada	$45.00 - 75.00
U.K.	£15.00 - 25.00

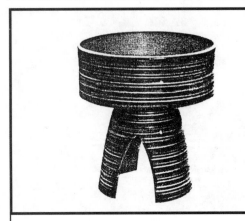

Shape 2158 Bowl on feet

Modeller:	Albert Hallam in 1967
Issued:	1968 - 1972
Height:	6 ½″, 16.4 cm
Diameter:	6″, 15 cm
Colour:	1. Solid lime green
	2. Solid forest green

Market	Range
U.S.A.	$30.00 - 50.00
Canada	$45.00 - 75.00
U.K.	£15.00 - 25.00

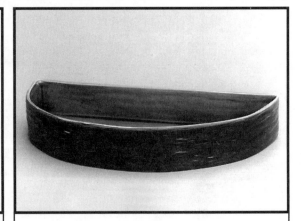

Shape 2159 Semi-circular bowl

Modeller:	Albert Hallam in 1967
Issued:	1968 - by 1972
Size:	12″ x 6″ x 2″, 30.5 x 15 x 5 cm
Colour:	1. Charcoal/celadon
	2. Matt grey/glossy blue

Market	Range
U.S.A.	$30.00 - 50.00
Canada	$45.00 - 75.00
U.K.	£15.00 - 25.00

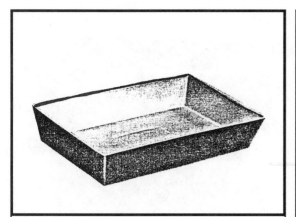

Shape 2160 Rectangular tray

Modeller:	Albert Hallam in 1967
Issued:	1968 - by 1972
Size:	13″ x 8″ x 2 ¼″, 33 x 20.3 x 5.7 cm
Colour:	1. Matt golden green/celadon
	2. Matt sage green/mustard

Market	Range
U.S.A.	$30.00 - 50.00
Canada	$45.00 - 75.00
U.K.	£15.00 - 25.00

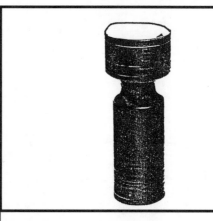

Shape 2161 Bowl on pedestal

Modeller:	Albert Hallam in 1967
Issued:	1968 - 1972
Height :	10 ½″, 26.7 cm
Diameter:	4, 10.1 cm
Colour:	1. Solid celadon
	2. Charcoal/celadon

Market	Range
U.S.A.	$30.00 - 50.00
Canada	$45.00 - 75.00
U.K.	£15.00 - 25.00

Shape 2162 Bowl

Modeller:	Albert Hallam in 1967
Issued:	1968 - 1972
Height:	7″, 17.8 cm
Diameter:	8 ½″, 21.6 cm
Colour:	Matt golden/celadon

Description	U.S.$	Can. $	U.K.£
Bowl	50.00	75.00	25.00

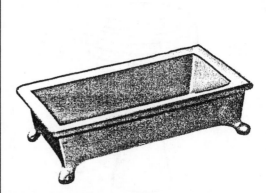

Shape 2163 Footed tray

Modeller:	Albert Hallam in 1967
Issued:	1968 - by 1972
Size:	11 ½″ x 7″ x 3″, 29.2 x 17.8 x 7.6 cm
Colour:	1. Forest green/celadon
	2. Solid celadon

Market	Range
U.S.A.	$40.00 - 60.00
Canada	$60.00 - 90.00
U.K.	£20.00 - 30.00

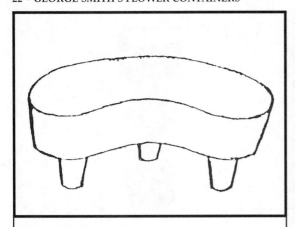

Shape 2335 Bowl

Modeller: Albert Hallam in 1970
Issued: 1971 - 1972
Size: 11 ¾" x 4", 29.8 x 10.1 cm
Colour: 1. Mushroom/olive green
          2. White - matt

Market	Range
U.S.A.	$40.00 - 40.00
Canada	$60.00 - 60.00
U.K.	£20.00 - 30.00

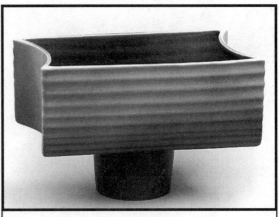

Shape 2336 Bowl

Modeller: Albert Hallam in 1970
Issued: 1971 - 1972
Size :   9" x 6", 22.9 x 15 cm
Colour: 1. Brown/blue
          2. White - matt

Market	Range
U.S.A.	$30.00 - 50.00
Canada	$45.00 - 75.00
U.K.	£15.00 - 25.00

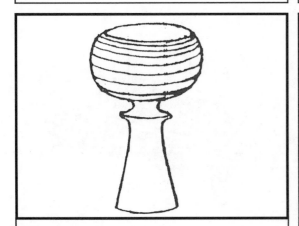

Shape 2337 Bowl

Modeller: Albert Hallam in 1970
Issued: 1971 - 1972
Height: 8", 20.3 cm
Colour: 1. Brown/blue, green
          2. White - matt

Market	Range
U.S.A.	$30.00 - 50.00
Canada	$45.00 - 75.00
U.K.	£15.00 - 25.00

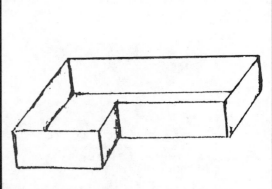

Shape 2338 Bowl

Modeller: Graham Tongue in 1970
Issued: 1971 - 1972
Size: 11" x 2", 27.9 x 5 cm
Colour: 1. Green/celadon
          2. White - matt

Market	Range
U.S.A.	$30.00 - 60.00
Canada	$45.00 - 90.00
U.K.	£15.00 - 30.00

HEATHER AND GORSE

This series consisted of fourteen shapes, all with a gloss finish. The background colour was either shaded peach or a shaded green. The heather decoration was raised and showed a spray of purple and yellow heather with green foliage and brown stems.

There were also seven undecorated shapes which corresponded with Heather and Gorse shapes as follows:

1900 with 1907, 1901 with 1908, 1902 with 1909, 1903 with 1911, 1904 with 1910, 1905 with 1916 and 1906 with 1912. These shapes (1900-1906) were possibly not put into production.

Shape 1907 Elongated dish

Designer:	Albert Hallam in 1963
Issued:	1964 - 1966/67
Length :	10", 25.4 cm
Colour:	Light peach or light green background, purple, yellow and green heather

Market	Range
U.S.A.	$50.00 - 75.00
Canada	$75.00 - 100.00
U.K.	£25.00 - 35.00

Shape 1908 Elongated dish

Designer:	Albert Hallam in 1963
Issued:	1964 - 1966/67
Length:	10", 25.4 cm
Colour:	Light peach or light green background, purple, yellow and green heather

Market	Range
U.S.A.	$50.00 - 75.00
Canada	$75.00 - 100.00
U.K.	£25.00 - 35.00

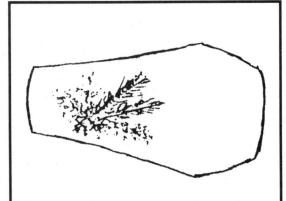

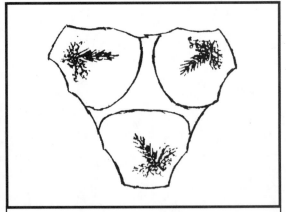

Shape 1909 Dish

Designer:	Albert Hallam in 1963
Issued:	1964 - 1966/67
Length:	12", 30.5 cm
Colour:	Light peach or light green background, purple, yellow and green heather

Market	Range
U.S.A.	$50.00 - 75.00
Canada	$75.00 - 100.00
U.K.	£25.00 - 35.00

Shape 1910 Triple dish

Designer:	Albert Hallam in 1963
Issued:	1964 - 1966/67
Length:	12", 30.5 cm
Colour:	Light peach or light green background, purple, yellow and green heather

Market	Range
U.S.A.	$60.00 - 90.00
Canada	$90.00 - 125.00
U.K.	£30.00 - 45.00

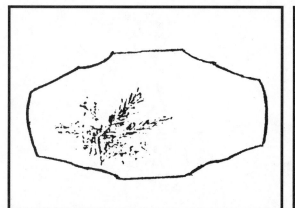

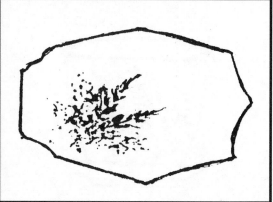

Shape 1911 Dish

Designer: Albert Hallam in 1963
Issued: 1964 - 1966/67
Lenght: 13", 33.0 cm
Colour: Light peach or light green background,
            purple, yellow and green heather

Market	Range
U.S.A.	$50.00 - 75.00
Canada	$75.00 - 100.00
U.K.	£25.00 - 35.00

Shape 1912 Dish

Designer: Albert Hallam in 1963
Issued: 1964 - 1966/67
Length: 8", 20.3 cm
Colour: Light peach or light green background,
            purple, yellow and green heather

Market	Range
U.S.A.	$40.00 - 60.00
Canada	$60.00 - 90.00
U.K.	£20.00 - 30.00

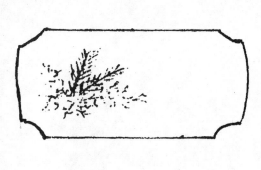

Shape 1916 Double dish

Designer: Albert Hallam in 1963
Issued: 1964 - 1966/67
Length: 13", 33.0 cm
Colour: Light peach or light green background,
            purple, yellow and green heather

Market	Range
U.S.A.	$50.00 - 75.00
Canada	$75.00 - 125.00
U.K.	£25.00 - 40.00

Shape 1924 Sandwich tray

Designer: Albert Hallam in 1964
Issued: 1964 - 1966/67
Length: 11", 27.9 cm
Colour: Light peach or light green background,
            purple, yellow and green heather

Market	Range
U.S.A.	$50.00 - 75.00
Canada	$75.00 - 125.00
U.K.	£25.00 - 35.00

Shape 1925 Preserve with lid

Designer: Albert Hallam in 1964
Issued: 1964 - 1966/67
Height: 3", 7.6 cm
Colour: Light peach or light green background,
               purple, yellow and green heather

Market	Range
U.S.A.	$50.00 - 75.00
Canada	$75.00 - 100.00
U.K.	£25.00 - 35.00

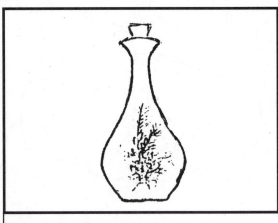

Shape 1926 Vinegar with stopper

Designer: Albert Hallam in 1964
Issued: 1964 - 1966/67
Height: 6", 15.0 cm
Colour: Light peach or light green background,
               purple, yellow and green heather

Market	Range
U.S.A.	$30.00 - 40.00
Canada	$45.00 - 60.00
U.K.	£30.00 - 40.00

Shape 1927-1928 Salt and pepper

Designer: Albert Hallam in 1964
Issued: 1964 - 1966/67
Height: 5 ½", 14.0 cm
Colour: Light peach or light green background,
               purple, yellow and green heather

Market	Range
U.S.A.	$60.00 - 75.00
Canada	$90.00 - 125.00
U.K.	£30.00 - 40.00

Note: Price listed is for pair.

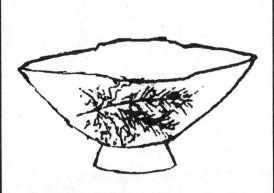

Shape 1929 Salad bowl, footed

Designer: Albert Hallam in 1964
Issued: 1964 - 1966/67
Size: Unknown
Colour: Light peach or light green background,
               purple, yellow and green heather

Market	Range
U.S.A.	$60.00 - 100.00
Canada	$90.00 - 125.00
U.K.	£35.00 - 50.00

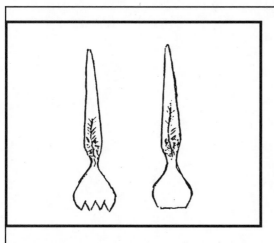

Shape 1930 Salad servers, decorated with a sprig of heather only

Designer:	Albert Hallam in 1964
Issued:	1964 - 1966/67
Length:	9", 22.9 cm
Colour:	Light peach or light green background, purple, yellow and green heather

Market	Range
U.S.A.	$60.00 - 90.00
Canada	$90.00 - 125.00
U.K.	£30.00 - 45.00

Heather and Gorse Series Ware
Shape 1908 Elongated dish

Shape 1927 Salt

Shape 1928 Pepper

HORS-D'OEUVRE

The decoration for this attractive and colourful series included combinations of the following fruit and vegetables: bananas, grapes, lemons, pineapples, tomatoes, strawberries, cherries, onions, mushrooms, asparagus and aubergines (eggplant). Also a carafe of wine, a wine glass and a candlestick were used on some of the items. The background was white with a gloss finish, to set off the many colours used for the decorations.

Mostly the seventeen shapes listed here were new introductions styled for use as hors-d'oeuvre ware and decorated as above, others were existing shapes similarly decorated. Also, patterns such as oranges and lemons, and even a blue rose have been seen on Hors D' Oeuvre shapes.

Shape 1444 Plate, contemporary shape
Designer: Albert Hallam in 1956
Issued: 1960 - 1963
Width: 8 ½", 21.6 cm
Colour: White with multi-coloured design

Description	U.S. $	Can. $	U.K. £
Plate, contemporary shape	30.00	45.00	15.00

Shape 1586 Dish with four sections
Designer: Albert Hallam in 1959
Issued: 1960 - 1963
Size: 9 ¾" x 6 ¾", 24.7 x 17.2 cm
Colour: White with multi-coloured designs

Description	U.S. $	Can. $	U.K. £
Dish, four sections	60.00	90.00	30.00

Shape 1617 Dish, square
Designer: Mr. Wood in 1959
Issued: 1960 - 1963
Width: 4", 10.1 cm
Colour: White with multi-coloured design

Description	U.S. $	Can. $	U.K. £
Dish, square	30.00	45.00	15.00

Shape 1623 Meat dish, contemporary shape
Designer: Mr. Wood in 1959
Issued: 1960 - 1963
Size: 12 ½" x 10 ¼", 31.7 x 26.0 cm
Colour: White with multi-coloured design

Description	U.S. $	Can. $	U.K. £
Meat dish, contemporary	50.00	75.00	25.00

Shape 1635 Rectangular dish
Designer: Albert Hallam in 1959
Issued: 1960 - 1963
Size: 7 ¾" x 5 ¼", 19.7 x 13.3 cm
Colour: White with multi-coloured design

Description	U.S. $	Can. $	U.K. £
Rectangular dish	30.00	45.00	15.00

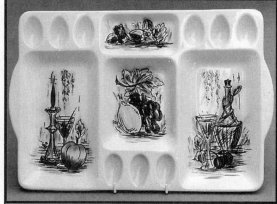

Shape 1636 Large rectangular dish with four sections plus egg holders
Designer: Albert Hallam in 1959
Issued: 1960 - 1963
Size: 18" x 11 ¾", 45.7 x 29.8 cm
Colour: White and light blue, with multi-coloured designs

Description	U.S. $	Can. $	U.K. £
Rectangular dish	100.00	150.00	50.00

Shape 1637 Large round dish with six sections around a centre one
Designer: Albert Hallam in 1959
Issued: 1960 - 1963
Diameter: 14 ½", 36.8 cm
Colour: White with multi-coloured designs

Description	U.S. $	Can. $	U.K. £
Round dish, six sections	90.00	125.00	45.00

Shape 1638 Large dish with five sections
Designer: Albert Hallam in 1959
Issued: 1960 - 1963
Size: 13 ¾" x 8 ¾", 34.9 x 22.2 cm
Colour: White with multi-coloured designs

Description	U.S. $	Can. $	U.K. £
Dish, five sections	60.00	90.00	30.00

Photograph not
available
at press time

Shape 1639 Dish with three sections
Designer: Albert Hallam in 1959
Issued: 1960 - 1963
Size: 10 ¼" x 9", 26.0 x 22.9 cm
Colour: White with multi-coloured designs

Description	U.S. $	Can. $	U.K. £
Dish, three sections	50.00	75.00	25.00

Shape 1640 Oval dish
Designer: Albert Hallam in 1959
Issued: 1960 - 1963
Size: 8" x 5", 20.3 x 12.7 cm
Colour: White with multi-coloured design

Description	U.S. $	Can. $	U.K. £
Oval dish	40.00	60.00	20.00

Shape 1665-1666 Pepper and Salt
Designer: Albert Hallam in 1959
Issued: 1960 - 1963
Height: 4 ½", 11.9 cm
Colour: White with multi-coloured designs

Description	U.S. $	Can. $	U.K. £
Pepper and Salt	50.00	75.00	25.00

Note: Price listed is for pair.

Shape 1667 Vinegar bottle marked with a "V"
Designer: Albert Hallam in 1959
Issued: 1960 - 1963
Height: 5", 12.7 cm including stopper
Colour: White with multi-coloured designs

Description	U.S. $	Can. $	U.K. £
Vinegar bottle	40.00	60.00	20.00

Note: This shape has also been seen without the "V" for
vinegar and would then have been intended for oil.
Priced listed is for each bottle.

Shape 1673 Fruit bowl, round

Designer:	Albert Hallam in 1960
Issued:	1960 - 1963
Size:	9 ¼" x 3 ½", 23.5 x 8.9 cm
Colour:	White with multi-coloured design

Description	U.S. $	Can. $	U.K. £
Fruit bowl, round	60.00	90.00	30.00

Shape 1674 Dish

Designer:	Albert Hallam in 1960
Issued:	1960 - 1963
Size:	10 ¼" x 9", 26.0 x 22.9 cm
Colour:	White with multi-coloured design

Description	U.S. $	Can. $	U.K. £
Dish	50.00	75.00	25.00

Shape 1689 Mexican hat, three sections

Designer:	Albert Hallam in 1960
Issued:	1960 - 1963
Size:	8 ¼" x 3 ½", 21.0 x 8.9 cm
Colour:	White with multi-coloured designs

Description	U.S. $	Can. $	U.K. £
Mexican hat, three sections	60.00	90.00	30.00

Shape 1693 Kidney-shaped dish

Designer:	Albert Hallam in 1960
Issued:	1960 - 1963
Size:	9 ½" x 4 ½", 24.0 x 11.9 cm
Colour:	White with multi-coloured design

Description	U.S. $	Can. $	U.K. £
Kidney-shaped dish	40.00	60.00	20.00

Hors-d'oeuvre Series Ware
Shape 1586 Dish with four sections

HUNTSMAN SERIES

The "Huntsman" series, sometimes referred to by collectors as the "Country" series, followed on closely after the Cottage Ware, and was designed in 1934.

The huntsman brandishing his crop and surrounded by his hounds created a colourful scene. The horse and hounds were in a pale brown. The leaves on the trees were green, and the grass was a paler green, with dark brown used for the tree trunks and the handles. The knobs were very attractive and made a lovely finishing touch, as they were in the shape of acorns.

There are only thirteen shapes in this series, all in a gloss finish. We believe that it would have been the intention to expand the set, but that the outbreak of war in 1939 brought about its early retirement. Except for the sugar dredger and the cruet set, where space was limited, the hunting scene was fully shown on all the pieces.

Shape 285   Jug

Designer:	Mr. Fletcher in 1934
Issued:	1935 - by 1954
Size:	Unknown
Colour:	Light cream and assorted colours

Description	U.S. $	Can. $	U.K. £
Jug	100.00	150.00	50.00

Shape 325   Teapot

Designer:	Mr. Fletcher in 1934
Issued:	1935 - by 1954
Height :	6 ¼″, 15.9 cm
Colour:	Light cream and assorted colours

Description	U.S. $	Can. $	U.K. £
Teapot	150.00	225.00	75.00

Shape 326   Hot water jug

Designer:	Mr. Fletcher in 1934
Issued:	1935 - by 1954
Size:	Unknown
Colour:	Light cream and assorted colours

Description	U.S. $	Can. $	U.K. £
Hot water jug	150.00	225.00	75.00

Shape 327/336 Covered cheese dish in two sizes

Designer:	Mr. Fletcher in 1934
Issued:	1935 - by 1954
Size:	1. Large — unknown
	2. Small — unknown
Colour:	Light cream and assorted colours

Description	U.S. $	Can. $	U.K. £
1. Shape 327, large	125.00	175.00	60.00
2. Shape 336, small	100.00	150.00	55.00

Shape 328   Biscuit barrel, wicker covered handle

Designer: Mr. Fletcher in 1934
Issued: 1935 - by 1954
Size: Unknown
Colour: Light cream and assorted colours

Description	U.S. $	Can. $	U.K. £
Biscuit barrel	175.00	225.00	85.00

Shape 329   Sugar bowl

Designer: Mr. Fletcher in 1934
Issued: 1935 - by 1954
Size: Unknown
Colour: Light cream and assorted colours

Description	U.S. $	Can. $	U.K. £
Sugar bowl	100.00	150.00	50.00

Shape 330   Cream jug

Designer: Mr. Fletcher in 1934
Issued: 1935 - by 1954
Size: Unknown
Colour: Light cream and assorted colours

Description	U.S. $	Can. $	U.K. £
Cream jug	100.00	150.00	50.00

Shape 331   Preserve pot with lid

Designer: Mr. Fletcher in 1934
Issued: 1935 - by 1954
Size: Unknown
Colour: Light cream and assorted colours

Description	U.S. $	Can. $	U.K. £
Preserve with lid	125.00	175.00	60.00

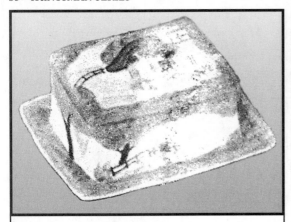

Shape 332   **Covered butter**

Designer:	Mr. Fletcher in 1934
Issued:	1935 - by 1954
Size:	Unknown
Colour:	Light cream and assorted colours

Description	U.S. $	Can. $	U.K. £
Covered butter	125.00	175.00	60.00

Shape 333   **Sugar dredger**

Designer:	Mr. Fletcher in 1934
Issued:	1935 - by 1954
Height:	5 ¼", 13.3 cm
Colour:	Light cream and assorted colours

Description	U.S. $	Can. $	U.K. £
Sugar dredger	90.00	125.00	45.00

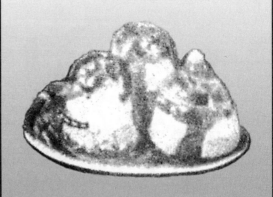

Shape 334   **Covered muffin dish**

Designer:	Mr. Fletcher in 1934
Issued:	1935 - by 1954
Size:	Unknown
Colour:	Light cream and assorted colours

Description	U.S. $	Can. $	U.K. £
Covered muffin dish	150.00	225.00	75.00

Shape 335   **Cruet set, salt, pepper and mustard on base**

Designer:	Mr. Fletcher in 1934
Issued:	1935 - by 1954
Size:	Unknown
Colour:	Light cream and assorted colours

Description	U.S. $	Can. $	U.K. £
Cruet set	150.00	225.00	75.00

KASHAN

This range of ornamental ware was almost the last to be modelled and produced under the Beswick backstamp, following the change of ownership from Beswick to Royal Doulton in 1969. The origin of the name Kashan has not yet come to light, but the name probably relates to the style of the pottery, which is somewhat oriental in character. The designs, which are strongly incised, produce an immediate visual impact.

The range consisted of twelve items, of which nine were vases. All the items were available in four decorations: Turquoise/stone, solid green or pewter - gloss; white - matt.

Shape 2250 Vase
Designer: James Hayward, Albert Hallam in 1968
Issued: 1969 - 1972
Height: 9", 22.9 cm
Colour: 1. Pewter   3. Turquoise/stone
        2. Solid green   4. White

Colour	U.S. $	Can. $	U.K. £
1. Pewter	60.00	90.00	30.00
2. Solid green	60.00	90.00	30.00
3. Turquoise/stone	75.00	110.00	40.00
4. White		Rare	

Shape 2251 Vase
Designer: J. Hayward, A. Hallam, G. Tongue in 1968
Issued: 1969 - 1972
Height : 7", 17.8 cm
Colour: 1. Pewter   3. Turquoise/stone
        2. Solid green   4. White

Colour	U.S. $	Can. $	U.K. £
1. Pewter	60.00	90.00	30.00
2. Solid green	60.00	90.00	30.00
3. Turquoise/stone	75.00	110.00	40.00
4. White		Rare	

Shape 2252 Vase
Designer: James Hayward, Albert Hallam in 1968
Issued: 1969 - 1972
Height: 5 ½", 14.0 cm
Colour: 1. Pewter   3. Turquoise/stone
        2. Solid green   4. White

Colour	U.S. $	Can. $	U.K. £
1. Pewter	50.00	75.00	25.00
2. Solid green	50.00	75.00	25.00
3. Turquoise/stone	75.00	100.00	35.00
4. White		Rare	

Shape 2255 Vase
Designer: James Hayward, Graham Tongue in 1968
Issued: 1969 - 1972
Height: 10", 25.4 cm
Colour: 1. Pewter   3. Turquoise/stone
        2. Solid green   4. White

Colour	U.S. $	Can. $	U.K. £
1. Pewter	60.00	90.00	30.00
2. Solid green	60.00	90.00	30.00
3. Turquoise/stone	75.00	110.00	40.00
4. White		Rare	

Shape 2256 Vase
Designer: James Hayward, Graham Tongue in 1969
Issued: 1969 - 1972
Height: 8", 20.3 cm
Colour: 1. Pewter   3. Turquoise/stone
            2. Solid green   4. White

Colour	U.S. $	Can. $	U.K. £
1. Pewter	60.00	90.00	30.00
2. Solid green	60.00	90.00	30.00
3. Turquoise/stone	75.00	110.00	40.00
4. White		Rare	

Shape 2257 Vase
Designer: James Hayward, Albert Hallam in 1969
Issued: 1969 - 1972
Height :   11", 27.9 cm
Colour: 1. Pewter   3. Turquoise/stone
            2. Solid green   4. White

Colour	U.S. $	Can. $	U.K. £
1. Pewter	60.00	90.00	30.00
2. Solid green	60.00	90.00	30.00
3. Turquoise/stone	75.00	110.00	40.00
4. White		Rare	

Shape 2258 Bowl oval
Designer: James Hayward, Graham Tongue in 1969
Issued: 1969 - 1972
Size: 5" x 12" x 6", 12.7 x 30.5 x 15.0 cm
Colour: 1. Pewter   3. Turquoise/stone
            2. Solid green   4. White

Colour	U.S. $	Can. $	U.K. £
1. Pewter	70.00	100.00	35.00
2. Solid green	70.00	100.00	35.00
3. Turquoise/stone	90.00	125.00	45.00
4. White		Rare	

Shape 2259 Vase
Designer: J. Hayward, A. Hallam, G. Tongue in 1969
Issued: 1969 - 1972
Height :   6 ½", 16.5 cm
Colour: 1. Pewter   3. Turquoise/stone
            2. Solid green   4. White

Colour	U.S. $	Can. $	U.K. £
1. Pewter	50.00	75.00	25.00
2. Solid green	50.00	75.00	25.00
3. Turquoise/stone	75.00	100.00	35.00
4. White		Rare	

Photograph not
available
at press time

Shape 2266 Plant Pot
Designer: Graham Tongue in 1969
Issued: 1969 - 1972
Height: 4 ½″, 11.9 cm
Colour: 1. Pewter   3. Turquoise/stone
               2. Solid green   4. White

Colour	U.S. $	Can. $	U.K. £
1. Pewter	40.00	40.00	20.00
2. Solid green	40.00	40.00	20.00
3. Turquoise/stone	60.00	90.00	30.00
4. White		Rare	

Shape 2296 Vase
Designer: Graham Tongue in 1969
Issued: 1970 - 1972
Height :   6 ½″ x 16.5 cm
Colour: 1. Pewter   3. Turquoise/stone
               2. Solid green   4. White

Colour	U.S. $	Can. $	U.K. £
1. Pewter	50.00	50.00	25.00
2. Solid green	50.00	50.00	25.00
3. Turquoise/stone	75.00	100.00	35.00
4. White		Rare	

Photograph not
available
at press time

Shape 2296C Ginger jar with cover
Designer: Graham Tongue in 1969
Issued: 1970 - 1972
Height: 7 ¼″, 18.4 cm
Colour: 1. Pewter   3. Turquoise/stone
               2. Solid green   4. White

Colour	U.S. $	Can. $	U.K. £
1. Pewter	60.00	90.00	30.00
2. Solid green	60.00	90.00	30.00
3. Turquoise/stone	75.00	110.00	40.00
4. White		Rare	

Shape 2303 Vase
Designer: Graham Tongue in 1970
Issued: 1971 - 1972
Height :   11 ¾″, 29.8 cm
Colour: 1. Pewter   3. Turquoise/stone
               2. Solid green   4. White

Colour	U.S. $	Can. $	U.K. £
1. Pewter	70.00	100.00	35.00
2. Solid green	70.00	100.00	35.00
3. Turquoise/stone	80.00	125.00	40.00
4. White		Rare	

PALM TREE

This distinctive series containing eighteen shapes was produced in the following colourways:

1. Biscuit, light blue or white - matt
2. Turquoise with gilt, grey with gilt, cobalt with gilt or ruby with gilt - gloss
3. British racing green, yellow, light green - gloss; pale green - matt

In the pricing tables, the numbers 1, 2 and 3 refer to the colourways as listed above.

The matt glazes were satin finished and the shaded colouring was soft and very pleasing. On the darker background, for example ruby, much gilding was used and more colours - such as black, blue and green - appeared on the palm leaves, which created a very dramatic effect. This is a popular series with collectors and it is quite a challenge to find the rare colourways.

Shape 1063 Wall vase with two drums

Designer: James Hayward in 1946
Issued: 1947 - by 1963
Height: 9 ½", 24 cm
Colour: See title page

Colourway	U.S. $	Can. $	U.K. £
1. Colour/matt	60.00	90.00	30.00
2. Gilt/gloss	90.00	125.00	45.00
3. Colour/gloss/matt		Rare	

Shape 1064 Vase, large

Designer: James Hayward in 1946
Issued: 1947 - by 1963
Height :   11 ½", 29.2 cm
Colour: See title page

Colourway	U.S. $	Can. $	U.K. £
1. Colour/matt	77.00	110.00	35.00
2. Gilt/gloss	125.00	175.00	65.00
3. Colour/gloss/matt		Rare	

Shape 1065 Vase with oval top

Designer: Albert Hallam in 1946
Issued: 1947 - by 1963
Height: 8", 20.3 cm
Colour: See title page

Colourway	U.S. $	Can. $	U.K. £
1. Colour/matt	60.00	90.00	30.00
2. Gilt/gloss	125.00	175.00	60.00
3. Colour/gloss/matt		Rare	

Shape 1066 Bowl

Designer: Albert Hallam in 1946
Issued: 1947 - by 1963
Diameter: 12", 30.5 cm
Colour: See title page

Colourway	U.S. $	Can. $	U.K. £
1. Colour/matt	75.00	100.00	35.00
2. Gilt/gloss	125.00	175.00	65.00
3. Colour/gloss/matt		Rare	

Shape 1067 Jug, large			
Designer:	Albert Hallam in 1946		
Issued:	1947 - by 1963		
Height:	11", 27.9 cm		
Colour:	See title page		

Colourway	U.S. $	Can. $	U.K. £
1. Colour/matt	60.00	90.00	30.00
2. Gilt/gloss	125.00	175.00	60.00
3. Colour/gloss/matt		Rare	

Shape 1068 Jug			
Designer:	Albert Hallam in 1946		
Issued:	1947 - by 1963		
Height :	9", 22.9 cm		
Colour:	See title page		

Colourway	U.S. $	Can. $	U.K. £
1. Colour/matt	60.00	90.00	30.00
2. Gilt/gloss	100.00	150.00	55.00
3. Colour/gloss/matt		Rare	

Shape 1069 Vase with wide curly oval top			
Designer:	Albert Hallam in 1946		
Issued:	1947 - by 1963		
Height:	8 ½", 21.6 cm		
Colour:	See title page		

Colourway	U.S. $	Can. $	U.K. £
1 Colour/matt	60.00	90.00	30.00
2. Gilt/gloss	125.00	175.00	60.00
3. Colour/gloss/matt		Rare	

Shape 1070 Basket			
Designer:	Albert Hallam in 1946		
Issued:	1947 - by 1963		
Height :	10 ¼", 26.0 cm		
Colour:	See title page		

Colourway	U.S. $	Can. $	U.K. £
1. Colour/matt	75.00	100.00	35.00
2. Gilt/gloss	125.00	175.00	60.00
3. Colour/gloss/matt		Rare	

Shape 1071 Vase on square base

Designer:	Albert Hallam in 1946
Issued:	1947 - by 1963
Height:	10 ¼", 26 cm
Colour:	See title page

Colourway	U.S. $	Can. $	U.K. £
1. Colour/matt	60.00	90.00	30.00
2. Gilt/gloss	125.00	175.00	65.00
3. Colour/gloss/matt		Rare	

Shape 1072 Vase

Designer:	Albert Hallam in 1946
Issued:	1947 - by 1963
Height:	6 ¼", 15.9 cm
Colour:	See title page

Colourway	U.S. $	Can. $	U.K. £
1. Colour/matt	60.00	90.00	30.00
2. Gilt/gloss	125.00	175.00	60.00
3. Colour/gloss/matt		Rare	

Shape 1073 Jug, medium

Designer:	Albert Hallam in 1946
Issued:	1947 - by 1963
Height:	8 ½", 21.6 cm
Colour:	See title page

Colourway	U.S. $	Can. $	U.K. £
1. Colour/matt	60.00	90.00	30.00
2. Gilt/gloss	125.00	175.00	60.00
3. Colour/gloss/matt		Rare	

Shape 1074 Jug, small

Designer:	Albert Hallam in 1946
Issued:	1947 - by 1963
Height:	7 ½" 19.1 cm
Colour:	See title page

Colourway	U.S. $	Can. $	U.K. £
1. Colour/matt	75.00	100.00	35.00
2. Gilt/gloss	125.00	175.00	60.00
3. Colour/gloss/matt		Rare	

Photograph not
available
at press time

Photograph not
available
at press time

Shape 1267 Bowl

Designer:	James Hayward, Albert Hallam in 1952		
Issued:	1953 - by 1963		
Size:	7 ½" x 5 ½", 19.1 x 14 cm		
Colour:	See title page		

Colourway	U.S. $	Can. $	U.K. £
1. Colour/matt	60.00	90.00	30.00
2. Gilt/gloss	125.00	175.00	65.00
3. Colour/gloss/matt		Rare	

Shape 1268 Jug, round with straight sides

Designer:	James Hayward, Albert Hallam in 1952		
Issued:	1953 - by 1963		
Height:	8", 20.3 cm		
Colour:	See title page		

Colourway	U.S. $	Can. $	U.K. £
1. Colour/matt	60.00	90.00	30.00
2. Gilt/gloss	125.00	175.00	60.00
3. Colour/gloss/matt		Rare	

Shape 1269 Vase standing with two drums

Designer:	James Hayward, Albert Hallam in 1952		
Issued:	1953 - by 1963		
Height:	7", 17.8 cm		
Colour:	See title page		

Colourway	U.S. $	Can. $	U.K. £
1. Colour/matt	75.00	100.00	35.00
2. Gilt/gloss	125.00	175.00	60.00
3. Colour/gloss/matt		Rare	

Shape 1270 Horn of Plenty

Designer:	Albert Hallam in 1952		
Issued:	1953 - by 1963		
Height:	7 ½", 19.1 cm		
Colour:	See title page		

Colourway	U.S. $	Can. $	U.K. £
1. Colour/matt	75.00	100.00	35.00
2. Gilt/gloss	125.00	175.00	65.00
3. Colour/gloss/matt		Rare	

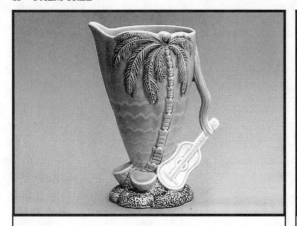

Shape 1271 Jug with guitar and drums

Designer: Albert Hallam in 1952
Issued: 1953 - by 1963
Height: 7 ¾", 19.7 cm
Colour: See title page

Colourway	U.S. $	Can. $	U.K. £
1. Colour/matt	75.00	100.00	35.00
2. Gilt/gloss	150.00	200.00	70.00
3. Colour/gloss/matt		Rare	

Shape 1272 Scorpion jug

Designer: James Hayward, Albert Hallam in 1952
Issued: 1953 - by 1963
Height : 6 ½", 16.5 cm
Colour: See title page

Colourway	U.S. $	Can. $	U.K. £
1. Colour/matt	75.00	125.00	40.00
2. Gilt/gloss	150.00	200.00	75.00
3. Colour/gloss/matt		Rare	

PETIT POINT

A new range of tableware in a gloss finish was introduced in 1939 which was plain except for an embossed border design. The pattern, which appeared on all the pieces, represented a type of embroidery stitch commonly known as petit point, and gave its name to the series. See for example the teapot, shape 641.

The items were also available with different lithograph designs applied. One known as "Windmill," was a very colourful and ornate Dutch scene (see shape 630), reminiscent of embroidery, while another named "Romance" was very different in style (see shape 681), and was more in the nature of a painting. The plain background varied between cream and white and on some examples the Dutch scene was heavily overlaid with gilt tracery.

As with most of the other series introduced pre-war, information is scarce, however it is likely that the twenty-three shapes of Petit Point were not in production for very long.

Shape 630, Windmill design

Shape 641, Plain white design

Shape 630-631 Teapot in two sizes

Designer:	Mr. Owen in 1938
Issued:	1939 - by 1954
Height:	1. Shape 630 — 8 ¼", 21 cm
	2. Shape 631 — unknown
Colour:	a. Plain
	b. Plain with multi-coloured decoration

Colour	U.S. $	Can. $	U.K. £
1a. Shape 630 - plain	75.00	100.00	35.00
1b. Shape 630 - multi-coloured	90.00	125.00	45.00
2a. Shape 631 - plain	60.00	90.00	30.00
2b. Shape 631 - multi-coloured	75.00	125.00	40.00

Shape 632/1/2/3 Jugs in three sizes

Designer:	Mr. Owen in 1938
Issued:	1939 - by 1954
Height:	1. Shape 632/1, large — 6 ¾", 17.2 cm
	2. Shape 632/2, medium — 6", 15 cm
	3. Shape 632/3, small — unknown
Colour:	a. Plain
	b. Plain with multi-coloured decoration

Colour	U.S. $	Can. $	U.K. £
1a. Large - plain	50.00	75.00	25.00
1b. Large - multi-coloured	60.00	90.00	30.00
2a. Medium - plain	40.00	60.00	20.00
2b. Medium - multi-coloured	50.00	75.00	25.00
3a. Small - plain	30.00	50.00	15.00
3b. Small - multi-coloured	40.00	60.00	20.00

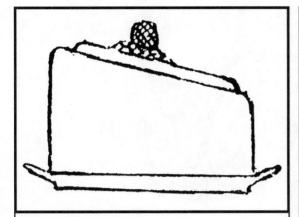

Shape 633-634 Cheese dish in two sizes

Designer:	Mr. Owen in 1938
Issued:	1939 - by 1954
Size:	1. Shape 633, small — unknown
	2. Shape 634, large — unknown
Colour:	a . Plain
	b. Plain with multi-coloured decoration

Colour	U.S. $	Can. $	U.K. £
1a. Shape 633 - plain	50.00	75.00	25.00
1b. Shape 633 - multi-coloured	60.00	90.00	30.00
2a. Shape 634 - plain	60.00	90.00	30.00
2b. Shape 634 - multi-coloured	75.00	110.00	35.00

Photograph not
available
at press time

Shape 635   Bread and butter plate

Designer:	Mr. Owen in 1938
Issued:	1939 - by 1954
Size:	Unknown
Colour:	a. Plain
	b. Plain with multi-coloured decoration

Colour		U.S. $	Can. $	U.K. £
a.	Plain	40.00	60.00	20.00
b.	Multi-coloured	50.00	75.00	25.00

Photograph not
available
at press time

Shape 636   Cup and saucer

Designer:	Mr. Owen in 1938
Issued:	1939 - by 1954
Size:	Unknown
Colour:	a. Plain
	b. Plain with multi-coloured decoration

Colour		U.S. $	Can. $	U.K. £
a.	Plain	40.00	60.00	20.00
b.	Multi-coloured	50.00	75.00	25.00

Photograph not
available
at press time

Shape 637   Muffin

Designer:	Mr. Owen in 1938
Issued:	1939 - by 1954
Size:	Unknown
Colour:	a. Plain
	b. Plain with multi-coloured decoration

Colour		U.S. $	Can. $	U.K. £
a.	Plain	60.00	90.00	30.00
b.	Multi-coloured	75.00	100.00	35.00

Photograph not
available
at press time

Shape 638/1/2 Sugar in two sizes

Designer: Mr. Owen in 1938
Issued: 1939 - by 1954
Size: Unknown
Colour: a. Plain
            b. Plain with multi-coloured decoration

Colour	U.S. $	Can. $	U.K. £
638/1a. Plain	50.00	75.00	25.00
638/1b. Multi-coloured	60.00	90.00	30.00
638/2a. Plain	40.00	60.00	20.00
638/2b. Multi-coloured	50.00	75.00	25.00

Shape 639 Cream jug

Designer: Mr. Owen in 1938
Issued: 1939 - by 1954
Height: 3 ¼", 8.3 cm
Colour: a. Plain
            b. Plain with multi-coloured decoration

Colour	U.S. $	Can. $	U.K. £
a. Plain	40.00	60.00	20.00
b. Multi-coloured	50.00	75.00	25.00

Photograph not
available
at press time

Shape 640 Breakfast cup and saucer

Designer: Mr. Owen in 1938
Issued: 1939 - by 1954
Size: Unknown
Colour: a. Plain
            b. Plain with multi-coloured decoration

Colour	U.S. $	Can. $	U.K. £
a. Plain	50.00	75.00	25.00
b. Multi-coloured	60.00	90.00	30.00

Shape 641 Teapot

Designer: Mr. Owen in 1938
Issued: 1939 - by 1954
Size: 6 ½", 16.5 cm
Colour: a. Plain
            b. Plain with multi-coloured decoration

Colour	U.S. $	Can. $	U.K. £
a. Plain	60.00	90.00	30.00
b. Multi-coloured	75.00	125.00	40.00

Photograph not
available
at press time

Photograph not
available
at press time

Shape 642   Coffee pot

Designer: Mr. Owen in 1938
Issued: 1939 - by 1954
Size: Unknown
Colour: a. Plain
            b. Plain with multi-coloured decoration

Colour	U.S. $	Can. $	U.K. £
a. Plain	75.00	100.00	35.00
b. Multi-coloured	100.00	150.00	50.00

Shape 643   Butter dish

Designer: Mr. Owen in 1938
Issued: 1939 - by 1954
Size: Unknown
Colour: a. Plain
            b. Plain with multi-coloured decoration

Colour	U.S. $	Can. $	U.K. £
a. Plain	60.00	90.00	30.00
b. Multi-coloured	75.00	100.00	35.00

Photograph not
available
at press time

Photograph not
available
at press time

Shape 644   Egg stand

Designer: Mr. Owen in 1938
Issued: 1939 - by 1954
Size: Unknown
Colour: a. Plain
            b. Plain with multi-coloured decoration

Colour	U.S. $	Can. $	U.K. £
a. Plain	60.00	90.00	30.00
b. Multi-coloured	75.00	100.00	35.00

Shape 645   Fruit bowl

Designer: Mr. Owen in 1938
Issued: 1939 - by 1954
Size: Unknown
Colour: a. Plain
            b. Plain with multi-coloured decoration

Colour	U.S. $	Can. $	U.K. £
a. Plain	75.00	100.00	35.00
b. Multi-coloured	90.00	125.00	45.00

Photograph not
available
at press time

Photograph not
available
at press time

Shape 646   Fruit saucer

Designer:	Mr. Owen in 1938
Issued:	1939 - by 1954
Size:	Unknown
Colour:	a. Plain
	b. Plain with multi-coloured decoration

Colour	U.S. $	Can. $	U.K. £
a. Plain	30.00	45.00	15.00
b. Multi-coloured	40.00	60.00	20.00

Shape 647   Coffee cup and saucer

Designer:	Mr. Owen in 1938
Issued:	1939 - by 1954
Size:	Unknown
Colour:	a. Plain
	b. Plain with multi-coloured decoration

Colour	U.S. $	Can. $	U.K. £
a. Plain	40.00	60.00	20.00
b. Multi-coloured	50.00	75.00	25.00

Photograph not
available
at press time

Photograph not
available
at press time

Shape 648   Muffin

Designer:	Mr. Owen in 1938
Issued:	1939 - by 1954
Size:	4", 10.1 cm
Colour:	a. Plain
	b. Plain with multi-coloured decoration

Colour	U.S. $	Can. $	U.K. £
a. Plain	80.00	125.00	40.00
b. Multi-coloured	70.00	110.00	35.00

Shape 649   Sugar, small

Designer:	Mr. Owen in 1938
Issued:	1939 - by 1954
Size:	Unknown
Colour:	a. Plain
	b. Plain with multi-coloured decoration

Colour	U.S. $	Can. $	U.K. £
a. Plain	40.00	60.00	20.00
b. Multi-coloured	50.00	75.00	25.00

Photograph not
available
at press time

Photograph not
available
at press time

Shape 670   Cream jug, small

Designer: Mr. Owen in 1938
Issued: 1939 - by 1954
Size: Unknown
Colour: a. Plain
             b. Plain with multi-coloured decoration

Colour	U.S. $	Can. $	U.K. £
a. Plain	40.00	60.00	20.00
b. Multi-coloured	50.00	75.00	25.00

Shape 671   Toast rack

Designer: Mr. Owen in 1938
Issued: 1939 - by 1954
Size: Unknown
Colour: a. Plain
             b. Plain with multi-coloured decoration

Colour	U.S. $	Can. $	U.K. £
a. Plain	50.00	75.00	25.00
b. Multi-coloured	75.00	100.00	35.00

Photograph not
available
at press time

Shape 672   Cress tray and drainer

Designer: Mr. Owen in 1938
Issued: 1939 - by 1954
Size: Unknown
Colour: a. Plain
             b. Plain with multi-coloured decoration

Colour	U.S. $	Can. $	U.K. £
a. Plain	60.00	90.00	30.00
b. Multi-coloured	80.00	125.00	40.00

Shape 681   Preserve with lid

Designer: Mr. Owen in 1939
Issued: 1939 - by 1954
Height: 5 ¾", 14.6 cm
Colour: a. Plain
             b. Plain with multi-coloured decoration

Colour	U.S. $	Can. $	U.K. £
a. Plain	40.00	60.00	20.00
b. Multi-coloured	60.00	90.00	30.00

Photograph not
available
at press time

Photograph not
available
at press time

Shape 682   Triple Tray

Designer: Mr. Owen in 1939
Issued: 1939 - by 1954
Size: Unknown
Colour: a. Plain
            b. Plain with multi-coloured decoration

Colour		U.S. $	Can. $	U.K. £
a	Plain	60.00	90.00	30.00
b.	Multi-coloured	75.00	110.00	35.00

Shape 683   Double Tray

Designer: Mr. Owen in 1939
Issued: 1939 - by 1954
Size: Unknown
Colour: a. Plain
            b. Plain with multi-coloured decoration

Colour		U.S. $	Can. $	U.K. £
a.	Plain	50.00	75.00	25.00
b.	Multi-coloured	60.00	90.00	30.00

Shape 685/1/2/3 Sweet dish in three sizes

Designer: Mr. Owen in 1939
Issued: 1939 - by 1954
Size :   1. Unknown
            2. 7 ½″ x 5 ¾″, 19.1 x 14.6 cm
            3. Unknown
Colour: a. Plain
            b. Plain with multi-coloured decoration

Colour	U.S. $	Can. $	U.K. £
1a. 685/1 - plain	50.00	75.00	25.00
1b. 685/1 - multi-coloured	60.00	90.00	30.00
2a. 685/2 - plain	40.00	60.00	20.00
2b. 685/2 - multi-coloured	50.00	75.00	25.00
3a. 685/3 - plain	30.00	45.00	15.00
3b. 685/3 - multi-coloured	40.00	60.00	20.00

SALAD WARE

A range of lettuce-leafed embossed salad ware in a gloss finish, was introduced during 1932, a time when funds were scarce, so that items of domestic tableware which were both useful and ornamental had an obvious attraction. The last piece (shape 2029) was added to the range in 1965, by which time thirty-seven pieces had been modelled. It is likely that production was interrupted during the war years and that some pieces were not reintroduced afterwards. Except for the round salad bowl (shape 210), which is listed in opaque white glaze for 1971, all the remaining range was withdrawn in 1970.

The very first decoration was a darkish solid green ground, but a primrose ground was very soon added. Later, around 1936, the solid green ground was replaced by a lighter shaded green, giving a more delicate effect. The shaded green decoration remained to the end, but other decorations exist, such as white, cream, and a deep yellow-orange. These date from before the war until the fifties. One piece has even been found decorated in three shaded colours, pink, mauve and green!

Shape 210   Salad bowl, round

Designer:	Mr. Symcox in 1932
Issued:	1. 1932 - 1971
	2. 1971 - 1971
Diameter:	9", 22.9 cm
Colour:	a. Background solid green, shaded green, white, cream or yellow-orange
	b. Opaque

Description	U.S. $	Can. $	U.K. £
Salad bowl, round	125.00	175.00	60.00

Note: Servers available, 9" long. Price is for bowl only.

Shape 211   Salad bowl, octagonal

Designer:	Mr. Symcox in 1932
Issued:	1932 - by 1965
Diameter:	7 ¾", 19.7 cm
Colour:	Background solid green, shaded green, white, cream or yellow-orange

Description	U.S. $	Can. $	U.K. £
Salad bowl, octagonal	100.00	150.00	55.00

Note: Supplied with or without servers which were 9", 22.9 cm long. Price is for bowl only.

Shape 212   Tomato dish

Designer:	Mr. Symcox in 1932
Issued:	1932 - 1970
Size:	8" x 9", 20.3 x 22.9 cm
Colour:	Background solid green, shaded green, white, cream or yellow-orange

Description	U.S. $	Can. $	U.K. £
Tomato dish	75.00	100.00	35.00

Note: Early pieces have a "cut-out."

Shape 213   Tomato dish, round

Designer:	Mr. Symcox in 1932
Issued:	1932 - 1970
Diameter:	6 ¾", 17.2 cm
Colour:	Background solid green, shaded green, white, cream or yellow-orange

Description	U.S. $	Can. $	U.K. £
Tomato dish, round	60.00	90.00	30.00

Shape 214-215 Tomato dish, leaf shape, in two sizes

Designer:	Mr. Symcox in 1932
Issued:	1932 - 1970
Size:	1. Shape 214 — 7" x 5 ¾", 17.8 x 14.6 cm
	2. Shape 215 — 5 ½" x 4 ¼", 14 x 10.8 cm
Colour:	Background solid green, shaded green, white, cream or yellow-orange

Description	U.S. $	Can. $	U.K. £
1. Shape 214	40.00	60.00	20.00
2. Shape 215	30 .00	45.00	15.00

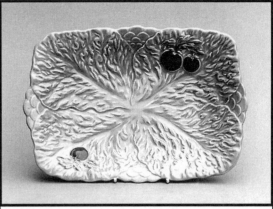

Shape 216   Tomato dish, rectangular

Designer:	Mr. Symcox in 1932
Issued:	1932 - 1970
Size:	10 ½" x 7 ¼", 26.7 x18.4 cm
Colour:	Background solid green, shaded green, white, cream or yellow-orange

Description	U.S. $	Can. $	U.K. £
Tomato dish, rectangular	75.00	100.00	35.00

Shape 217   Tomato dish

Designer:	Mr. Symcox in 1932
Issued:	1932 - 1970
Size :	9" x 7 ½", 22.9 x 19.1 cm
Colour:	Background solid green, shaded green, white, cream or yellow-orange

Description	U.S. $	Can. $	U.K. £
Tomato dish	75.00	100.00	35.00

Shape 218   Tomato dish, diamond shape

Designer:	Mr. Symcox in 1932
Issued:	1932 - 1965
Size:	7 ¾" x 4 ¼", 19.7 x 10.8 cm
Colour:	Background solid green, shaded green, white, cream or yellow-orange

Description	U.S. $	Can. $	U.K. £
Tomato dish, diamond	50.00	75.00	25.00

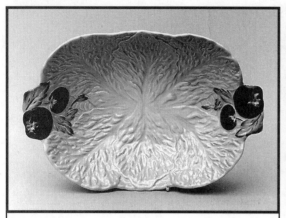

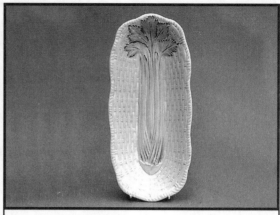

Shape 219   Tomato dish, oblong

Designer:	Mr. Symcox in 1932
Issued:	1932 - 1970
Size:	12" x 8", 30.5 x 20.3 cm
Colour:	Background solid green, shaded green, white, cream or yellow-orange

Description	U.S. $	Can. $	U.K. £
Tomato dish, oblong	75.00	100.00	35.00

Shape 220   Celery dish

Designer:	Mr. Symcox in 1932
Issued:	1932 - 1970
Size :	12" x 5 ¾", 30.5 x 14.6 cm
Colour:	Background solid green, shaded green, white, cream or yellow-orange

Description	U.S. $	Can. $	U.K. £
Celery dish	60.00	90.00	30.00

Shape 221   Cucumber tray

Designer:	Mr. Symcox in 1932
Issued:	1932 - 1970
Size :	12 ½" x 5 ¼", 31.7 x 13.3 cm
Colour:	Background solid green, shaded green, white, cream or yellow-orange

Description	U.S. $	Can. $	U.K. £
Cucumber tray	60.00	90.00	30.00

Shape 222   Triple tray

Designer:	Mr. Symcox in 1932
Issued:	1932 - by 1965
Size:	9 ½" x 10", 24 x 25.4 cm
Colour:	Background solid green, shaded green, white, cream or yellow-orange

Description	U.S. $	Can. $	U.K. £
Triple tray	80.00	125.00	40.00

Shape 223   Triple tray

Designer:	Mr. Symcox in 1932
Issued:	1932 - 1970
Diameter:	8 ¾", 22.2 cm
Colour:	Background solid green, shaded green, white, cream or yellow-orange

Description	U.S. $	Can. $	U.K. £
Triple tray	80.00	125.00	40.00

Shape 224   Strawberry double tray

Designer:	Mr. Symcox in 1932
Issued:	1932 - by 1965
Size:	12 ¾" x 6 ¼", 32.4 x 15.9 cm
Colour:	Background solid green, shaded green, white, cream or yellow-orange

Description	U.S. $	Can. $	U.K. £
Strawberry double tray	60.00	90.00	30.00

Shape 225   Lettuce cheese dish

Designer:	Mr. Symcox in 1932
Issued:	1932 - 1970
Size:	7 ¼" x 6" x 4", 18.4 x 15 x 10.1 cm
Colour:	Background solid green, shaded green, white, cream or yellow-orange

Description	U.S. $	Can. $	U.K. £
Cheese dish	90.00	125.00	45.00

Shape 226   Lettuce cheese dish

Designer:	Mr. Symcox in 1932
Issued:	1932 - 1970
Size:	6 ½" x 5' x 3 ½", 16.5 x 12.7 x 8.9 cm
Colour:	Background solid green, shaded green, white, cream or yellow-orange

Description	U.S. $	Can. $	U.K. £
Cheese dish	80.00	125.00	40.00

Shape 227   Lettuce butter dish

Designer: Mr. Symcox in 1932
Issued: 1932 - by 1954
Size: 6 ½" x 3", 16.5 x 7.6 cm
Colour: Background solid green, shaded green, white, cream or yellow-orange

Description	U.S. $	Can. $	U.K. £
Lettuce butter dish	100.00	150.00	50.00

Shape 228   Lettuce toast rack

Designer: Mr. Symcox in 1932
Issued: 1932 - 1968
Size: 6" x 4 ¾", 15 x 12.1 cm
Colour: Background solid green, shaded green, white, cream or yellow-orange

Description	U.S. $	Can. $	U.K. £
Toast rack	50.00	75.00	25.00

Photograph not
available
at press time

Shape 229   Lettuce sauce holder

Designer: Mr. Symcox in 1932
Issued: 1932 - by 1954
Size: 3 ½" x 3" , 8.9 x 7.6 cm
Colour: Background solid green, shaded green, white, cream or yellow-orange

Description	U.S. $	Can. $	U.K. £
Sauce holder	50.00	75.00	25.00

Shape 230   Lettuce preserve

Designer: Mr. Symcox in 1932
Issued: 1932 - 1962
Size: 4 ½" x 3 ½", 11.9 x 8.9 cm
Colour: Background solid green, shaded green, white, cream or yellow-orange

Description	U.S. $	Can. $	U.K. £
Lettuce preserve	60.00	80.00	30.00

Shape 231   Cherry preserve

Designer:	Mr. Symcox in 1932
Issued:	1932 - by 1954
Size	3 ½" x 4", 8.9 x 10.1 cm
Colour:	Background solid green, shaded green, white, cream or yellow-orange

Description	U.S. $	Can. $	U.K. £
Cherry preserve	90.00	125.00	45.00

Shape 232   Lettuce sauce boat and stand, large

Designer:	Mr. Symcox in 1932
Issued:	1932 - by 1965
Size:	6 ¾" x 3", 17.2 x 7.6 cm
Colour:	Background solid green, shaded green, white, cream or yellow-orange

Description	U.S. $	Can. $	U.K. £
Sauce boat and stand, large	60.00	90.00	30.00

Shape 233   Lettuce sauce boat and stand, small

Designer:	Mr. Symcox in 1932
Issued:	1932 - 1970
Size:	5" x 2 ¼", 12.7 x 5.7 cm
Colour:	Background solid green, shaded green, white, cream or yellow-orange

Description	U.S. $	Can. $	U.K. £
Sauce boat and stand, small	50.00	75.00	25.00

Shape 234   Lettuce cress tray and stand

Designer:	Mr. Symcox in 1932
Issued:	1932 - by 1954
Size:	8 ¼" x 2 ½", 21 x 6.4 cm
Colour:	Background solid green, shaded green, white, cream or yellow-orange

Description	U.S. $	Can. $	U.K. £
Cress tray and stand	90.00	125.00	45.00

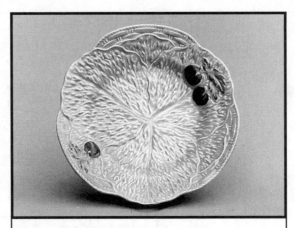

Shape 235   Lettuce dessert plate, round

Designer:	Mr. Symcox in 1932
Issued:	1932 - by 1954
Diameter:	8 ½", 21.6 cm
Colour:	Background solid green, shaded green, white, cream or yellow-orange

Description	U.S. $	Can. $	U.K. £
Dessert plate, round	60.00	90.00	30.00

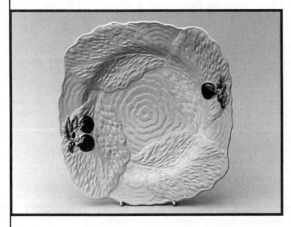

Shape 236/1/2/3 Lettuce plates, square three sizes

Designer:	Mr. Symcox in 1932
Issued:	1932 - by 1965
Length:	1. Shape 236/1 — 9 ½", 24 cm
	2. Shape 236/2 — 8 ½", 21.6 cm
	3. Shape 236/3 — 8", 20.3 cm
Colour:	Background solid green, shaded green, white, cream or yellow-orange

Description	U.S. $	Can. $	U.K. £
1. Shape 236/1	60.00	90.00	30.00
2. Shape 236/2	50.00	75.00	25.00
3. Shape 236/3	40.00	60.00	20.00

Photograph not
available
at press time

Shape 237   Tomato comport, rectangular

Designer:	Mr. Symcox in 1932
Issued:	1932 - by 1965
Size:	10 ½" x 7", 26.7 x 17.8 cm
Colour:	Background solid green, shaded green, white, cream or yellow-orange

Description	U.S. $	Can. $	U.K. £
Tomato comport, rectangular	60.00	90.00	30.00

Shape 238   Tomato cruet set, salt, pepper, mustard and base

Designer:	Mr. Symcox in 1932
Issued:	1932 - 1970
Size:	6" x 3 ¼", 15 x 8.3 cm
Colour:	Background solid green, shaded green, white, cream or yellow-orange

Description	U.S. $	Can. $	U.K. £
Tomato cruet set	60.00	90.00	30.00

Shape 269-270-271 Tomato dish, oval in three sizes

Designer:	Mr. Symcox in 1932
Issued:	1932 - 1970
Size:	1. Shape 269 — 7" x 5 ½", 17.8 x 14 cm
	2. Shape 270 — 8 ¼" x 6 ¼", 21 x 15.9
	3. Shape 271 — 10 ¼" x 8", 26 x 20.3 cm
Colour:	Background solid green, shaded green, white, cream or yellow-orange

Description	U.S. $	Can. $	U.K. £
1. Shape 269	40.00	60.00	20.00
2. Shape 270	50.00	75.00	25.00
3. Shape 271	60.00	90.00	30.00

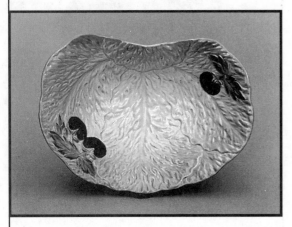

Shape 337-338-339 Tomato dish, kidney-shape, 3 sizes

Designer:	Mr. Symcox c.1934
Issued:	1934 - 1970
Size:	1. Shape 337 — 12" x 8", 30.5 x 20.3 cm
	2. Shape 338 — 10 ½" x 7", 26.7 x 17.8 cm
	3. Shape 339 — 9" x 6", 22.9 x 15 cm
Colour:	Background solid green, shaded green, white, cream or yellow-orange

Description	U.S. $	Can. $	U.K. £
1. Shape 337	75.00	100.00	35.00
2. Shape 338	60.00	90.00	30.00
3. Shape 339	50.00	75.00	25.00

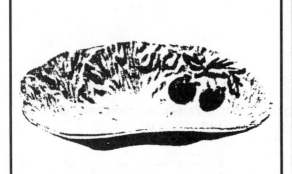

Shape 463   Tomato dish, kidney-shape, large

Designer:	Mr. Symcox in 1937
Issued:	1937 - 1970
Size:	7" x 4 ½", 17.8 x 11.9 cm
Colour:	Background solid green, shaded green, white, cream or yellow-orange

Description	U.S. $	Can. $	U.K. £
Tomato dish, kidney-shape	40.00	60.00	20.00

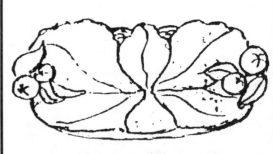

Shape 2029 Individual salad dish

Designer:	Albert Hallam in 1965
Issued:	1965 - 1970
Length:	7 ½", 19.1 cm
Colour:	Background solid green, shaded green, white, cream or yellow-orange

Description	U.S. $	Can. $	U.K. £
Individual salad dish		Rare	

SPRINGTIME

This series brought a "breath of spring" when it first appeared in 1961, and was aptly named. The range included items decorated with narcissi, with daffodils, with crocus and with anemones, all in their natural colours. The individual pieces were supplied with either a yellow or a green background in a gloss finish. The Double Dish (shape 1704) however was a hybrid, being half yellow and half green.

There was a total of twenty-two items in the series, of which eight were listed as dishes. Several of these were quite large, with novel shapes and scalloped edges. One small difference in detail to note is that in the case of shape 1710, the petals were yellow on the green version, and pale cream on the yellow version. This was necessary to provide a contrast with the background colour.

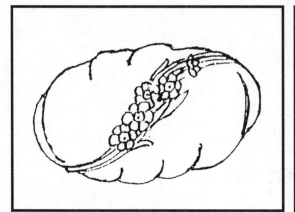

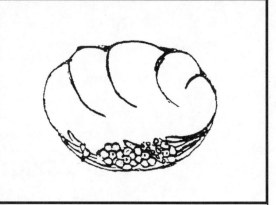

Shape 1704 Double dish, Narcissi

Designer: Albert Hallam in 1960
Issued: 1961 - by 1966
Size :   12″ x 8″, 30.5 x 20.3 cm
Colour: Yellow or green background with flowers
              in natural colours

Description	U.S. $	Can. $	U.K. £
Double dish, Narcissi	125.00	175.00	60.00

Shape 1705 Oval dish, Narcissi

Designer: Albert Hallam in 1960
Issued: 1961 - by 1966
Size: 11″ x 9″, 27.9 x 22.9 cm
Colour: Yellow or green background with flowers
              in natural colours

Description	U.S. $	Can. $	U.K. £
Oval dish, Narcissi	75.00	125.00	40.00

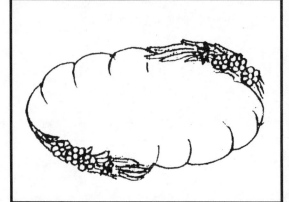

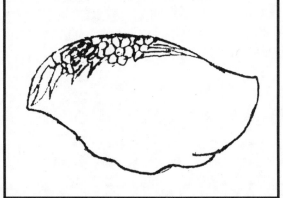

Shape 1706 Bowl, Narcissi

Designer: Albert Hallam in 1960
Issued: 1961 - by 1966
Size: 13″ x 8 ½″, 33 x 21.6 cm
Colour: Yellow or green background with flowers
              in natural colours

Description	U.S. $	Can. $	U.K. £
Bowl, Narcissi	75.00	125.00	45.00

Shape 1707 Dish, Narcissi

Designer: Albert Hallam in 1960
Issued: 1961 - by 1966
Size: 10″ x 7″, 25.4 cm x 17.8 cm
Colour: Yellow or green background with flowers
              in natural colours

Description	U.S. $	Can. $	U.K. £
Dish, Narcissi	75.00	125.00	40.00

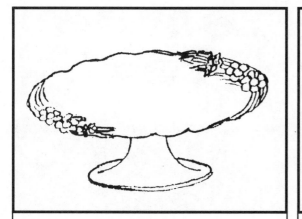

Shape 1708 Comport, Narcissi

Designer: Albert Hallam in 1960
Issued: 1961 - by 1966
Size: 11" x 4", 27.9 x 10.1 cm
Colour: Yellow or green background with flowers
            in natural colours

Description	U.S. $	Can. $	U.K. £
Comport, Narcissi	100.00	150.00	55.00

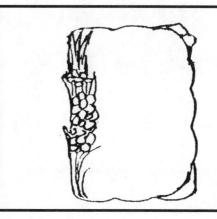

Shape 1709 Dish, Narcissi

Designer: Albert Hallam in 1960
Issued: 1961 - by 1966
Size: 8 ½" x 5 ¾", 21.6 x 14.6 cm
Colour: Yellow or green background with flowers
            in natural colours

Description	U.S. $	Can. $	U.K. £
Dish, Narcissi	60.00	90.00	30.00

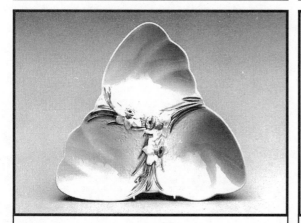

Shape 1710 Triple dish, Daffodil

Designer: Albert Hallam in 1960
Issued: 1961 - by 1966
Size: 11 ½" x 10 ½", 29.2 x 26.7 cm
Colour: Yellow or green background with flowers
            in natural colours

Description	U.S. $	Can. $	U.K. £
Triple dish, Daffodil	90.00	125.00	45.00

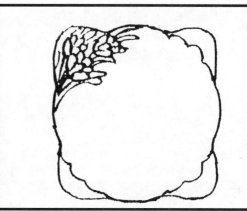

Shape 1711 Dish, Crocus

Designer: Albert Hallam in 1960
Issued: 1961 - by 1966
Width: 6 ½", 16.5 cm
Colour: Yellow or green background with flowers
            in natural colours

Description	U.S. $	Can. $	U.K. £
Dish, Crocus	50.00	75.00	25.00

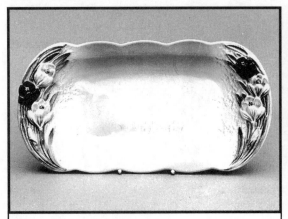

Shape 1712 Sandwich tray, Crocus

Designer:	Albert Hallam in 1960
Issued:	1961 - by 1966
Size :	11" x 5 ¾", 27.9 x 14.6 cm
Colour:	Yellow or green background with flowers in natural colours

Description	U.S. $	Can. $	U.K. £
Sandwich tray, Crocus	60.00	90.00	30.00

Shape 1713 Covered butter dish, Anemone

Designer:	Albert Hallam in 1960
Issued:	1961 - by 1966
Size:	5 ½" x 2 ¼", 14.0 x 5.7 cm
Colour:	Yellow or green background with flowers in natural colours

Description	U.S. $	Can. $	U.K. £
Covered butter dish, Anemone	75.00	100.00	35.00

Shape 1714 Cheese dish, Anemone

Designer:	Albert Hallam in 1960
Issued:	1961 - by 1966
Size:	6 ½" x 3 ½", 16.5 x 8.9 cm
Colour:	Yellow or green background with flowers in natural colours

Description	U.S. $	Can. $	U.K. £
Cheese dish, Anemone	90.00	125.00	45.00

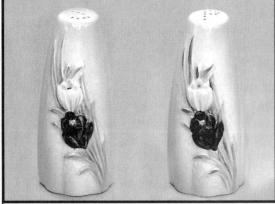

Shape 1715-1716 Salt and pepper, Crocus

Designer:	Albert Hallam in 1960
Issued:	1961 - by 1966
Height :	4 ½", 11.9 cm
Colour:	Yellow or green background with flowers in natural colours

Description	U.S. $	Can. $	U.K. £
1. Shape 1715 — Salt	50.00	75.00	25.00
2. Shape 1716 — Pepper	50.00	75.00	25.00

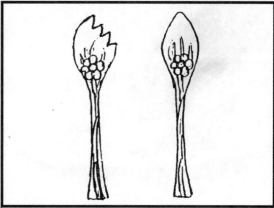

Shape 1717 Preserve with lid, Crocus

Designer:	Albert Hallam in 1960
Issued:	1961 - by 1966
Size:	4 ¼″ x 3 ½″, 10.8 x 8.9 cm
Colour:	Yellow or green background with flowers in natural colours

Description	U.S. $	Can. $	U.K. £
Preserve with lid	50.00	75.00	25.00

Shape 1718 Servers, Narcissi

Designer:	Albert Hallam in 1960
Issued:	1961 - by 1966
Length:	9″, 22.9 cm
Colour:	Yellow or green background with flowers in natural colours

Description	U.S. $	Can. $	U.K. £
Servers, Narcissi	100.00	150.00	50.00

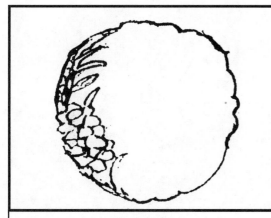

Shape 1725 Sweet dish, Daffodil

Designer:	Albert Hallam in 1960
Issued:	1961 - by 1966
Size:	5 ½″ x 5 ½″, 14 x 14 cm
Colour:	Yellow or green background with flowers in natural colours

Description	U.S. $	Can. $	U.K. £
Sweet dish, Daffodil	60.00	90.00	30.00

Shape 1726 Hostess set, Daffodil

Designer:	Albert Hallam in 1960
Issued:	1961 - by 1966
Size:	Unknown
Colour:	Yellow or green background with flowers in natural colours

Description	U.S. $	Can. $	U.K. £
Hostess set, Daffodil		Rare	

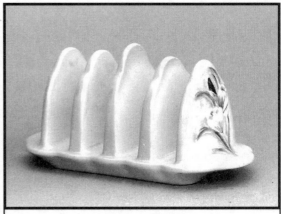

**Shape 1727 Cruet set — Salt, Pepper, Mustard
and Base, Crocus**

Designer: Albert Hallam in 1960
Issued: 1961 - by 1966
Size: 5 ½" x 3" x 2 ¾", 14 x 7.6 x 7 cm
Colour: Yellow or green background with flowers
in natural colours

Description	U.S. $	Can. $	U.K. £
Cruet set, Crocus	90.00	125.00	45.00

Shape 1728 Toast rack, Crocus

Designer: Albert Hallam in 1960
Issued: 1961 - by 1966
Size: 6" x 3", 15 x 7.6 cm
Colour: Yellow or green background with flowers
in natural colours

Description	U.S. $	Can. $	U.K. £
Toast rack, Crocus	75.00	100.00	35.00

Shape 1729 Jug (one pint), Anemone

Designer: Albert Hallam in 1960
Issued: 1961 - by 1966
Size: Unknown
Colour: Yellow or green background with flowers
in natural colours

Description	U.S. $	Can. $	U.K. £
Jug (one pint), Anemone	90.00	125.00	45.00

Shape 1747 Vinegar with stopper, Crocus

Designer: Albert Hallam in 1961
Issued: 1961 - by 1966
Height: 6", 15 cm
Colour: Yellow or green background with flowers
in natural colours

Description	U.S. $	Can. $	U.K. £
Vinegar with stopper, Crocus	75.00	100.00	35.00

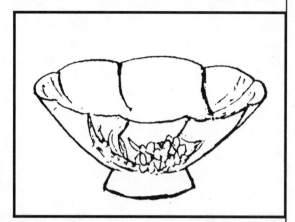

Shape 1795 Salad bowl, Daffodil

Designer:	Albert Hallam in 1961
Issued:	1962 - by 1966
Size:	Unknown
Colour:	Yellow or green background with flowers in natural colours

Description	U.S. $	Can. $	U.K. £
Salad bowl, Daffodil	150.00	225.00	75.00

Springtime Series Ware
Shape 1710 Triple dish, Daffodil
Shape 1728, 1715, 1716, 1747 Toast rack, salt, pepper and vinegar, Crocus
Shape 1714 Cheese dish, Anemone   Shape 1712 Sandwich tray, Crocus

STRAWBERRY FAIR

Strawberry Fair, as the name suggests, was decorated with a motif of red strawberries, white flowers with a blue edge, and leaves shaded in different greens, on a white background. The pattern was raised and overall there was a design of strings formed as part of the background and carried over to the outside of pieces where appropriate, e.g. the Salad Bowl (shape 1573).

The series consisted of twenty-two pieces, all in a gloss finish. It was a very attractive design and the shapes of many of the dishes were made more interesting by being irregular in shape. Nevertheless, however delightful the design, it would appear to have been wrong for the period, and the series had gone by 1963.

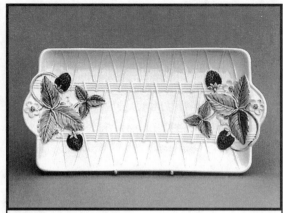

Shape 1565 Teapot

Designer:	Albert Hallam in 1958	
Issued:	1959 - by 1963	
Size:	Unknown	
Colour:	White background, red strawberries, white daisies, green leaves	

Description	U.S. $	Can. $	U.K. £
Teapot	125.00	175.00	60.00

Shape 1566 Sandwich tray

Designer:	Albert Hallam in 1958	
Issued:	1959 - by 1963	
Size:	11″ x 5 ½″, 27.9 x 14 cm	
Colour:	White background, red strawberries, white daisies, green leaves	

Description	U.S. $	Can. $	U.K. £
Sandwich tray	75.00	100.00	35.00

Shape 1567 Sandwich plate

Designer:	Albert Hallam in 1958	
Issued:	1959 - by 1963	
Width:	5″, 12.7 cm	
Colour:	White background, red strawberries, white daisies, green leaves	

Description	U.S. $	Can. $	U.K. £
Sandwich plate	40.00	60.00	20.00

Shape 1568 Cruet set - salt, pepper, mustard on a base

Designer:	Albert Hallam in 1958	
Issued:	1959 - by 1963	
Size:	4 ½″ x 4 ¼″ x 2 ¾″, 11.9 x 10.8 x 7.0 cm	
Colour:	White background, red strawberries, white daisies, green leaves	

Description	U.S. $	Can. $	U.K. £
Cruet set	75.00	110.00	40.00

Note: The above photo is missing the mustard pot.

Photograph not
available
at press time

Shape 1569 Cream jug

Designer: Albert Hallam in 1958
Issued: 1959 - by 1963
Size: Unknown
Colour: White background, red strawberries, white daisies, green leaves

Description	U.S. $	Can. $	U.K. £
Cream jug	60.00	90.00	30.00

Photograph not
available
at press time

Shape 1570 Sugar

Designer: Albert Hallam in 1958
Issued: 1959 - by 1963
Size: Unknown
Colour: White background, red strawberries, white daisies, green leaves

Description	U.S. $	Can. $	U.K. £
Sugar	60.00	90.00	30.00

Photograph not
available
at press time

Shape 1571 Stand for teapot

Designer: Albert Hallam in 1958
Issued: 1959 - by 1963
Size: Unknown
Colour: White background, red strawberries, white daisies, green leaves

Description	U.S. $	Can. $	U.K. £
Stand for teapot	40.00	60.00	20.00

Photograph not
available
at press time

Shape 1572 Cheese dish

Designer: Albert Hallam in 1958
Issued: 1959 - by 1963
Size: Unknown
Colour: White background, red strawberries, white daisies, green leaves

Description	U.S. $	Can. $	U.K. £
Cheese dish	100.00	150.00	50.00

Photograph not
available
at press time

Shape 1573 Salad bowl, footed

Designer:	Albert Hallam in 1958
Issued:	1959 - by 1963
Diameter:	9 ¼", 23.5 cm
Colour:	White background, red strawberries, white daisies, green leaves

Description	U.S. $	Can. $	U.K. £
Salad bowl, footed	90.00	125.00	45.00

Shape 1574 Salad servers

Designer:	Albert Hallam in 1958
Issued:	1959 - by 1963
Size:	Unknown
Colour:	White background, red strawberries, white daisies, green leaves

Description	U.S. $	Can. $	U.K. £
Salad servers	75.00	110.00	40.00

Shape 1575 Preserve with lid

Designer:	Albert Hallam in 1958
Issued:	1959 - by 1963
Size:	4" x 3 ¾", 10.1 x 9.5 cm
Colour:	White background, red strawberries, white daisies, green leaves

Description	U.S. $	Can. $	U.K. £
Preserve with lid	60.00	90.00	30.00

Shape 1576 Butter dish, rectangular

Designer:	Albert Hallam in 1958
Issued:	1959 - by 1963
Size:	5" x 3 ¼" , 12.7 x 8.3 cm
Colour:	White background, red strawberries, white daisies, green leaves

Description	U.S. $	Can. $	U.K. £
Butter dish, rectangular	90.00	125.00	45.00

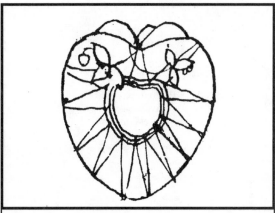

Shape 1577 Dish

Designer:	Albert Hallam in 1959
Issued:	1959 - by 1963
Size:	10" x 8 ¾", 25.4 x 22.2 cm
Colour:	White background, red strawberries, white daisies, green leaves

Description	U.S. $	Can. $	U.K. £
Dish	50.00	75.00	25.00

Shape 1578 Sweet dish

Designer:	Albert Hallam in 1959
Issued:	1959 - by 1963
Size:	5", 12.7 cm
Colour:	White background, red strawberries, white daisies, green leaves

Description	U.S. $	Can. $	U.K. £
Dish	50.00	75.00	25.00

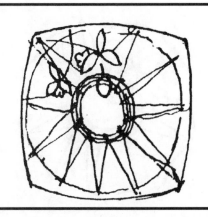

Photograph not
available
at press time

Shape 1579 Sweet dish, square

Designer:	Albert Hallam in 1959
Issued:	1959 - by 1963
Size:	4 ½", 11.9 cm
Colour:	White background, red strawberries, white daisies, green leaves

Description	U.S. $	Can. $	U.K. £
Sweet dish, square	50.00	75.00	25.00

Shape 1580 Toast rack

Designer:	Albert Hallam in 1959
Issued:	1959 - by 1963
Size:	Unknown
Colour:	White background, red strawberries, white daisies, green leaves

Description	U.S. $	Can. $	U.K. £
Toast rack	75.00	110.00	40.00

Photograph not
available
at press time

Shape 1581/1/2/3 Jugs in three sizes

Designer:	Mr. Garbet in 1959
Issued:	1959 - by 1963
Size:	Unknown
Colour:	White background, red strawberries, white daisies, green leaves

Description	U.S. $	Can. $	U.K. £
1. Shape 1581/1	100.00	150.00	50.00
2. Shape 1581/2	75.00	125.00	40.00
3. Shape 1581/3	65.00	100.00	35.00

Shape 1582 T.V. Set

Designer:	Albert Hallam in 1959
Issued:	1959 - by 1963
Size:	Unknown
Colour:	White background, red strawberries, white daisies, green leaves

Description	U.S. $	Can. $	U.K. £
TV Set	90.00	125.00	45.00

Photograph not
available
at press time

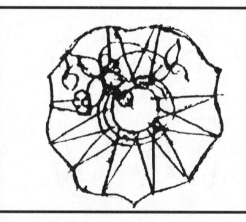

Shape 1583 Dish

Designer:	Albert Hallam in 1959
Issued:	1959 - by 1963
Size:	11 ½", 29.2 cm
Colour:	White background, red strawberries, white daisies, green leaves

Description	U.S. $	Can. $	U.K. £
Dish	75.00	100.00	35.00

Shape 1584 Dish

Designer:	Albert Hallam in 1959
Issued:	1959 - by 1963
Size:	5 ½", 14.0 cm
Colour:	White background, red strawberries, white daisies, green leaves

Description	U.S. $	Can. $	U.K. £
Dish	50.00	75.00	25.00

Photograph not
available
at press time

Shape 1585 Contemporary cup with new handle

Designer: Albert Hallam in 1959
Issued: 1959 - by 1963
Size: Unknown
Colour: Plain

Description	U.S. $	Can. $	U.K. £
Contemporary cup with new handle	50.00	75.00	25.00

Note: This shape is part of the TV Set (shape 1582).

Shape 1629 Spoon

Designer: Albert Hallam in 1959
Issued: 1959 - by 1963
Length: 4 ½", 11.9 cm
Colour: White background, red strawberries, white daisies, green leaves

Description	U.S. $	Can. $	U.K. £
Spoon		Rare	

Strawberry Ware Series Ware
Shape 1582 TV Set

Shape 1568 Pepper

Shape 1568 Salt

SUNDIAL

The Sundial tableware formed one of the more stylized ranges from the Beswick factory. Modelled in the then popular "Aztec" style, production was unlikely to have survived long after the outbreak of the Second World War.

The range consisted of eighteen items, all in gloss finish, including three different sizes of teapots, two sizes of butter dishes and two sizes of cheese dishes, but lacked teacups, saucers and plates.

In this colourful and distinctive group the colours are honey-beige (wall), green (grass), with orange and brown used on every piece. The flowers represent a herbaceous border, and are orange, dark red and blue in colour. A rose tree featured on all the designs, and a common feature where it could be incorporated was a sundial, hence the name. The dial and Roman numerals around the perimeter were painted dark brown while the gnomon (the piece that casts the shadow, when the sun is shining) was painted black and served as a knob.

The backstamp on some items read - "As purchased by H.M. Queen Mary" with the registration number 826924, corresponding to the year 1938.

Shape 530   Sugar dredger

Designer: Mr. Watkin in 1938
Issued: 1938 - by 1954
Height: 5", 12.7 cm
Colour: Cream, yellow, red, green, brown and black

Description	U.S. $	Can. $	U.K. £
Sugar dredger	100.00	150.00	50.00

Shape 531-541-579 Teapot in three sizes

Designer: Mr. Watkin, 541 in 1937, 531-579 in 1938
Issued: 1938 - by 1954
Height: 1. Shape 531 — 6 ½", 16.5 cm
             2. Shape 541 — unknown
             3. Shape 579 — unknown
Colour: Cream, yellow, red, green, brown and black

Description	U.S. $	Can. $	U.K. £
1. Shape 531, large	100.00	150.00	55.00
2. Shape 541, small	100.00	150.00	50.00
3. Shape 579, medium	100.00	150.00	45.00

Shape 532   Hot water jug

Designer: Mr. Watkin in 1937
Issued: 1938 - by 1954
Height: 6", 15 cm
Colour: Cream, yellow, red, green, brown and black

Description	U.S. $	Can. $	U.K. £
Hot water jug	100.00	150.00	55.00

Shape 533   Cream jug

Designer: Mr. Watkin in 1937
Issued: 1938 - by 1954
Height: 3 ½", 8.9 cm
Colour: Cream, yellow, red, green, brown and blue

Description	U.S. $	Can. $	U.K. £
Cream jug	75.00	100.00	35.00

Shape 534   Covered sugar

Designer: Mr. Watkin in 1937
Issued: 1938 - by 1954
Height: 4", 10.1 cm
Colour: Cream, yellow, red, green, brown and black

Description	U.S. $	Can. $	U.K. £
Covered sugar	75.00	100.00	40.00

Shape 535   Preserve with lid

Designer: Mr. Watkin in 1937
Issued: 1938 - by 1954
Height: 4", 10.1 cm
Colour: Cream, yellow, red, green, brown and black

Description	U.S. $	Can. $	U.K. £
Preserve with lid	75.00	100.00	40.00

Shape 536   Biscuit jar with lid

Designer: Mr. Watkin in 1937
Issued: 1938 - by 1954
Height: 6 ½", 16.5 cm
Colour: Cream, yellow, red, green, brown and black

Description	U.S. $	Can. $	U.K. £
Biscuit jar with lid	100.00	150.00	55.00

Shape 537-542 Cheese dish, two sizes

Designer:	Mr. Watkin in 1937
Issued:	1938 - by 1954
Size:	1. Shape 537 — 5", 12.7 cm
	2. Shape 542 — 4", 10.1 cm
Colour:	Cream, yellow, red, green, brown and black

Description	U.S. $	Can. $	U.K. £
1. Shape 537, large	100.00	150.00	55.00
2. Shape 542, small	100.00	150.00	50.00

Shape 538 Covered butter

Designer:	Mr. Watkin in 1937
Issued:	1938 - by 1954
Size:	4", 10.1 cm
Colour:	Cream, yellow, red, green, brown and black

Description	U.S. $	Can. $	U.K. £
Covered butter	100.00	150.00	55.00

Shape 539 Cruet set, salt, pepper, mustard on base

Designer:	Mr. Watkin in 1937
Issued:	1938 - by 1954
Size:	6 ¼" x 2 ¼" x 3", 15.9 x 5.7 x 7.6 cm
Colour:	Cream, yellow, red, green, brown and black

Description	U.S. $	Can. $	U.K. £
Cruet set	100.00	150.00	45.00

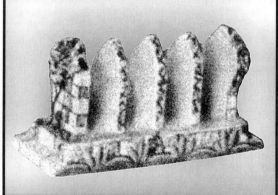

Shape 540 Toast rack, four slice

Designer:	Mr. Watkin in 1937
Issued:	1938 - by 1954
Size:	Unknown
Colour:	Cream, yellow, red, green, brown and black

Description	U.S. $	Can. $	U.K. £
Toast rack, four slice	100.00	150.00	45.00

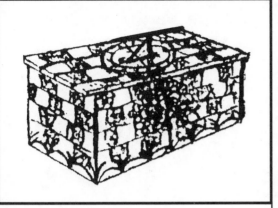

Shape 580   Covered butter, rectangular

Designer: Mr. Watkin in 1938
Issued: 1938 - by 1954
Size: Unknown
Colour: Cream, yellow, red, green, brown and black

Description	U.S. $	Can. $	U.K. £
Covered butter, rectangular	100.00	150.00	45.00

Photograph not
available
at press time

Shape 581   Covered muffin

Designer: Mr. Watkin in 1938
Issued: 1938 - by 1954
Size: Unknown
Colour: Cream, yellow, red, green, brown and black

Description	U.S. $	Can. $	U.K. £
Covered muffin		Rare	

Shape 582   Bowl

Designer: Mr. Watkin in 1938
Issued: 1938 - by 1954
Size: 10 ½" x 5", 26.7 x 12.7 cm
Colour: Cream, yellow, red, green, brown and black

Description	U.S. $	Can. $	U.K. £
Bowl	100.00	150.00	55.00

Shape 586   Stand for teapot

Designer: Mr. Watkin in 1938
Issued: 1938 - by 1954
Width: 5 ¼", 13.3 cm
Colour: Green and cream

Description	U.S. $	Can. $	U.K. £
Stand for teapot	35.00	50.00	20.00

Note: This stand was designed to be used with teapot
shapes 531 and 579.

Tit-Willow Series Ware

Shape 1832 Dish

Shape 1838 Dish
Shape 1841 Salad servers

Shape 1843 Dish

TIT-WILLOW

This series of eighteen items, all in a gloss finish, was in production for a very short time, which seems rather surprising to us, as we think it is very appealing. It is the only example of a realistic bird being used as part of the design on tableware. The bird, together with the willow in a raised motif, all on a subtle shaded background, combined to produce a most pleasing effect.

The background is a blend of shaded yellow and turquoise with a touch of pink. The bird was mainly brown, with a black head and blue wings, and brown again featured in the colour of the foliage. It is interesting to note how the position of the bird varies in relation to the willow branch. However alone among the items, the salt, pepper and servers were birdless!

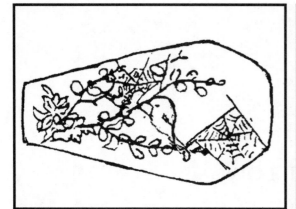

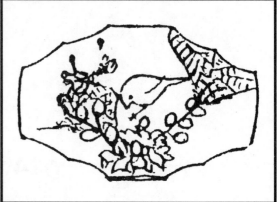

Shape 1830 Dish

Designer:	Albert Hallam in 1962
Issued:	1963 - by 1966
Length:	12", 30.5 cm
Colour:	Yellow, turquoise, pink, brown and black

Description	U.S. $	Can. $	U.K. £
Dish	100.00	150.00	50.00

Shape 1831 Dish

Designer:	Albert Hallam in 1962
Issued:	1963 - by 1966
Length:	10", 25.4 cm
Colour:	Yellow, turquoise, pink, brown and black

Description	U.S. $	Can. $	U.K. £
Dish	100.00	150.00	50.00

Shape 1832 Dish

Designer:	Albert Hallam in 1962
Issued:	1963 - by 1966
Size:	7" x 6 ½", 17.8 x 16.5 cm
Colour:	Yellow, turquoise, pink, brown and black

Description	U.S. $	Can. $	U.K. £
Dish	75.00	100.00	40.00

Shape 1833 Double dish

Designer:	Albert Hallam in 1962
Issued:	1963 - by 1966
Size:	13" x 8", 33 x 20.3 cm
Colour:	Yellow, turquoise, pink, brown and black

Description	U.S. $	Can. $	U.K. £
Double dish	125.00	175.00	60.00

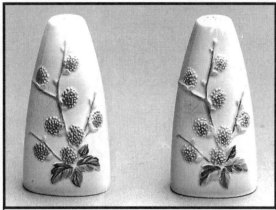

Shape 1834 Sandwich tray

Designer:	Albert Hallam in 1962		
Issued:	1963 - by 1966		
Length:	11", 27.9 cm		
Colour:	Yellow, turquoise, pink, brown and black		

Description	U.S. $	Can. $	U.K. £
Sandwich tray	90.00	125.00	45.00

Shape 1835-1836 Salt and pepper

Designer:	Albert Hallam in 1962		
Issued:	1963 - by 1966		
Height:	4 ½", 11.9 cm		
Colour:	Yellow, turquoise, pink and brown		

Description	U.S. $	Can. $	U.K. £
Salt	60.00	90.00	30.00
Pepper	60.00	90.00	30.00

Shape 1837 Preserve with lid

Designer:	Albert Hallam 1962		
Issued:	1963 - by 1966		
Size:	3", 7.6 cm		
Colour:	Yellow, turquoise, pink, brown and black		

Description	U.S. $	Can. $	U.K. £
Preserve with lid	75.00	125.00	40.00

Shape 1838 Dish

Designer:	Albert Hallam in 1962		
Issued:	1963 - by 1966		
Size:	13" x 8", 33 x 20.3 cm		
Colour:	Yellow, turquoise, pink, brown and black		

Description	U.S. $	Can. $	U.K. £
Dish	125.00	175.00	60.00

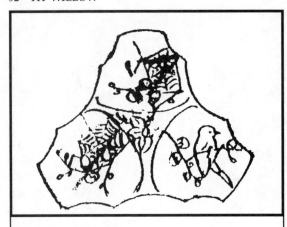

Shape 1839   Triple dish

Designer: Albert Hallam in 1962
Issued: 1963 - by 1966
Size: Unknown
Colour: Yellow, turquoise, pink, brown and black

Description	U.S. $	Can. $	U.K. £
Triple dish	125.00	175.00	60.00

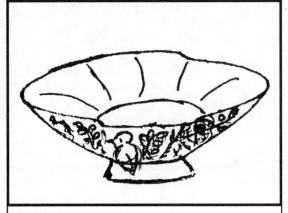

Shape 1840   Salad bowl

Designer: Albert Hallam in 1962
Issued: 1963 - by 1966
Diameter: 10 ½", 26.7 cm
Colour: Yellow, turquoise, pink, brown and black

Description	U.S. $	Can. $	U.K. £
Salad bowl	125.00	175.00	60.00

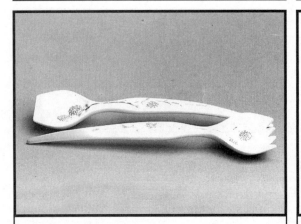

Shape 1841   Salad servers

Designer: Albert Hallam in 1962
Issued: 1963 - by 1966
Lenght: 9", 22.9 cm
Colour: Yellow, turquoise, pink and brown

Description	U.S. $	Can. $	U.K. £
Salad servers	100.00	150.00	50.00

Shape 1842   Dish

Designer: Albert Hallam in 1962
Issued: 1963 - by 1966
Length: 8", 20.3 cm
Colour: Yellow, turquoise, pink, brown and black

Description	U.S. $	Can. $	U.K. £
Dish	90.00	125.00	45.00

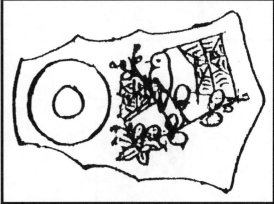

Shape 1843 Dish

Designer: Albert Hallam in 1962
Issued: 1963 - by 1966
Size: 6" x 5 ½", 15 x 14 cm
Colour: Yellow, turquoise, pink, brown and black

Description	U.S. $	Can. $	U.K. £
Dish	75.00	100.00	40.00

Shape 1844 Hostess or TV set
            (TV tray plus Eton cup)

Designer: Albert Hallam in 1962
Issued: 1963 - by 1966
Size: Unknown
Colour: Yellow, turquoise, pink, brown and black

Description	U.S. $	Can. $	U.K. £
Hostess or TV set		Rare	

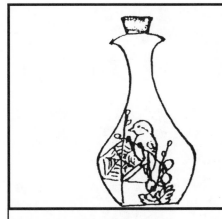

Shape 1846 Vinegar with stopper

Designer: Albert Hallam in 1962
Issued: 1963 - by 1966
Height: 5 ½", 14 cm
Colour: Yellow, turquoise, pink, brown and black

Description	U.S. $	Can. $	U.K. £
Vinegar with stopper	75.00	100.00	35.00

Shape 1864 Vase

Designer: Albert Hallam in 1963
Issued: 1963 - by 1966
Height: 7 ½", 19.1 cm
Colour: Yellow, turquoise, pink, brown and black

Description	U.S. $	Can. $	U.K. £
Vase	100.00	150.00	50.00

Shape 1865 Covered jar

Designer: Albert Hallam in 1963
Issued: 1963 - by 1966
Height: 6 ½″, 16.5 cm
Colour: Yellow, turquoise, pink, brown and black

Description	U.S. $	Can. $	U.K. £
Covered jar	100.00	150.00	55.00

TURQUOISE CATHAY

Turquoise Cathay was a new series of giftware announced for 1972. The items were in a delicate pale aquamarine colour glaze with a gloss finish, which became deeper as it radiated towards the edge of a lid or the base of a vase. The design of raised floral and geometric motifs had its origin in the early Chinese dynastic ceramics. The amalgamation of ancient and modern design combined with modern technology produced the unusual effect of this attractive range.

There were 12 items in the series, all of which are now difficult to find, because they were available for such a short time.

Shape 2382 Candlestick

Designer:	Graham Tongue in 1971
Issued:	1972 - 1972
Diameter:	2 ½", 6.4 cm
Height:	3 ½", 8.9 cm
Colour:	Aquamarine

Description	U.S. $	Can. $	U.K. £
Candlestick	50.00	75.00	25.00

Shape 2383 Candlestick

Designer:	Graham Tongue in 1971
Issued:	1972 - 1972
Diameter:	3 ½", 8.9 cm
Height:	2", 5 cm
Colour:	Aquamarine

Description	U.S. $	Can. $	U.K. £
Candlestick	40.00	60.00	20.00

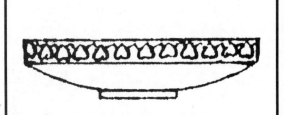

Shape 2384 Bowl

Designer:	Graham Tongue in 1971
Issued:	1972 - 1972
Diameter:	5", 12.7 cm
Height:	1 ¼", 3.1 cm
Colour:	Aquamarine

Description	U.S. $	Can. $	U.K. £
Bowl	75.00	100.00	35.00

Shape 2385 Vase

Designer:	Graham Tongue, Harry Sales in 1971
Issued:	1972 - 1972
Height:	7 ½", 19.1 cm
Colour:	Aquamarine

Description	U.S. $	Can. $	U.K. £
Vase	75.00	100.00	35.00

Shape 2386 Covered box with lid

Designer:	Graham Tongue in 1971
Issued:	1972 - 1972
Diameter:	4", 10.1 cm
Height:	3 ½", 8.9 cm
Colour:	Aquamarine

Description	U.S. $	Can. $	U.K. £
Covered box with lid	75.00	100.00	40.00

Shape 2387 Bowl

Designer:	Graham Tongue, Harry Sales in 1971
Issued:	1972 - 1972
Diameter:	6", 15 cm
Height:	2 ¾", 7 cm
Colour:	Aquamarine

Description	U.S. $	Can. $	U.K. £
Bowl	75.00	100.00	35.00

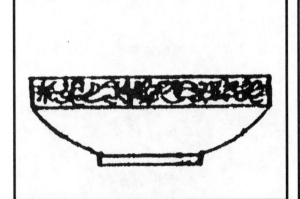

Shape 2388 Bowl

Designer:	Graham Tongue in 1971
Issued:	1972 - 1972
Diameter:	4 ¼", 10.8 cm
Height:	1 ¾", 4.4 cm
Colour:	Aquamarine

Description	U.S. $	Can. $	U.K. £
Bowl	60.00	90.00	30.00

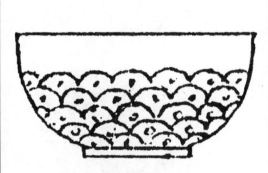

Shape 2389 Bowl

Designer:	Graham Tongue in 1971
Issued:	1972 - 1972
Diameter:	4 ½", 11.9 cm
Height:	2", 5 cm
Colour:	Aquamarine

Description	U.S. $	Can. $	U.K. £
Bowl	60.00	90.00	30.00

Shape 2390 Preserve with lid

Designer:	Graham Tongue in 1971
Issued:	1972 - 1972
Height:	4 ½″, 11.9 cm
Colour:	Aquamarine

Description	U.S. $	Can. $	U.K. £
Preserve with lid	75.00	100.00	35.00

Shape 2392 Vase

Designer:	Graham Tongue in 1971
Issued:	1972 - 1972
Height:	7 ½″, 19.1 cm
Colour:	Aquamarine

Description	U.S. $	Can. $	U.K. £
Vase	90.00	125.00	45.00

Shape 2408 Ginger jar, large

Designer:	Graham Tongue in 1972
Issued:	1972 - 1972
Height:	7″, 17.8 cm
Colour:	Aquamarine

Description	U.S. $	Can. $	U.K. £
Ginger jar, large	100.00	150.00	55.00

Shape 2409 Ginger jar, small

Designer:	Graham Tongue, Harry Sales in 1972
Issued:	1972 - 1972
Height:	4″, 10.1 cm
Colour:	Aquamarine

Description	U.S. $	Can. $	U.K. £
Ginger jar, small	100.00	150.00	50.00

VENETIAN WARE

The Venetian Series was designed soon after the beginning of the war in order to replace in overseas markets the particular types of ornamental wares previously available from Germany, Czecho-Slovakia and Italy. Two distinct styles of gloss decoration were used, one design incorporating scrolls and a stylistic bird, the other floral and leaf patterns. Three of the floral designs were illustrated in the Pottery Gazette for September, 1940 on a page with the caption :

"Britain **CAN** Export - Buy British Ware."

The decorations were carried out in a scratched or Sgraffito style in green, blue, yellow and red on a white or beige ground, and were typically Italian in character. Except perhaps for the large tray/plaques, all the floral designs were also produced in white matt.

Information is scarce on these early pieces, of which there were thirty-five in the series. The bird design was withdrawn earlier than the floral pattern and each is identified against the shapes in which it was produced, "Bird" with a (B), and "Floral" with an (F). Since the series was produced initially for export, examples rarely appear.

Shape 770 (B)   Vase, two handles each consisting of three loops

Designer:	Unknown in 1939	
Issued:	1940 - by 1954	
Size:	Unknown	
Colour:	Green, blue, yellow and red on beige background	

Description	U.S. $	Can. $	U.K. £
Vase	175.00	275.00	95.00

Shape 771 (B)   Jug, handle consisting of two loops

Designer:	Mr. Symcox in 1939	
Issued:	1940 - by 1954	
Size:	Unknown	
Colour:	Green, blue, yellow and red on beige background	

Description	U.S. $	Can. $	U.K. £
Jug	175.00	250.00	85.00

Photograph not
availabe
at press time

Shape 772 (B)   Jug

Designer:	Unknown in 1939	
Issued:	1940 - by 1954	
Size:	Unknown	
Colour:	Green, blue, yellow and red on beige background	

Description	U.S. $	Can. $	U.K. £
Jug	150.00	225.00	80.00

Shape 773 (B)   Vase

Designer:	Mr. Symcox in 1939	
Issued:	1940 - by 1954	
Size:	Unknown	
Colour:	Green, blue, yellow and red on beige background	

Description	U.S. $	Can. $	U.K. £
Vase	150.00	225.00	75.00

Shape 774 (B) Jug

Designer: Mr. Symcox in 1939
Issued: 1940 - by 1954
Size: Unknown
Colour: Green, blue, yellow and red on beige
background

Description	U.S. $	Can. $	U.K. £
Jug	150.00	225.00	80.00

Shape 775 (B) Vase

Designer: Mr. Symcox in 1940
Issued: 1940 - by 1954
Size: Unknown
Colour: Green, blue, yellow and red on beige
background

Description	U.S. $	Can. $	U.K. £
Vase	150.00	225.00	70.00

Shape 776 (B) Vase with 2 handles

Designer: Mr. Watkin in 1940
Issued: 1940 - by 1954
Size: Unknown
Colour: Green, blue, yellow and red on beige
background

Description	U.S. $	Can. $	U.K. £
Vase	150.00	225.00	75.00

Shape 777 (B) Jug

Designer: Mr. Watkin in 1940
Issued: 1940 - by 1954
Size: Unknown
Colour: Green, blue, yellow and red on beige
background

Description	U.S. $	Can. $	U.K. £
Jug	150.00	225.00	75.00

Photograph not
available
at press time

Shape 778 (B)   Bowl with fancy edge

Designer: Mr. Symcox in 1940
Issued: 1940 - by 1954
Diameter: 12 ½ ", 31.7 cm
Colour: Green, blue, yellow and red on beige
             background

Description	U.S. $	Can. $	U.K. £
Bowl	175.00	275.00	95.00

Shape 779 (B)   Vase with 2 handles

Designer: Unknown in 1940
Issued: 1940 - by 1954
Size: Unknown
Colour: Green, blue, yellow and red on beige
             background

Description	U.S. $	Can. $	U.K. £
Vase	150.00	225.00	75.00

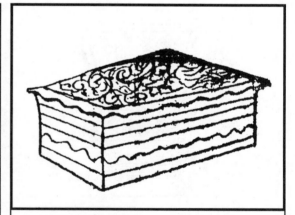

Shape 780 (B)   Jug

Designer: Mr. Symcox in 1940
Issued: 1940 - by 1954
Size: Unknown
Colour: Green, blue, yellow and red on beige
             background

Description	U.S. $	Can. $	U.K. £
Jug	150.00	225.00	75.00

Shape 781 (B)   Cigarette box , bird design on lid

Designer: Unknown in 1940
Issued: 1940 - by 1954
Size :   Unknown
Colour: Green, blue, yellow and red on beige
             background

Description	U.S. $	Can. $	U.K. £
Cigarette box	150.00	225.00	80.00

Photograph not
available
at press time

Shape 782 (B) Tray/Plaque

Designer:	Unknown in 1940
Issued:	1940 - by 1954
Diameter:	12 ¼", 31.1 cm
Colour:	Green, blue, yellow and red on beige background

Description	U.S. $	Can. $	U.K. £
Tray/Plaque	175.00	275.00	90.00

Shape 783 (B) Ashtray

Designer:	Unknown in 1940
Issued:	1940 - by 1954
Size:	Unknown
Colour:	Green, blue, yellow and red on beige background

Description	U.S. $	Can. $	U.K. £
Ashtray	75.00	100.00	40.00

Shape 784 (B) Wall pocket

Designer:	Unknown in 1940
Issued:	1940 - by 1954
Size:	Unknown
Colour:	Green, blue, yellow and red on beige background

Description	U.S. $	Can. $	U.K. £
Wall pocket	125.00	175.00	65.00

Shape 785 (F) Vase with 2 handles

Designer:	Unknown in 1939
Issued:	1940 - by 1963
Height:	9 ¾", 24.7 cm
Colour:	Green, blue, yellow and red on beige background

Description	U.S. $	Can. $	U.K. £
Vase	150.00	225.00	75.00

Shape 786 (F) Jug

Designer:	Unknown in 1939		
Issued:	1940 - by 1963		
Height:	12 ¼", 31.1 cm		
Colour:	Green, blue, yellow and red on beige background		

Description	U.S. $	Can. $	U.K. £
Jug	150.00	225.00	80.00

Shape 787 (F) Vase

Designer:	Unknown in 1939		
Issued:	1940 - by 1963		
Height:	7", 17.8 cm		
Colour:	Green, blue, yellow and red on beige background		

Description	U.S. $	Can. $	U.K. £
Vase	150.00	225.00	70.00

Shape 788 (F) Vase with 2 handles

Designer:	Mr. Watkin in 1939		
Issued:	1940 - by 1963		
Height:	10 ½", 26.7 cm		
Colour:	Green, blue, yellow and red on beige background		

Description	U.S. $	Can. $	U.K. £
Vase	150.00	225.00	75.00

Shape 789 (F) Vase

Designer:	Mr. Watkin in 1939		
Issued:	1940 - by 1963		
Height:	10 ¾", 27.8 cm		
Colour:	Green, blue, yellow and red on beige background		

Description	U.S. $	Can. $	U.K. £
Vase	150.00	225.00	70.00

Shape 790 (F)   Jug

Designer: Mr. Watkin in 1939
Issued: 1940 - by 1963
Height: 8 ½", 21.6 cm
Colour: Green, blue, yellow and red on beige
             background

Description	U.S. $	Can. $	U.K. £
Jug	150.00	225.00	75.00

Shape 791 (F)   Vase with 2 handles

Designer: Mr. Symcox in 1939
Issued: 1940 - by 1963
Height: 7 ½", 19.1 cm
Colour: Green, blue, yellow and red on beige
             background

Description	U.S. $	Can. $	U.K. £
Vase	150.00	225.00	75.00

Shape 792 (F)   Vase / Lamp base

Designer: Mr. Symcox in 1939
Issued: 1940 - by 1963
Height: 15 ¼", 38.7 cm
Colour: Green, blue, yellow and red on beige
             background

Description	U.S. $	Can. $	U.K. £
Vase / lamp base	150.00	225.00	80.00

Shape 793 (F)   Vase with 2 handles

Designer: Mr. Watkin in 1939
Issued: 1940 - by 1963
Height: 6", 15 cm
Colour: Green, blue, yellow and red on beige
             background

Description	U.S. $	Can. $	U.K. £
Vase	125.00	175.00	65.00

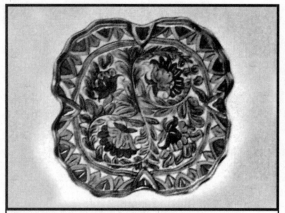

Shape 794 (F) Bowl

Designer:	Unknown in 1939	
Issued:	1940 - by 1963	
Diameter:	11″, 27.9 cm	
Colour:	Green, blue, yellow and red on beige background	

Description	U.S. $	Can. $	U.K. £
Bowl	175.00	225.00	95.00

Shape 795 (F) Jug

Designer:	Mr. Symcox in 1940	
Issued:	1940 - by 1963	
Height:	9″, 22.9 cm	
Colour:	Green, blue, yellow and red on beige background	

Description	U.S. $	Can. $	U.K. £
Jug	150.00	225.00	75.00

Shape 796 (F) Jug

Designer:	Mr. Symcox in 1940	
Issued:	1940 - by 1963	
Height:	7″, 17.8 cm	
Colour:	Green, blue, yellow and red on beige background	

Description	U.S. $	Can. $	U.K. £
Jug	125.00	200.00	70.00

Shape 797 (F) Ashtray, large

Designer:	Mr. Watkin in 1940	
Issued:	1940 - by 1963	
Diameter:	5 ¼″, 13.3 cm	
Colour:	Green, blue, yellow and red on beige background	

Description	U.S. $	Can. $	U.K. £
Ashtray	75.00	100.00	40.00

Photograph not
available
at press time

Shape 798 (F)   Wall Vase

Designer:	Mr. Watkin in 1940
Issued:	1940 - by 1963
Height:	6 ½", 16.5 cm
Colour:	Green, blue, yellow and red on beige background

Description	U.S. $	Can. $	U.K. £
Wall Vase	125.00	175.00	65.00

Shape 799 (F)   Ashtray, small

Designer:	Unknown in 1940
Issued:	1940 - by 1963
Diameter:	3 ½", 8.9 cm
Colour:	Green, blue, yellow and red on beige background

Description	U.S. $	Can. $	U.K. £
Ashtray, small	75.00	100.00	40.00

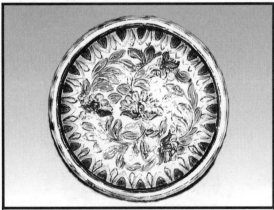

Shape 814 (F)   Cigarette box

Designer:	Mr. Watkin in 1940
Issued:	1940 - by 1963
Size:	5 ½" x 4 ¼", 14.0 x 10.8 cm
Colour:	Green, blue, yellow and red on beige background

Description	U.S. $	Can. $	U.K. £
Cigarette box	175.00	250.00	80.00

Shape 816 (F)   Tray / Plaque

Designer:	James Hayward, Albert Hallam in 1940
Issued:	1940 - by 1963
Diameter:	12 ¼", 31.7 cm
Colour:	Green, blue, yellow and red on beige background

Description	U.S. $	Can. $	U.K. £
Tray/Plaque	175.00	275.00	90.00

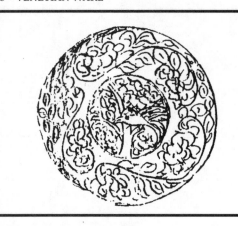

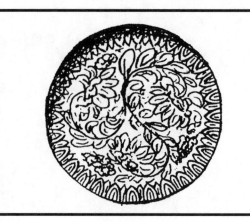

Shape 838 (B) Tray / Plaque

Designer: Albert Hallam, James Hayward in 1940
Issued: 1940 - by 1954
Diameter: 14", 35.5 cm
Colour: Green, blue, yellow and red on beige
background

Description	U.S. $	Can. $	U.K. £
Tray/Plaque	250.00	350.00	125.00

Shape 839 (F) Tray / Plaque

Designer: Albert Hallam, James Hayward in 1940
Issued: 1940 - by 1954
Diameter: 14", 35.5 cm
Colour: Green, blue, yellow and red on beige
background

Description	U.S. $	Can. $	U.K. £
Tray/Plaque	250.00	350.00	125.00

Shape 921 (B) Vase / Lamp base

Designer: Albert Hallam, James Hayward in 1941
Issued: 1941 - by 1954
Height: 7 ½", 19.1 cm
Colour: Green, blue, yellow and red on beige
background

Description	U.S. $	Can. $	U.K. £
Vase / Lamp base	175.00	250.00	85.00

WAYSIDE

The name "Wayside" brings to mind a picture of a typical country lane, and this series surely was inspired by the wonder of nature in the countryside. The background colour chosen for this pretty and attractive series was either a turquoise or primrose with red, purple, pink, yellow and green flowers. Variations have been found in the background, e.g. a pastel turquoise blue or an almost white. A feature of the design were the harebell knobs in blue and yellow. These were used on the butter, preserve and on the teapots. Some of the flowers represented in the decoration were poppies, harebells and violets.

There were twenty-three items in the series, which could be purchased separately or in sets, all in a gloss finish. The sets were put together at the time of purchase. If a Morning Set was ordered, the shop would gather the appropriate pieces to create the set. The four sets were:

1. A fruit set comprising six fruit saucers and a fruit bowl
2. A tea set comprising 21 pieces
3. A tea set comprising 18 pieces
4. A morning set comprising two cups and saucers, a plate, a sugar, a cream jug and a teapot

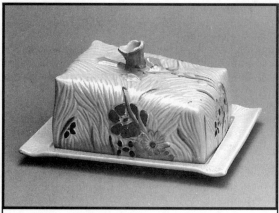

Shape 870-871 Teapot, two sizes

Designer:	Mr. Watkin in 1940
Issued:	1941 - by 1963
Height:	1. Shape 870 — 6", 15 cm
	2. Shape 871 — 5 ¼", 13.3 cm
Colour:	See title page

Description	U.S. $	Can. $	U.K. £
1. Shape 870	150.00	225.00	75.00
2. Shape 871	150 .00	225.00	80.00

Shape 872-873 Cheese dish, two sizes

Designer:	Mr. Watkin in 1940
Issued:	1941 - by 1963
Base Size:	1. Shape 872 — 7" x 8 ¼", 17.8 x 21 cm
	2. Shape 873 — 6" x 6 ¾", 15 x 17.2 cm
Height :	1. Shape 872 — 3 ½, 8.9 cm
	2. Shape 873 — 3", 7.6 cm
Colour:	See title page

Description	U.S. $	Can. $	U.K. £
1. Shape 872	150.00	225.00	75.00
2. Shape 873	125.00	200.00	65.00

Photograph not
available
at press time

Shape 874 /1/2/3 Jug, three sizes

Designer:	Mr. Watkin in 1940
Issued:	1941 - by 1963
Heights:	1. Shape 874/1 — 6 ½", 16.5 cm
	2. Shape 874/2 — 6", 15 cm
	3. Shape 874/3 — 5 ¼", 13.3 cm
Colour:	See title page

Description	U.S. $	Can. $	U.K. £
1. Large	100.00	150.00	50.00
2. Medium	75.00	125.00	40.00
3. Small	65.00	100.00	35.00

Shape 875 Covered butter

Designer:	Mr. Watkin in 1940
Issued:	1941 - by 1963
Size:	6" x 4" x 3 ¾", 15 x 10.1 x 9.5 cm
Colour:	See title page

Description	U.S. $	Can. $	U.K. £
Covered butter	100.00	150.00	55.00

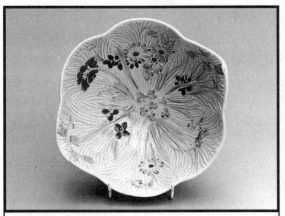

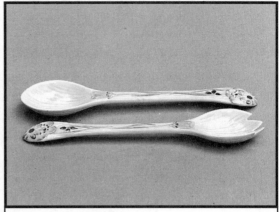

Shape 876	**Salad bowl**
Designer:	Mr. Watkin in 1940
Issued:	1941 - by 1963
Size:	9 ¾″ x 4″, 24.7 x 10.1 cm
Colour:	See title page

Description	U.S. $	Can. $	U.K. £
Salad bowl	150.00	225.00	75.00

Shape 877	**Salad servers**
Designer:	Mr. Watkin in 1940
Issued:	1941 - by 1963
Length:	9″, 22.9 cm
Colour:	See title page

Description	U.S. $	Can. $	U.K. £
Salad servers	100.00	150.00	50.00

Note: Price listed above is for the pair.

Shape 878	**Open sugar bowl, large**
Designer:	Mr. Watkin in 1940
Issued:	1941 - by 1963
Diameter:	3 ¼″, 8.3 cm
Colour:	See title page

Description	U.S. $	Can. $	U.K. £
Open sugar bowl, large	60.00	90.00	30.00

Shape 879	**Cream jug**
Designer:	Mr. Watkin in 1940
Issued:	1941 - by 1963
Height :	4″, 10.1 cm
Colour:	See title page

Description	U.S. $	Can. $	U.K. £
Cream jug	60.00	90.00	30.00

Shape 880 **Preserve with lid**

Designer: Mr. Watkin in 1940
Issued: 1941 - by 1963
Size: 3 ½" x 4 ½", 8.9 x11.9 cm
Colour: See title page

Description	U.S. $	Can. $	U.K. £
Preserve with lid	75.00	100.00	40.00

Shape 881 **Egg set (4 egg cups on a base)**

Designer: Mr. Watkin in 1941
Issued: Unknown
Size: Unknown
Colour: See title page

Description	U.S. $	Can. $	U.K. £
Egg set		Rare	

Note: Possibly not put into production.

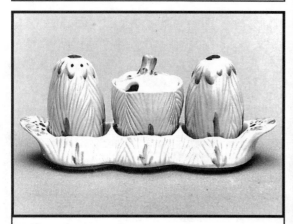

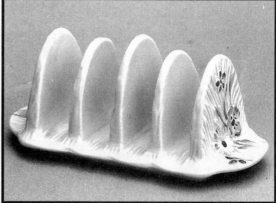

Shape 882 **Cruet set, salt, pepper and mustard on base (four pieces)**

Designer: Mr. Watkin in 1941
Issued: 1941 - by 1963
Length: 6 ½", 16.5 cm
Colour: See title page

Description	U.S. $	Can. $	U.K. £
Cruet set	90.00	125.00	45.00

Note: These pieces were also supplied as separate items.

Shape 883 **Toast rack, four slice**

Designer: Mr. Watkin in 1941
Issued: 1941 - by 1963
Size: 2 ½" x 6", 6.4 x 15 cm
Colour: See title page

Description	U.S. $	Can. $	U.K. £
Toast rack, four slice	80.00	125.00	40.00

Shape 884/1/2 Sweet dish, two sizes

Designer:	Mr. Watkin in 1941
Issued:	1941 - by 1963
Length:	1. Shape 884/1 — 9 ¼", 23.5 cm
	2. Shape 884/2 — 7", 17.8 cm
Colour:	See title page

Description	U.S. $	Can. $	U.K. £
1. Shape 884/1	75.00	100.00	35.00
2. Shape 884/2	50.00	75.00	25.00

Photograph not
available
at press time

Shape 885 Cup and saucer

Designer:	Mr. Watkin in 1941
Issued:	1941 - by 1963
Size:	Cup - 3 ¾", 9.5 cm
	Saucer - unknown
Colour:	See title page

Description	U.S. $	Can. $	U.K. £
Cup and saucer		Rare	

Photograph not
available
at press time

Shape 886-887 Plate, two sizes

Designer:	Mr. Watkin in 1941
Issued:	1941 - by 1963
Size:	1. Shape 886 — 5", 12.7 cm
	2. Shape 887 — 6 ¾", 17.2 cm
Colour:	See title page

Description	U.S. $	Can. $	U.K. £
1. Shape 886	60.00	90.00	30.00
2. Shape 887	50.00	75.00	25.00

Photograph not
available
at press time

Shape 888 Bread and butter plate

Designer:	Mr. Watkin in 1941
Issued:	1941 - by 1963
Diameter:	9", 22.9 cm
Colour:	See title page

Description	U.S. $	Can. $	U.K. £
Bread and butter plate	75.00	100.00	40.00

Photograph not
available
at press time

Shape 889 Fruit bowl

Designer: Mr. Watkin in 1941
Issued: 1941 - by 1963
Diameter: 9", 22.9 cm
Colour: See title page

Description	U.S. $	Can. $	U.K. £
Fruit bowl	135.00	175.00	70.00

Shape 890 Fruit saucer

Designer: Mr. Watkin in 1941
Issued: 1941 - by 1963
Diameter: 6 ½", 16.5 cm
Colour: See title page

Description	U.S. $	Can. $	U.K. £
Fruit saucer	50.00	75.00	25.00

Photograph not
available
at press time

Photograph not
available
at press time

Shape 1323 Cream, for the morning set

Designer: Albert Hallam in 1954
Issued: 1954 - by 1963
Size: Unknown
Colour: See title page

Description	U.S. $	Can. $	U.K. £
Cream	75.00	100.00	35.00

Shape 1324 Sugar, for the morning set

Designer: Albert Hallam in 1954
Issued: 1954 - by 1963
Size: Unknown
Colour: See title page

Description	U.S. $	Can. $	U.K. £
Sugar	75.00	100.00	35.00

WILLOW

1938 saw the introduction of the "Willow" series, which was modelled in relief. There were two distinct colourways, the first being in both light and dark blue, on a white background and the second using green, orange, brown and blue also on a white background.

The novelty of the design was that the component subjects of the old willow-pattern plate story were used separately as motifs for the decoration. For example, on the lids of both the teapot (shape 511) and the hot water jug (shape 512), it is possible to see embossed on the lid, the two lovers turned into birds and flying away.

There are eighteen items in this series and all were produced in a gloss finish. Again, as with many series which were modelled around this time, the war intervened and they were discontinued after only a few years. Examples of the more highly coloured decoration have turned up, but the blue version appears to be very rare indeed.

Shape 511   Teapot on stand

Designer:	Mr. Watkin in 1937
Issued:	1938 - by 1954
Height:	7", 17.8 cm
Colour:	1. Green, orange, brown and blue on a white background
	2. Light and dark blue on white background

Description	U.S. $	Can. $	U.K. £
Teapot on stand	250.00	350.00	125.00

Shape 512   Hot water jug

Designer:	Mr. Watkin in 1937
Issued:	1938 - by 1954
Size:	4 ¾" x 3 ¾" x 6 ½", 12.1 x 9.5 x 16.5 cm
Colour:	1. Green, orange, brown and blue on a white background
	2. Light and dark blue on white background

Description	U.S. $	Can. $	U.K. £
Hot water jug	200.00	300.00	100.00

Shape 513   Cream jug

Designer:	Mr. Watkin in 1937
Issued:	1938 - by 1954
Height:	3 ½", 8.9 cm
Colour:	1. Green, orange, brown and blue on a white background
	2. Light and dark blue on white background

Description	U.S. $	Can. $	U.K. £
Cream jug	100.00	150.00	55.00

Shape 514   Sugar

Designer:	Mr. Watkin in 1937
Issued:	1938 - by 1954
Height :	3 ¾", 9.5 cm
Colour:	1. Green, orange, brown and blue on a white background
	2. Light and dark blue on white background

Description	U.S. $	Can. $	U.K. £
Sugar	135.00	200.00	70.00

Shape 515   Preserve with lid

Designer: Mr. Watkin in 1937
Issued: 1938 - by 1954
Size: 4 ½" x 3 ¼" x 4", 11.9 x 8.3 x 10.1 cm
Colour: 1. Green, orange, brown and blue on a
               white background
            2. Light and dark blue on white background

Description	U.S. $	Can. $	U.K. £
Preserve with lid	135.00	200.00	70.00

Shape 516   Cheese dish

Designer: Mr. Watkin in 1937
Issued: 1938 - by 1954
Size: Unknown
Colour: 1. Green, orange, brown and blue on a
               white background
            2. Light and dark blue on white background

Description	U.S. $	Can. $	U.K. £
Cheese dish	200.00	300.00	100.00

Shape 517   Toast rack

Designer: Mr. Watkin in 1937
Issued: 1938 - by 1954
Size: Unknown
Colour: 1. Green, orange, brown and blue on a
               white background
            2. Light and dark blue on white background

Description	U.S. $	Can. $	U.K. £
Toast rack	200.00	300.00	110.00

Shape 518   Biscuit jar with lid

Designer: Mr. Watkin in 1937
Issued: 1938 - by 1954
Size: Unknown
Colour: 1. Green, orange, brown and blue on a
               white background
            2. Light and dark blue on white background

Description	U.S. $	Can. $	U.K. £
Biscuit jar with lid	250.00	350.00	125.00

Shape 519   Cruet Set, Salt, Pepper, Mustard and Base

Designer: Mr. Watkin in 1937
Issued: 1938 - by 1954
Size: Unknown
Colour: 1. Green, orange, brown and blue on a
                white background
             2. Light and dark blue on white background

Description	U.S. $	Can. $	U.K. £
Cruet set	200.00	300.00	100.00

Shape 520   Teapot

Designer: Mr. Watkin in 1937
Issued: 1938 - by 1954
Size: Unknown
Colour: 1. Green, orange, brown and blue on a
                white background
             2. Light and dark blue on white background

Description	U.S. $	Can. $	U.K. £
Teapot	200.00	300.00	100.00

Shape 521   Covered muffin

Designer: Mr. Watkin in 1937
Issued: 1938 - by 1954
Size :   Unknown
Colour: 1. Green, orange, brown and blue on a
                white background
             2. Light and dark blue on white background

Description	U.S. $	Can. $	U.K. £
Covered muffin	250.00	375.00	125.00

Shape 522   Cheese dish

Designer: Mr. Watkin in 1937
Issued: 1938 - by 1954
Size: Unknown
Colour: 1. Green, orange, brown and blue on a
                white background
             2. Light and dark blue on white background

Description	U.S. $	Can. $	U.K. £
Cheese dish	250.00	375.00	120.00

Shape 523   Salad / Fruit bowl

Designer:	Mr. Watkin in 1937
Issued:	1938 - by 1954
Size :	Unknown
Colour:	1. Green, orange, brown and blue on a white background
	2. Light and dark blue on white background

Description	U.S. $	Can. $	U.K. £
Salad / Fruit bowl	200.00	275.00	95.00

Shape 524   Butter dish

Designer:	Mr. Watkin in 1937
Issued:	1938 - by 1954
Size:	Unknown
Colour:	1. Green, orange, brown and blue on a white background
	2. Light and dark blue on white background

Description	U.S. $	Can. $	U.K. £
Butter dish	250.00	375.00	125.00

Shape 525   Cup and saucer

Designer:	Mr. Watkin in 1937
Issued:	1938 - by 1954
Size:	Unknown
Colour:	1. Green, orange, brown and blue on a white background
	2. Light and dark blue on white background

Description	U.S. $	Can. $	U.K. £
Cup and saucer	175.00	200.00	85.00

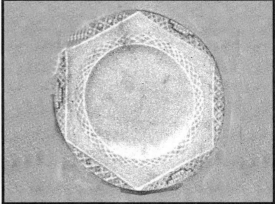

Shape 526   Plate, small

Designer:	Mr. Watkin in 1937
Issued:	1938 - by 1954
Size:	Unknown
Colour:	1. Green, orange, brown and blue on a white background
	2. Light and dark blue on white background

Description	U.S. $	Can. $	U.K. £
Plate, small	100.00	150.00	50.00

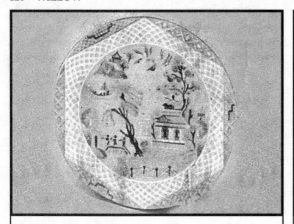

Photograph not
available
at press time

Shape 527 **Plate, large**

Designer:	Mr. Watkin in 1937
Issued:	1938 - by 1954
Size:	Unknown
Colour:	1. Green, orange, brown and blue on a white background
	2. Light and dark blue on white background

Description	U.S. $	Can. $	U.K. £
Plate, large	175.00	275.00	95.00

Shape 528 **Slop bowl**

Designer:	Mr. Watkin in 1937
Issued:	1938 - by 1954
Size:	Unknown
Colour:	1. Green, orange, brown and blue on a white background
	2. Light and dark blue on white background

Description	U.S. $	Can. $	U.K. £
Slop bowl	150.00	225.00	75.00

ZORBA

There were thirty-two items in this large series and the shapes were produced in two colourways, brown and olive green, both in a gloss finish. The decoration used geometric shapes of circles and triangles to create a border pattern for the various "modern" shapes. At some time, probably as production was drawing to a close, some pieces were produced in white, these are rare.

The brown finish, called "bronze," was probably the "in colour" at the time, and this is the colourway most often found today. It is amazing to think that so many of these items, which would have been in everyday use, have survived so well. The brown came in different combinations, one shade all over, dark brown and light brown, or in some cases three shades of brown. The dark brown was a satin matt finish. In addition to the individual pieces, Zorba was available in Coffee Sets or Tea Sets. Until a saucer (shape 2344) became available, the Orbit shape was used.

The name for the series conjures up Greek origins and perhaps the inspiration for this design came from that country?

Shape 2211 Coffee pot

Designer:	Graham Tongue in 1968
Issued:	1970 - 1973
Base Dia:	4 ½", 11.9 cm
Height:	9", 22.9 cm
Colour:	Brown (bronze) or olive green

Description	U.S. $	Can. $	U.K. £
Coffee pot	25.00	35.00	15.00

Shape 2212 Cup

Designer:	Graham Tongue in 1968
Issued:	1970 - 1973
Top Dia:	3", 7.6 cm
Height :	3", 7.6 cm
Colour:	Brown (bronze) or olive green

Description	U.S. $	Can. $	U.K. £
Cup	10.00	15.00	5.00

Shape 2224 Open sugar

Designer:	Graham Tongue in 1968
Issued:	1970 - 1973
Diameter:	3 ¾", 9.5 cm
Height:	2 ½", 6.4 cm
Colour:	Brown (bronze) or olive green

Description	U.S. $	Can. $	U.K. £
Open sugar	10.00	15.00	5.00

Shape 2225 Cream jug

Designer:	Graham Tongue in 1968
Issued:	1970 - 1973
Height:	3 ¾", 9.5 cm
Colour:	Brown (bronze) or olive green

Description	U.S. $	Can. $	U.K. £
Cream jug	10.00	15.00	5.00

Shape 2228 Cheese dish

Designer:	Graham Tongue in 1968
Issued:	1970 - 1973
Height:	3 ¾", 9.5 cm
Colour:	Brown (bronze) or olive green

Description	U.S. $	Can. $	U.K. £
Cheese dish	20.00	30.00	12.00

Shape 2229 Hot milk jug

Designer:	Graham Tongue in 1968
Issued:	1970 - 1973
Base:	4", 10.1 cm
Height :	7 ¼", 18.4 cm
Colour:	Brown (bronze) or olive green

Description	U.S. $	Can. $	U.K. £
Hot milk jug	25.00	35.00	15.00

Shape 2234 Covered butter with wide rim

Designer:	Graham Tongue in 1968
Issued:	1970 - 1973
Size:	6 ½" x 5" x 4", 16.5 x 12.7 x 10.1 cm
Colour:	Brown (bronze) or olive green

Description	U.S. $	Can. $	U.K. £
Covered butter	20.00	30.00	12.00

Shape 2245 Preserve with cover

Designer:	Graham Tongue in 1968
Issued:	1970 - 1973
Diameter:	3 ¼", 8.3 cm
Height :	3 ½", 8.9 cm
Colour:	Brown (bronze) or olive green

Description	U.S. $	Can. $	U.K. £
Preserve with cover	15.00	20.00	8.00

Note: The above picture has cover missing.

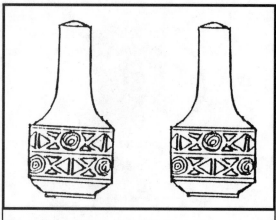

Shape 2248-2249 Pepper and Salt

Designer:	Graham Tongue in 1968
Issued:	1970 - 1973
Height:	5", 12.7 cm
Colour:	Brown (bronze) or olive green

Description	U.S. $	Can. $	U.K. £
1. Shape 2248, Pepper	7.00	10.00	4.00
2. Shape 2249, Salt	7.00	10.00	4.00

Photograph not
available
at press time

Shape 2322 Casserole with cover, (3 ½ pint) oval

Designer:	Graham Tongue in 1970
Issued:	1971 - 1973
Size:	9" x 6 ½", 5", 22.9 x 16.5 x 12.7 cm
Colour:	Brown (bronze) or olive green

Description	U.S. $	Can. $	U.K. £
Casserole with cover	40.00	60.00	22.00

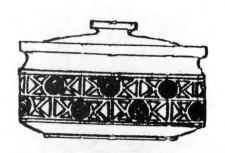

Casserole (6 pint) with cover

Casserole (4 pint) cover missing

Shape 2319-2320-2321 Casserole with cover

Designer:	Shape 2319 — Albert Hallam in 1970
	Shape 2320 - 2321 — Graham Tongue in 1970
Issued:	1971 - 1973
Diameter:	1. Shape 2319, 6 pint — 9", 22.9 cm
	2. Shape 2320, 4 pint — 8", 20.3 cm
	3. Shape 2321, 2 ½ pint — 6 ½", 16.5 cm
Height :	1. Shape 2319, 6 pint — 6", 15 cm
	2. Shape 2320, 4 pint — 5", 12.7 cm
	3. Shape 2321, 2 ½ pint — Unknown
Colour:	Brown (bronze) or olive green

Description	U.S. $	Can. $	U.K. £
1. Shape 2319, 6 pint	50.00	75.00	25.00
2. Shape 2320, 4 pint	40.00	60.00	20.00
3. Shape 2321, 2 ½ pint	30.00	40.00	15.00

Shape 2323 Gravy boat

Designer:	Graham Tongue in 1970
Issued:	1971 - 1973
Height:	3", 7.6 cm
Colour:	Brown (bronze) or olive green

Description	U.S. $	Can. $	U.K. £
Gravy boat	20.00	30.00	10.00

Shape 2324 Mug, ½ pint

Designer:	Graham Tongue in 1970
Issued:	1971 - 1973
Height :	3 ½", 8.9 cm
Colour:	Brown (bronze) or olive green

Description	U.S. $	Can. $	U.K. £
Mug, ½ pint	10.00	15.00	5.00

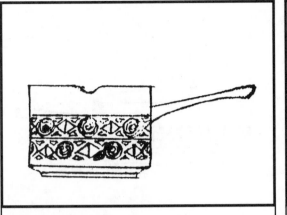

Shape 2325 Teapot

Designer:	Graham Tongue in 1970
Issued:	1971 - 1973
Height:	6 ½", 16.5 cm
Colour:	White

Description	U.S. $	Can. $	U.K. £
Teapot	25.00	35.00	15.00

Shape 2326-2327-2328 Plate, three sizes

Designer:	Graham Tongue in 1970
Issued:	1971 - 1973
Size:	1. Shape 2326, small - 7", 17.8 cm
	2. Shape 2327, medium - 8 ¾", 22.2 cm
	3. Shape 2328, large - 10 ¾", 27.8 cm
Colour:	Brown (bronze) or olive green

Description	U.S. $	Can. $	U.K. £
1. Shape 2326	10.00	15.00	4.00
2. Shape 2327	10.00	15.00	5.00
3. Shape 2328	10.00	15.00	6.00

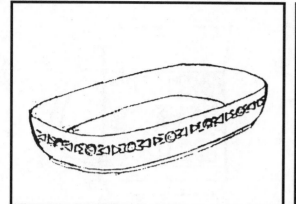

Shape 2329 Gratin dish

Designer: Graham Tongue in 1970
Issued: 1971 - 1973
Size: 10 ½" x 9 ½" x 2", 26.7 x 24 x 5 cm
Colour: Brown (bronze) or olive green

Description	U.S. $	Can. $	U.K. £
Gratin dish	20.00	30.00	12.00

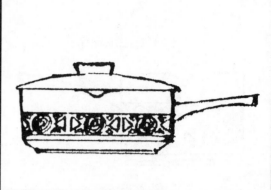

Shape 2330 Ramekin dish

Designer: Graham Tongue in 1970
Issued: 1971 - 1973
Diameter: 5 ¼", 13.3 cm
Height :   3", 7.6 cm
Colour: Brown (bronze) or olive green

Description	U.S. $	Can. $	U.K. £
Ramekin dish	20.00	30.00	12.00

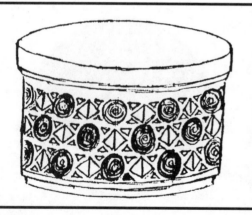

Shape 2331 Soufflé dish, large

Designer: Graham Tongue in 1970
Issued: 1971 - 1973
Diameter: 6 ½", 16.5 cm
Height: 3 ½", 8.9 cm
Colour: Brown (bronze) or olive green

Description	U.S. $	Can. $	U.K. £
Soufflé dish, large	20.00	30.00	12.00

Shape 2332 Soufflé dish, individual

Designer: Graham Tongue in 1970
Issued: 1971 - 1973
Diameter: 3 ½", 8.9 cm
Height :   2", 5.0 cm
Colour: Brown (bronze) or olive green

Description	U.S. $	Can. $	U.K. £
Soufflé dish, individual	10.00	15.00	5.00

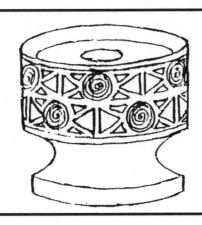

Shape 2341 Candlestick

Designer: Graham Tongue in 1970
Issued: 1971 - 1973
Height: 2 ½", 6.4 cm
Colour: Brown (bronze) or olive green

Description	U.S. $	Can. $	U.K. £
Candlestick	10.00	15.00	5.00

Shape 2342 Egg cup

Designer: Graham Tongue in 1970
Issued: 1971 - 1973
Diameter: 2 ¼", 5.7 cm
Height :   2 ¾", 7.0 cm
Colour: Brown (bronze) or olive green

Description	U.S. $	Can. $	U.K. £
Egg cup	10.00	15.00	5.00

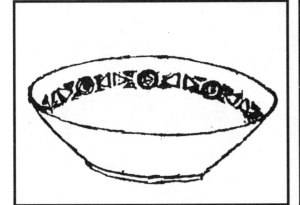

Shape 2343 Coupe

Designer: Graham Tongue in 1970
Issued: 1971 - 1973
Diameter: 6 ¾", 17.2 cm
Colour: Brown (bronze) or olive green

Description	U.S. $	Can. $	U.K. £
Coupe	10.00	15.00	5.00

Shape 2344 Saucer

Designer: Graham Tongue in 1970
Issued: 1971 - 1973
Diameter: 5 ¾", 14.6 cm
Colour: Brown (bronze) or olive green

Description	U.S. $	Can. $	U.K. £
Saucer	7.00	10.00	4.00

Shape 2353 Lug soup

Designer:	Graham Tongue in 1971
Issued:	1972 - 1973
Diameter:	4 ¼", 10.8 cm
Height:	3" x 7.6 cm
Colour:	Brown (bronze) or olive green

Description	U.S. $	Can. $	U.K. £
Lug soup	10.00	15.00	5.00

Photograph not
available
at press time

Shape 2400 Meat dish

Designer:	Graham Tongue in 1972
Issued:	1972 - 1973
Size:	13 ½" x 10 ½", 34.3 x 26.7 cm
Colour:	Brown (bronze) or olive green

Description	U.S. $	Can. $	U.K. £
Meat dish	20.00	30.00	12.00

Photograph not
available
at press time

Shape 2401 Fruit saucer

Designer:	Graham Tongue in 1972
Issued:	1972 - 1973
Diameter:	5 ½", 14 cm
Colour:	Brown (bronze) or olive green

Description	U.S. $	Can. $	U.K. £
Fruit saucer	10.00	15.00	5.00

Photograph not
available
at press time

Shape 2402 Covered sugar

Designer:	Graham Tongue in 1972
Issued:	1972 - 1973
Size:	Unknown
Colour:	Brown (bronze) or olive green

Description	U.S. $	Can. $	U.K. £
Covered sugar	20.00	30.00	10.00

SECTION TWO

This part of the book has been divided into chapters to make it easier to locate and identify a particular piece. Within these chapters are series and sets, which we have listed separately here for quick reference. The details for an individual piece can be found under the appropriate chapter and shape number.

THE MODELLE RANGE

The style of modelling and the colour unites these shapes. They were:

No. 653 Jug, No. 654 Jug, No. 655 Vase, No. 656 Vase, No. 657 Bowl, No. 675 Vase, No. 676 Jug, No. 677 Vase, No. 678 Vase, No.679 Jug, No. 680 Vase. A total of eleven shapes.

THE FESTIVAL SERIES

This series was so named as it was sold to coincide with the Festival of Britain in 1951. The items were selected from production shapes and were not in any specific colourways. They were:

No. 977 Candlestick, No. 978 Ashtray, No. 979/1/2 Bowl, No. 1051 Deer Vase, No. 1083 Galleon Vase, No. 1095 Nymph Vase, No. 1176 Jug, No. 1184 Column Vase, No. 1185 Flamingo Vase, No. 1186 Shell Vase, No. 1187/1/2/3 Handled Bowl, No. 1189 Square Chequered Vase, No. 1190 Large Urn Vase, No. 1191 Fern Vase, No. 1192 Low fluted bowl, No. 1193 Bellflower Vase, No. 1194 Magnolia Vase, No. 1236 Bowl, No. 1264 Bowl. A total of nineteen shapes.

THE ELIZABETHAN SERIES

All the items in this series, which was launched for the new Elizabethan era in 1953, were in a gloss finish. There were only three colourways under this name: Maroon, Holly Green and Chartreuse. The shapes in this series were:

No. 1191 Vase, No. 1284 Trout Vase, No. 1287 Skater Vase, No. 1288 "Dog Rose" Bowl, No. 1290 "Book" Bowl, No. 1292 Leaf Bowl, No. 1293 Doves Vase, No. 1295 "Maple Bud" Vase, No. 1297 Fan Bowl, No. 1298 Apple Vase, No. 1300 Stardust Vase, No. 1305 Mallard Vase, No. 1306 Pinewood Vase. A total of thirteen shapes.

Note these pieces can also be found in other colourways.

CAPRICE

There were only three colourways under this name — turquoise, orange and yellow. The shapes available were:

No. 128 Vase, No. 1498-2 Bowl, No. 1502/2/3 Vase, No. 1316 Vase, No. 1651 Vase, No. 1654 Vase, No. 1656 Vase, No. 1749 Vase, No. 1750 Vase, No. 1751 Vase, No. 1752 Vase, No. 1896 Plant Pot Holder. A total of twelve shapes issued under this name, between 1968 and 1972 only.

CHRYSANTHEMUM

A set of nine shapes, which were:

No. 1602 Vase, No. 1603 Bowl, No. 1604 Vase, No. 1605 Vase, No. 1606 Vase, No. 1607 Vase, No. 1608 Vase, No. 1609 Wall Vase, No. 1668 Basket.

ROSE

A set of six shapes, which were:

No. 1658 Vase, No. 1659 Basket, No. 1660 Vase, No. 1661 Vase, No. 1662 Vase, No. 1663 Vase.

SHELL

A set of eight shapes, which were:

No. 1996 Bowl, No. 2003 Plant Pot Holder, No. 2012 Vase, No. 2014 Vase, No. 2015 Vase, No. 2016 Plant Pot Holder, No. 2020 Vase, No. 2021 Vase.

KATHI URBACH

A set of seven shapes, which were:

No. 1555 Swan Vase, No. 1556 Swan Vase, No. 1589 Bowl, No. 1590 Vase, No. 1591 Vase, No. 1592 Vase, No. 1593 Bowl.

SHAKESPEARE

A series of ten shapes, which were:

Jugs Nos. 1126, 1146, 1214 and 1366, Mugs Nos. 1127, 1147, 1215 and 1368 plus two wall plaques Nos. 1209 and 1210.

TULIP

A set of six shapes, all vases similar in style, which were:

Nos. 843, 846, 847, 848, 851 and 852.

TRENTHAM ART WARES

A large number of the early Beswick shapes, mostly vases or jugs, with some bowls, wall masks and ashtrays etc., can be found backstamped "Trentham Art Ware." They had the Beswick shape number together with "Made in England," impressed on the base. The origin of these pieces was an agreement made between Beswick and G. Hardy and Company, wholesalers, of Walnut Tree Lane, Nottingham. At the time of the introduction of the matt glaze decoration in 1933, Hardy's were looking to replace foreign ornamental wares with British designs and turned to Beswick as a supplier.

The agreement lasted until 1941 when Beswick were free to market them with their own backstamp.

GENERAL GUIDE TO COLOURS

Many colours were used by Beswick over the years to decorate their pottery — to name a few — blues, greens, browns, yellows, pinks, oranges etc. Shapes were decorated in subtle shades of a single colour, several colours blended together, with definite or indistinct patterns, Art Deco handpainted designs using several colours — the list is endless.

Countless colour combinations were used to decorate the Beswick shapes and the colourways were so varied that we can only give a general guide to changes over the years.

Early 1930s	—	Assorted handpainted decorations, matt glazes (today referred to as satin matt) and matt white.
1963	—	Four new colourways were introduced to the range, these were pink pearl, noire, juniper and black matt.
1966	—	Juniper discontinued. Copper lustre introduced in June.
1967	—	Noire discontinued and pewter introduced.
1968	—	Caprice Series introduced on certain items — colours orange, turquoise or yellow.
1970	—	Pink pearl discontinued.
1972	—	Matt white and pewteramic only.

ASHTRAYS — ASH-BOWLS

A total of sixty-one shapes were designed between about 1934 and 1971. They were produced in a variety of colours and colour combinations with matt glaze (satin matt), gloss, matt and lustre finishes.

Fourteen of these were produced as special commissions, from 1959 onwards, mostly for tobacco companies, and therefore there is little detailed information available. The highlights of this group are the Timpson's Shoemaker, with the delightful figure, and the interesting Les Leston Steering Wheel.

Not surprisingly thirteen shapes incorporated animal and bird models, some of which could be purchased separately (see *The Charlton Standard Catalogue of Beswick Animals*) and six shapes were actually modelled in the shapes of fish or birds.

Shape 83   Ash-bowl

Designer:	Albert Hallam c.1934
Issued:	c.1934 - by 1963
Diameter:	4", 10.1 cm
Colour:	1. Assorted decos, solid colours - satin matt
	2. White - matt

Colour	U.S. $	Can. $	U.K. £
1. Assorted decorations	30.00	45.00	15.00
2. White	20.00	30.00	10.00

Shape 84   Ashtray

Designer:	Mr. Symcox c.1934
Issued:	c.1934 - by 1954
Length:	4 ½", 11.9 cm
Colour:	1. Assorted decos, solid colours - satin matt
	2. White - matt

Colour	U.S. $	Can. $	U.K. £
1. Assorted decorations	50.00	75.00	25.00
2. White	40.00	60.00	20.00

Photograph not
available
at press time

Shape 88   Scottie, ashtray

Designer:	Unknown
Issued:	1934 - 1965
Height :	3 ¼", 8.3 cm
Colour:	1. Assorted decos, solid colours - satin matt
	2. Blue - gloss
	3. White - matt

Colour	U.S. $	Can. $	U.K. £
1. Assorted decorations	50.00	75.00	25.00
2. Blue	50.00	75.00	25.00
3. White	75.00	95.00	30.00

Shape 112   Mona, ashtray

Designer:	Unknown
Issued:	1932 - by 1940
Size:	Unknown
Colour:	1. Assorted decos - satin matt
	2. White - matt

Colour	U.S. $	Can. $	U.K. £
1. Assorted decorations	50.00	75.00	25.00
2. White	40.00	60.00	20.00

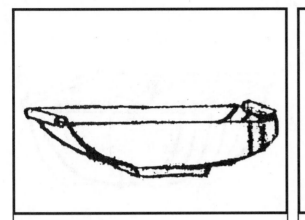

Shape 165   Ashtray

Designer:	Mr. Symcox c.1934
Issued:	c.1934 - by 1954
Size:	Unknown
Colour:	1. Assorted decos, solid colours - satin matt
	2. White- matt

Colour	U.S. $	Can. $	U.K. £
1. Assorted decorations	40.00	60.00	20.00
2. White	30.00	45.00	15.00

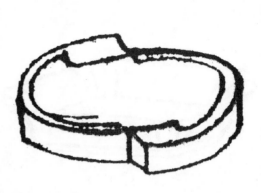

Shape 299   Ashtray

Designer:	Mr. Symcox c.1935
Issued:	c.1935 - by 1954
Size:	Unknown
Colour:	1. Assorted decos, solid colours - satin matt
	2. White - matt

Colour	U.S. $	Can. $	U.K. £
1. Assorted decorations	40.00	60.00	20.00
2. White	30.00	45.00	15.00

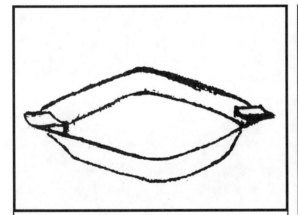

Shape 305   Ashtray

Designer:	Mr. Symcox c.1935
Issued:	c.1935 - by 1963
Length:	6 ¼", 15.9 cm
Colour:	1. Assorted decos, solid colours - satin matt
	2. White - matt

Colour	U.S. $	Can. $	U.K. £
1. Assorted decorations	40.00	60.00	20.00
2. White	30.00	45.00	15.00

Shape 309   Ashtray

Designer:	Mr. Watkin c.1935
Issued:	c.1935 - by 1954
Size:	4" x 3", 10.1 x 7.6 cm
Colour:	1. Assorted decos, solid colours - satin matt
	2. White - matt

Colour	U.S. $	Can. $	U.K. £
1. Assorted decorations	50.00	75.00	25.00
2. White	40.00	60.00	20.00

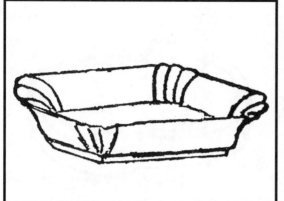

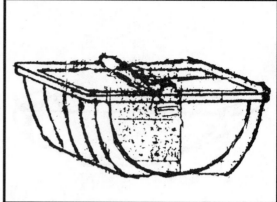

Shape 320/1/2 Ashtray

Designer:	Mr. Symcox c. 1935
Issued:	c.1935 - by 1954
Size:	Unknown
Colour:	1. Assorted decos, solid colours - satin matt
	2. White - matt

Colour	U.S. $	Can. $	U.K. £
1. Assorted decorations	40.00	60.00	20.00
2. White	30.00	45.00	15.00

Shape 321 Ashtray with cover

Designer:	Mr. Symcox in 1935
Issued:	c.1935 - by 1954
Size:	Unknown
Colour:	1. Assorted decos, solid colours - satin matt
	2. White - matt

Colour	U.S. $	Can. $	U.K. £
1. Assorted decorations	50.00	75.00	25.00
2. White	40.00	60.00	20.00

Shape 360 Seal ash bowl

Designer:	Miss Greaves in 1936
Issued:	1936 - by 1954
Size:	5 ¼" x 4 ¾" - 13.3 cm x 12.1 cm
Colour:	1. Assorted decos, solid colours - satin matt
	2. Blue - gloss
	3. White - matt

Colour	U.S. $	Can. $	U.K. £
1. Assorted decorations	125.00	175.00	60.00
2. Blue	150.00	200.00	70.00
3. White	75.00	110.00	40.00

Shape 440 Ashtray

Designer:	Mr. Symcox in 1936
Issued:	1936 - by 1954
Diameter:	4 ¾", 12.1 cm
Height:	2 ¾", 7 cm
Colour:	1. Assorted decos, solid colours - satin matt
	2. White - matt

Colour	U.S. $	Can. $	U.K. £
1. Assorted decorations	50.00	75.00	25.00
2. White	40.00	60.00	20.00

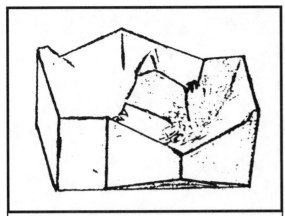

Shape 464   Crompton ashtray

Designer: Albert Hallam in 1937
Issued: 1937 - by 1954
Size: Unknown
Colour: 1. Assorted decos, solid colours - satin matt
             2. White - matt

Colour	U.S. $	Can. $	U.K. £
1. Assorted decorations	50.00	75.00	25.00
2. White	40.00	60.00	20.00

Note: Similar in shape to No. 309.

Shape 497   Pelican match holder and ash-bowl

Designer: Mr. Watkin in 1937
Issued: 1937 - by 1954
Height: 4", 10.1 cm
Colour: 1. Assorted decos, solid colours - satin matt
             2. Blue - gloss
             3. White - matt

Colour	U.S. $	Can. $	U.K. £
1. Assorted decorations	150.00	200.00	65.00
2. Blue	175.00	225.00	75.00
3. White	150.00	200.00	60.00

Shape 617   Duck ashtray

Designer: Mr. Watkin in 1938
Issued: 1938 - by 1954
Height :   3", 7.6 cm
Colour: 1. Assorted decos, solid colours - satin matt
             2. Blue - gloss
             3. White - matt

Colour	U.S. $	Can. $	U.K. £
1. Assorted decorations	150.00	200.00	85.00
2. Blue	175.00	225.00	100.00
3. White	110.00	150.00	65.00

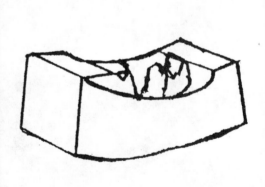

Shape 669   Crompton ashtray

Designer: Mr. Owen in 1939
Issued: 1939 - by 1954
Size: Unknown
Colour: 1. Assorted decos, solid colours - satin matt
             2. White - matt

Colour	U.S. $	Can. $	U.K. £
1. Assorted decorations	50.00	75.00	25.00
2. White	40.00	60.00	20.00

Shape 754 **Pheasant ashtray**

Designer:	Mr. Watkin in 1939
Issued:	1939 - 1970
Height :	3 ½", 8.9 cm
Colour:	Teal green and brown - gloss

Description	U.S. $	Can. $	U.K. £
Pheasant ashtray	50.00	75.00	30.00

Note: Pheasant shape 767A was used for this ashtray.

Shape 755 **Duck ashtray**

Designer:	Mr. Watkin in 1939
Issued:	1939 - 1969
Height:	4", 10.1 cm
Colour:	Teal green, brown and white - gloss

Description	U.S. $	Can. $	U.K. £
Duck ashtray	50.00	75.00	30.00

Note: Duck shape 756-3 was used for this ashtray.

Shape 764 **Soldier ashtray**

Designer:	Arthur Gredington in 1939
Issued:	1939 - by 1954
Size:	Unknown
Colour:	Tan/brown hat and collar; green and brown bowl - gloss

Description	U.S. $	Can. $	U.K. £
Soldier ashtray		Rare	

Shape 810 **Bulldog ashtray**

Designer:	Arthur Gredington in 1940
Issued:	1940 - by 1954
Height:	4", 10.1 cm
Colour:	White dog wearing a white sailor cap with a blue band, biscuit coloured base - gloss

Description	U.S. $	Can. $	U.K. £
Bulldog ashtray	275.00	350.00	150.00

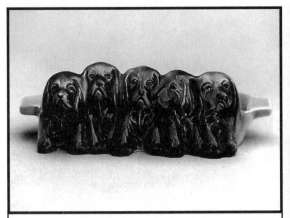

Shape 869   Five puppy ashtray

Designer: Mr. Watkin in 1940
Issued: 1940 - 1967
Height: 2", 5 cm
Colour: 1. Brown puppies, green ashtray - gloss
              2. Light tan puppies, green ashtray - gloss

Colour	U.S. $	Can. $	U.K. £
1. Brown puppies	65.00	90.00	40.00
2. Light tan puppies	65.00	90.00	40.00

Shape 916   Three puppy ashtray

Designer: Mr. Watkin in 1941
Issued: 1941 - 1967
Height: 2", 5.0 cm
Colour: 1. Brown puppies, green ashtray - gloss
              2. Light tan puppies, green ashtray - gloss

Colour	U.S. $	Can. $	U.K. £
1. Brown puppies	55.00	75.00	25.00
2. Light tan puppies	55.00	75.00	25.00

Note: Dog shape 917 was used for this ashtray.

Shape 918   Ashtray

Designer: Mr. Watkin in 1941
Issued: 1941 - by 1954
Size: Unknown
Colour: 1. Assorted decos, solid colours - satin matt
              2. White - matt

Colour	U.S. $	Can. $	U.K. £
1. Assorted decorations	60.00	75.00	30.00
2. White	50.00	90.00	25.00

Shape 934   Ashtray

Designer: Mr. Watkin in 1941
Issued: 1941 - by 1954
Size: Unknown
Colour: 1. Assorted decos, solid colours - satin matt
              2. White - matt

Colour	U.S. $	Can. $	U.K. £
1. Assorted decorations	50.00	75.00	25.00
2. White	40.00	60.00	20.00

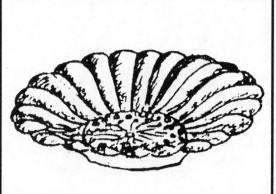

Shape 978   Ashtray

Designer:	Mr. Symcox in 1942
Issued:	1942 - by 1962
Diameter:	4", 10.1 cm
Colour:	1. Assorted decos, solid colours - satin matt
	2. White - matt

Colour	U.S. $	Can. $	U.K. £
1. Assorted decorations	50.00	75.00	25.00
2. White	40.00	60.00	20.00

Note: This ashtray later became part of the Festival Series.

Shape 1212   Three duck ashtray

Designer:	Arthur Gredington in 1951
Issued:	1. 1951 - 1965
Issued:	2. 1951 - 1970
Height:	2 ¾", 7 cm
Colour:	1. Blue - gloss
	2. Teal green, white and brown - gloss

Colour	U.S. $	Can. $	U.K. £
1. Blue	55.00	75.00	40.00
2. Teal green	55.00	75.00	35.00

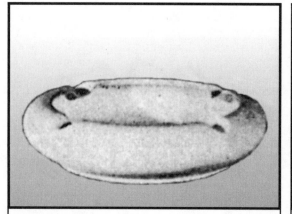

Shape 1547   Ashtray

Designer:	Albert Hallam in 1958
Issued:	1958 - 1971
Diameter:	6", 15 cm
Colour:	1. Assorted decos, solid colours - satin matt
	2. Copper lustre
	3. White or black - matt

Colour	U.S. $	Can. $	U.K. £
1. Assorted decorations	40.00	60.00	20.00
2. Copper lustre	40.00	60.00	20.00
3. White or black	30.00	45.00	15.00

Shape 1599   Trout ash-bowl

Designer:	Graham Tongue in 1959
Issued:	1959 - 1970
Height:	5", 12.7 cm
Colour:	Fish in naturalistic colours;
	turquoise blue bowl - gloss

Colour	U.S. $	Can. $	U.K. £
Natural, turquoise blue	175.00	250.00	85.00

Photograph not
available
at press time

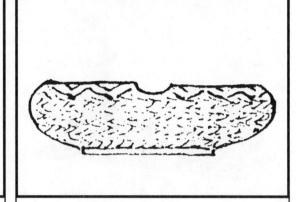

Shape 1625 Woodbine ashtray

Designer:	Albert Hallam in 1959
Issued:	1959
Size:	Unknown
Colour:	Unknown

Description	U.S. $	Can. $	U.K. £
Woodbine, ashtray	30.00	45.00	15.00

Note: Special Commission.

Shape 1722 Mexican ashtray

Designer:	Albert Hallam in 1960
Issued:	1960 - unknown
Diameter:	6", 15 cm
Colour:	Unknown

Description	U.S. $	Can. $	U.K. £
Mexican	40.00	60.00	20.00

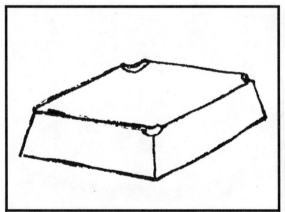

Shape 1866 Ashtray

Designer:	Albert Hallam in 1963
Issued:	1963 - unknown
Width:	3", 7.6 cm
Colours:	1. Assorted decos, solid colours - satin matt
	2. Copper - lustre
	3. White or black - matt

Colour	U.S. $	Can. $	U.K. £
1. Assorted decorations	30.00	45.00	15.00
2. Copper	30.00	45.00	15.00
3. White or black	20.00	30.00	10.00

Shape 1918 Ashbowl

Designer:	Albert Hallam in 1963
Issued:	1963 - 1971
Size:	11" x 8", 27.9 cm x 20.3 cm
Colour:	1. Pale brown bowl with animal - gloss
	2. Blue bowl with animal - gloss
	3. White and blue bowl with transfer print of Babycham - gloss

Colour	U.S. $	Can. $	U.K. £
1. Blue bowl with animal	250.00	350.00	125.00
2. Pale brown bowl/ animal	75.00	125.00	40.00
3. White/blue/Babycham	30.00	45.00	15.00

Shape 1932 Dachshund ashtray

Designer:	Albert Hallam in 1962
Issued:	1962 - 1969
Base size:	8" x 3", 20.3 cm x 7.6 cm
Height :	5", 12.7 cm
Colour:	1. Black and tan dog on charcoal base - gloss
	2. Tan dog on charcoal base - gloss

Colour	U.S. $	Can. $	U.K. £
1. Black/tan dog	150.00	150.00	65.00
2. Tan dog	150.00	150.00	65.00

Note: Dog Shape 1460 was used for this ashtray.

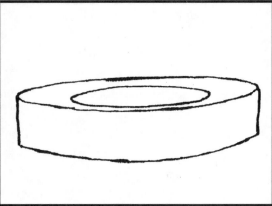

Shape 1934 Ashtray, round

Designer:	Albert Hallam in 1964
Issued:	1964 - unknown
Diameter:	10", 25.4 cm
Colour:	1. Assorted decos, solid colours - satin matt
	2. White or black - matt

Colour	U.S. $	Can. $	U.K. £
1. Assorted decorations	30.00	45.00	15.00
2. White or black	20.00	30.00	10.00

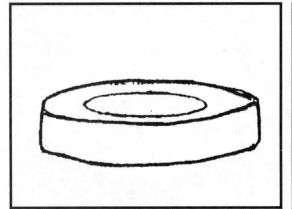

Shape 1938 Ashtray, round

Designer:	Albert Hallam in 1964
Issued:	1964 - unknown
Diameter:	5", 12.7 cm
Colour:	1. Assorted decos, solid colours - satin matt
	2. White or black - matt

Colour	U.S. $	Can. $	U.K. £
1. Assorted decorations	30.00	45.00	15.00
2. White or black	20.00	30.00	10.00

Shape 1946 Timpson's Shoemaker - ashbowl

Designer:	Albert Hallam in 1964
Issued:	c.1964
Height:	4 ½", 11. 9 cm
Colour:	Shoemaker wears a white apron, blue trousers, light green shirt, darker waistcoat; blue base - gloss

Colour	U.S. $	Can. $	U.K. £
Base blue	175.00	225.00	85.00

Note: Special Centenary Commission. Backstamped "Timpson fine shoes 1865 - 1965."

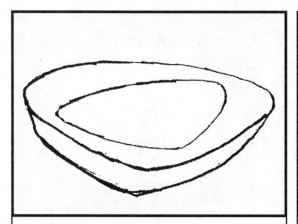

Shape 1983   Canada Dry ashtray

Designer: Mr. Murphy in 1964
Issued: c.1964
Diameter: 9", 22.9 cm
Colour: Unknown

Description	U.S. $	Can. $	U.K. £
Canada Dry	30.00	45.00	15.00

Note: Special Commission.

Shape 2001   Benson and Hedges ashtray

Designer: Mr. Murphy in 1964
Issued: c.1964
Size: 8" x 6 ½", 20.3 cm x 16.5 cm
Colour: Charcoal/bronze with gold lettering - lustre

Colour	U.S. $	Can. $	U.K. £
Charcoal/bronze	30.00	45.00	15.00

Note: Special Commission.

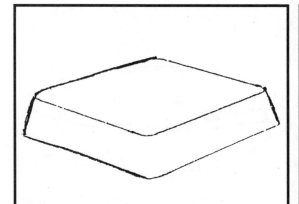

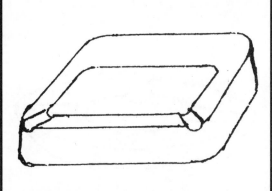

Shape 2007   Ashtray

Designer: Mr. Murphy in 1965
Issued: 1965 - unknown
Width: 8 ¾", 22.2 cm
Colour: 1. Assorted decos, solid colours - satin matt
              2. White or black - matt

Colour	U.S. $	Can. $	U.K. £
1. Assorted decorations	30.00	45.00	15.00
2. White or black	20.00	30.00	10.00

Shape 2024   Ashtray

Designer: Albert Hallam in 1965
Issued: 1965 - unknown
Size: 5 ½", 14 cm
Colour: 1. Assorted decos, solid colours - satin matt
              2. White or black - matt

Colour	U.S. $	Can. $	U.K. £
1. Assorted decorations	30.00	45.00	15.00
2. White or black	20.00	30.00	10.00

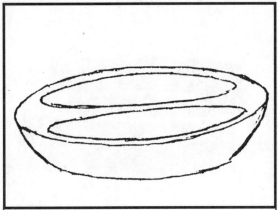

Shape 2047 Gallaher ashtray

Designer: Albert Hallam in 1965
Issued: c.1965
Size: 9″ x 7″, 22.9 cm x 17.8 cm
Colour: Unknown

Description	U.S. $	Can. $	U.K. £
Gallaher	30.00	45.00	15.00

Note: Special commission.

Shape 2048 Les Leston ashtray

Designer: Albert Hallam in 1965
Issued: c.1965
Diameter: 7 ¼″, 18.4 cm
Colour: White bowl, brown edges and silver
             spokes - gloss

Colour	U.S. $	Can. $	U.K. £
White, brown and silver	100.00	150.00	50.00

Note: Special commission. Les Leston was a top 500cc Formula 3 driver in the early 1950s. Later he drove for Connaught and BRM.

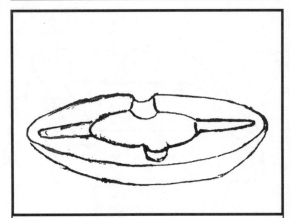

Shape 2052 Piccadilly ashtray

Designer: Albert Hallam in 1965
Issued: c.1965
Diameter: 8″, 20.3 cm
Colour: Unknown

Description	U.S. $	Can. $	U.K. £
Piccadilly	30.00	45.00	15.00

Note: Special commission.

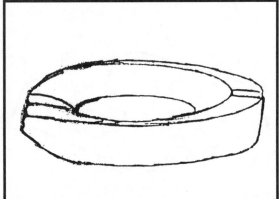

Shape 2055 Craven "A" ashtray

Designer: Albert Hallam in 1966
Issued: c.1966
Size: 11″ x 6 ½″, 27.9 x 16.5 cm
Colour: Unknown

Description	U.S. $	Can. $	U.K £.
Craven "A"	30.00	45.00	15.00

Note: Special commission.

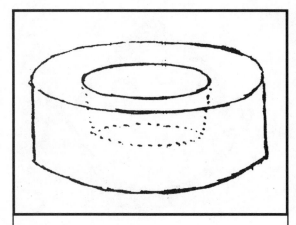

Shape 2114 Ashtray

Designer:	Albert Hallam in 1967
Issued:	1967 - unknown
Size:	5" x 2", 12.7 x 5 cm
Colour:	1. Assorted decos, solid colours - satin matt
	2. Copper - lustre
	3. White or black - matt

Colour	U.S. $	Can. $	U.K. £
1. Assorted decorations	30.00	45.00	15.00
2. Copper	30.00	45.00	15.00
3. White or black	20.00	30.00	10.00

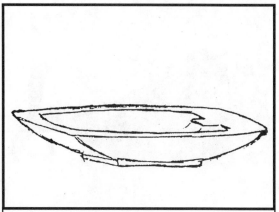

Shape 2115 Pall Mall ashtray

Designer:	Albert Hallam in 1967
Issued:	c.1967
Size:	9 ¾" x 4 ¾", 24.7 x 12.1 cm
Colour:	Unknown

Description	U.S. $	Can. $	U.K. £
Pall Mall	30.00	45.00	15.00

Note: Special Commission.

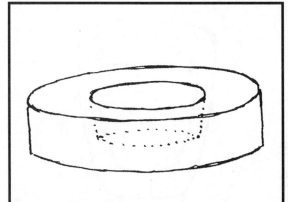

Shape 2119 Ashtray

Designer:	Albert Hallam in 1967
Issued:	1967 - unknown
Size:	8" x 2", 20.3 x 5 cm
Colour:	1. Assorted decos, solid colours - satin matt
	2. Copper - lustre
	3. White or black - matt

Colour	U.S. $	Can. $	U.K. £
1. Assorted decorations	30.00	45.00	15.00
2. Copper	30.00	45.00	15.00
3. White or black	20.00	30.00	10.00

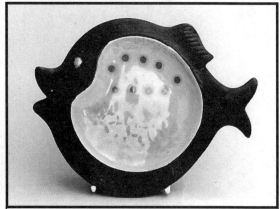

Shape 2128 Fish ashtray

Designer:	Graham Tongue in 1967
Issued:	1968 - c.1970
Length:	7", 17.8 cm
Colour:	Dark brown matt outer colour, turquoise gloss inner surface with orange spots

Colour	U.S. $	Can. $	U.K. £
Dark brown	75.00	100.00	35.00

Shape 2129 Whale ashtray

Designer:	Graham Tongue in 1967
Issued:	1968 - c.1970
Length:	7 ¼″, 18.4 cm
Colour:	Dark brown matt outer colour, red gloss inner surface

Colour	U.S. $	Can. $	U.K. £
Dark brown, red	60.00	90.00	30.00

Shape 2133 Fish ashtray

Designer:	Graham Tongue in 1967
Issued:	1968 - c.1970
Length:	9 ½″, 24 cm
Colour:	Dark brown matt outer colour, lime green gloss inner surface

Colour	U.S. $	Can. $	U.K. £
Dark brown, lime green	75.00	100.00	35.00

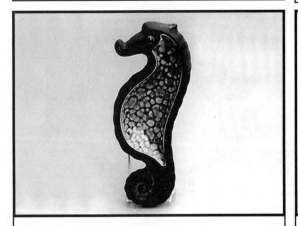

Shape 2169 Sea horse ashtray

Designer:	Graham Tongue in 1967
Issued:	1968 - c.1970
Length:	10 ½″, 26.7 cm
Colour:	Dark brown matt outer colour, green/blue coloured mottled gloss inner surface

Colour	U.S. $	Can. $	U.K. £
Dark brown, green/blue	75.00	100.00	40.00

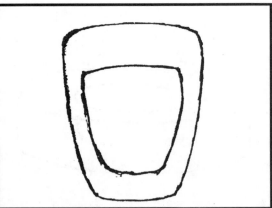

Shape 2175 Ashtray

Designer:	Graham Tongue in 1967
Issued:	1967, remodelled in 1968 - unknown
Size:	8″ x 6″, 20.3 x 15 cm
Colour:	1. Assorted decos, solid colours - satin matt
	2. Copper - lustre
	3. White or black - matt

Colour	U.S. $	Can. $	U.K. £
1. Assorted decorations	30.00	45.00	15.00
2. Copper	30.00	45.00	15.00
3. White or black	20.00	30.00	10.00

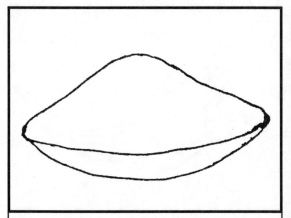

Shape 2176 Ashtray

Designer: Graham Tongue in 1968
Issued: 1968 - unknown
Size: 5 ¾", 14.6 cm
Colour: 1. Assorted decos, solid colours - satin matt
             2. Copper - lustre
             3. White or black - matt

Colour	U.S. $	Can. $	U.K. £
1. Assorted decorations	30.00	45.00	15.00
2. Copper	30.00	45.00	15.00
3. White or black	20.00	30.00	10.00

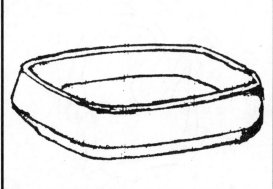

Shape 2177 Ashtray

Designer: Albert Hallam in 1968
Issued: 1968 - unknown
Size: 10" x 7 ½", 25.4 cm x 19.1 cm
Colour: 1. Assorted decos, solid colours - satin matt
             2. Copper - lustre
             3. White or black - matt

Colour	U.S. $	Can. $	U.K. £
1. Assorted decorations	30.00	45.00	15.00
2. Copper	30.00	45.00	15.00
3. White or black	20.00	30.00	10.00

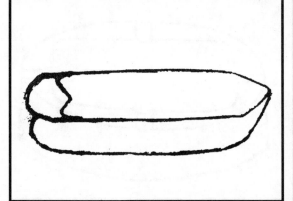

Shape 2178 Ashtray

Designer: Albert Hallam in 1968
Issued: 1968 - unknown
Size: 10" x 7 ½", 25.4 x 19.1 cm
Colour: 1. Assorted decos, solid colours - satin matt
             2. Copper - lustre
             3. White or black - matt

Colour	U.S. $	Can. $	U.K. £
1. Assorted decorations	30.00	45.00	15.00
2. Copper	30.00	45.00	15.00
3. White or black	20.00	30.00	10.00

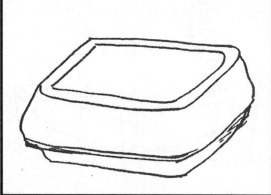

Shape 2192 Benson and Hedges ashtray

Designer: Albert Hallam in 1968
Isuued: c.1968
Width: 5", 12.7 cm
Colour: Unknown

Description	U.S. $	Can. $	U.K. £
Benson and Hedges	30.00	45.00	15.00

Note: Special Commission.

Shape 2199 Cockerel ashtray

Designer:	Graham Tongue in 1968
Issued:	1968 - Unknown
Length:	8", 20.3 cm
Colour:	Unknown

Description	U.S. $	Can. $	U.K. £
Cockerel	90.00	125.00	45.00

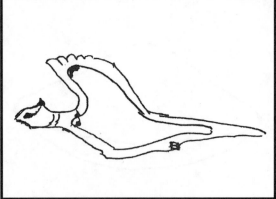

Shape 2209 Pheasant ashtray

Designer:	Graham Tongue in 1968
Issued:	1968 - Unknown
Length:	12 ¾", 32.4 cm
Colour:	Unknown

Description	U.S. $	Can. $	U.K. £
Pheasant	100.00	150.00	50.00

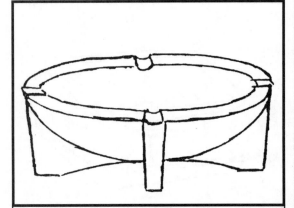

Shape 2218 Benson and Hedges orb ashtray

Designer:	Albert Hallam in 1968
Issued:	c.1968
Diameter:	7", 17.8 cm
Colour:	Unknown

Description	U.S. $	Can. $	U.K. £
Benson and Hedges orb	30.00	45.00	15.00

Note: Special Commission.

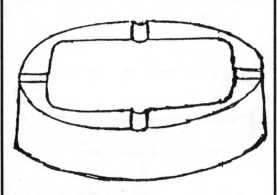

Shape 2219 Craven "A" ashtray

Designer:	Albert Hallam in 1968
Issued:	c.1968
Diameter:	8", 20.3 cm
Colour:	Unknown

Description	U.S. $	Can. $	U.K. £
Craven "A"	30.00	45.00	15.00

Note: Special Commission.

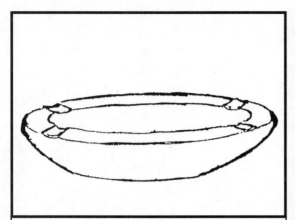

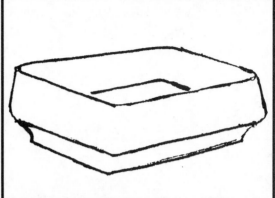

Shape 2241 Hamlet, oval ashtray

Designer: Albert Hallam in 1968
Issued: c.1968
Size: 7 ½" x 5", 19.1 x 12.7 cm
Colour: Unknown

Description	U.S. $	Can. $	U.K. £
Hamlet, oval ashtray	30.00	45.00	15.00

Note: Special Commission.

Shape 2261 Hamlet Cigars ashtray

Designer: Albert Hallam in 1969
Issued: c.1969
Size :   6" x 6", 15.0 x 15.0 cm
Colour: Unknown

Description	U.S. $	Can. $	U.K. £
Hamlet cigars	30.00	45.00	15.00

Note: Special Commission.

Shape 1918 — Ashbowl

BASKETS AND BOWLS

There are a hundred shapes in this large group, spanning the production years from the early thirties to 1972. These shapes are mainly decorative bowls, some handled, some on feet, some large and some small. Two bulb bowls were also produced and thirteen baskets, i.e. with the handle over the top.

As can be seen here we list some members of the Festival, Elizabethan, Caprice, Rose, Chrysanthemum, Kathi Urbach, Modelle and Shell Series - a quick reference to these series is given at the beginning of this section of the book.

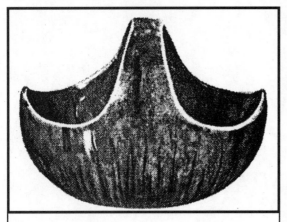

Shape 78	Basket
Designer:	Mr. Symcox c.1933
Issued:	c.1933 - by 1940
Length:	10 ½″, 26.7 cm
Colour:	1. Assorted decorations - satin matt
	2. White - matt

Market	Range
U.S.A.	$40.00 - 100.00
Canada	$60.00 - 150.00
U.K.	£20.00 - 50.00

Shape 81	Footed bowl
Designer:	Mr. Symcox c.1933
Issued:	c.1933 - by 1940
Diameter:	11 ½″, 29.2 cm
Colour:	1. Assorted decorations - satin matt
	2. White - matt

Market	Range
U.S.A.	$40.00 - 100.00
Canada	$60.00 - 150.00
U.K.	£20.00 - 50.00

Shape 86	Basket
Designer:	Mr. Symcox c.1933
Issued:	c.1933 - by 1940
Length:	7″, 17.8 cm
Colour:	1. Assorted decorations - satin matt
	2. White - matt

Market	Range
U.S.A.	$40.00 - 75.00
Canada	$60.00 - 100.00
U.K.	£20.00 - 40.00

Shape 99	Bowl
Designer:	Mr. Symcox c.1933
Issued:	c.1933 - by 1940
Diameter:	11 ½″, 29.2 cm
Colour:	1. Assorted decorations - satin matt
	2. White - matt

Market	Range
U.S.A.	$40.00 - 100.00
Canada	$60.00 - 150.00
U.K.	£20.00 - 50.00

BOWLS AND BASKETS • 151

Shape 123	Bowl
Designer:	Albert Hallam c.1933
Issued:	c.1933 - by 1959
Length:	11 ½", 29.2 cm
Colour:	1. Assorted decorations - satin matt
	2. White - matt

Market	Range
U.S.A.	$40.00 - 100.00
Canada	$60.00 - 150.00
U.K.	£20.00 - 50.00

Shape 157	Handled bowl
Designer:	Mr. Symcox c.1933
Issued:	c.1933 - by 1940
Diameter:	11", 27.9 cm
Colour:	1. Assorted decorations - satin matt
	2. White - matt

Market	Range
U.S.A.	$40.00 - 100.00
Canada	$60.00 - 150.00
U.K.	£20.00 - 50.00

Photograph not
available
at press time

Shape 199	Posy bowl
Designer:	Mr. Symcox c.1933
Issued:	c.1933 - by 1940
Size:	Unknown
Colour:	1. Assorted decorations - satin matt
	2. White - matt

Market	Range
U.S.A.	$40.00 - 100.00
Canada	$60.00 - 150.00
U.K.	£20.00 - 50.00

Shape 256/1/2 Bowl Troon

Designer:	Unknown
Issued:	c.1933 - by 1940
Size:	Unknown
Colour:	1. Assorted decorations - satin matt
	2. White - matt

Market	Range
U.S.A.	$40.00 - 100.00
Canada	$60.00 - 150.00
U.K.	£20.00 - 50.00

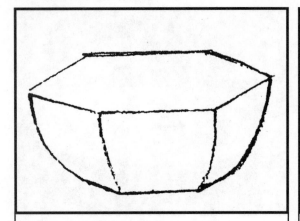

Shape 257   Octagon bulb bowl

Designer:	Unknown
Issued:	c.1933 - by 1940
Size:	Unknown
Colour:	1. Assorted decorations - satin matt
	2. White - matt

Market	Range
U.S.A.	$30.00 - 75.00
Canada	$45.00 - 100.00
U.K.	£15.00 - 35.00

Shape 258   Round bulb bowl

Designer:	Unknown
Issued:	c.1933 - by 1940
Size:	Unknown
Colour:	1. Assorted decorations - satin matt
	2. White - matt

Market	Range
U.S.A.	$30.00 - 75.00
Canada	$45.00 - 100.00
U.K.	£15.00 - 35.00

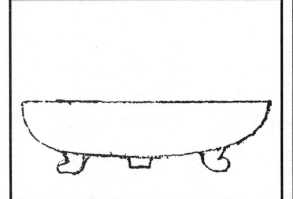

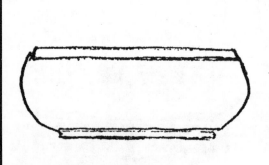

Shape 259   Trentham bowl

Designer:	Unknown
Issued:	c.1933 - by 1940
Size:	Unknown
Colour:	1. Assorted decorations - satin matt
	2. White - matt

Market	Range
U.S.A.	$30.00 - 75.00
Canada	$45.00 - 100.00
U.K.	£15.00 - 35.00

Shape 262   Louis bowl, New Hall

Designer:	Unknown
Issued:	c.1933 - by 1940
Size:	Unknown
Colour:	1. Assorted decorations - satin matt
	2. White - matt

Market	Range
U.S.A.	$30.00 - 75.00
Canada	$45.00 - 100.00
U.K.	£15.00 - 35.00

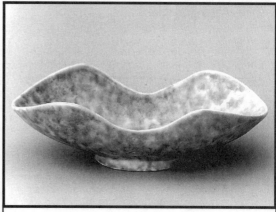

Shape 288   Bowl

Designer:	Mr. Symcox c.1934
Issued:	c.1934 - by 1959
Length:	8", 20.3 cm
Colour:	1. Assorted decorations - satin matt
	2. White - matt

Market	Range
U.S.A.	$40.00 - 100.00
Canada	$60.00 - 150.00
U.K.	£20.00 - 50.00

Shape 291   Bowl

Designer:	Mr. Symcox c.1934
Issued:	c.1934 - by 1940
Size:	Unknown
Colour:	1. Assorted decorations - satin matt
	2. White - matt

Market	Range
U.S.A.	$40.00 - 100.00
Canada	$60.00 - 150.00
U.K.	£20.00 - 50.00

Shape 300   Bowl

Designer:	Mr. Symcox c.1934
Issued:	c.1934 - by 1940
Size:	Unknown
Colour:	1. Assorted decorations - satin matt
	2. White - matt

Market	Range
U.S.A.	$40.00 - 100.00
Canada	$60.00 - 150.00
U.K.	£20.00 - 50.00

Shape 306   Bowl

Designer:	Mr. Symcox c.1934
Issued:	1935 - by 1940
Diameter:	13", 33 cm
Colour:	1. Assorted decorations - satin matt
	2. White - matt

Market	Range
U.S.A.	$40.00 - 100.00
Canada	$60.00 - 150.00
U.K.	£20.00 - 50.00

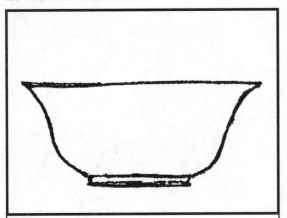

Photograph not
available
at press time

Shape 322   Bowl

Designer:	Unknown
Issued:	1935 - by 1940
Size:	Unknown
Colour:	1. Assorted decorations - satin matt
	2. White - matt

Market	Range
U.S.A.	$30.00 - 90.00
Canada	$45.00 - 125.00
U.K.	£15.00 - 45.00

Shape 342   Bowl, comport

Designer:	Mr. Symcox in 1935
Issued:	1935 - by 1940
Size:	Unknown
Colour:	1. Assorted decorations - satin matt
	2. White - matt

Market	Range
U.S.A.	$40.00 - 100.00
Canada	$60.00 - 150.00
U.K.	£20.00 - 50.00

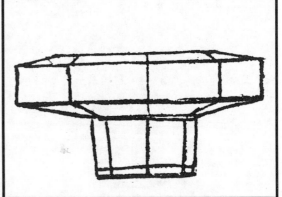

Shape 379   Bowl

Designer:	Mr. Symcox in 1936
Issued:	1936 - by 1959
Diameter:	12", 30.5 cm
Colour:	1. Assorted decorations - satin matt
	2. White - matt

Market	Range
U.S.A.	$40.00 - 100.00
Canada	$60.00 - 150.00
U.K.	£20.00 - 50.00

Shape 384   Bowl

Designer:	Mr. Symcox in 1936
Issued:	1936 - by 1940
Size:	Unknown
Colour:	1. Assorted decorations - satin matt
	2. White - matt

Market	Range
U.S.A.	$40.00 - 100.00
Canada	$60.00 - 150.00
U.K.	£20.00 - 50.00

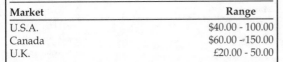

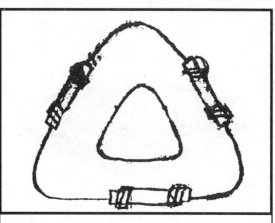

Shape 419   Bowl

Designer:	Mr. Symcox in 1936
Issued:	1936 - by 1959
Length:	12″, 30.5 cm
Colour:	1. Assorted decorations - satin matt
	2. White - matt

Market	Range
U.S.A.	$40.00 - 100.00
Canada	$60.00 - 150.00
U.K.	£20.00 - 55.00

Shape 420   Bowl

Designer:	Mr. Symcox in 1936
Issued:	1936 - by 1940
Size:	Unknown
Colour:	1. Assorted decorations - satin matt
	2. White - matt

Market	Range
U.S.A.	$40.00 - 100.00
Canada	$60.00 - 150.00
U.K.	£20.00 - 50.00

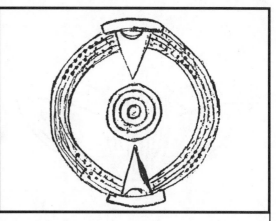

Shape 425   Bowl

Designer:	Mr. Symcox in 1936
Issued:	1936 - by 1959
Length:	11 ½″, 29.2 cm
Colour:	1. Assorted decorations - satin matt
	2. White - matt

Market	Range
U.S.A.	$40.00 - 100.00
Canada	$60.00 - 150.00
U.K.	£20.00 - 50.00

Shape 427   Bowl

Designer:	Mr. Symcox in 1936
Issued:	1936 - by 1959
Length:	12 ½″, 31.7 cm
Colour:	1. Assorted decorations - satin matt
	2. White - matt

Market	Range
U.S.A.	$40.00 - 100.00
Canada	$60.00 - 150.00
U.K.	£20.00 - 50.00

Shape 434   Bowl

Designer:	Mr. Symcox in 1936
Issued:	1936 - by 1940
Diameter:	14 ¼", 36.2 cm
Colour:	1. Assorted decorations - satin matt
	2. White - matt

Market	Range
U.S.A.	$40.00 - 100.00
Canada	$60.00 - 150.00
U.K.	£20.00 - 50.00

Shape 444   Bowl

Designer:	Mr. Symcox in 1936
Issued:	1936 - by 1940
Diameter:	15", 38.1 cm
Colour:	1. Assorted decorations - satin matt
	2. White - matt

Market	Range
U.S.A.	$40.00 - 100.00
Canada	$60.00 - 150.00
U.K.	£20.00 - 50.00

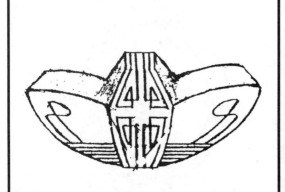

Shape 475   Basket

Designer:	Mr. Symcox in 1937
Issued:	1937 - by 1954
Length:	11", 27.9 cm
Colour:	1. Assorted decorations - satin matt
	2. White - matt

Market	Range
U.S.A.	$40.00 - 100.00
Canada	$60.00 - 150.00
U.K.	£20.00 - 50.00

Shape 476   Basket

Designer:	Mr. Symcox in 1937
Issued:	1937 - by 1940
Length:	6", 15 cm
Colour:	1. Assorted decorations - satin matt
	2. White - matt

Market	Range
U.S.A.	$40.00 - 100.00
Canada	$60.00 - 150.00
U.K.	£20.00 - 50.00

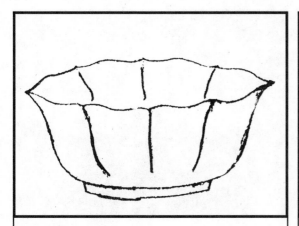

Shape 554   Bowl

Designer:	Unknown
Issued:	1937 - by 1940
Size:	Unknown
Colour:	1. Assorted decorations - satin matt
	2. White - matt

Market	Range
U.S.A.	$20.00 - 75.00
Canada	$45.00 - 125.00
U.K.	£15.00 - 40.00

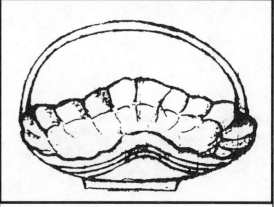

Shape 570   Basket

Designer:	Mr. Symcox in 1938
Issued:	1938 - by 1940
Size:	Unknown
Colour:	1. Assorted decorations - satin matt
	2. White - matt

Market	Range
U.S.A.	$40.00 - 100.00
Canada	$60.00 - 150.00
U.K.	£20.00 - 50.00

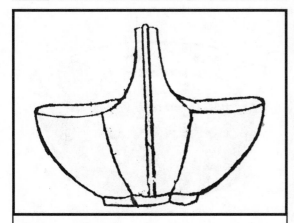

Shape 605   Basket

Designer:	Mr. Symcox in 1938
Issued:	1938 - by 1940
Size:	Unknown
Colour:	1. Assorted decorations - satin matt
	2. White - matt

Market	Range
U.S.A.	$40.00 - 100.00
Canada	$60.00 - 150.00
U.K.	£20.00 - 50.00

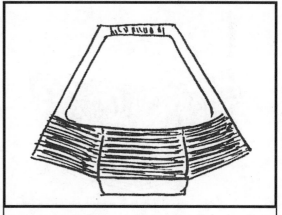

Shape 606   Basket

Designer:	Mr. Watkin in 1938
Issued:	1938 - by 1940
Length:	6 ½" 16.5 cm
Colour:	1. Assorted decorations - satin matt
	2. White - matt

Market	Range
U.S.A.	$40.00 - 100.00
Canada	$60.00 - 150.00
U.K.	£20.00 - 50.00

Shape 607	Bowl
Designer:	Mr. Symcox in 1938
Issued:	1938 - by 1940
Length:	4", 10.1 cm
Colour:	1. Assorted decorations - satin matt
	2. White - matt

Market	Range
U.S.A.	$30.00 - 75.00
Canada	$45.00 - 100.00
U.K.	£15.00 - 40.00

Shape 623	Basket
Designer:	Mr. Symcox in 1938
Issued:	1938 - by 1940
Length:	5", 12.7 cm
Colour:	1. Assorted decorations - satin matt
	2. White - matt

Market	Range
U.S.A.	$30.00 - 75.00
Canada	$45.00 - 100.00
U.K.	£15.00 - 40.00

Shape 657	Bowl, Modelle series
Designer:	Mr. Watkin in 1938
Issued:	1938 - by 1959
Size:	13 ½" x 5 ½", 34.3 x 14cm
Colour:	1. Assorted decorations - satin matt
	2. White - matt

Market	Range
U.S.A.	$50.00 - 125.00
Canada	$75.00 - 175.00
U.K.	£25.00 - 65.00

Shape 745	Bowl
Designer:	Mr. Watkin in 1939
Issued:	1939 - by 1940
Size:	Unknown
Colour:	1. Assorted decorations - satin matt
	2. White - matt

Market	Range
U.S.A.	$30.00 - 75.00
Canada	$45.00 - 100.00
U.K.	£15.00 - 40.00

Photograph not
available
at press time

Shape 758   Bowl

Designer:	Mr. Watkin in 1939
Issued:	1940 - by 1954
Size:	9 ½" x 3 ¾", 24 x 9.5 cm
Colour:	1. Assorted decorations - satin matt
	2. White - matt

Market	Range
U.S.A.	$40.00 - 75.00
Canada	$60.00 - 100.00
U.K.	£20.00 - 40.00

Shape 759   Bowl

Designer:	Mr. Watkin in 1939
Issued:	1939 - by 1959
Diameter:	12", 30.5 cm
Colour:	1. Assorted decorations - satin matt
	2. White - matt

Market	Range
U.S.A.	$40.00 - 100.00
Canada	$60.00 - 150.00
U.K.	£20.00 - 50.00

Shape 808   Bowl

Designer:	Mr. Symcox in 1940
Issued:	1940 - 1969
Height:	6 ½", 16.5 cm
Colour:	1. Assorted decorations, solid colours - satin matt
	2. Copper lustre
	3. White or black - matt

Market	Range
U.S.A.	$40.00 - 75.00
Canada	$60.00 - 100.00
U.K.	£20.00 - 40.00

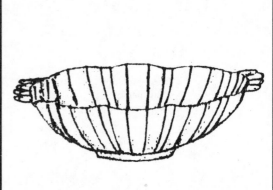

Shape 819   Basket

Designer:	Mr. Watkin in 1940
Issued:	1940 - 1972
Height :	12", 30.5 cm
Colour:	1. Assorted decos, solid colours - satin matt
	2. Copper lustre
	3. White or black - matt

Market	Range
U.S.A.	$40.00 - 75.00
Canada	$60.00 - 100.00
U.K.	£20.00 - 40.00

Shape 835   Bowl

Designer:	Mr. Symcox in 1940
Issued:	1940 - by 1969
Length:	17", 43.2 cm
Colour:	1. Assorted decos, solid colours - satin matt
	2. Copper lustre
	3. White or black - matt

Market	Range
U.S.A.	$40.00 - 100.00
Canada	$60.00 - 150.00
U.K.	£20.00 - 50.00

Shape 900 /1/2/3 Basket

Designer:	Mr. Symcox in 1940
Issued:	1941 - by 1959
Height:	1. Shape 900/1 — 8", 20.3 cm
	2. Shape 900/2 — 6 ¼", 15.9 cm
	3. Shape 900/3 — 4 ½" , 11.9 cm
Colour:	1. Assorted decorations - satin matt
	2. White - matt

Market	Range
Shape 900/1	
U.S.A.	$40.00 - 100.00
Canada	$60.00 - 150.00
U.K.	£20.00 - 50.00
Shape 900/2	
U.S.A.	$20.00 - 60.00
Canada	$30.00 - 40.00
U.K.	£10.00 - 20.00
Shape 900/3	
U.S.A.	$20.00 - 60.00
Canada	$30.00 - 40.00
U.K.	£10.00 - 20.00

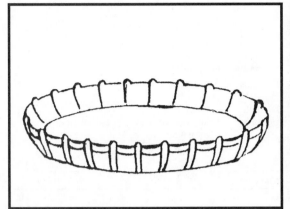

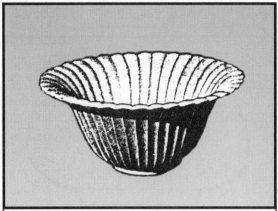

Shape 933 Bowl

Designer:	Mr. Symcox in 1941
Issued:	1941 - by 1954
Size:	Unknown
Colour:	1. Assorted decorations - satin matt
	2. White - matt

Market	Range
U.S.A.	$40.00 - 100.00
Canada	$60.00 - 150.00
U.K.	£20.00 - 50.00

Shape 979/1/2 Bowl - Festival series

Designer:	Mr. Symcox in 1941
Issued:	1942 - by 1962
Size:	1. Shape 979/1 — 8 ½", 21.6 cm
	2. Shape 979/2 — 7", 17.8 cm
Colour:	1. Assorted decorations - satin matt
	2. White - matt

Market	Range
U.S.A.	$20.00 - 75.00
Canada	$30.00 - 100.00
U.K.	£10.00 - 40.00

Shape 1079 Posy bowl

Designer:	Albert Hallam in 1946
Issued:	1947 - by 1959
Diameter:	4 ½", 11.9 cm
Colour:	1. Assorted decorations - satin matt
	2. White - matt

Market	Range
U.S.A.	$30.00 - 50.00
Canada	$20.00 - 75.00
U.K.	£10.00 - 25.00

Shape 1080 Posy bowl

Designer:	Albert Hallam in 1946
Issued:	1947 - 1972
Diameter:	4 ½", 11.9 cm
Colour:	1. Assorted decos, solid colours - satin matt
	2. Copper - lustre
	3. White or black - matt

Market	Range
U.S.A.	$20.00 - 50.00
Canada	$30.00 - 75.00
U.K.	£10.00 - 25.00

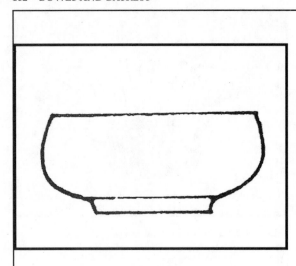

Shape 1081 Posy bowl

Designer: Albert Hallam in 1946
Issued: 1946 - 1971
Diameter: 4 ½″, 11.9 cm
Colour: 1. Assorted decorations, solid colours -
                satin matt
             2. White or black - matt
             3. Copper - lustre

Market	Range
U.S.A.	$20.00 - 50.00
Canada	$30.00 - 75.00
U.K.	£10.00 - 25.00

Shape 1187/1/2/3 Handled Bowl - Festival series

Designer: 1. Shape 1187/1/2 — Albert Hallam,
                James Hayward in 1950
             2. Shape 1187/2 — Albert Hallam,
                James Hayward in 1953
             3. Shape 1187/3 — Albert Hallam in 1953
Issued: 1. Shape 1187/1 — 1950 - 1972
             2. Shape 1187/2 — 1953 - 1972
             3. Shape 1187/3 — 1953 - 1972
Size: 1. Shape 1187/1 — 13″, 33 cm
             2. Shape 1187/2 — 9″, 22.9 cm
             3. Shape 1187/3 — 7″, 17.8 cm
Colour: 1. Various decorations - satin matt
             2. White or black - matt
             3. Copper lustre

Market	Range
Shape 1187/1	
U.S.A.	$40.00 - 100.00
Canada	$60.00 - 150.00
U.K.	£20.00 - 50.00
Shape 1187/2	
U.S.A.	$45.00 - 75.00
Canada	$30.00 - 100.00
U.K.	£15.00 - 40.00
Shape 1187/3	
U.S.A.	$20.00 - 60.00
Canada	$30.00 - 90.00
U.K.	£10.00 - 30.00

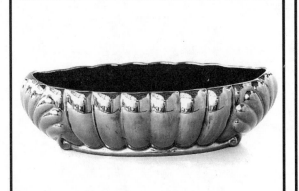

Shape 1192 Low fluted bowl - Festival series

Designer:	Albert Hallam, James Hayward in 1950
Issued:	1950 - 1971
Size:	12", 30.5 cm
Colour:	1. Assorted decorations - satin matt
	2. White or black - matt
	3. Copper lustre

Market	Range
U.S.A.	$40.00 - 100.00
Canada	$60.00 - 150.00
U.K.	£20.00 - 50.00

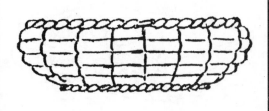

Shape 1236 Conversation piece - Festival series, bowl round wicker

Designer:	Albert Hallam, James Hayward in 1952
Issued:	1952 - 1962
Diameter:	7 ½", 19.1 cm
Colour:	1. Assorted decorations - satin matt
	2. White - matt

Market	Range
U.S.A.	$40.00 - 100.00
Canada	$60.00 - 150.00
U.K.	£20.00 - 50.00

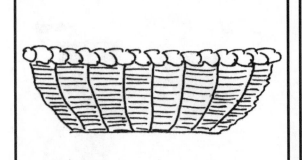

Shape 1264 Bowl, oval - Festival series

Designer:	Albert Hallam, James Hayward in 1952
Issued:	1952 - 1962
Size:	6 ½", 16.5 cm
Colour:	1. Assorted decorations - satin matt
	2. White - matt

Market	Range
U.S.A.	$20.00 - 60.00
Canada	$30.00 - 90.00
U.K.	£10.00 - 30.00

Shape 1288 Dog rose bowl - Elizabethan series

Designer:	Albert Hallam, James Hayward in 1953
Issued:	1954 - 1962
Size:	12 ½", 31.7 cm
Colour:	1. Chartreusse, holly green or maroon - gloss
	2. White - matt

Market	Range
U.S.A.	$40.00 - 100.00
Canada	$60.00 - 150.00
U.K.	£20.00 - 50.00

Shape 1290   Book bowl - Elizabethan series

Designer:	Albert Hallam, James Hayward in 1953
Issued:	1954 - by 1959
Size:	10" x 7", 25.4 x 17.8 cm
Colour:	1. Chartreuse, holly green or maroon - gloss
	2. White - matt

Market	Range
U.S.A.	$40.00 - 100.00
Canada	$60.00 - 150.00
U.K.	£20.00 - 50.00

Photograph not
available
at press time

Shape 1292   Leaf bowl large - Elizabethan series

Designer:	Albert Hallam, James Hayward in 1953
Issued:	1954 - by 1962
Size:	14", 35.5 cm
Colour:	1. Chartreuse, holly green or maroon - gloss
	2. White - matt

Market	Range
U.S.A.	$40.00 - 100.00
Canada	$60.00 - 150.00
U.K.	£20.00 - 50.00

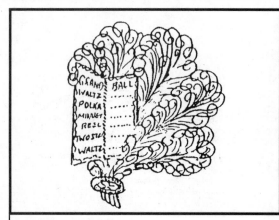

Shape 1297   Fan bowl - Elizabethan series

Designer:	Albert Hallam, James Hayward in 1953
Issued:	1954 - by 1959
Size:	14" x 12", 35.5 x 30.5 cm
Colour:	1. Chartreuse, holly green or maroon - gloss
	2. White - matt

Market	Range
U.S.A.	$40.00 - 100.00
Canada	$60.00 - 150.00
U.K.	£20.00 - 50.00

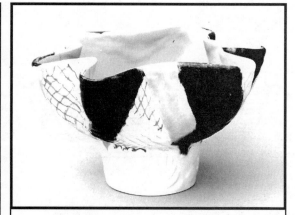

Shape 1338   Bowl

Designer:	Albert Hallam in 1954
Issued:	1954 - by 1962
Height :	4 ¾", 12.1 cm
Colour:	1. Assorted decorations - satin matt
	2. White - matt

Market	Range
U.S.A.	$30.00 - 75.00
Canada	$45.00 - 100.00
U.K.	£15.00 - 40.00

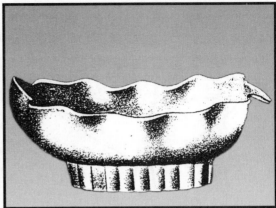

Shape 1340 Bowl

Designer:	Albert Hallam, James Hayward in 1954
Issued:	1954 - by 1962
Height :	5 ¾", 14.6 cm
Colour:	1. Assorted decorations - satin matt
	2. White - matt

Market	Range
U.S.A.	$40.00 - 100.00
Canada	$60.00 - 150.00
U.K.	£20.00 - 50.00

Shape 1346 Oval bowl

Designer:	Albert Hallam in 1954
Issued:	1954 - by 1962
Length:	14" , 35.5 cm
Height :	5", 12.7 cm
Colour:	1. Assorted decorations - satin matt
	2. White - matt

Market	Range
U.S.A.	$40.00 - 100.00
Canada	$60.00 - 150.00
U.K.	£20.00 - 50.00

Shape 1353 Bowl

Designer:	Albert Hallam in 1954
Issued:	1954 - 1969
Size:	10 ½" x 2 ½", 26.7 x 6.4 cm
Colour:	1. Assorted decos, solid colours - satin matt
	2. Copper - lustre
	3. White or black - matt

Market	Range
U.S.A.	$30.00 - 75.00
Canada	$45.00 - 100.00
U.K.	£15.00 - 40.00

Shape 1354 Bowl

Designer:	Albert Hallam in 1954
Issued:	1954 - by 1965
Size :	5", 12.7 cm
Colour:	1. Assorted decos, solid colours - satin matt
	2. White or black - matt

Market	Range
U.S.A.	$30.00 - 75.00
Canada	$45.00 - 100.00
U.K.	£15.00 - 40.00

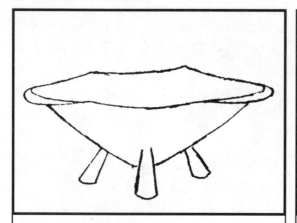

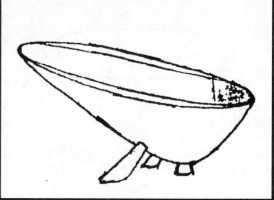

Shape 1387 Bowl on three feet

Designer: Albert Hallam in 1955
Issued: 1955 - by 1962
Height: 4 ½", 11.9 cm
Colour: 1. Assorted decorations - satin matt
            2. White - matt

Market	Range
U.S.A.	$30.00 - 75.00
Canada	$45.00 - 100.00
U.K.	£15.00 - 40.00

Shape 1388 Bowl on three feet

Designer: Albert Hallam in 1955
Issued: 1955 - by 1962
Height :   3 ¾", 9.5 cm
Colour: 1. Assorted decorations - satin matt
            2. White - matt

Market	Range
U.S.A.	$30.00 - 75.00
Canada	$45.00 - 100.00
U.K.	£15.00 - 40.00

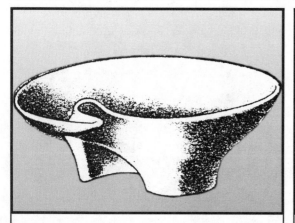

Shape 1458 Bowl

Designer: Albert Hallam in 1956
Issued: 1957 - by 1962
Size :   3 ¼" x 9", 8.3 x 22.9 cm
Colour: 1. Assorted decorations - satin matt
            2. White - matt

Market	Range
U.S.A.	$30.00 - 75.00
Canada	$45.00 - 100.00
U.K.	£15.00 - 40.00

Shape 1497 Bowl, round, on foot with two handles

Designer: Albert Hallam in 1957
Issued: 1957 - by 1966
Size: 10" x 6", 25.4 x 15cm
Colour: 1. Assorted decos, solid colours - satin matt
            2. Copper - lustre
            3. White or black - matt

Market	Range
U.S.A.	$30.00 - 75.00
Canada	$45.00 - 100.00
U.K.	£15.00 - 40.00

Shape 1498/1/2 Bowl, footed, oval

Designer:	Albert Hallam in 1957
Issued:	1. Shape 1498/1 — 1957 - 1971
	2. Shape 1498/2 — 1957 - 1972
Size:	1. Shape 1498/1 — 16" x 7", 41.9 x 17.8 cm
	2. Shape 1498/2 — 13" x 6", 33 x 15cm
Colour:	1. Assorted decorations - satin matt
	2. White or black - matt
	3. Copper - lustre

Market	Range
Shape 1498/1	
U.S.A.	$30.00 - 75.00
Canada	$45.00 - 100.00
U.K.	£15.00 - 40.00
Shape 1498/2	
U.S.A.	$30.00 - 75.00
Canada	$45.00 - 100.00
U.K.	£15.00 - 40.00

Note: Introduced in 1968 Caprice Series (size 2 only)
Colours: Orange, turquoise or yellow

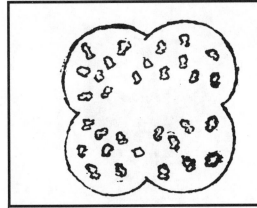

Shape 1589 Bowl

Designer:	Kathi Urbach
Modeller:	Albert Hallam in 1959
Issued:	1959 - 1965
Size:	8", 20.3 cm
Colour:	Various colours incl. black with green/blue
	or white - gloss

Market	Range
U.S.A.	$40.00 - 75.00
Canada	$60.00 - 100.00
U.K.	£20.00 - 40.00

Shape 1593 Oval fluted bowl footed

Designer:	Kathi Urbach
Modeller:	Albert Hallam in 1959
Issued:	1959 - 1965
Length:	12" x 5", 30.5 x 12.7 cm
Colour:	Black with green/blue or white - gloss

Market	Range
U.S.A.	$40.00 - 75.00
Canada	$60.00 - 100.00
U.K.	£20.00 - 40.00

Shape 1593A   Oval fluted bowl footed

Designer:	Kathi Urbach
Modeller:	Albert Hallam in 1959
Reissued:	1966 - 1968
Size:	12″ x 5″, 30.5 x 12.7 cm
Colour:	1. Assorted decos; solid colours - satin matt
	2. Copper - lustre
	3. White or black - matt

Market	Range
U.S.A.	$60.00 - 100.00
Canada	$90.00 - 150.00
U.K.	£30.00 - 50.00

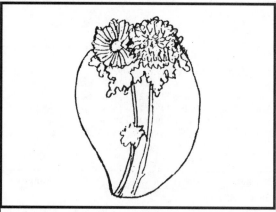

Shape 1603   Chrysanthemum, bowl

Designer:	Albert Hallam in 1959
Issued:	1959 - by 1963
Size:	14″, 35.5 cm
Colour:	Coloured flowers on white background - gloss

Description	U.S. $	Can. $	U.K. £
Chrysanthemum bowl	100.00	150.00	50.00

Shape 1620   Bowl footed

Designer:	Albert Hallam in 1959
Issued:	1959 - 1968
Size:	12 ½″ x 5 ½″, 31.7 x 14 cm
Colour:	1. Assorted decos; solid colours - satin matt
	2. Copper - lustre
	3. White or black - matt

Market	Range
U.S.A.	$40.00 - 100.00
Canada	$60.00 - 150.00
U.K.	£20.00 - 50.00

Shape 1650   Basket

Designer:	Albert Hallam in 1959
Issued:	1959 - 1968
Length:	11″, 27.9 cm
Colour:	1. Assorted decos; solid colours - satin matt
	2. Copper - lustre
	3. White or black - matt

Market	Range
U.S.A.	$40.00 - 100.00
Canada	$60.00 - 150.00
U.K.	£20.00 - 50.00

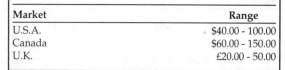

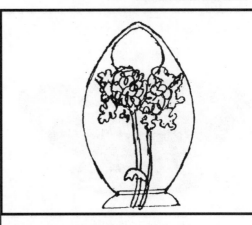

Shape 1659   Rose, basket

Designer:	Albert Hallam in 1959
Issued:	1959 - 1965
Size:	11 ¼″, 28.5 cm
Colour:	Rose, green leaves on cream background - satin matt

Market	Range
U.S.A.	$50.00
Canada	$75.00
U.K.	£25.00

Shape 1668   Chrysanthemum, basket

Designer:	Albert Hallam in 1960
Issued:	1960 - by 1963
Size:	Unknown
Colour:	Coloured flowers on a white background - gloss

Market	Range
U.S.A.	$100.00
Canada	$150.00
U.K.	£50.00

Shape 1683/1/2 Bowl

Designer:	Albert Hallam in 1960
Issued:	1. Shape 1683/1 — 1960 - 1968
	2. Shape 1683/2 — 1960 - 1971
Size:	1. Shape 1683/1 — 14 ¾″ x 6 ½″, 37.5 x 16.5 cm
	2. Shape 1683/2 — 10″ x 5″, 25.4 x 12.7 cm
Colour:	1. Assorted decorations; solid colours - satin matt
	2. Copper - lustre
	3. White or black - matt

Market	Range
U.S.A.	$40.00 - 100.00
Canada	$60.00 - 150.00
U.K.	£20.00 - 50.00

Shape 1721   Oval bowl

Designer:	Albert Hallam in 1960
Issued:	1960 - 1971
Size:	4 ½", 11.9 cm
Colour:	1. Assorted decos; solid colours - satin matt
	2. White or black - matt
	3. Copper - lustre

Market	Range
U.S.A.	$20.00 - 60.00
Canada	$30.00 - 90.00
U.K.	£10.00 - 30.00

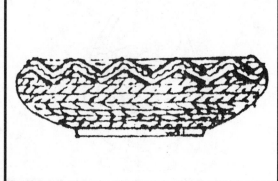

Shape 1735   Mexican flower bowl

Designer:	Albert Hallam in 1961
Issued:	Unknown
Height:	5", 12.7 cm
Colour:	1. Assorted decorations - satin matt
	2. White - matt

Market	Range
U.S.A.	$40.00 - 75.00
Canada	$60.00 - 100.00
U.K.	£20.00 - 40.00

Shape 1788   Bowl on pedestal

Designer:	Albert Hallam in 1961
Issued:	1961 - 1972
Size:	6 ½", 16.5 cm
Colour:	1. Assorted decorations - satin matt
	2. Copper - lustre
	3. White or black - matt

Market	Range
U.S.A.	$30.00 - 75.00
Canada	$50.00 - 100.00
U.K.	£15.00 - 40.00

Shape 1789   Shell bowl

Designer:	Albert Hallam in 1961
Issued:	1961 - 1971
Size:	7" x 4 ¼", 17.8 x 10.8 cm
Colour:	1. Assorted decos; solid colours - satin matt
	2. Copper - lustre
	3. White or black - matt

Market	Range
U.S.A.	$40.00 - 75.00
Canada	$60.00 - 100.00
U.K.	£20.00 - 40.00

Shape 1790 Shell bowl on pedestal

Designer:	Albert Hallam in 1961
Issued:	1961 - 1969
Height :	6 ½", 16.5 cm
Colour:	1. Assorted decos; solid colours - satin matt
	2. Copper - lustre
	3. White or black - matt

Market	Range
U.S.A.	$40.00 - 100.00
Canada	$60.00 - 150.00
U.K.	£20.00 - 50.00

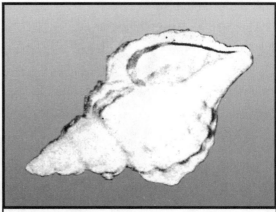

Shape 1794 Shell bowl, large

Designer:	Albert Hallam in 1961
Issued:	1961 - 1970
Size:	10" x 5 ¾", 25.4 x 14.6 cm
Colour:	1. Assorted decos; solid colours - satin matt
	2. Copper - lustre
	3. White or black - matt

Market	Range
U.S.A.	$60.00 - 100.00
Canada	$90.00 - 150.00
U.K.	£30.00 - 50.00

Shape 1798 Bowl, with or without candle holders and snuffers

Designer:	Albert Hallam in 1962
Issued:	1962 - 1969
Length:	15", 38.1 cm
Colour:	1. Assorted decos; solid colours - satin matt
	2. Copper - lustre 3. White or black - matt

Market	Range
U.S.A.	$40.00 - 100.00
Canada	$60.00 - 150.00
U.K.	£20.00 - 50.00

Shape 1800 Pineapple comport

Designer:	Albert Hallam in 1962
Issued:	1962 - 1968
Height:	9", 22.9 cm
Colour:	1. Assorted decos; solid colours - satin matt
	2. Copper - lustre
	3. White or black - matt

Market	Range
U.S.A.	$40.00 - 100.00
Canada	$60.00 - 150.00
U.K.	£20.00 - 50.00

Shape 1860 Bowl on pedestal

Designer:	Albert Hallam in 1963
Issued:	1963 - 1971
Height :	7″, 17.8 cm
Colour:	1. Assorted decos; solid colours - satin matt
	2. Copper - lustre
	3. White or black - matt

Market	Range
U.S.A.	$40.00 - 100.00
Canada	$60.00 - 150.00
U.K.	£20.00 - 50.00

Shape 1861 Bowl

Designer:	Albert Hallam in 1962
Issued:	1963 - 1972
Size:	16 ½″ x 7 ½, 41.9 x 19.1 cm
Colour:	1. Assorted decos, sold colours - satin matt
	2. Copper - lustre
	3. White or black - matt

Market	Range
U.S.A.	$60.00 - 125.00
Canada	$90.00 - 175.00
U.K.	£30.00 - 60.00

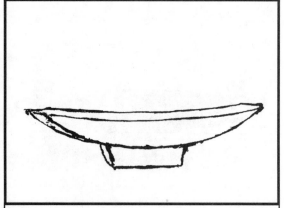

Shape 1996 Bowl, Shell series

Designer:	Albert Hallam in 1964
Issued:	1965 - 1968
Size:	10 ½″ x 7 ½, 26.7 x 19.1 cm
Colour:	Soft variegated pastel colours - gloss

Description	U.S. $	Can. $	U.K. £
Bowl, Shell series	75.00	100.00	40.00

Shape 2142 Bowl

Designer:	Graham Tongue in 1967
Issued:	1968 - 1970
Length:	11 ¼″, 28.5 cm
Colour:	1. Assorted decos; solid colours - satin matt
	2. Copper - lustre
	3. White or black - matt

Market	Range
U.S.A.	$30.00 - 75.00
Canada	$45.00 - 100.00
U.K.	£15.00 - 40.00

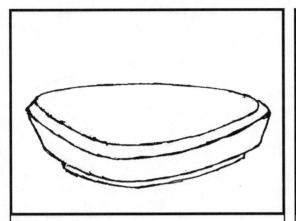

Shape 2143 Bowl

Designer:	Albert Hallam in 1967
Issued:	1968 - 1970
Length:	13 ½", 34.3 cm
Colour:	1. Assorted decos; solid colours - satin matt
	2. Copper - lustre
	3. White or black - matt

Market	Range
U.S.A.	$30.00 - 75.00
Canada	$45.00 - 100.00
U.K.	£15.00 - 40.00

Shape 2144 Bowl

Designer:	Graham Tongue in 1967
Issued:	1968 - 1970
Size:	8" x 4", 20.3 x 10.1cm
Colour:	1. Assorted decos; solid colours - satin matt
	2. Copper - lustre
	3. White or black - matt

Market	Range
U.S.A.	$30.00 - 75.00
Canada	$45.00 - 100.00
U.K.	£15.00 - 40.00

Shape 2145 Bowl

Designer:	Graham Tongue in 1967
Issued:	1968 - 1970
Size:	5" x 2 ½", 12.7 x 6.4 cm
Colour:	1. Assorted decos; solid colours - satin matt
	2. Copper - lustre
	3. White or black - matt

Market	Range
U.S.A.	$30.00 - 60.00
Canada	$45.00 - 90.00
U.K.	£15.00 - 30.00

Shape 2146 Bowl

Designer:	Graham Tongue in 1967
Issued:	1968 - 1970
Diameter:	10 ½", 26.7 cm
Colour:	1. Assorted decos; solid colours - satin matt
	2. Copper - lustre
	3. White or black - matt

Market	Range
U.S.A.	$40.00 - 75.00
Canada	$60.00 - 100.00
U.K.	£20.00 - 40.00

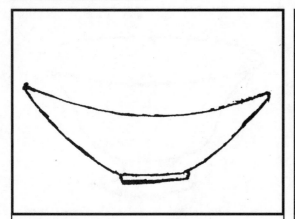

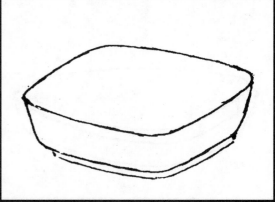

Shape 2147 Oval bowl

Designer: Albert Hallam in 1967
Issued: 1968 - 1970
Size   10 ½" x 4 ¾", 26.7 x 12.1 cm
Colour: 1. Assorted decos; solid colours - satin matt
              2. Copper - lustre
              3. White or black - matt

Market	Range
U.S.A.	$40.00 - 75.00
Canada	$60.00 - 100.00
U.K.	£20.00 - 40.00

Shape 2148 Bowl

Designer: Graham Tongue in 1967
Issued: 1968 - 1970
Size: 7 ½" x 1 ½", 19.1 x 3.1 cm
Colour: 1. Assorted decos; solid colours - satin matt
              2. Copper - lustre
              3. White or black - matt

Market	Range
U.S.A.	$40.00 - 75.00
Canada	$60.00 - 100.00
U.K.	£20.00 - 40.00

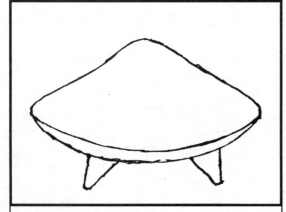

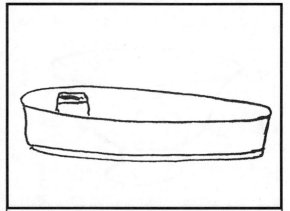

Shape 2149 Bowl

Designer: Graham Tongue in 1967
Issued: 1968 - 1970
Width: 9 ½", 24.0 cm
Colour: 1. Assorted decos; solid colours - satin matt
              2. Copper - lustre
              3. White or black - matt

Market	Range
U.S.A.	$40.00 - 75.00
Canada	$60.00 - 100.00
U.K.	£20.00 - 40.00

Shape 2150 Bowl with candleholder

Designer: Albert Hallam in 1967
Issued: 1968 - 1970
Length: 12 ½", 31.7 cm
Colour: 1. Assorted decos; solid colours - satin matt
              2. Copper - lustre
              3. White or black - matt

Market	Range
U.S.A.	$40.00 - 75.00
Canada	$60.00 - 100.00
U.K.	£20.00 - 40.00

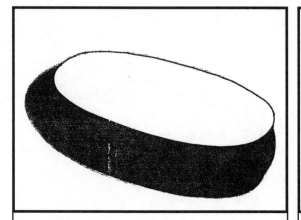

Shape 2153 Oval bowl

Designer:	Graham Tongue in 1967
Issued:	1968 - 1972
Size:	13 ½" x 3 ½", 34.3 x 8.9 cm
Colour:	1. Assorted decos; solid colours - satin matt
	2. Copper - lustre
	3. White or black - matt

Market	Range
U.S.A.	$40.00 - 75.00
Canada	$60.00 - 100.00
U.K.	£20.00 - 40.00

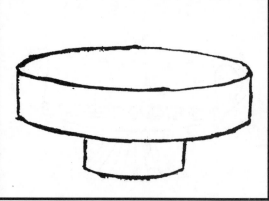

Shape 2168 Bowl

Designer:	Albert Hallam in 1967
Issued:	1968 - 1970
Size:	7" x 3", 17.8 x 7.6 cm
Colour:	1. Assorted decos; solid colours - satin matt
	2. Copper - lustre
	3. White or black - matt

Market	Range
U.S.A.	$30.00 - 60.00
Canada	$45.00 - 90.00
U.K.	£15.00 - 30.00

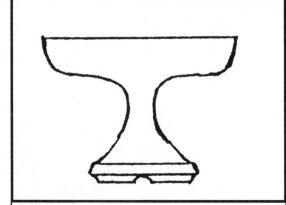

Shape 2278 Bowl, comport

Designer:	Albert Hallam in 1969
Issued:	1969 - 1970
Height:	4", 10.1 cm
Colour:	1. Assorted decos; solid colours - satin matt
	2. Copper - lustre
	3. White or black - matt

Market	Range
U.S.A.	$20.00 - 60.00
Canada	$30.00 - 60.00
U.K.	£10.00 - 30.00

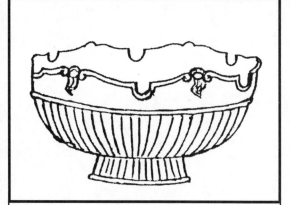

Shape 2374 Bowl, round

Designer:	Graham Tongue in 1971
Issued:	1971 - 1972
Size:	10" x 5 ½", 25.4 x 14.0 cm
Colour:	1. Assorted decos; solid colours - satin matt
	2. Copper - lustre
	3. White or black - matt

Market	Range
U.S.A.	
Canada	Rare
U.K.	

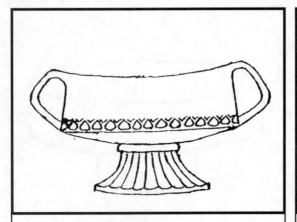

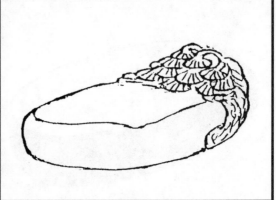

Shape 2380 Bowl, oval handled

Designer: Graham Tongue in 1971
Issued: 1971 - 1972
Size :   14" x 6 ¼", 35.5 x 15.9 cm
Colour: 1. Assorted decos; solid colours - satin matt
            2. Copper - lustre
            3. White or black - matt

Market	Range
U.S.A.	
Canada	Rare
U.K.	

Shape 2396 Bowl

Designer: Graham Tongue in 1971
Issued: 1972 only
Size: 7 ½" x 3 ¾", 19.1 x 9.5 cm
Colour: 1. Pewteramic - satin matt
            2. White - matt

Market	Range
U.S.A.	
Canada	Rare
U.K.	

CANDLEHOLDERS

Thirty-one candleholders were designed over the years spanning the early 1930s to the late 1960s. One represented three ducks (shape 370) and another was in the shape of a pig (shape 2294).

Mostly they were produced in the matt glaze (satin matt) finish with an enormous variety of subtle colour combinations. Later, dark colours were introduced, which included pewter, black matt and copper lustre. Some were handled and one, shape 1798 in the form of a long bowl, even had candle snuffers.

Shape 23   **Candlestick**

Designer: Unknown
Issued: c.1932 - by 1954
Size: Unknown
Colour: 1. Assorted decos; solid colours - satin matt
           2. White - matt

Market	Range
U.S.A.	$40.00 - 75.00
Canada	$60.00 - 100.00
U.K.	£20.00 - 35.00

Shape 48   **Aladdin's lamp candleholder**

Designer: Mr. Symcox c.1933
Issued: c.1933 - by 1954
Length: 8″, 20.3 cm
Colour: 1. Assorted decos; solid colours - satin matt
           2. White - matt

Market	Range
U.S.A.	$40.00 - 75.00
Canada	$60.00 - 100.00
U.K.	£25.00 - 35.00

Shape 82   **Candleholder with handle**

Designer: Mr. Symcox c.1933
Issued: c.1933 - by 1954
Size: 5 ½″ x 2″, 14 x 5 cm
Colour: 1. Assorted decos; solid colours - satin matt
           2. White - matt

Market	Range
U.S.A.	$40.00 - 75.00
Canada	$60.00 - 100.00
U.K.	£20.00 - 35.00

Shape 85   **Candleholder with handle**

Designer: Mr. Symcox c.1933
Issued: c.1933 - by 1954
Size: 4″ x 2 ½″, 10.1 x 6.4 cm
Colour: 1. Assorted decos; solid colours - satin matt
           2. White - matt

Market	Range
U.S.A.	$40.00 - 75.00
Canada	$60.00 - 100.00
U.K.	£25.00 - 35.00

Shape 156   Candleholder with handle

Designer:	Mr. Symcox c.1933
Issued:	c.1933 - by 1954
Size:	Unknown
Colour:	1. Assorted decos; solid colours - satin matt
	2. White - matt

Market	Range
U.S.A.	$30.00 - 50.00
Canada	$45.00 - 75.00
U.K.	£15.00 - 25.00

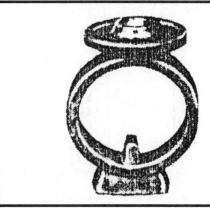

Shape 160   Candleholder

Designer:	Unknown c.1933
Issued:	c.1933 - by 1954
Height:	7", 17.8 cm
Colour:	1. Assorted decos; solid colours - satin matt
	2. White - matt

Market	Range
U.S.A.	$40.00 - 75.00
Canada	$60.00 - 100.00
U.K.	£20.00 - 35.00

Shape 203   Candlestick

Designer:	Mr. Symcox c.1933
Issued:	1933 - by 1954
Height:	9 ½", 24 cm
Colour:	1. Assorted decos; solid colours - satin matt
	2. White - matt

Market	Range
U.S.A.	$40.00 - 75.00
Canada	$60.00 - 100.00
U.K.	£20.00 - 35.00

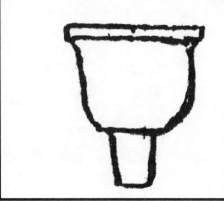

Shape 295   Candleholder

Designer:	Mr. Symcox in 1935
Issued:	1935 - by 1954
Diameter:	2", 5 cm Height: 2 ¼", 5.7 cm
Colour:	1. Assorted decos; solid colours - satin matt
	2. White - matt

Market	Range
U.S.A.	$30.00 - 40.00
Canada	$45.00 - 60.00
U.K.	£15.00 - 20.00

Note: Made to slide into the posy troughs (eg. shape 294).

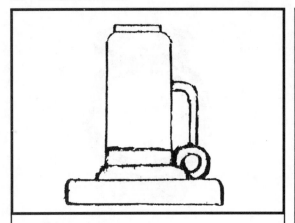

Shape 304 **Candleholder**

Designer:	Mr. Symcox in 1935
Issued:	1935 - by 1954
Size:	Unknown
Colour:	1. Assorted decos; solid colours - satin matt
	2. White - matt

Market	Range
U.S.A.	$40.00 - 85.00
Canada	$60.00 - 125.00
U.K.	£20.00 - 40.00

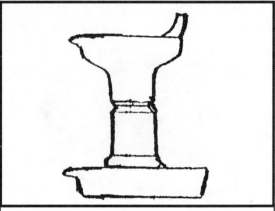

Shape 354 **Candlestick**

Designer:	Mr. Symcox in 1935
Issued:	1935 - by 1954
Size:	Unknown
Colour:	1. Assorted decos; solid colours - satin matt
	2. White - matt

Market	Range
U.S.A.	$40.00 - 85.00
Canada	$60.00 - 125.00
U.K.	£20.00 - 40.00

Shape 370 **Ducks, candleholder**

Designer:	James Hayward in 1935
Issued:	1935 - by 1954
Height:	3 ½", 8.9 cm
Colours:	1. Assorted decos; solid colours - satin matt
	2. White - matt

Market	Range
U.S.A.	$50.00 - 90.00
Canada	$75.00 - 125.00
U.K.	£25.00 - 45.00

Shape 422 **Candleholder**

Designer:	Mr. Symcox in 1936
Issued:	1936 - by 1954
Size:	Unknown
Colour:	1. Assorted decos; solid colour - satin matt
	2. White - matt

Market	Range
U.S.A.	$40.00 - 75.00
Canada	$60.00 - 100.00
U.K.	£20.00 - 35.00

Shape 423   Candleholder

Designer:	Mr. Symcox in 1936
Issued:	1936 - by 1963
Height:	5", 12.7 cm
Colour:	1. Assorted decos; solid colours - satin matt
	2. White - matt

Market	Range
U.S.A.	$40.00 - 75.00
Canada	$60.00 - 100.00
U.K.	£20.00 - 35.00

Shape 435   Candleholder and match holder

Designer:	Mr. Owen in 1936
Issued:	1936 - by 1954
Length:	7", 17.8 cm
Colour:	1. Assorted decos; solid colours - satin matt
	2. White - matt

Market	Range
U.S.A.	$40.00 - 75.00
Canada	$60.00 - 100.00
U.K.	£20.00 - 35.00

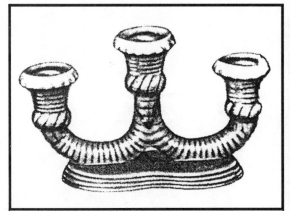

Shape 447   Candleholder

Designer:	Mr. Symcox in 1936
Issued:	1936 - by 1963
Height:	6 ½", 16.5 cm
Colour:	1. Assorted decos; solid colours - satin matt
	2. White - matt

Market	Range
U.S.A.	$40.00 - 85.00
Canada	$60.00 - 125.00
U.K.	£20.00 - 40.00

Shape 502   Candlestick

Designer:	Mr. Symcox in 1937
Issued:	1938 - by 1963
Height:	2 ½", 6.4 cm
Colour:	1. Assorted decos; solid colour - satin matt
	2. White - matt

Market	Range
U.S.A.	$30.00 - 50.00
Canada	$45.00 - 75.00
U.K.	£15.00 - 25.00

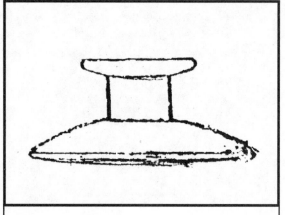

Shape 549 **Candleholder**

Designer: Mr. Symcox in 1937
Issued: 1938 - by 1954
Size: Unknown
Colour: 1. Assorted decos; solid colours - satin matt
2. White - matt

Market	Range
U.S.A.	$40.00 - 85.00
Canada	$60.00 - 125.00
U.K.	£20.00 - 40.00

Shape 611 **Candlestick**

Designer: Mr. Symcox in 1938
Issued: 1938 - by 1954
Size: Unknown
Colour: 1. Assorted decos; solid colour - satin matt
2. White - matt

Market	Range
U.S.A.	$30.00 - 50.00
Canada	$45.00 - 75.00
U.K.	£15.00 - 25.00

Photograph not
available
at press time

Shape 712 **Candleholder**

Designer: Mr. Symcox in 1939
Issued: 1939 - by 1954
Base Size: 10 ½" x 4 ¾", 26.7 cm x 12.1 cm
Height: 6 ¾", 17.2 cm
Colour: 1. Assorted decos; solid colours - satin matt
2. White - matt

Market	Range
U.S.A.	$40.00 - 85.00
Canada	$60.00 - 100.00
U.K.	£20.00 - 40.00

Shape 748 **Candleholder**

Designer: Mr. Symcox in 1939
Issued: 1939 - by 1954
Size: Unknown
Colour: 1. Assorted decos; solid colour - satin matt
2. White - matt

Market	Range
U.S.A.	$40.00 - 85.00
Canada	$60.00 - 100.00
U.K.	£20.00 - 40.00

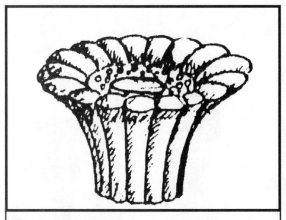

Shape 977   Candlestick

Designer:	Mr. Symcox in 1942
Issued:	1942 - by 1963
Size:	Unknown
Colour:	1. Assorted decos; solid colours - satin matt
	2. White - matt

Market	Range
U.S.A.	$40.00 - 75.00
Canada	$60.00 - 100.00
U.K.	£20.00 - 35.00

Note: This shape later became part of the Festival series.

Shape 1237 Candlestick

Designer:	James Hayward and Albert Hallam in 1952
Issued:	1952 - by 1963
Size:	3" x 2", 7.6 cm x 5 cm
Height:	2 ¼", 5.7 cm
Colour:	1. Assorted decos; solid colours - satin matt
	2. White - matt

Market	Range
U.S.A.	$30.00 - 40.00
Canada	$45.00 - 60.00
U.K.	£15.00 - 20.00

Shape 1798   Bowl with two candle holders (1798C)
Bowl with candle holders and snuffers (1798CS)

Designer:	Albert Hallam in 1962
Issued:	1962 - 1969
Length:	15", 38.1 cm
Colour:	1. Assorted decos; solid colours - satin matt
	2. White or black - matt
	3. Copper lustre

Market	Range
U.S.A.	$40.00 - 75.00
Canada	$60.00 - 95.00
U.K.	£20.00 - 35.00

Note: Also listed in Bowls and Basket section on page 171.

Shape 2072/2080 Candlestick

Designer:	Graham Tongue in 1966
Issued:	1967 - 1972
Height:	1. Shape 2072 — 7″, 17.8
	2. Shape 2080 — 9″, 22.9 cm
Colour:	1. Pink pearl or pewter - satin matt
	2. Copper - lustre
	3. White or black - matt

Market	Range
U.S.A.	$40.00 - 75.00
Canada	$60.00 - 100.00
U.K.	£20.00 - 35.00

Shape 2141 Candlestick

Designer:	Albert Hallam in 1967
Issued:	1968 - 1970
Height:	4 ½″, 11.9 cm
Colour:	1. Assorted decos; solid colours - satin matt
	2. Copper - lustre
	3. White or black - matt

Market	Range
U.S.A.	$30.00 - 60.00
Canada	$45.00 - 90.00
U.K.	£15.00 - 30.00

Shape 2203 Candleholder

Designer:	Graham Tongue in 1968
Issued:	1970 - 1972
Height:	2 ½″, 6.4 cm
Colour:	1. Black - matt
	2. Opaque white or green glaze - gloss

Market	Range
U.S.A.	$20.00 - 30.00
Canada	$30.00 - 45.00
U.K.	£10.00 - 15.00

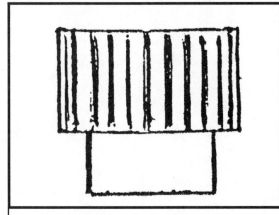

Shape 2204 Candleholder

Designer: Graham Tongue in 1968
Issued: 1970 only
Height :   2 ½", 6.4 cm
Colour: 1. Black - matt
           2. Opaque white or green glaze - gloss

Market	Range
U.S.A.	$20.00 - 30.00
Canada	$30.00 - 45.00
U.K.	£10.00 - 15.00

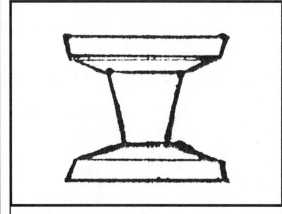

Shape 2246 Candlestick

Designer: Graham Tongue in 1968
Issued: 1970 only
Height: 2 ½", 6.4 cm
Colour: 1. Black - matt
           2. Opaque white or green glaze - gloss

Market	Range
U.S.A.	$20.00 - 30.00
Canada	$30.00 - 45.00
U.K.	£10.00 - 15.00

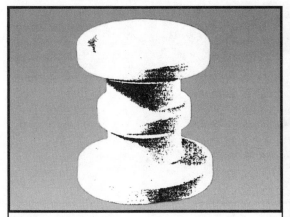

Shape 2247 Candlestick

Designer: Albert Hallam in 1968
Issued: 1970 - 1972
Height: 3 ¼", 8.3 cm
Colour: 1. Black - matt
           2. Opaque white or green glaze - gloss

Market	Range
U.S.A.	$30.00 - 40.00
Canada	$45.00 - 60.00
U.K.	£15.00 - 20.00

Shape 2294 Piglet candleholder

Designer: Harry Sales in 1969
Issued: 1970 - 1972
Size: 11" x 3 ½", 27.9 cm x 8.9 cm
Colour: 1. Blue and white gloss
           2. Brown gloss

Market	Range
U.S.A.	$100.00 - 125.00
Canada	$125.00 - 175.00
U.K.	£50.00 - 65.00

Note: This shape has four candle holders.

Shape 423 Candleholder

Shape 418 Vase   Shape 934 Ashtray   Shape 509 Vase

DECORATIVE DISHES AND TRAYS

In this list there are forty-one shapes, most of which belong to the attractive "Afternoon Tea" style, used in the days when four o'clock tea was one of the main traditions and a highlight of the day. These dishes could have been purchased boxed, for use as gifts, complete with a decorative knife, (Shape 598) or spoon, (Shape 599). An additional spoon was Shape 730.

Shapes 1907 to 1912 and shape 1916 can be found on pages 24 and 25 in the Heather and Gorse chapter. Shape 1689, a three-sectioned Mexican Hat, can be found on page 33 in the Hors-d'oeuvre chapter.

Other decorative dishes can also be found in the Tableware section. These dishes belong to the individual groups and conform to the style and decorations mentioned in that section.

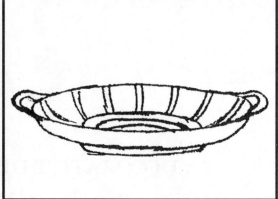

Shape 343   Dish/Dessert plate

Designer:	Mr. Symcox in 1935
Issued:	1935 - by 1940
Diameter:	8 ¼", 21 cm
Colour:	1. Assorted decorations - satin matt
	2. White - matt

Market	Range
U.S.A.	$30.00 - 60.00
Canada	$45.00 - 90.00
U.K.	£15.00 - 30.00

Shape 344   Nut tray

Designer:	Mr. Symcox in 1935
Issued:	1935 - by 1940
Size:	Unknown
Colour:	1. Assorted decorations - satin matt
	2. White - matt

Market	Range
U.S.A.	$30.00 - 75.00
Canada	$45.00 - 95.00
U.K.	£15.00 - 35.00

Shape 359   Nut tray

Designer:	Mr. Symcox in 1935
Issued:	1935 - by 1963
Length:	10 ¼, 26 cm
Colour:	1. Assorted decorations - satin matt
	2. White - matt

Market	Range
U.S.A.	$40.00 - 90.00
Canada	$60.00 - 125.00
U.K.	£20.00 - 45.00

Shape 591   Buttercup and apricot, double tray

Designer:	Mr. White in 1938
Issued:	1938 - by 1963
Length:	7 ¾", 19.7 cm
Colour:	Shades of yellow with green - gloss

Description	U.S. $	Can. $	U.K. £
Double tray	40.00	60.00	20.00

Note: Could be purchased separately, or boxed with a
knife and spoon or with one knife or one spoon.

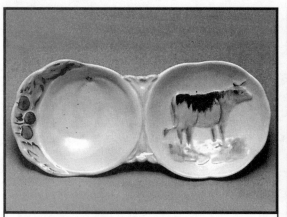

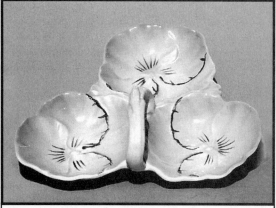

Shape 592   Cow and apple double tray

Designer:	Mr. White in 1938
Issued:	1938 - by 1963
Length:	7 ¾", 19.7 cm
Colour:	Green, yellow, brown and mauve - gloss

Description	U.S. $	Can. $	U.K. £
Double tray	40.00	60.00	20.00

Note: Could be purchased separately, or boxed with a knife and spoon or with one knife or one spoon.

Shape 593   Pansies triple tray

Designer:	Mr. White in 1938
Issued:	1938 - by 1963
Size:	7 ½", 19.1 cm triangular
Colour:	1. Yellow flowers with green - gloss
	2. White - matt

Market	Range
U.S.A.	$30.00 - 100.00
Canada	$45.00 - 125.00
U.K.	£15.00 - 35.00

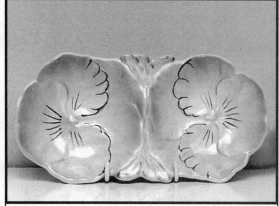

Shape 594   Butterfly tray

Designer:	Mr. White in 1938
Issued:	1938 - by 1954
Size:	6 ¾" x 5 ½", 17.2 x 14 cm
Colour:	Green, yellow, orange and black - gloss

Description	U.S. $	Can. $	U.K. £
Butterfly tray	60.00	90.00	30.00

Shape 595   Pansies double tray

Designer:	Mr. White in 1938
Issued:	1938 - by 1963
Length:	7 ¾", 19.7 cm
Colour:	Pink, yellow and mauve with green - gloss or lustre

Description	U.S. $	Can. $	U.K. £
Pansies double tray	40.00	60.00	20.00

Shape 600   Pansy dish

Designer: Mr. White in 1938
Issued: 1938 - by 1963
Size: 5", 12.7 cm
Colour: Yellow and oranges with green - gloss

Description	U.S. $	Can. $	U.K. £
Pansy dish	30.00	45.00	15.00

Note: Could be purchased separately, or boxed with one knife or one spoon.

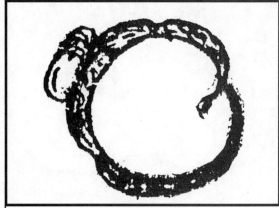

Shape 601   Apricot dish

Designer: Mr. White in 1938
Issued: 1938 - by 1963
Size: 5", 12.7 cm
Colour: Shades of yellow - gloss

Description	U.S. $	Can. $	U.K. £
Apricot dish	30.00	45.00	15.00

Note: Could be purchased separately, or boxed with one knife or one spoon.

Shape 602   Buttercup dish

Designer;   Mr. White in 1938
Issued: 1938 - by 1963
Size: 5", 12.7 cm
Colour: Yellow, green, with orange centre - gloss or lustre

Market	Range
U.S.A.	$30.00 - 60.00
Canada	$45.00 - 90.00
U.K.	£15.00 - 30.00

Shape 603   Cow dish

Designer: Mr. White in 1938
Issued: 1938 - by 1963
Size: 5", 12.7 cm
Colour: Yellow, brown with green grass - gloss

Description	U.S. $	Can. $	U.K. £
Cow dish	30.00	45.00	15.00

Note: Could be purchased separately, or boxed with one knife or one spoon.

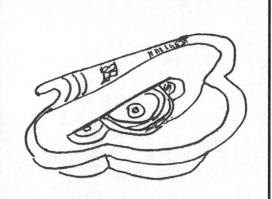

Shape 604   Apple dish

Designer:	Mr. White in 1938
Issued:	1938 - 1963
Size:	5", 12.7 cm
Colour:	Pink, green and yellow/orange - gloss or lustre

Description	U.S. $	Can. $	U.K. £
Apple dish	30.00	45.00	15.00

Note: Could be purchased separately or boxed with one knife or one spoon.

Shape 627   Dish tray

Designer:	Mr. Symcox in 1938
Issued:	1938 - by 1954
Size:	9" x 6 ½", 22.9 x 16.5 cm
Colour:	1. Assorted decorations - satin matt
	2. White - matt

Market	Range
U.S.A.	$30.00 - 75.00
Canada	$45.00 - 100.00
U.K.	£15.00 - 35.00

Shape 628   Daisy sweet dish

Designer:	Mr. Watkin in 1938
Issued:	1938 - by 1963
Diameter:	6 ¼", 15.9 cm
Colour:	Pink and green with pink, yellow, green or white centre - gloss

Description	U.S. $	Can. $	U.K. £
Daisy sweet dish	50.00	75.00	25.00

Note: Could be purchased separately, or boxed with a knife.

Shape 629   Chrysanthemum sweet dish

Designer:	Mr. Watkin in 1938
Issued:	1938 - by 1963
Size:	6 ¼" x 4 ¾", 15.9 x 12.1 cm
Colour:	Pink and yellow flowers with green - gloss

Description	U.S. $	Can. $	U.K. £
Chrysanthemum sweet dish	50.00	75.00	25.00

Note: Could be purchased separately, or boxed with a knife.

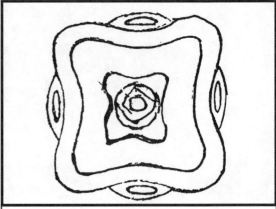

Shape 659   Narcissus sweet dish

Designer:	Unknown
Issued:	1938 - by 1963
Size:	9 ¼" x 5.3/4", 23.5 x 14.6 cm
Colour:	White and yellow, with green - gloss

Description	U.S. $	Can. $	U.K. £
Narcissus sweet dish	50.00	75.00	25.00

Shape 660   Dish

Designer:	Mr. Symcox in 1938
Issued:	1938 - by 1940
Width:	10 ½", 26.7 cm
Colour:	1. Assorted decorations - satin matt
	2. White - matt

Market	Range
U.S.A.	$30.00 - 75.00
Canada	$45.00 - 100.00
U.K.	£15.00 - 35.00

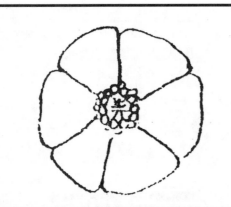

Shape 716   Daisy butter pat dish

Designer:	Mr. Hayward in 1939
Issued:	1939 - by 1963
Diameter:	3 ½", 8.9 cm
Colour:	Assorted decorations - satin matt

Market	Range
U.S.A.	$30.00 - 50.00
Canada	$45.00 - 75.00
U.K.	£15.00 - 25.00

Shape 722   Love in a mist, sweet dish

Designer:	Mr. Watkin in 1939
Issued:	1939 - by 1963
Size:	6" x 4 ¾", 15.0 x 12.1 cm
Colour:	Green and pink with green, pink, yellow or white centre - gloss

Market	Range
U.S.A.	$30.00 - 50.00
Canada	$45.00 - 75.00
U.K.	£15.00 - 25.00

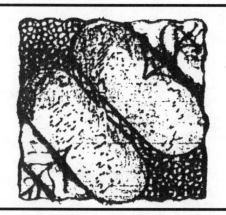

Shape 727   Forget-me-not sweet dish

Designer:	Mr. Watkin in 1939
Issued:	1939 - by 1963
Width:	5 ¼", 13.3 cm
Colour:	Assorted shades of green, pink, yellow or white - gloss

Market	Range
U.S.A.	$30.00 - 60.00
Canada	$45.00 - 75.00
U.K.	£15.00 - 25.00

Shape 932   Leaf dish

Designer:	Mr. Watkin in 1941
Issued:	1941 - by 1954
Size:	Unknown
Colour:	1. Assorted decorations - satin matt
	2. White - matt

Market	Range
U.S.A.	$30.00 - 60.00
Canada	$45.00 - 90.00
U.K.	£15.00 - 30.00

Photograph not
available
at press time

Photograph not
available
at press time

Shape 1253   Elizabeth II Coronation tray, large

Designer:	Albert Hallam, James Hayward in 1952
Issued:	1953 - 1953
Size:	Unknown
Colour:	Assorted colours on white background - gloss

Description	U.S. $	Can. $	U.K. £
Coronation tray, large	60.00	90.00	30.00

Shape 1254   Elizabeth II Coronation tray, small

Designer:	Albert Hallam, James Hayward in 1952
Issued:	1953 - 1953
Size:	Unknown
Colour:	Assorted colours on white background - gloss

Description	U.S. $	Can. $	U.K. £
Coronation tray, small	50.00	75.00	25.00

Shape 1304 Fish tray/trinket dish

Designer:	Arthur Gredington in 1953
Issued:	1953 - 1966
Length:	5", 12.7 cm
Colour:	Blues, yellow, browns and pink with black - gloss

Description	U.S. $	Can. $	U.K. £
Fish tray/trinket dish	90.00	125.00	45.00

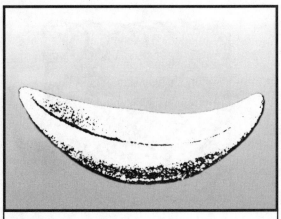

Shape 1358 Small oval dish

Designer:	Albert Hallam in 1954
Issued:	1954 - by 1962
Size:	6" x 2 ½", 15.0 x 6.4 cm
Colour:	1. Assorted decorations - satin matt
	2. White - matt

Market	Range
U.S.A.	$30.00 - 50.00
Canada	$45.00 - 75.00
U.K.	£15.00 - 25.00

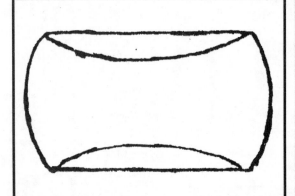

Shape 1537 Dish

Designer:	Albert Hallam in 1958
Issued:	1958 - by 1965
Size:	Unknown
Colour:	1. Assorted decorations - satin matt
	2. White - matt

Market	Range
U.S.A.	$30.00 - 50.00
Canada	$45.00 - 75.00
U.K.	£15.00 - 25.00

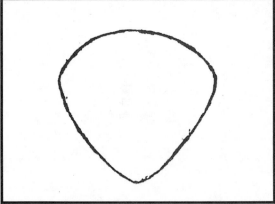

Shape 1538 Dish

Designer:	Albert Hallam in 1958
Issued:	1958 - by 1965
Size:	Unknown
Colour:	1. Assorted decorations - satin matt
	2. White - matt

Market	Range
U.S.A.	$30.00 - 50.00
Canada	$45.00 - 75.00
U.K.	£15.00 - 25.00

Shape 1635 Dish, rectangular

Designer:	Albert Hallam in 1959
Issued:	1960 - by 1963
Size:	7 ¾" x 5 ¼", 19.7 x 13.3 cm
Colour:	1. Assorted decorations - satin matt
	2. White - matt

Market	Range
U.S.A.	$20.00 - 30.00
Canada	$30.00 - 45.00
U.K.	£10.00 - 15.00

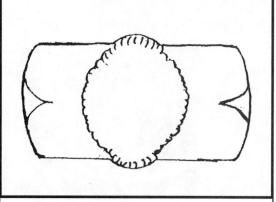

Shape 1690 Dish, rectangular

Designer:	Albert Hallam in 1960
Issued:	1960 - by 1962
Length:	14", 35.5 cm
Colour:	1. Assorted decorations - satin matt
	2. White - matt

Market	Range
U.S.A.	$30.00 - 75.00
Canada	$45.00 - 100.00
U.K.	£15.00 - 35.00

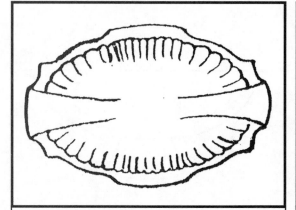

Shape 1691 Dish, oval

Designer:	Albert Hallam in 1960
Issued:	1960 - by 1962
Length:	12", 30.5 cm
Colour:	1. Assorted decorations - satin matt
	2. White - matt

Market	Range
U.S.A.	$30.00 - 75.00
Canada	$45.00 - 100.00
U.K.	£15.00 - 35.00

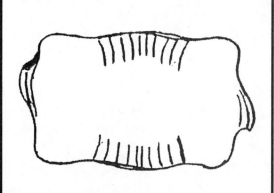

Shape 1692 Dish, rectangular

Designer:	Albert Hallam in 1960
Issued:	1960 - by 1962
Length:	12 ½", 31.7 cm
Colour:	1. Assorted decorations - satin matt
	2. White - matt

Market	Range
U.S.A.	$30.00 - 75.00
Canada	$45.00 - 100.00
U.K.	£15.00 - 35.00

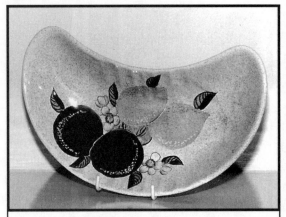

Shape 1693 Dish, kidney shape

Designer: Albert Hallam in 1960
Issued: 1960 - by 1963
Size: 9 ½" x 4 ½", 24 x 11.9 cm
Colour: 1. Assorted decorations - satin matt
  2. White - matt

Market	Range
U.S.A.	$20.00 - 50.00
Canada	$30.00 - 75.00
U.K.	£10.00 - 25.00

Shape 1701 Dish, Mexican hat (four sections)

Designer: Albert Hallam in 1960
Issued: 1960 - by 1963
Size: 8 ¼" x 3 ½", 21 x 8.9 cm
Colour: Yellow hat with blue, white and
  brown trim - gloss

Description	U.S. $	Can. $	U.K. £
Dish, Mexican hat	75.00	100.00	40.00

Photograph not
available
at press time

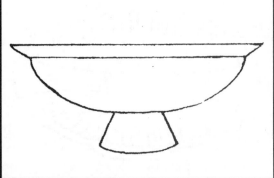

Shape 1856 Double Diamond dish

Designer: Unknown
Issued: 1962
Size: Unknown
Colour: 1. Assorted solid colours - matt
  2. White - matt

Market	Range
U.S.A.	$30.00 - 50.00
Canada	$45.00 - 75.00
U.K.	£15.00 - 25.00

Note: Special Commission.

Shape 1889 Dish on foot

Designer: Albert Hallam in 1963
Issued: 1963 - by 1965
Length: 12" x 4 ¾", 30.5 x 12.1 cm
Colour: 1. Assorted decorations - satin matt
  2. White - matt

Market	Range
U.S.A.	$30.00 - 50.00
Canada	$45.00 - 75.00
U.K.	£15.00 - 25.00

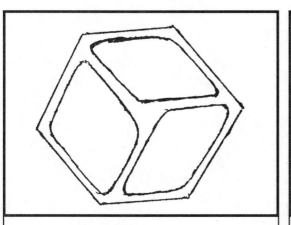

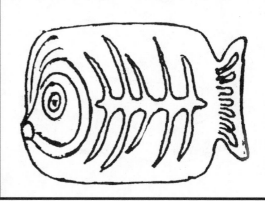

Shape 2013 Dish in three sections

Designer: Mr. Murphy in 1964
Issued: 1964 - unknown
Size: Unknown
Colour: 1. Assorted decos; solid colours - satin matt
            2. White or black - matt

Market	Range
U.S.A.	$30.00 - 50.00
Canada	$45.00 - 75.00
U.K.	£15.00 - 25.00

Shape 2167 Fish dish

Designer: Albert Hallam in 1967
Issued: 1967 - 1969
Size: 7 ½" x 6", 19.1 x 15 cm
Colour: Assorted decorations, solid colours - gloss

Market	Range
U.S.A.	$30.00 - 60.00
Canada	$45.00 - 90.00
U.K.	£15.00 - 30.00

Shape 2170 Fish dish

Designer: Albert Hallam in 1967
Issued: 1967 - 1969
Size: 7 ½" x 5 ½", 19.1 x 14 cm
Colour: Assorted decorations, solid colours - gloss

Market	Range
U.S.A.	$30.00 - 60.00
Canada	$45.00 - 90.00
U.K.	£15.00 - 30.00

Shape 2171 Fish dish

Designer: Albert Hallam in 1967
Issued: 1967 - 1969
Size: 12" x 4", 30.5 x 10.1 cm
Colour: Assorted decorations, solid colours - gloss

Market	Range
U.S.A.	$30.00 - 60.00
Canada	$45.00 - 90.00
U.K.	£15.00 - 30.00

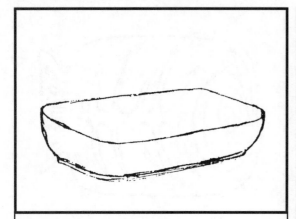

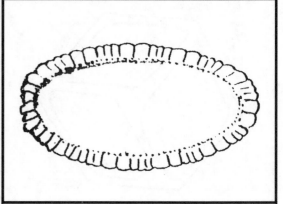

Shape 2277 Dish

Designer:	Albert Hallam in 1969
Issued:	1969 - 1970
Size:	9 ½" x 7 ¼", 24 x 18.4 cm
Colour:	1. Assorted decos; solid colours - satin matt
	2. Copper - lustre
	3. White or black - matt

Market	Range
U.S.A.	$20.00 - 50.00
Canada	$30.00 - 75.00
U.K.	£10.00 - 25.00

Shape 2291 Oval tray, pair with shape 2292

Designer:	Graham Tongue in 1969
Issued:	1969 - unknown
Size:	5 ½" x 8 ½", 14 x 21.6 cm
Colour:	1. Assorted decos; solid colours - satin matt
	2. Copper - lustre
	3. White or black - matt

Market	Range
U.S.A.	$20.00 - 60.00
Canada	$30.00 - 90.00
U.K.	£10.00 - 30.00

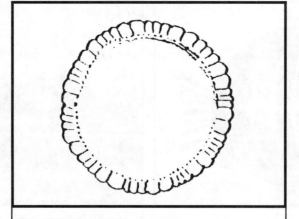

Shape 2292 Sweet dish

Designer:	Graham Tongue in 1969
Issued:	1969 - unknown
Diameter:	5", 12.7 cm
Colour:	1. Assorted decos; solid colours - satin matt
	2. Copper - lustre
	3. White or black - matt

Market	Range
U.S.A.	$20.00 - 50.00
Canada	$30.00 - 75.00
U.K.	£10.00 - 25.00

JUGS

There are ninety-six shapes listed in this section, most of which could be called "jug-vases," since they appear to have been designed for use as flower holders, or simply for ornamental purposes only. Because of this, they have been listed separately from the jugs which form part of named series or small sets, for example, milk or cream jugs, which are to be found listed with the appropriate named series or in the Tableware Section.

The early assorted decorations used for these jugs varied considerably - ranging from the soft blended colours with subtle shading of the matt glazes, (satin matt), to dynamic Art deco styles (often backstamped - "Handpainted"). Very detailed decorations were used on the four Shakespeare Jugs, which were embossed and decorated with many colours. Other jugs were quite plain, yet still very striking, such as the copper lustre finish with black gloss inners. There are also some very interesting shapes to note, eg. Shape 94 with a spout pourer, and even a jug with feet! Quite a selection?

Shape 22   Jug

Designer:	Mr. Symcox in 1933
Issued:	1933 - by 1954
Height:	12 ¼", 31.1 cm
Colour:	1. Assorted decorations - satin matt
	2. White - matt

Market	Range
U.S.A.	$75.00 - 150.00
Canada	$100.00 - 200.00
U.K.	£35.00 - 70.00

Shape 26   Jug

Designer:	Mr. Symcox in 1933
Issued:	1933 - by 1954
Height :	10 ½", 26.7 cm
Colour:	1. Assorted decorations - satin matt
	2. White - matt

Market	Range
U.S.A.	$75.00 - 150.00
Canada	$100.00 - 200.00
U.K.	£35.00 - 70.00

Shape 28   Jug

Designer:	Mr. Symcox in 1933
Issued:	1933 - by 1959
Height:	9 ½", 24 cm
Colour:	1. Assorted decorations - satin matt
	2. White - matt

Market	Range
U.S.A.	$75.00 - 150.00
Canada	$100.00 - 200.00
U.K.	£35.00 - 70.00

Shape 72   Ruth jug

Designer:	Unknown
Issued:	1932 - by 1954
Height :	10 ¼", 26 cm
Colour:	1. Assorted decorations - satin matt
	2. White - matt

Market	Range
U.S.A.	$75.00 - 150.00
Canada	$100.00 - 200.00
U.K.	£35.00 - 70.00

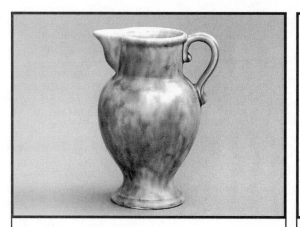

Shape 91   Jug

Designer:	Mr. Symcox in 1933
Issued:	1933 - by 1954
Height:	8", 20.3 cm
Colour:	1. Assorted decorations - satin matt
	2. White - matt

Market	Range
U.S.A.	$60.00 - 125.00
Canada	$90.00 - 175.00
U.K.	£30.00 - 60.00

Shape 92   Jug

Designer:	Mr. Symcox in 1933
Issued:	1933 - by 1954
Height :	6 ½", 16.5 cm
Colour:	1. Assorted decorations - satin matt
	2. White - matt

Market	Range
U.S.A.	$50.00 - 100.00
Canada	$75.00 - 150.00
U.K.	£25.00 - 50.00

Shape 94   Jug

Designer:	Mr. Symcox in 1933
Issued:	1933 - by 1954
Height:	9", 22.9 cm
Colour:	1. Assorted decorations - satin matt
	2. White - matt

Market	Range
U.S.A.	$75.00 - 150.00
Canada	$100.00 - 200.00
U.K.	£35.00 - 70.00

Shape 98/1/2 Jug

Designer:	Mr. Symcox in 1933
Issued:	1933 - by 1954
Height :	1. Shape 98/1 — 10", 25.4 cm
	2. Shape 98/2 — Unknown
Colour:	1. Assorted decorations - satin matt
	2. White - matt

Market	Range
U.S.A.	$50.00 - 150.00
Canada	$75.00 - 200.00
U.K.	£25.00 - 70.00

Shape 119   Jug

Designer: Mr. Symcox in 1933
Issued: 1934 - by 1954
Height: 11", 27.9 cm
Colour: 1. Assorted decorations - satin matt
              2. White - matt

Market	Range
U.S.A.	$75.00 - 150.00
Canada	$100.00 - 200.00
U.K.	£35.00 - 70.00

Shape 125   Jug

Designer: Mr. Owen in 1934
Issued: 1934 - by 1954
Height :   7", 17.8 cm
Colour: 1. Assorted decorations - satin matt
              2. White - matt

Market	Range
U.S.A.	$60.00 - 125.00
Canada	$90.00 - 175.00
U.K.	£30.00 - 60.00

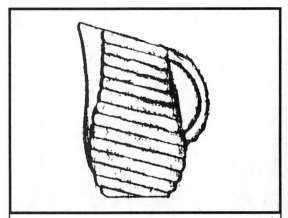

Shape 129/1/2 Jug

Designer: Mr. Symcox in 1933
Issued: 1934 - by 1954
Size :   Unknown
Colour: 1. Assorted decorations - satin matt
              2. White - matt

Market	Range
U.S.A.	$60.00 - 125.00
Canada	$90.00 - 175.00
U.K.	£30.00 - 60.00

Shape 131   Jug

Designer: Mr. Symcox in 1933
Issued: 1934 - by 1963
Height :   6 ¼", 15.9 cm
Colour: 1. Assorted decorations - satin matt
              2. White - matt

Market	Range
U.S.A.	$50.00 - 100.00
Canada	$75.00 - 150.00
U.K.	£25.00 - 50.00

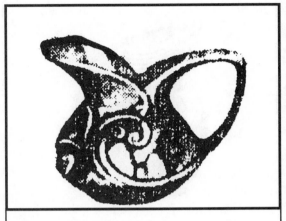

Shape 136 Jug

Designer: Mr. Symcox in 1933
Issued: 1934 - by 1954
Height: 4 ½", 11.9 cm
Colour: 1. Assorted decorations - satin matt
2. White - matt

Market	Range
U.S.A.	$40.00 - 75.00
Canada	$60.00 - 100.00
U.K.	£20.00 - 40.00

Shape 137 Jug

Designer: Mr. Symcox in 1933
Issued: 1934 - by 1963
Height: 4 ½", 11.9 cm
Colour: 1. Assorted decorations - satin matt
2. White - matt

Market	Range
U.S.A.	$40.00 - 75.00
Canada	$60.00 - 100.00
U.K.	£20.00 - 40.00

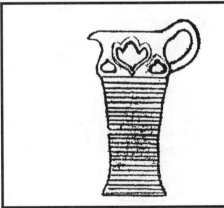

Shape 140 Jug

Designer: Mr. Symcox in 1933
Issued: 1934 - by 1954
Size: Unknown
Colour: 1. Assorted decorations - satin matt
2. White - matt

Market	Range
U.S.A.	$60.00 - 125.00
Canada	$90.00 - 175.00
U.K.	£30.00 - 60.00

Shape 141 Jug

Designer: Mr. Symcox in 1933
Issued: 1934 - by 1954
Height: 11", 27.9 cm
Colour: 1. Assorted decorations - satin matt
2. White - matt

Market	Range
U.S.A.	$60.00 - 125.00
Canada	$90.00 - 175.00
U.K.	£30.00 - 60.00

Shape 146   Jug

Designer:	Mr. Symcox in 1933
Issued:	1934 - by 1954
Height:	9 ¼", 23.5 cm
Colour:	1. Assorted decorations - satin matt
	2. White - matt

Market	Range
U.S.A.	$60.00 - 125.00
Canada	$90.00 - 175.00
U.K.	£30.00 - 60.00

Shape 148   Jug

Designer:	Mr. Symcox in 1933
Issued:	1934 - by 1962
Height :	9", 22.9 cm
Colour:	1. Assorted decorations - satin matt
	2. White - matt

Market	Range
U.S.A.	$60.00 - 125.00
Canada	$90.00 - 175.00
U.K.	£30.00 - 60.00

Shape 150   Jug

Designer:	Mr. Symcox in 1933
Issued:	1934 - by 1954
Height:	8 ½", 21.6 cm
Colour:	1. Assorted decorations - satin matt
	2. White - matt

Market	Range
U.S.A.	$60.00 - 125.00
Canada	$90.00 - 175.00
U.K.	£30.00 - 60.00

Shape 151   Jug

Designer:	Mr. Symcox in 1933
Issued:	1934 - by 1954
Height :	10 ½", 26.7 cm
Colour:	1. Assorted decorations - satin matt
	2. White - matt

Market	Range
U.S.A.	$75.00 - 150.00
Canada	$100.00 - 225.00
U.K.	£35.00 - 70.00

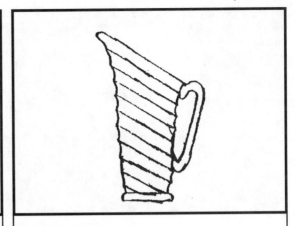

Shape 155	**Jug**
Designer:	Mr. Owen in 1933
Issued:	1934 - by 1954
Height:	5 ½", 14 cm
Colour:	1. Assorted decorations - satin matt
	2. White - matt

Market	Range
U.S.A.	$40.00 - 75.00
Canada	$60.00 - 100.00
U.K.	£20.00 - 40.00

Shape 162	**Jug**
Designer:	Mr. Symcox in 1933
Issued:	1934 - by 1963
Height :	11 ¼", 28.5
Colour:	1. Assorted decorations - satin matt
	2. White - matt

Market	Range
U.S.A.	$60.00 - 125.00
Canada	$90.00 - 175.00
U.K.	£30.00 - 60.00

Shape 163	**Jug**
Designer:	Mr. Symcox in 1933
Issued:	1934 - by 1954
Size :	Unknown
Colour:	1. Assorted decorations - satin matt
	2. White - matt

Market	Range
U.S.A.	$60.00 - 125.00
Canada	$90.00 - 175.00
U.K.	£30.00 - 60.00

Shape 173	**Jug**
Designer:	Mr. Symcox in 1933
Issued:	1934 - by 1954
Height :	9", 22.9 cm
Colour:	1. Assorted decorations - satin matt
	2. White - matt

Market	Range
U.S.A.	$60.00 - 125.00
Canada	$90.00 - 175.00
U.K.	£30.00 - 60.00

Shape 174   Jug

Designer: Mr. Owen in 1934
Issued: 1934 - by 1954
Height: 8", 20.3 cm
Colour: 1. Assorted decorations - satin matt
            2. White - matt

Market	Range
U.S.A.	$50.00 - 100.00
Canada	$75.00 - 150.00
U.K.	£25.00 - 50.00

Shape 175   Jug

Designer: Mr. Symcox in 1933
Issued: 1934 - by 1954
Height :   11", 27.9 cm
Colour: 1. Assorted decorations - satin matt
            2. White - matt

Market	Range
U.S.A.	$60.00 - 125.00
Canada	$90.00 - 175.00
U.K.	£30.00 - 60.00

Shape 176   Jug

Designer: Mr. Symcox in 1933
Issued: 1934 - by 1954
Height: 7 ½", 19.1 cm
Colour: 1. Assorted decorations - satin matt
            2. White - matt

Market	Range
U.S.A.	$50.00 - 100.00
Canada	$75.00 - 150.00
U.K.	£25.00 - 50.00

Shape 177/1/2 Jug

Designer: Mr. Symcox in 1933
Issued: 1934 - by 1954
Height :   1. Shape 177/1 — 10 ½", 26.7 cm
            2. Shape 177/2 — Unknown
Colour: 1. Assorted decorations - satin matt
            2. White - matt

Market	Range
U.S.A.	$40.00 - 125.00
Canada	$60.00 - 175.00
U.K.	£20.00 - 60.00

Shape 178   Jug

Designer:	Mr. Symcox in 1933
Issued:	1934 - by 1954
Height:	8 ½", 21.6 cm
Colour:	1. Assorted decorations - satin matt
	2. White - matt

Market	Range
U.S.A.	$50.00 - 100.00
Canada	$75.00 - 150.00
U.K.	£25.00 - 50.00

Shape 179   Jug

Designer:	Mr. Symcox in 1933
Issued:	1934 - by 1954
Size:	Unknown
Colour:	1. Assorted decorations - satin matt
	2. White - matt

Market	Range
U.S.A.	$75.00 - 150.00
Canada	$100.00 - 200.00
U.K.	£35.00 - 70.00

Shape 260/1/2/3 Jug

Designer:	Albert Hallam in 1933
Issued:	1934 - by 1954
Height:	1. Shape 260/1 — 7 ½", 19.1 cm
	2. Shape 260/2 — 6 ½", 16.5 cm
	3. Shape 260/3 — 5 ½", 14 cm
Colour:	1. Assorted decorations - satin matt
	2. White - matt

Market	Range
Shape 260/1	
U.S.A.	$50.00 - 150.00
Canada	$75.00 - 200.00
U.K.	£25.00 - 70.00
Shape 260/2	
U.S.A.	$40.00 - 75.00
Canada	$60.00 - 100.00
U.K.	£20.00 - 40.00
Shape 260/3	
U.S.A.	$30.00 - 50.00
Canada	$45.00 - 75.00
U.K.	£15.00 - 25.00

Shape 261/1/2/3 Jug

Designer: Mr. Symcox in 1934
Issued: 1934 - by 1954
Height :   6 ¼", 15 cm
Colour: 1. Assorted decorations - satin matt
             2. White - matt

Market	Range
U.S.A.	$30.00 - 150.00
Canada	$45.00 - 200.00
U.K.	£15.00 - 70.00

Shape 265/1/2/3 Jug in three sizes

Designer: Unknown
Issued: 1934 - by 1959
Reissued: 1962 - by 1970
Height: See below
Colour: 1. Assorted decorations - satin matt
             2. White - matt

Shape No.	Height	Colour	U.S. $	Can. $	U.K. £
265/1	5", 12.7 cm	Assorted	50.00	75.00	25.00
265/1	5", 12.7 cm	White	30.00	45.00	15.00
265/2	4 ½", 11.9 cm	Assorted	40.00	60.00	20.00
265/2	4 ½", 11.9 cm	White	25.00	35.00	12.00
265/3	4", 10.1 cm	Assorted	30.00	45.00	15.00
265/3	4", 10.1 cm	White	20.00	30.00	10.00

Note: First issued in 1934 with a plain design, this jug was reissued in 1962 with a ribbed design.

Shape 266   **Wolstan jug**

Designer:	Unknown
Issued:	1933 - by 1954
Height :	6 ½", 16.5 cm
Colour:	1 Assorted decorations - satin matt
	2. White - matt

Market	Range
U.S.A.	$40.00 - 75.00
Canada	$60.00 - 100.00
U.K.	£20.00 - 40.00

Shape 292   **Jug**

Designer:	Mr. Symcox in 1934
Issued:	1935 - by 1954
Height:	4 ½", 11.9 cm
Colour:	1. Assorted decorations - satin matt
	2. White - matt

Market	Range
U.S.A.	$30.00 - 60.00
Canada	$45.00 - 90.00
U.K.	£15.00 - 30.00

Shape 293   **Jug**

Designer:	Mr. Symcox in 1934
Issued:	1935 - by 1954
Size:	Unknown
Colour:	1. Assorted decorations - satin matt
	2. White - matt

Market	Range
U.S.A.	$30.00 - 60.00
Canada	$45.00 - 90.00
U.K.	£15.00 - 30.00

Shape 346   **Jug**

Designer:	Mr. Symcox in 1934
Issued:	1935 - by 1954
Height:	5 ½",14 cm
Colour:	1. Assorted decorations - satin matt
	2. White - matt

Market	Range
U.S.A.	$40.00 - 75.00
Canada	$60.00 - 100.00
U.K.	£20.00 - 40.00

Shape 348   Jug

Designer:	Mr. Symcox in 1934
Issued:	1935 - by 1954
Height :	7 ¾", 19.7 cm
Colour:	1. Assorted decorations - satin matt
	2. White - matt

Market	Range
U.S.A.	$50.00 - 100.00
Canada	$75.00 - 150.00
U.K.	£25.00 - 50.00

Shape 349   Jug

Designer:	Mr. Symcox in 1934
Issued:	1935 - by 1954
Size :	Unknown
Colour:	1. Assorted decorations - satin matt
	2. White - matt

Market	Range
U.S.A.	$50.00 - 100.00
Canada	$75.00 - 150.00
U.K.	£25.00 - 50.00

Shape 350   Jug

Designer:	Mr. Symcox in 1935
Issued:	1935 - by 1965
Height :	8 ½", 21.6 cm
Colour:	1. Assorted decorations, solid colours - satin matt
	2. White or black - matt

Market	Range
U.S.A.	$50.00 - 100.00
Canada	$75.00 - 175.00
U.K.	£25.00 - 50.00

Shape 355   Jug

Designer:	Mr. Symcox in 1935
Issued:	1935 - by 1954
Height:	10", 25.4 cm
Colour:	1. Assorted decorations - satin matt
	2. White - matt

Market	Range
U.S.A.	$60.00 - 125.00
Canada	$90.00 - 175.00
U.K.	£30.00 - 60.00

Shape 356   Jug

Designer:	Mr. Symcox in 1935
Issued:	1935 - by 1954
Height :	10", 25.4 cm
Colour:	1. Assorted decorations - satin matt
	2. White - matt

Market	Range
U.S.A.	$60.00 - 125.00
Canada	$90.00 - 175.00
U.K.	£30.00 - 60.00

Shape 387   Jug

Designer:	Mr. Symcox in 1936
Issued:	1936 - by 1954
Size :	Unknown
Colour:	1. Assorted decorations - satin matt
	2. White - matt

Market	Range
U.S.A.	$60.00 - 125.00
Canada	$90.00 - 175.00
U.K.	£30.00 - 60.00

Shape 394/1/2 Jug

Designer:	Mr. Symcox in 1936
Issued:	1936 - by 1959
Height:	1. Shape 394/1 — 10", 25.4 cm
	2. Shape 394/2 — 8", 20.3 cm
Colour:	1. Assorted decorations - satin matt
	2. White - matt

Market	Range
U.S.A.	$50.00 - 125.00
Canada	$75.00 - 175.00
U.K.	£25.00 - 60.00

Shape 421   Jug

Designer:	Mr. Symcox in 1936
Issued:	1936 - by 1954
Size:	Unknown
Colour:	1. Assorted decorations - satin matt
	2. White - matt

Market	Range
U.S.A.	$60.00 - 125.00
Canada	$90.00 - 175.00
U.K.	£30.00 - 60.00

Shape 424   **Jug**

Designer:	Mr. Owen in 1936
Issued:	1936 - by 1954
Height :	9 ½", 24 cm
Colour:	1. Assorted decorations - satin matt
	2. White - matt

Market	Range
U.S.A.	$60.00 - 125.00
Canada	$90.00 - 175.00
U.K.	£30.00 - 60.00

Shape 426   **Jug**

Designer:	Mr. Owen in 1936
Issued:	1936 - by 1954
Height:	7 ½", 19.1 cm
Colour:	1. Assorted decorations - satin matt
	2. White - matt

Market	Range
U.S.A.	$50.00 - 100.00
Canada	$75.00 - 150.00
U.K.	£25.00 - 50.00

Shape 430   **Jug**

Designer:	Mr. Symcox in 1936
Issued:	1936 - by 1954
Size:	Unknown
Colour:	1. Assorted decorations - satin matt
	2. White - matt

Market	Range
U.S.A.	$50.00 - 100.00
Canada	$75.00 - 150.00
U.K.	£25.00 - 50.00

Shape 448   **Jug**

Designer:	Mr. Symcox in 1936
Issued:	1936 - by 1954
Height:	12", 30.5 cm
Colour:	1. Assorted decorations - satin matt
	2. White - matt

Market	Range
U.S.A.	$75.00 - 150.00
Canada	$100.00 - 225.00
U.K.	£35.00 - 70.00

Shape 478 **Jug**

Designer: Mr. Symcox in 1937
Issued: 1937 - by 1962
Height : 6", 15 cm
Colour: 1. Assorted decorations - satin matt
2. White - matt

Market	Range
U.S.A.	$40.00 - 75.00
Canada	$60.00 - 100.00
U.K.	£20.00 - 40.00

Shape 480 **Jug**

Designer: Mr. Symcox in 1937
Issued: 1937 - by 1954
Size : Unknown
Colour: 1. Assorted decorations - satin matt
2. White - matt

Market	Range
U.S.A.	$50.00 - 100.00
Canada	$75.00 - 150.00
U.K.	£25.00 - 50.00

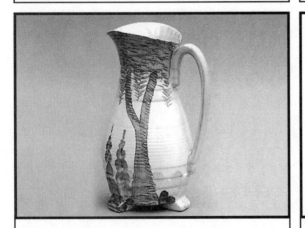

Shape 488 **Jug**

Designer: Mr. Symcox in 1937
Issued: 1937 - by 1954
Height: 10", 25.4 cm
Colour: 1. Assorted decorations - satin matt
2. White - matt

Market	Range
U.S.A.	$60.00 - 125.00
Canada	$90.00 - 175.00
U.K.	£30.00 - 60.00

Shape 493 **Jug**

Designer: Mr. Owen in 1937
Issued: 1937 - by 1954
Size : Unknown
Colour: 1. Assorted decorations - satin matt
2. White - matt

Market	Range
U.S.A.	$50.00 - 100.00
Canada	$75.00 - 150.00
U.K.	£25.00 - 50.00

Shape 505   Jug

Designer:	Mr. Owen in 1937
Issued:	1937 - by 1962
Height :	10", 25.4 cm
Colour:	1. Assorted decorations - satin matt
	2. White - matt

Market	Range
U.S.A.	$60.00 - 125.00
Canada	$90.00 - 175.00
U.K.	£30.00 - 60.00

Photograph not
available
at press time

Shape 510   Jug

Designer:	Mr. Symcox in 1937
Issued:	1937 - by 1954
Height:	10", 25.4 cm
Colour:	1. Assorted decorations - satin matt
	2. White - matt

Market	Range
U.S.A.	$60.00 - 125.00
Canada	$90.00 - 175.00
U.K.	£30.00 - 60.00

Photograph not
available
at press time

Shape 544   Jug

Designer:	Mr. Symcox in 1937
Issued:	1938 - by 1954
Size:	Unknown
Colour:	1. Assorted decorations - satin matt
	2. White - matt

Market	Range
U.S.A.	$60.00 - 125.00
Canada	$90.00 - 175.00
U.K.	£30.00 - 60.00

Shape 547   Jug

Designer:	Mr. Symcox in 1937
Issued:	1938 - by 1954
Size :	9", 23.0 cm
Colour:	1. Assorted decorations - satin matt
	2. White - matt

Market	Range
U.S.A.	$50.00 - 100.00
Canada	$75.00 - 150.00
U.K.	£25.00 - 50.00

Shape 550   Jug

Designer: Mr. Symcox in 1937
 Issued: 1938 - by 1954
Size: Unknown
Colour: 1. Assorted decorations - satin matt
              2. White - matt

Market	Range
U.S.A.	$50.00 - 100.00
Canada	$75.00 - 150.00
U.K.	£25.00 - 50.00

Shape 555   Jug

Designer: Mr. Symcox in 1937
Issued: 1938 - by 1954
Size::   Unknown
Colour: 1. Assorted decorations - satin matt
              2. White - matt

Market	Range
U.S.A.	$60.00 - 125.00
Canada	$90.00 - 175.00
U.K.	£30.00 - 60.00

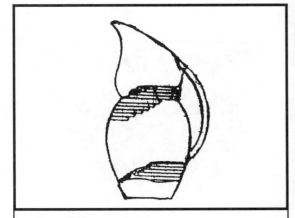

Shape 561   Jug

Designer: Mr. Owen in 1937
Issued: 1938 - by 1962
Height :   12 ¼", 31.1 cm
Colour: 1. Assorted decorations - satin matt
              2. White - matt

Market	Range
U.S.A.	$75.00 - 150.00
Canada	$100.00 - 200.00
U.K.	£35.00 - 70.00

Shape 567   Jug

Designer: Mr. Owen in 1937
Issued: 1938 - by 1954
Height: 8", 20.3 cm
Colour: 1. Assorted decorations - satin matt
              2. White - matt

Market	Range
U.S.A.	$60.00 - 125.00
Canada	$90.00 - 175.00
U.K.	£30.00 - 60.00

Shape 578   Jug

Designer:	Mr. Newman in 1938
Issued:	1938 - by 1954
Size:	Unknown
Colour:	1. Assorted decorations - satin matt
	2. White - matt

Market	Range
U.S.A.	$60.00 - 125.00
Canada	$90.00 - 175.00
U.K.	£30.00 - 60.00

Shape 616   Jug

Designer:	Mr. Symcox in 1938
Issued:	1938 - by 1954
Height:	8", 20.3 cm
Colour:	1. Assorted decorations - satin matt
	2. White - matt

Market	Range
U.S.A.	$50.00 - 100.00
Canada	$75.00 - 150.00
U.K.	£25.00 - 50.00

Shape 652   Jug

Designer:	Mr. Symcox in 1938
Issued:	1938 - by 1954
Height :	9", 22.9 cm
Colour:	1. Assorted decorations - satin matt
	2. White - matt

Market	Range
U.S.A.	$60.00 - 125.00
Canada	$90.00 - 175.00
U.K.	£30.00 - 60.00

Shape 653   Jug, Modelle Series

Designer:	Mr. Watkin in 1938
Issued:	1939 - by 1962
Size:	8 ½", 21.6 cm
Colour:	1. Assorted decorations - satin matt
	2. White - matt

Market	Range
U.S.A.	$100.00 - 150.00
Canada	$150.00 - 225.00
U.K.	£50.00 - 70.00

Shape 654   Jug, Modelle Series

Designer: James Hayward 1938
Issued: 1939 - by 1962
Size: 10", 25.4 cm
Colour: 1. Assorted decorations- satin matt
             2. White - matt

Market	Range
U.S.A.	$100.00 - 150.00
Canada	$150.00 - 225.00
U.K.	£50.00 - 70.00

Photograph not
available
at press time

Shape 662   Jug

Designer: Mr. Symcox in 1938
Issued: 1939 - by 1954
Size :   Unknown
Colour: 1. Assorted decorations - satin matt
             2. White - matt

Market	Range
U.S.A.	$60.00 - 125.00
Canada	$90.00 - 175.00
U.K.	£30.00 - 60.00

Shape 667   Jug

Designer: Mr. Symcox in 1938
Issued: 1939 - by 1962
Height :   4 ½", 11.9 cm
Colour: 1. Assorted decorations - satin matt
             2. White - matt

Market	Range
U.S.A.	$40.00 - 75.00
Canada	$60.00 - 100.00
U.K.	£20.00 - 40.00

Shape 676   Jug, Modelle Series

Designer: Mr. Watkin in 1939
Issued: 1939 - by 1962
Size: 10", 25.4 cm
Colour: 1. Assorted decorations - satin matt
             2. White - matt

Market	Range
U.S.A.	$100.00 - 150.00
Canada	$150.00 - 225.00
U.K.	£50.00 - 70.00

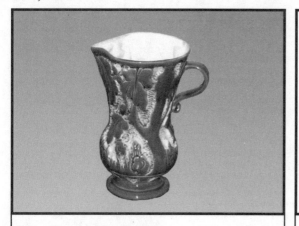

Shape 679 **Jug, Modelle Series**

Designer:	Mr. Watkin in 1939
Issued:	1939 - by 1962
Size:	8″, 20.3 cm
Colour:	1. Assorted decorations - satin matt
	2. White - matt

Market	Range
U.S.A.	$100.00 - 150.00
Canada	$150.00 - 225.00
U.K.	£50.00 - 70.00

Photograph not
available
at press time

Shape 694 **Jug, Modelle Series**

Designer:	Mr. Watkin in 1939
Issued:	1939 - by 1962
Size:	9 ¾″, 24.7 cm
Colour:	1. Assorted decorations - satin matt
	2. White - matt

Market	Range
U.S.A.	$100.00 - 150.00
Canada	$150.00 - 225.00
U.K.	£50.00 - 70.00

Shape 717 **Jug**

Designer:	Mr. Watkin in 1939
Issued:	1939 - by 1954
Height :	10″, 25.4 cm
Colour:	1. Assorted decorations - satin matt
	2. White - matt

Market	Range
U.S.A.	$60.00 - 125.00
Canada	$90.00 - 175.00
U.K.	£30.00 - 60.00

Shape 718 **Jug**

Designer:	Mr. Watkin in 1939
Issued:	1939 - by 1954
Height:	7 ½″, 19.1 cm
Colour:	1. Assorted decorations - satin matt
	2. White - matt

Market	Range
U.S.A.	$50.00 - 100.00
Canada	$75.00 - 175.00
U.K.	£25.00 - 50.00

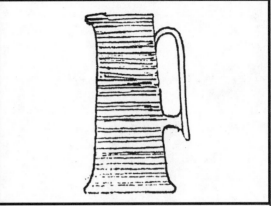

Shape 734   Jug

Designer: Mr. Symcox in 1939
Issued: 1939 - by 1962
Height :   12", 30.5 cm
Colour: 1. Assorted decorations - satin matt
             2. White - matt

Market	Range
U.S.A.	$75.00 - 150.00
Canada	$100.00 - 200.00
U.K.	£35.00 - 70.00

Shape 955   Jug

Designer: Albert Hallam in 1941
Issued: 1941 - by 1954
Size :   Unknown
Colour: 1. Assorted decorations - satin matt
             2. White - matt

Market	Range
U.S.A.	$50.00 - 100.00
Canada	$75.00 - 150.00
U.K.	£25.00 - 50.00

Note: Jug is pair with tankard shape 956, see page 244.

Shape 957/1/2 Soup Jugs

Designer: Albert Hallam in 1941
Issued: 1941 - by 1954
Size: Unknown
Colour: 1. Assorted decorations - satin matt
             2. White - matt

Market	Range
U.S.A.	$40.00 - 75.00
Canada	$60.00 - 100.00
U.K.	£20.00 - 40.00

Note: Set with shapes 958 (soup bowl)
             and shape 959 (soup saucer).

Shape 1045/1/2 Robert Burns, jug

Designer:	Unknown 1946
Issued:	1947 - 1966
Height :	1. Shape 1045/1 — 10", 25.4 cm
	2. Shape 1045/2 — 8", 20.3 cm
Colour:	1. Various colours on embossed white background - gloss
	2. Plain white, embossed - gloss

Market	Range
U.S.A.	$100.00 - 200.00
Canada	$150.00 - 300.00
U.K.	£50.00 - 150.00

Shape 1126 Falstaff jug, Shakespeare Series

Designer:	Albert Hallam, Arthur Gredington in 1948
Issued:	1948 - 1972
Hight:	8", 20.3 cm
Colour:	Maroon, black, yellow and green - gloss

Description	U.S.$	Can.$	U.K.£
Falstaff jug	200.00	250.00	100.00

Note: Set of four with jugs no. 1146, 1214 and 1366.

Shape 1146 Hamlet jug, Shakespeare Series

Designer:	Arthur Gredington in 1949
Issued:	1949 - 1972
Hight:	8 ¼", 21 cm
Colour:	Black, yellow and maroon - gloss

Description	U.S.$	Can.$	U.K.£
Hamlet jug	200.00	220.00	100.00

Note: Set of four with jugs no. 1126, 1214 and 1366.

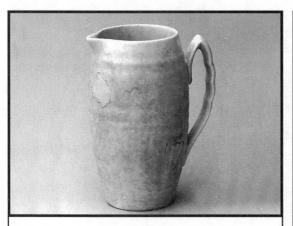

Shape 1176 Jug, Festival Series

Designer:	Albert Hallam in 1949
Issued:	1950 - by 1954
Height :	7 ½", 19.1 cm
Colour:	1. Assorted decorations - satin matt
	2. White - matt

Market	Range
U.S.A.	$50.00 - 100.00
Canada	$75.00 - 150.00
U.K.	£25.00 - 50.00

Shape 1177 Jug

Designer:	Albert Hallam in 1949
Issued:	1950 - by 1954
Size :	Unknown
Colour:	1. Assorted decorations - satin matt
	2. White - matt

Market	Range
U.S.A.	$50.00 - 100.00
Canada	$75.00 - 150.00
U.K.	£25.00 - 50.00

Shape 1214 Romeo and Juliet jug, Shakespeare Series

Designer:	Albert Hallam, Arthur Gredington in 1951
Issued:	1951 - 1972
Height:	8 ¼", 21 cm
Colour:	Maroon, blue, brown and green - gloss

Description	U.S.$	Can.$	U.K.£
Romeo and Juliet jug	200.00	250.00	100.00

Shape 1366 Midsummer Nights Dream jug, Shakespeare Series

Designer:	Albert Hallam, Mr. Orwell in 1955
Issued:	1955 - 1972
Height:	8", 20.3 cm
Colour:	Light blue, yellow, brown and black - gloss

Description	U.S.$	Can.$	U.K.£
Midsummer Nights Dream jug	250.00	300.00	125.00

Shape 1372 Jug, with handle not joined at the top

Designer: Albert Hallam in 1955
Issued: 1955 - 1973
Height :   6", 15 cm
Colour: 1. Assorted decorations - satin matt
             2. White - matt

Market	Range
U.S.A.	$40.00 - 75.00
Canada	$60.00 - 100.00
U.K.	£20.00 - 40.00

Shape 1441 Cutty Sark, jug

Designer: Albert Hallam in 1956
Issued: c.1956
Size: Unknown
Colour: Unknown

Market	Range
U.S.A.	$75.00 - 90.00
Canada	$100.00 - 125.00
U.K.	£35.00 - 45.00

Note: Special Commission. For the Contemporary shape
         see Tableware section page 265.

Shape 1550/1/2/3 Jugs

Designer: Albert Hallam in 1958
Issued: 1958 - 1967
Height: 1. Shape 1550/1 — 11", 27.9 cm
             2. Shape 1550/2 — 9", 22.9 cm
             3. Shape 1550/3 — 7", 17.8 cm
Colour: 1. Assorted decorations, solid colours -
                satin matt
             2. Copper - lustre
             3. White or black - matt

Market	Range
U.S.A.	$40.00 - 125.00
Canada	$60.00 - 175.00
U.K.	£20.00 - 60.00

Shape 1553/1/2/3 Jugs

Designer:	Albert Hallam in 1958
Issued:	1958 - 1971
Height:	1. Shape 1553/1 — 5", 12.7 cm
	2. Shape 1553/2 — 5 ½", 14 cm
	3. Shape 1553/3 — 4", 10.1 cm
Colour:	1. Assorted decorations, solid colours - satin matt
	2. Copper - lustre
	3. White or black - matt

Market	Range
U.S.A.	$20.00 - 60.00
Canada	$30.00 - 90.00
U.K.	£10.00 - 30.00

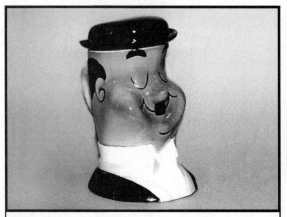

Shape 1672/1/2 Double Diamond, jug

Designer:	Albert Hallam in 1960
Issued:	1960 - 1965
Size:	6 ½", 16.5 cm
Colour:	Black hat and jacket, white shirt, green tie - gloss

Description	U.S. $	Can. $	U.K. £
Black, white and green	300.00	450.00	160.00

Shape 1741 Lord Mayor, water jug

Designer:	Albert Hallam in 1961
Issued:	1962 - 1967
Height:	8 ½", 21.6 cm
Colour:	Red robe, black jacket and hat, with gold chain of office; red top to bottle - gloss

Description	U.S. $	Can. $	U.K. £
Red, black and gold	150.00	200.00	70.00

Note: Re-issued green top to bottle 1986 - 1987. Special Commission.

Shape 1859 Jug

Designer: Albert Hallam in 1963
Issued: 1963 - 1971
Height :   8", 20.3 cm
Colour: 1. Assorted decos, solid colours - satin matt
             2. Copper - lustre
             3. White or black - matt

Market	Range
U.S.A.	$50.00 - 100.00
Canada	$75.00 - 150.00
U.K.	£25.00 - 50.00

Shape 2027 Soup jug

Designer: Albert Hallam in 1965
Issued: c. 1965
Height: 7 ¼", 18.4 cm
Colour: 1. Assorted decos, solid colours - satin matt
             2. White or black - matt

Market	Range
U.S.A.	$30.00 - 60.00
Canada	$45.00 - 90.00
U.K.	£15.00 - 30.00

Note: Pair with soup cup shape 2028 see page 283.

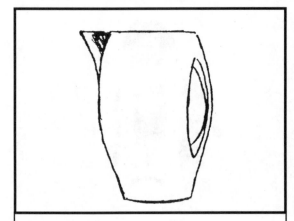

Shape 2053 Gallaher jug

Designer: Albert Hallam in 1965
Issued: c.1965
Height :   5 ½", 14 cm
Colour: Unknown

Description	U.S. $	Can. $	U.K. £
Gallagher jug	60.00	90.00	30.00

Note: Special Commission.

Shape 2118 Lemonade jug

Designer: Graham Tongue in 1967
Issued: c.1967
Height: 9 ½", 24 cm
Colour: 1. Assorted decos, solid colours - satin matt
             2. Copper - lustre
             3. White or black - matt

Market	Range
U.S.A.	$30.00 - 60.00
Canada	$45.00 - 90.00
U.K.	£15.00 - 30.00

Shape 2127 Ale jug

Designer:	Albert Hallam in 1967
Issued:	1968 - 1972
Height :	8 ¼", 21 cm
Colour:	1. Assorted decorations - satin matt
	2. Copper - lustre
	3. White or black - matt

Market	Range
U.S.A.	$30.00 - 60.00
Canada	$45.00 - 90.00
U.K.	£15.00 - 30.00

Shape 2280 Cockerel jug, Chante Clair

Designer:	Unknown
Issued:	Unknown
Height:	9 ¾", 24.7 cm
Colour:	Greens and browns, with red crest and comb - gloss

Description	U.S. $	Can. $	U.K. £
Cockerel jug	300.00	450.00	170.00

Shape 2506 Jug, Minton ewer, Bass Charrington

Designer:	Mr. Plant in 1976
Issued:	c.1976
Height :	6 ¾", 17.2 cm
Colour:	Logo with red triangle, and garland of pale green leaves with pale ochre flowers on white background - gloss

Description	U.S. $	Can. $	U.K. £
Jug, Minton ewer	75.00	125.00	40.00

Note: Special Commission.

Shape 1126 Falstaff Jug, Shakespeare Series

LAMPS AND LAMP BASES

There are only twenty-eight shapes in this section, of which the best known is the Peter Rabbit Tree Lamp Base (No. 1531). It is an attractive base and although the Beatrix Potter models, being the obvious choice, were supplied with it, of course, the owner could have added any figure or animal model of his or her choice.

Strangely, in our experience, over the many years that we have been involved with Beswick, lamps and lamp bases appear to be very elusive and have just not come to light! ... if they have, where are they hiding?

Six shapes were Special Commissions for the tobacco and brewing companies and due to lack of information at the present time, sadly we cannot indicate the colours for these items.

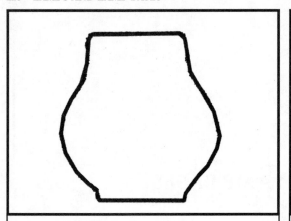

Shape 47   **Lamp base/vase**

Designer: Mr. Symcox c.1933
Issued: 1933 - by 1940
Size: Unknown
Colour: 1. Assorted decorations - satin matt
             2. White - matt

Market	Range
U.S.A.	$40.00 - 75.00
Canada	$60.00 - 100.00
U.K.	£20.00 - 35.00

Shape 75   **Lamp base/vase**

Designer: Mr. Symcox c.1933
Issued: 1933 - by 1940
Height :   6 ½", 16.5 cm
Colour: 1. Assorted decorations - satin matt or gloss
             2. White - matt

Market	Range
U.S.A.	$40.00 - 75.00
Canada	$60.00 - 100.00
U.K.	£20.00 - 35.00

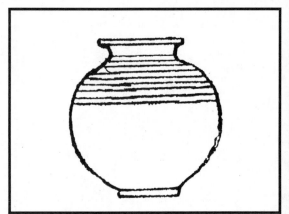

Shape 116   **Lamp base/vase**

Designer: Mr. Symcox c.1933
Issued: c.1934 - by 1940
Size: Unknown
Colour: 1. Assorted decorations - satin matt
             2. White - matt

Market	Range
U.S.A.	$40.00 - 75.00
Canada	$60.00 - 100.00
U.K.	£20.00 - 35.00

Shape 135   **Lamp base/vase**

Designer: Unknown
Issued: c.1934 - by 1940
Height :   5 ½", 14 cm
Colour: 1. Assorted decorations - satin matt
             2 White - matt

Market	Range
U.S.A.	$30.00 - 60.00
Canada	$45.00 - 90.00
U.K.	£15.00 - 30.00

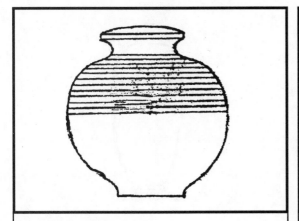

Shape 143   **Lamp base/vase**

Designer: Albert Hallam c.1934
Issued: c.1934 - by 1940
Height: 9", 22.9 cm
Colour: 1. Assorted decorations - satin matt
    2. White - matt

Market	Range
U.S.A.	$40.00 - 75.00
Canada	$60.00 - 100.00
U.K.	£20.00 - 35.00

Shape 144   **Lamp base/vase**

Designer: Albert Hallam c.1934
Issued: c.1934 - by 1940
Height :   10 ½", 26.7 cm
Colour: 1. Assorted decorations - satin matt
    2. White - matt

Market	Range
U.S.A.	$40.00 - 75.00
Canada	$60.00 - 100.00
U.K.	£20.00 - 35.00

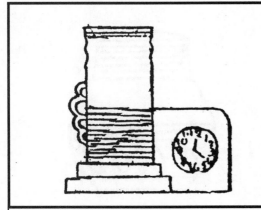

Shape 272   **Lamp base with clock**

Designer: Mr. Symcox c.1934
Issued: c.1934 - by 1940
Height: 8 ¾", 22.2 cm
Colour: 1. Assorted decorations - satin matt
    2. White - matt

Market	Range
U.S.A.	$60.00 - 100.00
Canada	$90.00 - 150.00
U.K.	£30.00 - 50.00

Shape 275   **Lamp**

Designer: Mr. Symcox c.1934
Issued: c.1934 - by 1940
Size: Unknown
Colour: 1. Assorted decorations - satin matt
    2. White - matt

Market	Range
U.S.A.	$50.00 - 100.00
Canada	$75.00 - 150.00
U.K.	£25.00 - 45.00

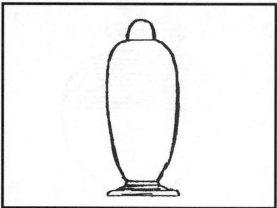

Shape 276   Lamp

Designer:	Mr. Symcox c.1934
Issued:	c.1934 - by 1940
Size:	Unknown
Colour:	1. Assorted decorations - satin matt
	2. White - matt

Market	Range
U.S.A.	$50.00 - 100.00
Canada	$75.00 - 150.00
U.K.	£25.00 - 45.00

Shape 477   Lamp

Designer:	Mr. Symcox in 1937
Issued:	1937 - by 1940
Size:	Unknown
Colour:	1. Assorted decorations - satin matt
	2. White - matt

Market	Range
U.S.A.	$30.00 - 50.00
Canada	$45.00 - 75.00
U.K.	£15.00 - 25.00

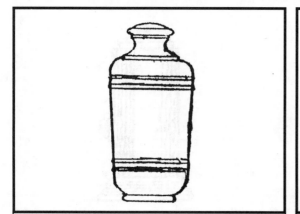

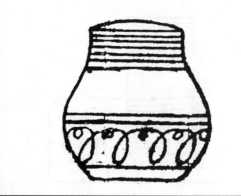

Shape 666   Lamp

Designer:	Mr. Symcox in 1938
Issued:	1938 - by 1940
Size:	Unknown
Colour:	1. Assorted decorations - satin matt
	2. White - matt

Market	Range
U.S.A.	$30.00 - 50.00
Canada	$45.00 - 75.00
U.K.	£15.00 - 25.00

Shape 703   Lamp base/vase

Designer:	Albert Hallam in 1939
Issued:	1939 - by 1940
Size:	Unknown
Colour:	1. Assorted decorations - satin matt
	2. White - matt

Market	Range
U.S.A.	$40.00 - 75.00
Canada	$60.00 - 100.00
U.K.	£20.00 - 35.00

Shape 1158 Lamp base

Designer:	Albert Hallam, JamesHayward in 1949
Issued:	1949 - by 1954
Size:	Unknown
Colour:	1. Assorted decorations - satin matt
	2. White - matt

Market	Range
U.S.A.	$40.00 - 75.00
Canada	$60.00 - 100.00
U.K.	£20.00 - 35.00

Shape 1231 Etched lamp base

Designer:	Albert Hallam, JamesHayward in 1952
Issued:	1952 - 1954
Size:	Unknown
Colour:	1. Assorted decorations - satin matt
	2. White - matt

Market	Range
U.S.A.	$50.00 - 100.00
Canada	$75.00 - 150.00
U.K.	£25.00 - 45.00

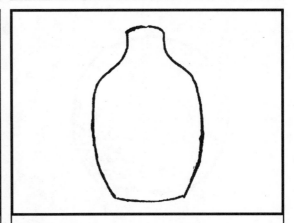

Shape 1459/1/2 Lamp

Designer:	Albert Hallam in 1956
Issued:	1957 - by 1963
Size:	Unknown
Colour:	1. Assorted decorations - satin matt
	2. White - matt

Market	Range
U.S.A.	$40.00 - 75.00
Canada	$60.00 - 100.00
U.K.	£20.00 - 35.00

Note: Lamp was taken from vase shape 1432.

Shape 1509 Lamp

Designer:	Colin Melbourne in 1956
Issued:	1957 - by 1963
Height:	6 ½", 16.5 cm
Colour:	1. Assorted decorations - satin matt
	2. White - matt

Market	Range
U.S.A.	$40.00 - 50.00
Canada	$60.00 - 75.00
U.K.	£15.00 - 25.00

Note: Lamp converted from CM Series shape 1399.

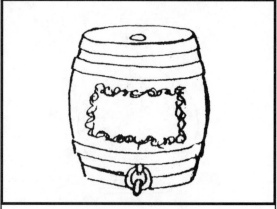

Shape 1531 Peter Rabbit tree-lamp base

Designer:	Albert Hallam, James Hayward in 1958
Issued:	1958 - 1969
Height :	7″, 17.8 cm
Colour:	Browns and greens - gloss

Description	U.S. $	Can. $	U.K. £
Peter Rabbit base	125.00	175.00	75.00

Note: This item was supplied with or without a Beatrix Potter figure attached at the base of the tree trunk.

Shape 1544 Lamp - barrel with tap (sherry, port or whisky)

Designer:	Albert Hallam in 1958
Issued:	1958 - by 1962
Height:	4 ½″, 11.9 cm
Colour:	Red or green on white background - gloss

Description	U.S. $	Can. $	U.K. £
Barrel lamp	60.00	75.00	40.00

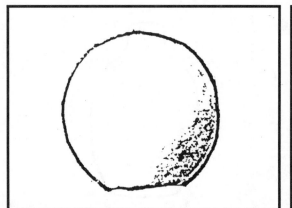

Shape 1808 Lamp

Designer:	Albert Hallam in 1962
Issued:	1962 - unknown
Size:	Unknown
Colour:	1. Assorted decorations - satin matt
	2. White - matt

Market	Range
U.S.A.	$20.00 - 40.00
Canada	$30.00 - 60.00
U.K.	£10.00 - 20.00

Shape 1850 Double Diamond lamp

Designer:	Albert Hallam in 1962
Issued:	Unknown
Size:	6″, 15 cm
Colour:	Unknown - gloss

Description	U.S. $	Can. $	U.K. £
Double Diamond	60.00	75.00	40.00

Note: Special commission.

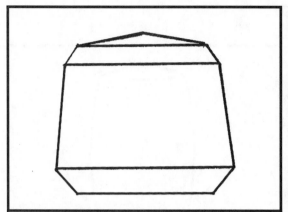

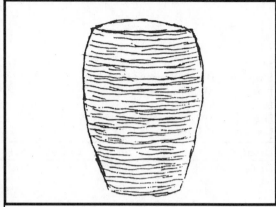

Shape 1984 Rothmans lamp

Designer: Albert Hallam in 1962
Issued: Unknown
Size: 4 ½", 11.9 cm
Colour: Unknown - gloss

Description	U.S. $	Can. $	U.K. £
Rothmans	60.00	75.00	40.00

Note: Special commission.

Shape 2009 Skol lamp

Designer: Albert Hallam in 1965
Issued: Unknown
Size: 6", 15 cm
Colour: Unknown - gloss

Description	U.S. $	Can. $	U.K. £
Skol	60.00	75.00	40.00

Note: Special commission.

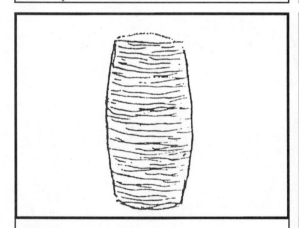

Shape 2010 Double Diamond lamp

Designer: Albert Hallam in 1965
Issued: Unknown
Size: 5 ½", 14 cm
Colour: Unknown - gloss

Description	U.S. $	Can. $	U.K. £
Double Diamond	60.00	75.00	40.00

Note: Special commission.

Shape 2011 Skol lamp

Designer: Albert Hallam in 1965
Issued: Unknown
Size: 6", 15 cm
Colour: Unknown - gloss

Description	U.S. $	Can. $	U.K. £
Skol	60.00	75.00	40.00

Note: Special commission.

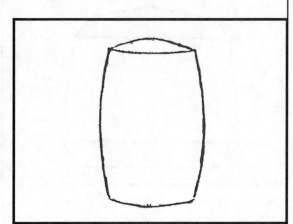

Shape 2018 Double Diamond lamp

Designer: Albert Hallam in 1965
Issued: Unknown
Size: 5 ½", 14 cm
Colour: Unknown - gloss

Description	U.S. $	Can. $	U.K. £
Double Diamond	60.00	75.00	40.00

Note: Special commission.

LIQUOR FLASKS AND CONTAINERS

The use of earthenware and china items to promote their products has long been the practice of the brewing, distilling and tobacco trades, and Beswick supplied a variety of items for this purpose during a period of over twenty years. Nineteen of them, mainly whisky flasks are listed here. In addition Beswick produced many other whisky containers, in the shape of animals and birds, and information on these can be obtained from *The Charlton Standard Catalogue of Beswick Animals*.

Other Beswick products used as promotional lines appear elsewhere in this book, and are listed in the appropriate sections.

Shape 1517   Double Diamond man container

Designer: Albert Hallam, James Hayward in 1958
Issued: c.1958
Height: 8", 20.3 cm
Colour: Black hat and suit, white shirt and green tie,
            striped trousers - gloss

Colour	U.S. $	Can. $	U.K. £
Black, white and green	250.00	350.00	175.00

Note: The hat is attached by a cork. Special commission.

Shape 1587   Barrel, container for port

Designer: Albert Hallam in 1959
Issued: 1959 - unknown
Size: 4 ¼", 10.8 cm
Colour: 1. Green and white - gloss
            2. Maroon and white - gloss

Colour	U.S. $	Can. $	U.K. £
1. Green and white	75.00	100.00	40.00
2. Maroon and white	75.00	100.00	40.00

Note: Also available with "Sherry" or "Whisky."

Shape 1598   Barrel, container for sherry

Designer: Albert Hallam in 1959
Issued: 1959 - unknown
Width: 5 ¼" x 5 ¼", 13.3 x 13.3 cm
Colour: 1. Green and white - gloss
            2 Maroon and white - gloss

Colour	U.S. $	Can. $	U.K. £
1. Green and white	75.00	100.00	45.00
2. Maroon and white	75.00	100.00	45.00

Note: Also available with "Port" or "Whisky."

Shape 1820   Barrel, Beneagles scotch whisky

Designer: Albert Hallam in 1962
Issued: 1962 - 1986
Height: 2", 5 cm
Colour: Brown - gloss

Colour	U.S. $	Can. $	U.K. £
Brown	15.00	20.00	10.00

Note: Special commission for Peter Thompson (Perth) Ltd.

Shape 1829 **The Sportsman's,**
Catto's scotch whisky flask

Designer: Mr. Folkard in 1962
Height: 11 ½", 29.2 cm
Colour: Green jacket and maroon waistcoat with
              yellow stripes, white trousers - gloss

Colour	U.S. $	Can. $	U.K. £
Green, maroon, yellow	325.00	375.00	185.00

Note: Special commission.

Shape 2033 Fisherman's Beneagles scotch whisky flask

Designer: Albert Hallam in 1965
Issued: c.1965
Height: 3 ¾", 9.5 cm
Colour: Blue - gloss

Colour	U.S. $	Can. $	U.K. £
Blue	35.00	50.00	20.00

Note: Special commission for Peter Thompson (Perth) Ltd.

Shape 2056 Pheasant, Beneagles scotch whisky flask

Designer: Albert Hallam in 1966
Issued: c.1966
Height: 3 ½", 8.9 cm
Colour: Blue - gloss

Colour	U.S. $	Can. $	U.K. £
Blue	40.00	60.00	25.00

Note: Replaced by shape 2208 in 1968. Special
commission for Peter Thompson (Perth) Ltd.

Shape 2057 Pike, Beneagles scotch whisky flask

Designer:	Albert Hallam in 1966
Issued:	c.1966
Height::	3 ½", 8.9 cm
Colour:	Unknown - gloss

Colour	U.S. $	Can. $	U.K. £
Unknown	40.00	60.00	25.00

Note: Replaced by Shape 2207 in 1968. Special commission for Peter Thompson (Perth) Ltd.

Shape 2058 Deer, Beneagles scotch whisky flask

Designer:	Albert Hallam in 1966
Issued:	c.1966
Height:	3 ½", 8.9 cm
Colour:	Green - gloss

Colour	U.S. $	Can. $	U.K. £
Green	40.00	60.00	25.00

Note: Replaced by Shape 2206 in 1968. Special commission for Peter Thompson (Perth) Ltd.

Shape 2076 Robert Burns cottage, Beneagles scotch whisky flask

Designer	Albert Hallam in 1966
Issued:	c.1966
Length:	3 ½", 8.9 cm
Colour:	Blue-grey - gloss

Colour	U.S. $	Can. $	U.K. £
Blue-grey	35.00	50.00	20.00

Note: Special commission for Peter Thompson (Perth) Ltd.

Shape 2077 Edinburgh Castle, Beneagles scotch whisky flask

Designer:	Albert Hallam in 1966
Isued:	c.1956
Length:	3 ½", 8.9 cm
Colour:	Olive-green - gloss

Colour	U.S. $	Can. $	U.K. £
Olive-green	35.00	50.00	20.00

Note: Special commission for Peter Thompson (Perth) Ltd.

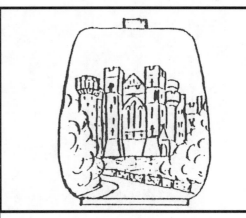

**Shape 2180 Tower Bridge,
Beneagles scotch whisky flask**

Designer:	Albert Hallam in 1968		
Issued:	c.1968		
Length:	3 ½", 8.9 cm		
Colour:	Blue - gloss		

Colour	U.S. $	Can. $	U.K. £
Blue	35.00	50.00	20.00

Note: Special commission for Peter Thompson (Perth) Ltd.

Shape 2185 Arundel castle flask

Designer:	Albert Hallam in 1968		
Issued:	c.1968		
Height:	4 ½", 11.9 cm		
Colour:	Unknown		

Colour	U.S. $	Can. $	U.K. £
Unknown	40.00	60.00	25.00

Note: Special commission for Merrydown Cider.

Shape 2206 Deer flask, Beneagles scotch whisky

Designer:	Albert Hallam in 1966. Re-modelled by Graham Tongue in 1968		
Issued:	c.1968		
Height:	3", 7.6 cm		
Colour:	Green - gloss		

Colour	U.S. $	Can. $	U.K. £
Green	35.00	50.00	20.00

Note: Replaced shape 2058. Special commission for Peter Thompson (Perth) Ltd.

Shape 2207 Trout flask, Beneagles scotch whisky

Designer:	Albert Hallam in 1966. Re-modelled by Graham Tongue in 1968		
Issued:	c.1968		
Height:	3", 7.6 cm		
Colour:	Blue - gloss		

Colour	U.S. $	Can. $	U.K. £
Blue	35.00	50.00	20.00

Note: Replaced shape 2057. Special commission for Peter Thompson (Perth) Ltd.

Shape 2208 Pheasant flask, Beneagles scotch whisky

Designer:	Albert Hallam in 1966. Re-modelled by Graham Tongue in 1968
Issued:	c.1968
Height:	3", 7.6 cm
Colour:	Blue - gloss

Colour	U.S. $	Can. $	U.K. £
Blue	35.00	50.00	20.00

Note: Replaced shape 2056. Special commission for Peter Thompson (Perth) Ltd.

Shape 2318 Golf ball, Beneagles scotch whisky flask

Designer:	Graham Tongue in 1970
Issued:	c.1970
Diameter:	1 ¼", 3.1 cm
Colour:	White with red lettering - gloss

Colour	U.S. $	Can. $	U.K. £
White with red lettering	40.00	60.00	25.00

Note: Special commission for Peter Thompson (Perth) Ltd.

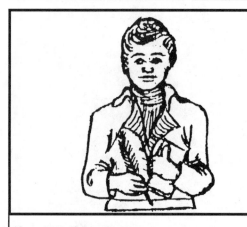

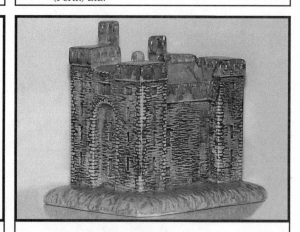

**Shape 2349 Robert Burns,
Beneagles scotch whisky flask**

Designer:	Albert Hallam in 1970
Issued:	c.1970
Height :	4", 10.1 cm
Colour:	Unknown

Colour	U.S. $	Can. $	U.K. £
Robert Burns flask	150.00	200.00	85.00

Note: Special commission for Peter Thompson (Perth) Ltd.

Shape 2670 Bunratty castle, flask

Designer:	Mr. Lyttleton in 1980
Issued:	c.1980
Height:	6", 15 cm
Colour:	Grey castle with green grass - gloss

Colour	U.S. $	Can. $	U.K. £
Grey and green	60.00	75.00	40.00

MUGS, BEAKERS AND TANKARDS

Forty-three shapes make up this group, which were produced between about 1933 and 1970.

Eight were Royal Commemoratives and although Edward's Coronation did not take place, surprisingly some shapes have been found. The twelve Christmas Carol Tankards are the most detailed in this group both in the modelling and the decoration, where many colours were used to illustrate the scenes from the book by Charles Dickens.

The three wartime mugs (numbers 735, 736 and 737) are very unusual and are also very rare. The Nursery Ware with coloured transfer prints are very attractive and we have listed the whole series at the beginning of the Tableware Section.

Shape 205   Beaker

Designer: Albert Hallam c.1933
Issued: c.1933 - by 1954
Size: Unknown
Colour: 1. Assorted decorations - satin matt
            2. White - matt

Colour	U.S. $	Can. $	U.K. £
1. Assorted decorations	30.00	45.00	15.00
2. White	20.00	30.00	10.00

Shape 445   Edward VIII Musical Coronation tankard

Designer: Mr. Roscoe in 1936
Issued: Not issued
Size: 5", 12.7 cm
Colour: Ivory glaze embossed

Description	U.S. $	Can. $	U.K. £
Musical jug		Not issued.	

Note: Although not issued, several pieces are known.

Shape 446   Edward VIII Coronation mug

Designer: Mr. Owen in 1936
Issued: Not issued
Size: 3 ½", 8.9 cm
Colour: Ivory glaze embossed

Description	U.S. $	Can. $	U.K. £
Edward VIII Coronation mug		Not issued	

Note: Although not issued, several pieces are known.

Photograph not
available
at press time

Shape 461   George VI Musical Coronation tankard

Designer: Unknown in 1937
Issued: 1937 - 1937
Size: 5", 12.7 cm
Colour: Ivory glaze embossed

Description	U.S. $	Can. $	U.K. £
Musical jug	200.00	300.00	100.00

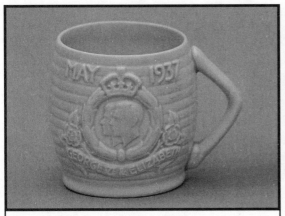

Shape 462   George VI Coronation mug

Designer:	Unknown in 1937
Issued:	1937 - 1937
Size:	3 ½", 8.9 cm
Colour:	Ivory glaze embossed

Description	U.S. $	Can. $	U.K. £
George VI Coronation mug	50.00	75.00	25.00

Shape 735   Army "Old Bill," mug

Designer:	Mr. Watkin in 1939
Issued:	1939 - by 1954
Size:	5", 12.7 cm
Colour:	Flesh tones, khaki cap - gloss

Description	U.S. $	Can. $	U.K. £
"Old Bill" mug	450.00	500.00	250.00

Note: Set of three with shape nos 736 and 737.

Shape 736   Navy "HMS Wink," mug

Designer:	Mr. Watkin in 1939
Issued:	1939 - by 1954
Size:	5", 12.7 cm
Colour:	Flesh tones, brown hair, blue and white hat - gloss

Description	U.S. $	Can. $	U.K. £
"HMS Wink" mug	450.00	500.00	250.00

Note: Set of three with shape nos. 735 and 737

Shape 737   Air Force, mug

Designer:	Mr. Watkin in 1939
Issued:	1939 - by 1954
Size	5", 12.7 cm
Colour:	Flesh tones, dark brown hair, blue hat - gloss

Description	U.S. $	Can. $	U.K. £
Air Force mug	450.00	500.00	250.00

Note: Set of three with shape nos. 735 and 736

Shape 956/1/2/3 Tankard

Designer: Albert Hallam in 1941
Issued: 1939 - by 1954
Size : Unknown
Colour: 1. Assorted decorations - satin matt
  2. White - matt

Colour	U.S. $	Can. $	U.K. £
1. Assorted decorations	30.00	45.00	15.00
2. White	20.00	30.00	10.00

Note: Tankard is pair with jug shape 955, see page 219.

Shape 987/1/2 Tankard

Designer: Unknown in 1942
Issued: 1942 - by 1954; re-issued 1966 - by 1971
Size: 1. Shape 987/1, 18 oz — 4", 10.1 cm
  2. Shape 987/2, 12 oz — 3 ½", 8.9 cm
Colour: 1. Transfer print on white - gloss
  2. Assorted decorations - matt glaze
  3. Copper - lustre

Description	U.S. $	Can. $	U.K. £
1. 18 oz	30.00	45.00	15.00
2. 12 oz	20.00	30.00	10.00

Note: Re-issued ribbed and with new handle in 1966.

Shape 987/3 Queen Elizabeth Coronation tankard

Designer: Unknown in 1942
Issued: 1953 - 1953
Height: 3 ¾", 9.5 cm
Colour: Transfer print on white

Description	U.S. $	Can. $	U.K. £
Coronation tankard	40.00	60.00	20.00

Shape 988   Mug, Newhall

Designer: Unknown
Issued: 1942 - by 1954
Height: Unknown
Colour: 1. Assorted decorations - satin matt
  2. White - matt

Colour	U.S. $	Can. $	U.K. £
1. Assorted decorations	30.00	45.00	15.00
2. White	20.00	30.00	10.00

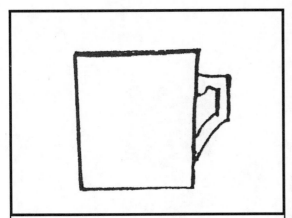

Shape 1056 Mug

Designer:	Unknown
Issued:	1946
Size:	Unknown
Colour:	Unknown - gloss

Colour	U.S. $	Can. $	U.K. £
Unknown	20.00	30.00	10.00

Note: Special commission for The Ministry of Works in 1946.

Shape 1127 Falstaff mug

Designer:	Arthur Gredington, Albert Hallam in 1948
Issued:	1948 - 1972
Size:	4", 10.1 cm
Colour:	Green, orange and blue - gloss
Series:	Shakespeare

Description	U.S. $	Can. $	U.K. £
Falstaff mug	90.00	90.00	45.00

Note: Set of four with shape nos. 1147, 1215, 1368.

Shape 1147 Hamlet mug

Designer:	Arthur Gredington in 1949
Issued:	1949 - 1972
Size:	4 ¼", 10.8 cm
Colour:	Browns, greens, black and yellow - gloss
Series:	Shakespeare

Description	U.S. $	Can. $	U.K. £
Hamlet mug	90.00	90.00	45.00

Note: Set of four with shape nos. 1127, 1215, 1368.

Shape 1215 Juliet mug

Designer:	Arthur Gredington, Albert Hallam in 1951
Issued:	1951 - 1972
Size:	4", 10.1 cm
Colour:	Browns, greens, maroon and blue - gloss
Series:	Shakespeare

Description	U.S. $	Can. $	U.K. £
Juliet mug	90.00	90.00	45.00

Note: Set of four with shape nos. 1127, 1215, 1368.

Shape 1250 Elizabeth II Federation Coronation mug

Designer:	Unknown in 1952
Issued:	1953 - 1953
Height:	3 ¼", 8.3 cm
Colour:	Colour transfer on white background - gloss

Description	U.S. $	Can. $	U.K. £
Coronation mug	40.00	60.00	20.00

Shape 1251 Elizabeth II Federation Coronation beaker

Designer:	Unknown in 1952
Issued:	1953 - 1953
Height :	4 ¼", 10.8 cm
Colour:	Colour transfer on white background - gloss

Description	U.S. $	Can. $	U.K. £
Coronation beaker	40.00	60.00	20.00

Shape 1252 Elizabeth II Coronation beaker

Designer:	Albert Hallam, James Hayward in 1952
Issued:	1953 - 1953
Height:	3 ½", 8.9 cm
Colour:	Ivory glaze embossed

Description	U.S. $	Can. $	U.K. £
Coronation beaker	50.00	75.00	25.00

Shape 1286 Baby mug with one handle   Shape 1286T Baby mug with two handles

Shape 1286   Baby mug with one handle
Shape 1286T   Baby mug with two handles

Designer: Albert Hallam in 1953
Issued: See below
Height: Unknown
Colour: Transfer print on white background - gloss

Shape No.	Description	Issued	U.S. $	Can. $	U.K. £
1286/1a	Disney image, Bambi	1954 - 1959	50.00	75.00	25.00
1286/1b	Disney image, Thumper	1954 - 1959	50.00	75.00	25.00
1286/2	Nursery rhyme images	1960 - 1963	30.00	45.00	15.00
1286/3	Jack and Jill comic series	1964 - 1970	30.00	45.00	15.00
1286T/1a	Disney image, Bambi	1954 - 1959	50.00	75.00	25.00
1286T/1b	Disney image, Thumper	1954 - 1959	50.00	75.00	25.00
1286T/2	Nursery rhyme images	1960 - 1963	30.00	45.00	15.00
1286T/3	Jack and Jill comic series	1964 - 1970	30.00	45.00	15.00

Shape 1368 Midsummer Night's Dream mug

Designer:	Albert Hallam, Mr. Orwell in 1955
Issued:	1951 - 1972
Size:	4 ¼", 10.8 cm
Colour:	Greens, browns, blue and maroon - gloss
Series:	Shakespeare

Description	U.S. $	Can. $	U.K. £
Midsummer Night's Dream mug	75.00	170.00	75.00

Note: Set of four with shape nos. 1127, 1147, 1215.

Shape 1596 Robert Burns, Mug

Designer:	Albert Hallam, James Hayward in 1959
Issued:	1959 - 1966
Height:	4 ¼", 10.8 cm
Colour:	1. Multi-coloured - gloss
	2. White - gloss

Colour	U.S. $	Can. $	U.K. £
1. Multi-coloured	100.00	150.00	50.00
2. White	60.00	90.00	30.00

Shape 1669 Nursery ware beaker

Designer:	Albert Hallam in 1960
Issued:	1. 1960 - 1963 2. 1964 - by 1966
Size:	Unknown
Colour:	1. Transfer print of nursery rhyme character on white background - gloss
	2. Transfer print of Jack and Jill comic character on white background - gloss

Description	U.S. $	Can. $	U.K. £
1. Nursery rhyme character	30.00	45.00	15.00
2. Jack and Jill comic series	30.00	45.00	15.00

Shape 1670 Nursery ware mug

Designer:	Albert Hallam in 1960
Issued:	1. 1960 - 1963 2. 1964 - 1970
Size:	Unknown
Colour:	1. Transfer print of nursery rhyme character on white background - gloss
	2. Transfer print of Jack and Jill comic character on white background - gloss

Description	U.S. $	Can. $	U.K. £
1. Nursery rhyme character	30.00	45.00	15.00
2. Jack and Jill comic series	30.00	45.00	15.00

Shape 1821 Tankard, one pint

Designer:	Harry Sales in 1962
Issued:	1963 - 1971
Height :	5 ¼", 13.3 cm
Colour:	1. Solid colours - gloss
	2. White or black - matt
	3. Copper - lustre

Colour	U.S. $	Can. $	U.K. £
1. Solid colours	30.00	45.00	15.00
2. White or black	20.00	30.00	10.00
3. Copper	25.00	35.00	12.00

Shape 1979 Beaker

Designer:	Albert Hallam in 1964
Issued:	1964 - 1970
Size:	3 ¾", 9.5 cm
Colour :	1. Transfer of characters from Jack and Jill comic - gloss
	2. Trendsetter series - gloss (illustrated)

Description	U.S. $	Can. $	U.K. £
1. Jack and Jill series	30.00	45.00	15.00
2. Trendsetter series	15.00	20.00	10.00

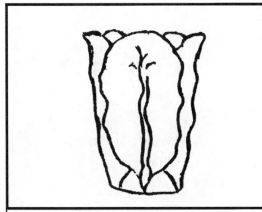

Shape 2044 Beaker

Designer:	Albert Hallam in 1965
Issued:	Unknown
Height:	4", 10.1 cm
Colour:	1. Solid colours - gloss
	2. White or black - matt
	3. Copper - lustre

Colour	U.S. $	Can. $	U.K. £
1. Solid colours	17.00	20.00	15.00
2. White or black	12.00	15.00	10.00
3. Copper	15.00	18.00	12.00

Shape 2073 Tankard

Designer:	Graham Tongue in 1966
Issued:	1967 - 1972
Height :	5 ½", 14 cm
Colour:	1. Solid colours - gloss
	2. White or black - matt
	3. Copper - lustre

Colour	U.S. $	Can. $	U.K. £
1. Solid colours	17.00	20.00	15.00
2. White or black	12.00	15.00	10.00
3. Copper	15.00	18.00	12.00

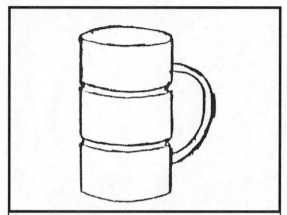

Shape 2125/ Pint tankard
Shape 2126 Half-pint tankard

Designer:	Graham Tongue in 1967
Issued:	c.1967
Height:	1. Shape 2125 — 5 ½", 14.0 cm
	2. Shape 2126 — 4 ½", 11.9 cm
Colour:	1. Solid colours - glosss
	2. White or black - matt
	3. Copper - lustre

Description	U.S. $	Can. $	U.K. £
Pint tankard	20.00	25.00	15.00
Half-pint tankard	15.00	17.00	10.00

Shape 2165/ Pint tankard
Shape 2166 Half-pint tankard

Designer:	Graham Tongue in 1967
Issued:	c.1967
Height:	1. Shape 2165 — 5", 12.7 cm
	2. Shape 2166 — 4 ½", 11.9 cm
Colour:	1. Solid colours - gloss
	2. White or black - matt
	3. Copper - lustre

Description	U.S. $	Can. $	U.K. £
Pint tankard	20.00	25.00	15.00
Half-pint tankard	15.00	17.00	10.00

Shape 2310 Shaving mug

Designer:	Graham Tongue in 1970
Issued:	c.1970
Height:	3 ½", 8.9 cm
Colour:	1. Solid colours - gloss
	2. White or black - matt
	3. Copper - lustre

Colour	U.S. $	Can. $	U.K. £
1. Solid colours	17.00	20.00	15.00
2. White or black	12.00	15.00	10.00
3. Copper	15.00	18.00	12.00

Shape 2351 Yule 1971, Latama Tankard
"Bob Cratchit and Scrooge"

Designer:	Graham Tongue in 1971
Issued:	1971 - 1971
Height:	5", 12.7 cm
Colour:	Multi-coloured - gloss
Series:	Christmas Carol Tankards

Description	U.S.$	Can. $	U.K.£
Yule 1971	75.00	100.00	50.00

Shape 2375 Yule 1972 - Latama Tankard
"The Carol Singers"

Designer:	Albert Hallam in 1971	
Issued:	1972 - 1972	
Height:	5", 12.7 cm	
Colour:	Multi-coloured - gloss	
Series:	Christmas Carol Tankards	

Description	U.S.$	Can.$	U.K.£
Yule 1972	75.00	100.00	50.00

Shape 2423 Yule 1973 - Latama Tankard, "Solicitation"

Designer:	Albert Hallam in 1972	
Issued:	1973 - 1973	
Height :	5", 12.7 cm	
Colour:	Multi-coloured - gloss	
Series:	Christmas Carol Tankards	

Description	U.S.$	Can.$	U.K.£
Yule 1973	75.00	100.00	50.00

Shape 2445 Yule 1974 - Latama Tankard
"The Ghost of Marley"

Designer:	Albert Hallam in 1973	
Issued:	1974 - 1974	
Height:	5", 12.7 cm	
Colour:	Multi-coloured - gloss	
Series:	Christmas Carol Tankards	

Description	U.S.$	Can.$	U.K.£
Yule 1974	75.00	100.00	45.00

Shape 2523 Yule 1975 - Latama Tankard
"The Ghost of Christmas Past"

Designer:	Graham Tongue in 1974	
Issued:	1975 - 1975	
Height :	5", 12.7 cm	
Colour:	Multi-coloured - gloss	
Series:	Christmas Carol Tankards	

Description	U.S.$	Can.$	U.K.£
Yule 1975	75.00	100.00	45.00

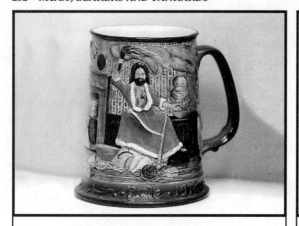

Shape 2539 Yule 1976, Latama Tankard
"The Ghost of Christmas Present"

Designer:	Mr. Plant, Mr. Lyttleton in 1975
Issued:	1976 - 1976
Height:	5", 12.7 cm
Colour:	Multi-coloured - gloss
Series:	Christmas Carol Tankards

Description	U.S.$	Can.$	U.K.£
Yule 1976	75.00	100.00	45.00

Shape 2568 Yule 1977, Latama Tankard
"The Ghost of Christmas Present"

Designer:	Mr. Plant, Mr. Lyttleton,
	Graham Tongue in 1976
Issued:	1977 - 1977
Height :	5", 12.7 cm
Colour:	Multi-coloured - gloss
Series:	Christmas Carol Tankards

Description	U.S.$	Can.$	U.K.£
Yule 1977	75.00	100.00	45.00

Shape 2599 Yule 1978, Latama Tankard
"The Ghost of Christmas Present"

Designer:	Mr. Lyttleton in 1977
Issued:	1978 - 1978
Height:	5", 12.7 cm
Colour:	Multi-coloured - gloss
Series:	Christmas Carol Tankards

Description	U.S.$	Can.$	U.K.£
Yule 1978	75.00	100.00	45.00

Shape 2624 Yule 1979, Latama Tankard
"The Ghost of Christmas Future"

Designer:	Mr. Lyttleton in 1978
Issued:	1979 - 1979
Height:	5", 12.7 cm
Colour:	Multi-coloured - gloss
Series:	Christmas Carol Tankards

Description	U.S.$	Can.$	U.K.£
Yule 1979	75.00	100.00	45.00

Shape 2657	Yule 1980, Latama Tankard "Scrooge sees his own Grave"		
Designer:	Mr. Lyttleton in 1979		
Issued:	1980 - 1980		
Height:	5", 12.7 cm		
Colour:	Multi-coloured - gloss		
Series:	Christmas Carol Tankards		

Desription	U.S.$	Can.$	U.K.£
Yule 1980	75.00	100.00	45.00

Shape 2692	Yule 1981, Latama Tankard "Scrooge goes to Church"		
Designer:	Mr. Lyttleton in 1980		
Issued:	1981 - 1981		
Height :	5", 12.7 cm		
Colour:	Multi-coloured - gloss		
Series:	Christmas Carol Tankards		

Desription	U.S.$	Can.$	U.K.£
Yule 1981	75.00	100.00	45.00

Photograph not
available
at press time

Shape 2764	Yule 1982 - Latama Tankard "Christmas with Bob Cratchit"		
Designer:	Mr. Lyttleton in 1981		
Issued:	1982 - 1982		
Height:	5", 12.7 cm		
Colour:	Multi-coloured - gloss		
Series:	Christmas Carol Tankards		

Description	U.S.$	Can.$	U.K.£
Yule 1982	100.00	125.00	55.00

Shape 1273 — Teapot

Shape 1273 — Tea Cup

TABLEWARE

Tableware was produced over many years in the Marie, Eton, Contemporary and Orbit shapes with the decorations often overlapping the shapes. Often the same decoration was applied to two shapes e.g. Contemporary and Orbit, and even in some cases, to all four shapes. We have used the decoration title in the listing to denote the patterns and colours used for the decorations, which in all cases had a gloss finish.

Beswick also produced Souvenir Ware e.g. Souvenir of Scotland with a Piper (see shape 2120 on page 284), Souvenir of Ireland with an Irish Harp and/or a Spinning Wheel and Present from Morecombe with sailing ships.

In addition to the shapes listed in this section there were two mugs (shape 1286 on page 247 and shape 1670 on page 248) and one beaker (shape 1669 on page 248), details of these are in the Mugs, Beakers and Tankards Section, but included here is the Childrens Tea Set (Shape 1273).

The following shapes have not been included in the listing as it is possible that they were never put into full commercial production - 1619 (Butter), 1621 (Covered Scallop), 1622 (Gravy Boat), 1679 (Mustard), 1698 (Salt), 1699 (Pepper), 1920 (Gravy Boat), 1921 (Sugar), 1961 (Sugar) and 1971 (Cheese).

Gilt Edges

The transfer decorations mostly had gilt edges, although examples have been found with silver or coloured rims, and some with no rim colouring at all. They included:

> A cottage scene
> Red rose pattern
> Yellow rose pattern
> Blue rose pattern
> Yellow flowers
> Red and white flowers
> Fruit pattern (e.g. oranges and lemons)
> Hazelnut
> Poppies
> Blue flowers
> Crinoline ladies
> Ladies in long dresses
> Ballerinas
> Dogs

Nursery Ware

Nursery ware, as the name suggests, was for the use of children. This ware consisted of three groups all in a light ivory coloured background and gloss finish:

Walt Disney	Coloured transfer prints of Disney characters. Issued 1954 - 1959.
Nursery	Coloured transfer prints of Nursery Rhyme characters. Issued 1960 - 1963.
Jack and Jill	Coloured transfer prints of characters from the comic Jack and Jill. Issued 1964 - 1970.

Transfer Designs

The Contemporary shaped tableware was decorated with "transfer designs" on a white background (with one exception), brief descriptions of the patterns are:

Ballet	Blue and pink dress, cream background
Moonlight	Blue bulrushes
Circus	Blue horse with bare-back rider
Dawn Chorus	Birds are blue, black and pink
Picnic	Oranges on tree, multi-coloured scene
Greenfingers	Willow tree, multi-coloured scene
Horses	Yellow sun, multi-coloured scene
Mexican Madness	Yellow hat with coloured flowers
Pavlova	Blue and pink dress

The Trend-Setters

"Trend-Setters" was the advertising slogan used for the series of tableware, which included the decorations known as Apollo, Lunar, Metric and Verona. These sets had their shapes in common, had transfer prints on to a white background and were in a gloss finish, but, of course, the designs for each set was individual. They were issued 1966 - 1970.

Metric	As the name suggests this was a geometric design and the colours were two shades of brown with mustard. The lids ad bases were solid brown.
Lunar	The shape in this series had a brown and mustard design with lids and bases in solid brown.
Apollo	Blue design with mustard foliage on brown stems with lids and bases in solid blue.
Verona	A foliage pattern with mustard and brown flowers, green leaves and solid brown lids and bases.

Plain Colours

The shapes used for the "trend-setters" series were also produced in plain colours - green, blue, mink and calypso.

REGAL FLUTED WARE

The sketch shown is of shape 1130 which serves as a guide to the style. Unfortunately, at this time we have no further information on these shapes.

Listed below are the shapes which occur in Regal Fluted ware without prices as all pieces must be considered extremely rare.

Shape 1130 Tall cup

Designer: Albert Hallam
Issued: 1948 - 1952
Colours: Unknown

Shape	Description	Shape	Description
Shape 1130	Tall cup and saucer	Shape 1140	Coffee sugar
Shape 1131	Low cup	Shape 1141	Coffee cream
Shape 1132	Coffee cup and saucer	Shape 1142	Fruit bowl
Shape 1133	Muffin, 4"	Shape 1143	Fruit saucer/oatmeal
Shape 1134	Muffin, 5"	Shape 1144	Sweet dish
Shape 1135	Muffin, 6"	Shape 1174	Teapot
Shape 1136	Muffin, 7"	Shape 1175	Coffee pot
Shape 1137	Bread and butter plate	Shape 1181	Dish
Shape 1138	Sugar	Shape 1213	Oatmeal, small
Shape 1139	Cream	Shape 1229	Bread and butter plate

MARIE

Shape 1161 Tea cup and saucer, Gilt edge design

Shape1165 Plate, Nursery Ware design

Shape 1169 Sugar, Gilt edge design

Shape1170 Cream, Gilt edge design

Shape 1228 Marie bread and butter plate

Shape 2019 Marie plate with flat, wide rim

Plate 1/1 — "Cuba" No. 2 deco 6661, "Durban" No. 1 deco 6663, "Egyptian" deco 5057

Plate 1/2 — "Holborn" deco 6591, "Victoria" No. 1 deco 6045, "Victoria" No. 2 deco 6456

Plate 2/1 — "Eric"

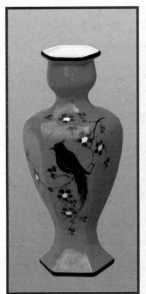

Plate 2/2 — "Deal"

Plate 2/3 — "Deal"

Plate 2/4 — "Blythe"
deco 5057

Plate 3/1 — "Troy" deco 6448

Plate 3/2 — "Sale" deco 6115

Plate 3/3 — "Octagon" deco 6451

Plate 3/4 — "Victory"

Plate 4/1 — "Gardena" deco 6997

Plate 4/2 — "Flowerkist" deco 7245

Plate 4/3 — "Louvain" No. 1 deco Garland

Plate 4/4 — "Victory"

Plate 5/1 — Shape 184

Plate 5/2 — Shape 484

Plate 5/3 — Shape 135

Plate 5/4 — Shape 70

Plate 6/1 — Handled bowl (shape 157)

Plate 6/2 — Caprice Series (shape 1656, shape 808, shape 101)

Plate 6/3 — Basket (shape 623)

Plate 6/4 — Shape 2039

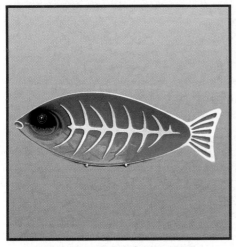

Plate 6/5 — Fish dish (shape 2171)

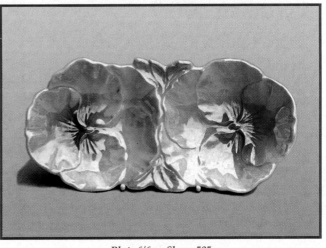

Plate 6/6 — Shape 595

Plate 7/1 — "Albany" deco 3072

Plate 7/2 — "Lynn" deco 6338

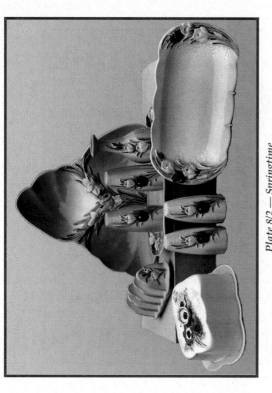

Plate 8/1 — *Willow*

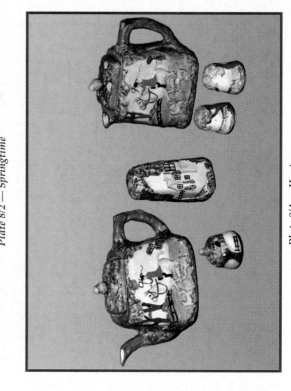

Plate 8/2 — *Springtime*

Plate 8/3 — *Sundial*

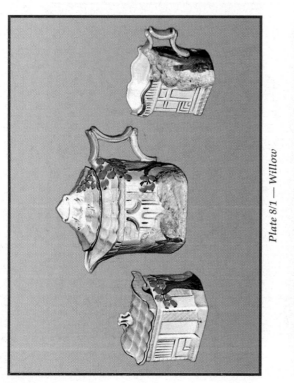

Plate 8/4 — *Huntsman*

Shape 2034 Marie plate, large size

Shape 2035 Marie plate, medium size

Designer:	Albert Hallam in 1949 except 1208 in 1950, 1228 in 1951, 2019 in 1964, 2034, 2035, 2036 in 1965			Design:	Gilt edge — shapes 1161, 1162, 1163, 1164, 1165, 1166, 1167, 1169, 1170, 1171, 1172, 1173, 1208, 1228, 2019, 2034, 2035, 1036	
Issued:	See below				Nursery Ware — shape 1165	
Size:	See below				Trend-setters — shapes 2019, 2034, 2035, 2036	

Shape	Name	Issued	Size	U.S. $	Can. $	U.K.£
1161	Tea cup and saucer	1949 - 1970	Cup — 3", 7.6 cm Saucer — 5 ½", 14.0 cm	10.00	15.00	7.00
1162	Breakfast cup and saucer	1949 - 1970	3 ½", 8.9 cm	15.00	20.00	10.00
1163	Coffee cup and saucer	1949 - unknown	Unknown	15.00	20.00	10.00
1164	Plate	1949 - 1961	6", 15.0 cm	7.50	10.00	5.00
1165	Plate (gilt edge)	1949 - 1961	6 ¾", 17.2 cm	7.50	10.00	5.00
1165	Plate (nursery ware)	1954 - 1963	6 ¾", 17.2 cm	25.00	35.00	15.00
1166	Plate	1949 - 1961	8 ¾", 22.2 cm	10.00	15.00	7.50
1167	Plate	1949 - 1961	9 ¾", 24.7 cm	15.00	20.00	10.00
1169	Sugar bowl	1949 - by 1959	3", 11.9 cm	10.00	15.00	7.50
1170	Cream jug	1949 - by 1959	3 ¼", 8.3 cm	10.00	15.00	7.50
1171	Fruit bowl	1949 - by 1959	Unknown	30.00	45.00	15.00
1172	Fruit saucer/oatmeal	1949 - by 1959	7", 17.8 cm	10.00	15.00	7.50
1173	Oval dish	1949 - by 1959	Unknown	20.00	30.00	10.00
1208	Oatmeal, small	1951 - by 1959	6", 12.7 cm	10.00	15.00	7.50
1228	Bread and butter plate	1952 - by 1959	9 ¾", 24.7 cm	20.00	30.00	10.00
2019	Plate with flat, wide rim	1964 - 1970	9 ¾", 24.7 cm	20.00	30.00	10.00
2034	Plate with flat, wide rim	1965 - 1970	8 ¾", 22.2 cm	20.00	30.00	10.00
2035	Plate with flat, wide rim	1965 - 1970	7 ¾", 19.7 cm	15.00	20.00	8.00
2036	Plate with flat, wide rim	1965 - 1970	6 ¾", 17.2 cm	12.00	15.00	6.00

SHAPE 1273
CHILDREN'S TEA SET

Designer:	Albert Hallam in 1952			Size:	See below	
Issued:	1953 - 1959			Design:	Nursery ware (© Walt Disney)	

Shape	Description	Height	Diameter	U.S. $	Can. $	U.K.£
1273	Teapot	3 ¾", 9.5 cm	3 ½", 8.9 cm	125.00	200.00	65.00
1273	Cream	2", 5.0 cm	1 ¾", 4.4 cm	25.00	35.00	12.00
1273	Sugar	1 ½", 3.8 cm	2 ½", 6.4 cm	25.00	35.00	12.00
1273	Cup	1 ¾", 4.4 cm	2", 5.0 cm	15.00	25.00	8.00
1273	Saucer		4 ½", 11.9 cm	15.00	20.00	7.00
1273	Plate		4 ½", 11.9 cm	15.00	20.00	7.00

Note: The first version cup and cream had supported handles.
In 1954 the cup was replaced by shape 1317, and the cream was replaced by shape 1318.

Shape 1285 Baby plate

Designer:	Albert Hallam in 1953
Issued:	1954 - 1970
Diameter:	6 ½", 16.5 cm
Design:	Nursery ware

Description	U.S. $	Can. $	U.K. £
Baby plate	50.00	75.00	25.00

Photograph not
available
at press time

Shape 1303 Baby cup

Designer:	Albert Hallam in 1953
Issued:	1954 - 1970
Size:	Unknown
Design:	Nursery ware

Description	U.S. $	Can. $	U.K. £
Baby cup	10.00	15.00	7.50

Shape 1317 Toy cup

Designer:	Albert Hallam in 1953
Issued:	1954 - 1959
Size:	Unknown
Design:	Nursery ware

Description	U.S. $	Can. $	U.K. £
Toy cup	10.00	15.00	5.00

Note: Shape 1317 replaced the cup in set 1273.

Shape 1318 Toy cream

Designer:	Albert Hallam in 1953
Issued:	1954 - 1959
Size:	Unknown
Design:	Nursery ware

Description	U.S. $	Can. $	U.K. £
Toy cream	10.00	15.00	5.00

Note: Shape 1318 replaced the cream in set 1273.

Photograph not
available
at press time

Shape 1423 Contemporary sugar bowl

Designer: Albert Hallam in 1956
Issued: 1956 - 1961
Diameter: 5", 12.7 cm
Design: Transfer designs

Description	U.S. $	Can. $	U.K. £
Sugar bowl	10.00	17.00	8.00

Shape 1424 Contemporary cream jug

Designer: Albert Hallam in 1956
Issued: 1956 - 1961
Height: 3 ½", 8.9 cm
Design: Transfer designs

Description	U.S. $	Can. $	U.K. £
Cream jug	10.00	15.00	8.00

Shape 1425/A/B Contemporary cup and saucer

Designer: Albert Hallam in 1956
Issued: 1956 - by 1962
Height: 2 ¾", 7.0 cm
Design: Transfer designs

Description	U.S. $	Can. $	U.K. £
1. Angled handle on cup	10.00	15.00	8.00
2. Rounded handle on cup	10.00	15.00	8.00

Note: The bottom of the cup is square.

Shape 1426 Contemporary plate, small size

Designer: Albert Hallam in 1956
Issued: 1956 - 1961
Size: 6 ¾", 17.2 cm
Design: Transfer designs

Description	U.S. $	Can. $	U.K. £
Plate, small	10.00	15.00	6.00

Shape 1427 Contemporary bread and butter plate

Designer: Albert Hallam in 1956
Issued: 1956 - 1961
Diameter: 9 ½", 24 cm
Design: Transfer designs

Description	U.S. $	Can. $	U.K. £
Bread/butter plate	10.00	15.00	8.00

Shape 1428 Contemporary fruit bowl

Designer: Albert Hallam in 1956
Issued: 1956 - 1961
Diameter: 9", 22.9cm
Design: Transfer designs

Description	U.S. $	Can. $	U.K. £
Fruit bowl	15.00	20.00	10.00

Shape 1429 Contemporary fruit saucer

Designer: Albert Hallam in 1956
Issued: 1956 - 1961
Diameter: 6 ½", 16.5 cm
Design: Transfer designs

Description	U.S. $	Can. $	U.K. £
Fruit saucer	10.00	12.00	6.00

Photograph not
available
at press time

Shape 1430 Contemporary TV set

Designer: Albert Hallam in 1956
Issued: 1956 - 1961
Size: Unknown
Design: Transfer designs

Description	U.S. $	Can. $	U.K. £
TV set	30.00	45.00	15.00

Shape 1431   Contemporary teapot,
First version — knob cut-out

Designer: Albert Hallam in 1956
Issued: 1956 - 1961
Size: Unknown
Design: Transfer designs

Description	U.S. $	Can. $	U.K. £
Teapot	50.00	75.00	25.00

Note: Shape 1431 was replaced by shape 1777.

Shape 1432   Contemporary cheese dish,
First version — knobcut-out

Designer: Albert Hallam in 1956
Issued: 1956 - 1961
Size: 5" x 4", 12.7 x 10.1 cm
Design: Transfer designs

Description	U.S. $	Can. $	U.K. £
Cheese dish	30.00	40.00	15.00

Note: Shape 1432 was replaced by shape 1776.

Shape 1433   Contemporary toast rack

Designer: Albert Hallam in 1956
Issued: 1956 - 1970
Size: 6 ½" x 3" x 3", 16.5 x 7.6 x 7.6 cm
Design: 1. Gilt edge
             2. Transfer designs
             3. Trend-setters

Description	U.S. $	Can. $	U.K. £
Toast rack	20.00	25.00	12.00

Shape 1434   Contemporary cruet
Salt, pepper and mustard on a base,
First version — knob cut-out

Designer: Albert Hallam in 1956
Issued: 1956 - 1961
Size: 5 ¼" x 2 ½", 13.3 x 6.4 cm
Design: Transfer designs

Description	U.S. $	Can. $	U.K. £
Cruet	50.00	75.00	25.00

Note: Shape 1434 was replaced by shape 1787.

Shape 1441/1/2/3 Contemporary jug, in three sizes

Designer:	Albert Hallam in 1956
Issued:	1956 - 1966
Height:	1. Unknown
	2. 5 ½″, 14.0 cm
	3. Unknown
Design:	Transfer designs

Description	U.S. $	Can. $	U.K. £
Jug	20.00	30.00	10.00

Shape 1442   Contemporary preserve with lid
First version — knob cut-out

Designer:	Albert Hallam in 1956
Issued:	1956 - 1961
Size:	3 ¼″ x 3 ¼″ x 4″, 8.3 x 8.3 x 10.1 cm
Design:	Transfer designs

Description	U.S. $	Can. $	U.K. £
Preserve with lid	50.00	75.00	25.00

Note: Shape 1442 was replaced by shape 1779.

Photograph not
available
at press time

Photograph not
available
at press time

Shape 1443   Contemporary breakfast cup and saucer

Designer:	Albert Hallam in 1956
Issued:	1956 - 1961
Size:	Unknown
Design:	Transfer designs

Description	U.S. $	Can. $	U.K. £
Breakfast cup/saucer	20.00	30.00	12.00

Shape 1444   Contemporary plate, medium size

Designer:	Albert Hallam in 1956
Issued:	1956 - 1961
Diameter:	8 ½″, 21.6 cm
Design:	Transfer designs

Description	U.S. $	Can. $	U.K. £
Plate, medium	10.00	15.00	8.00

Shape 1445 Contemporary tray/dish, rectangular,
large size

Designer: Albert Hallam in 1956
Issued: 1956 - 1970
Size: 7 ½" x 5 ¼", 19.1 x 13.3 cm
Design: 1. Gilt edge
2. Transfer designs
3. Trend-setters

Description	U.S. $	Can. $	U.K. £
Tray/dish, large	15.00	20.00	10.00

Shape 1446 Contemporary tray/dish, triangular,
medium size

Designer: Albert Hallam in 1956
Issued: 1956 - 1970
Size: 5" x 5 ½" x 5 ½", 12.7 x 14.0 x 14.0 cm
Design: 1. Gilt edge
2. Transfer designs

Colour	U.S. $	Can. $	U.K. £
Tray/dish, medium	10.00	15.00	8.00

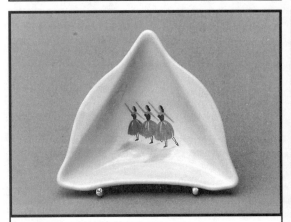

Shape 1447 Contemporary tray/dish, triangular,
small size

Designer: Albert Hallam in 1956
Issued: 1956 - 1970
Size: 4 ½" x 4 ½" x 4 ¼", 11.9 x 11.9 x 10.8 cm
Design: 1. Gilt edge
2. Transfer designs

Description	U.S. $	Can. $	U.K. £
Tray dish, small	8.00	12.00	5.00

Shape 1448 Contemporary butter with lid, large
First version — knob cut-out

Designer: Albert Hallam in 1956
Issued: 1956 - 1959
Size: 6 ¾" x 3 ½" x 3 ¼", 17.2 x 8.9 x 9.5 cm
Design: Transfer designs

Description	U.S. $	Can. $	U.K. £
Butter with lid	30.00	40.00	18.00

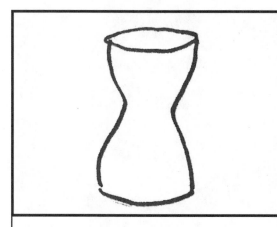

Shape 1449 Contemporary double egg cup

Designer:	Albert Hallam in 1956
Issued:	1956 - 1961
Size:	Unknown
Design:	Transfer designs

Description	U.S. $	Can. $	U.K. £
Double egg cup	15.00	20.00	8.00

Shape 1450 Contemporary coffee pot
First version — knob cut-out

Designer:	Albert Hallam in 1956
Issued:	1956 - 1961
Size:	Unknown
Design:	Transfer designs

Description	U.S. $	Can. $	U.K. £
Coffee pot	30.00	40.00	18.00

Note: The illustration shows a pot with the lid missing. Shape 1450 was replaced by shape 1778.

Shape 1464 Contemporary TV plate (small)
with location for cup shape 1425A

Designer:	Albert Hallam in 1957
Issued:	1957 - 1961
Size:	8 ½″ x 8 ½″, 21.6″ x 21.6 cm
Design:	Transfer designs

Description	U.S. $	Can. $	U.K. £
Contemporary TV plate	25.00	35.00	15.00

Shape 1535 Square dish

Designer:	Albert Hallam in 1958
Issued:	1958 - 1970
Size:	4 ½″ x 4 ½″, 11.9 x 11.9 cm
Design:	1. Gilt edge
	2. Transfer designs
	3. Trend-setters

Description	U.S. $	Can. $	U.K. £
Square dish	8.00	12.00	5.00

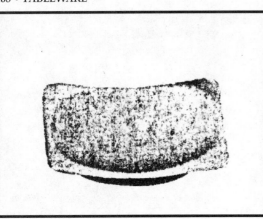

Shape 1536 Dish, small

Designer:	Albert Hallam in 1958
Issued:	1958 - 1970
Size:	3 ¼" x 3 ¼", 8.3 x 8.3 cm
Design:	1. Gilt edge
	2. Transfer designs
	3. Trend-setters

Description	U.S. $	Can. $	U.K. £
Dish, small	8.00	12.00	5.00

Shape 1539 Dish, large

Designer:	Albert Hallam in 1958
Issued:	1958 - 1965
Size:	5 ¾" x 4 ¼", 14.6 x 10.8 cm
Design:	1. Gilt edge
	2. Transfer designs

Description	U.S. $	Can. $	U.K. £
Dish, large	8.00	12.00	5.00

Shape 1540 Dish, small

Designer:	Albert Hallam in 1958
Issued:	1958 - 1965
Size:	3" x 4", 7.6 x 10.1 cm
Design:	1. Gilt edge
	2. Transfer designs

Description	U.S. $	Can. $	U.K. £
Dish, small	8.00	12.00	5.00

Photograph not
available
at press time

Shape 1594 Contemporary butter dish, ½ lb.
First version — knob cut-out

Designer:	Albert Hallam in 1959
Issued:	1959 - 1961
Size:	5" x 3 ¼" x 2", 12.7 x 8.3 x 5.0 cm
Design:	Transfer designs

Description	U.S. $	Can. $	U.K. £
Butter dish	30.00	40.00	18.00

Note: Shape 1594 was replaced by shape 1775.

**Shape 1595 TV set with location for cup
shape 1425B**

Designer: Albert Hallam in 1959
Issued: 1959 - 1961
Size: 8 ¾" x 7", 22.2 x 17.8 cm
Design: Transfer designs

Description	U.S. $	Can. $	U.K. £
TV set	25.00	35.00	15.00

Note: Shape 1595 was replaced by shape 1782.

Shape 1617 Square dish

Designer: Albert Hallam in 1959
Issued: 1959 - 1969
Size: 4" x 4", 10.1 x 10.1 cm
Design: 1. Gilt edge
           2. Transfer designs

Description	U.S. $	Can. $	U.K. £
Square dish	8.00	12.00	5.00

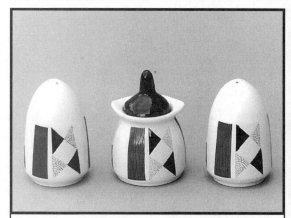

Shape 1618 Cruet, salt, pepper and mustard with lid

Designer: Mr. Wood in 1959
Issued: 1959 - 1970
Height: 3", 7.6 cm
Design: 1. Gilt edge
           2. Transfer designs
           3. Trend-setters

Description	U.S. $	Can. $	U.K. £
Cruet	25.00	40.00	15.00

Shape 1623 Contemporary meat dish

Designer: Mr. Wood in 1959
Issued: 1959 - 1961
Length: 12 ½", 31.7 cm
Design: Transfer designs

Description	U.S. $	Can. $	U.K. £
Meat dish	25.00	35.00	18.00

Shape 1665/1666 Pepper and salt

Designer:	Albert Hallam in 1959
Issued:	1959 - 1967
Height:	4 ½", 11.9 cm
Design:	1. Copper - lustre
	2. Transfer designs
	3. White - satin matt

Description	U.S. $	Can. $	U.K. £
Pepper and salt	8.00	12.00	5.00

Shape 1667 Vinegar with handle

Designer:	Albert Hallam in 1959
Issued:	1959 - 1967
Height:	5 ½", 14 cm incl. stopper
Design:	1. Copper - lustre
	2. Transfer designs
	3. White - satin matt

Description	U.S. $	Can. $	U.K. £
Vinegar	15.00	20.00	10.00

Shape 1674 Tray / Dish

Designer:	Albert Hallam in 1960
Issued:	1960 - 1963
Size:	10 ¼" x 9", 26.0 x 22.9 cm
Design:	Transfer designs

Description	U.S. $	Can. $	U.K. £
Tray/dish	20.00	30.00	10.00

Shape 1694 Vinegar with stopper

Designer:	Albert Hallam in 1960
Issued:	1960 - 1965
Height:	6", 15 cm
Design:	Transfer designs

Description	U.S. $	Can. $	U.K. £
Vinegar with stopper	20.00	30.00	10.00

Note: Top and stopper altered in 1961.

Shape 1695/1696 Salt and pepper

Designer:	Albert Hallam in 1960
Issued:	1960 - 1965
Height:	4 ½", 11.9 cm
Design:	Transfer designs

Description	U.S. $	Can. $	U.K. £
Salt and pepper	20.00	30.00	10.00

Shape 1703 Sandwich tray

Designer:	Albert Hallam in 1960
Issued:	1960 - 1965
Size:	10 ¾" x 5 ¼", 27.8 x 13.3 cm
Design:	Transfer designs

Description	U.S. $	Can. $	U.K. £
Sandwich tray	20.00	30.00	12.00

Shape 1719 Mustard

Designer:	Albert Hallam in 1960
Issued:	1960 - 1965
Height:	3", 7.6 cm
Design:	Gilt edge

Description	U.S. $	Can. $	U.K. £
Mustard	10.00	15.00	8.00

Shape 1732 Egg cup

Designer:	Albert Hallam in 1960
Issued:	1961 - 1970
Height:	1 ¾", 4.4 cm
Design:	1. Gilt edge
	2. Nursery ware
	3. Trend-setter

Description	U.S. $	Can. $	U.K. £
Egg cup	10.00	15.00	5.00

Shape 1755 Eton tea cup and saucer

Designer:	Albert Hallam in 1961
Issued:	1961 - 1965
Cup Dia.:	3 ¼", 8.3 cm
Height:	3", 7.6 cm
Saucer Dia.:	5 ¾", 14.6 cm
Design:	Transfer designs

Description	U.S. $	Can. $	U.K. £
Tea cup and saucer	15.00	20.00	10.00

Shape 1756 Eton sugar

Designer:	Albert Hallam in 1961
Issued:	1961 - 1970
Diameter:	4 ¼", 10.8 cm
Design:	1. Gilt edge
	2. Transfer designs

Description	U.S. $	Can. $	U.K. £
Sugar	10.00	15.00	8.00

Shape 1757 Eton cream

Designer:	Albert Hallam in 1961
Issued:	1961 - 1970
Size:	Unknown
Design:	1. Gilt edge
	2. Transfer designs

Description	U.S. $	Can. $	U.K. £
Cream	10.00	15.00	8.00

Shape 1758 Eton breakfast cup and saucer

Designer:	Albert Hallam in 1961
Issued:	1961 - 1965
Size:	Unknown
Design:	Transfer designs

Description	U.S. $	Can. $	U.K. £
Breakfast cup and saucer	15.00	20.00	10.00

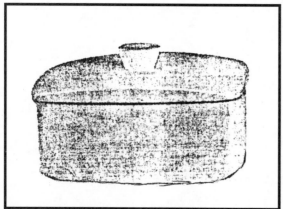

Shape 1775 Contemporary covered butter
            Second version — knob solid

Designer:	Albert Hallam in 1961
Issued:	1961 - 1965
Size:	5″ x 3 ¼″ x 2″, 12.7 x 8.3 x 5 cm
Design:	Transfer designs

Description	U.S. $	Can. $	U.K. £
Covered butter	25.00	40.00	15.00

Note: Shape 1775 replaced shape 1594.

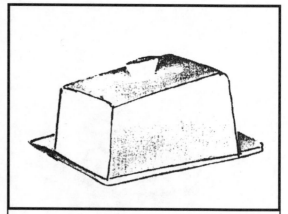

Shape 1776 Cheese dish
            Second version — knob solid

Designer:	Albert Hallam in 1961
Issued:	1961 - 1965
Size:	5″ x 4″, 12.7 x 10.1 cm
Design:	Transfer designs

Description	U.S. $	Can. $	U.K. £
Cheese dish	25.00	40.00	15.00

Note: Shape 1776 replaced shape 1432.

Shape 1777 Eton teapot
            Second version — knob solid

Designer:	Albert Hallam in 1961
Issued:	1961 - 1965
Size:	Unknown
Design:	Transfer designs

Description	U.S. $	Can. $	U.K. £
Teapot	40.00	60.00	20.00

Note: Shape 1777 replaced shape 1431.

Shape 1778 Eton coffee pot
            Second version — knob solid

Designer:	Albert Hallam in 1961
Issued:	1961 - 1965
Size:	Unknown
Design:	Transfer designs

Description	U.S. $	Can. $	U.K. £
Coffee pot	40.00	60.00	20.00

Note: Shape 1778 replaced shape 1450.

Shape 1779 Preserve
Second version — knob solid

Designer:	Albert Hallam in 1961
Issued:	1961 - 1965
Height:	3 ¾", 9.5 cm
Design:	Transfer designs

Description	U.S. $	Can. $	U.K. £
Preserve	20.00	30.00	15.00

Note: Shape 1779 replaced shape 1442.

Photograph not
available
at press time

Shape 1780 Oatmeal/Soup

Designer:	Albert Hallam in 1961
Issued:	1961 - 1965
Size:	1. 7", 17.8 cm
	2. 6", 15.0 cm
Design:	1. Nursery ware
	2. Transfer designs

Description	U.S. $	Can. $	U.K. £
Oatmeal/soup	10.00	15.00	8.00

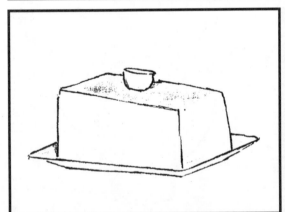

Shape 1781 Cheese dish, narrow
Second version — knob solid

Designer:	Albert Hallam in 1961
Issued:	1961 - 1965
Size:	5 ¼" x 3 ¼", 13.3 x 8.3 cm
Design:	Transfer designs

Description	U.S.$	Can. $	U.K.£
Cheese dish	25.00	35.00	15.00

Shape 1782 Eton TV set

Designer:	Albert Hallam in 1961
Issued:	1961 - 1965
Base size:	9" x 6", 22.9 x 15 cm
Design:	Transfer designs

Description	U.S.$	Can. $	U.K.£
TV set	25.00	35.00	15.00

Note: Cup replaced shape 1595.

Shape 1783 Eton plate, small

Designer	Albert Hallam in 1961
Issued:	1961 - 1970
Diameter:	6 ¾", 17.2 cm
Design:	1. Nursery ware
	2. Plain colours
	3. Transfer designs
	4. Trend-setters

Description	U.S.$	Can.$	U.K.£
Plate	20.00	30.00	10.00

Shape 1784 Eton plate, medium

Designer:	Albert Hallam in 1961
Issued:	1961 - 1970
Diameter:	8 ¾", 22.2 cm
Design:	1. Plain colours
	2. Transfer designs
	3. Trend-setters

Description	U.S.$	Can.$	U.K.£
Plate, medium	20.00	30.00	10.00

Shape 1785 Eton plate, large

Designer:	Albert Hallam in 1961
Issued:	1961 - 1970
Diameter:	9 ¾", 24.7 cm
Design:	1. Plain colours
	2. Transfer designs
	3. Trend-setters

Description	U.S.$	Can.$	U.K.£
Plate, large	20.00	30.00	12.00

Shape 1787 Cruet - salt, pepper, mustard on base

Designer:	Albert Hallam in 1961
Issued:	1962 - 1970
Size:	5 ¼" x 2 ½", 13.3 cm x 6.4 cm
Design:	1. Gilt edge
	2. Transfer designs
	3. Trend-setters

Description	U.S.$	Can.$	U.K.£
Cruet	50.00	75.00	25.00

Note: Shape 1787 replaced shape 1434.

Shape 1806 Fruit bowl

Designer: Unknown
Issued: 1962 - 1967
Diameter: 9", 22.9 cm
Design: 1. Gilt edge
2. Trend-setters

Description	U.S. $	Can. $	U.K. £
Fruit bowl	40.00	60.00	20.00

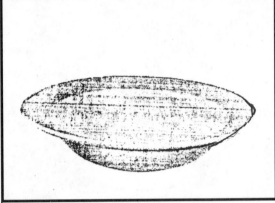

Shape 1807 Fruit saucer

Designer: Unknown
Issued: 1962 - 1967
Diameter: 6 ½", 16.5 cm
Design: 1. Gilt edge
2. Trend-setters

Description	U.S. $	Can. $	U.K. £
Fruit saucer	15.00	20.00	8.00

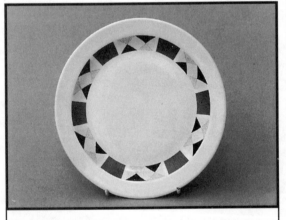

Shape 1822 Eton plate

Designer: Albert Hallam in 1961
Issued: 1961 - 1970
Diameter: 7 ¾", 19.7 cm
Design: 1. Plain colours
2. Transfer designs
3. Trend-setters

Description	U.S. $	Can. $	U.K. £
Plate	12.00	15.00	7.00

Photograph not
available
at press time

Shape 1913 Coupe soup

Designer: Albert Hallam in 1963
Issued: 1964 - 1970
Diameter: 7 ¾", 19.7 cm
Design: 1. Gilt edge
2. Plain colours
3. Trend-setters

Description	U.S. $	Can. $	U.K. £
Coupe soup	12.00	15.00	7.00

Photograph not
available
at press time

Shape 1915 Deep soup

Designer:	Albert Hallam in 1963
Issued:	1964 - 1970
Diameter:	9 ¼", 23.5 cm
Design:	1. Gilt edge
	2. Trend-setters

Description	U.S. $	Can. $	U.K. £
Deep soup	20.00	30.00	10.00

Shape 1919 Tureen

Designer:	Albert Hallam in 1963
Issued:	1964 - 1971
Diameter:	9 ¾", 24.7 cm
Design:	1. Gilt edge
	2. Pewter

Description	U.S. $	Can. $	U.K. £
Tureen	60.00	90.00	35.00

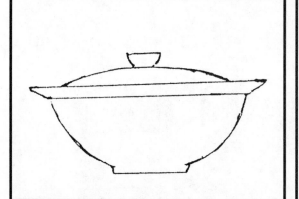

Shape 1922 Covered scallop

Designer:	Albert Hallam in 1964
Issued:	1964 - 1970
Size:	Unknown
Design:	Gilt edge

Description	U.S. $	Can. $	U.K. £
Covered scallop	50.00	75.00	25.00

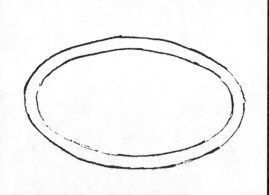

Shape 1923 Meat dish

Designer:	Albert Hallam in 1964
Issued:	1964 - 1969
Size:	12" x 9", 30.5 x 22.9 cm
Design:	Gilt edge

Description	U.S. $	Can. $	U.K. £
Meat dish	40.00	60.00	20.00

Shape 1958 Orbit coffee pot

Designer: Albert Hallam in 1964
Issued: 1964 - 1971
Height: 9", 22.9 cm
Design: 1. Gilt edge
          2. Plain colours
          3. Trend-setters

Description	U.S. $	Can. $	U.K. £
Coffee pot	40.00	60.00	20.00

Shape 1959 Orbit teapot

Designer: Albert Hallam in 1964
Issued: 1964 - 1970
Height: 6 ½", 15.0 cm
Design: 1. Gilt edge
          2. Plain colours
          3. Trend-setters

Description	U.S. $	Can. $	U.K. £
Teapot	40.00	60.00	20.00

Shape 1960 Orbit tea cup and saucer

Designer: Albert Hallam in 1964
Issued: 1964 - 1970
Cup Dia.:   3 ¼", 8.3 cm
Height: 2 ¾", 7.0 cm
Saucer Dia.:   5 ½", 14.0 cm
Design: 1. Gilt edge
          2. Trend-setters (not Verona)

Description	U.S. $	Can. $	U.K. £
Tea cup and saucer	20.00	30.00	12.00

Shape 1962 Orbit cream jug

Designer: Albert Hallam in 1964
Issued: 1964 - 1971
Height: 4", 10.1 cm
Design: 1. Plain colours
          2. Trend-setters

Description	U.S. $	Can. $	U.K. £
Cream jug	15.00	20.00	7.00

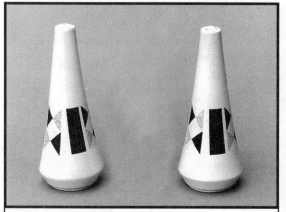

Shape 1963/1964 Pepper and salt

Designer:	Albert Hallam in 1964
Issued:	1964 - 1970
Height:	5 ½″, 14.0 cm
Design:	1. Gilt edge
	2. Plain colours
	3. Trend-setters

Description	U.S. $	Can. $	U.K. £
Pepper and salt	10.00	15.00	5.00

Shape 1965 Vinegar

Designer:	Albert Hallam in 1964
Issued:	1964 - 1970
Height:	5 ½″, 14.0 cm
Design:	1. Gilt edge
	2. Plain colours
	3. Trend-setters

Description	U.S. $	Can. $	U.K. £
Vinegar	10.00	15.00	6.00

Shape 1966 Orbit vegetable dish

Designer:	Albert Hallam in 1964
Issued:	1964 - 1970
Width:	10 ¼″, 26.0 cm
Design:	1. Gilt edge
	2. Trend-setters

Description	U.S. $	Can. $	U.K. £
Vegetable dish	40.00	60.00	20.00

Shape 1967 Orbit gravy boat and stand

Designer:	Albert Hallam in 1964
Issued:	1964 - 1970
Boat size:	9 ¼″ x 3″ x 3 ¾″, 23.5 x 7.6 x 9.5 cm
Design:	1. Gilt edge
	2. Trend-setters

Description	U.S. $	Can. $	U.K. £
Gravy boat and stand	40.00	60.00	20.00

Shape 1968 Orbit preserve

Designer: Albert Hallam in 1964
Issued: 1964 - 1970
Height: 3 ¾″, 9.5 cm
Design: 1. Gilt edge
           2. Plain colours
           3. Trend-setters

Description	U.S. $	Can. $	U.K. £
Preserve	30.00	40.00	15.00

Shape 1969 Orbit butter

Designer: Albert Hallam in 1964
Issued: 1964 - 1970
Size: 5 ¼″ x 3 ½″, 13.3 x 8.9 cm
Design: 1. Gilt edge
           2. Plain colours
           3. Trend-setters

Description	U.S. $	Can. $	U.K. £
Butter dish	30.00	40.00	15.00

Shape 1970 Orbit cheese dish

Designer: Albert Hallam in 1964
Issued: 1964 - 1970
Size: 6 ¾″ x 5 ¾″, 17.2 x 14.6 cm (base)
Height :   5″, 12.7 cm
Design: 1. Gilt edge
           2. Plain colours
           3. Trend-setters

Description	U.S. $	Can. $	U.K. £
Cheese dish	30.00	40.00	15.00

Shape 1972 Orbit coffee cup and saucer

Designer: Albert Hallam in 1964
Issued: 1964 - 1971
Size: Unknown
Design: 1. Gilt edge
           2. Plain colours
           3. Trend-setters

Description	U.S. $	Can. $	U.K. £
Cup and saucer	15.00	20.00	8.00

Shape 1973 Orbit hot milk jug

Designer:	Albert Hallam in 1964
Issued:	1964 - 1971
Height:	7 ¾", 19.7 cm
Design:	1. Gilt edge
	2. Plain colours
	3. Trend-setters

Description	U.S. $	Can. $	U.K. £
Hot milk jug	30.00	45.00	12.00

Photograph not
available
at press time

Shape 1974 Orbit fruit bowl

Designer:	Albert Hallam in 1964
Issued:	1964 - 1970
Diameter:	7 ¾", 19.7 cm
Design:	1. Gilt edge
	2. Trend-setters

Description	U.S. $	Can. $	U.K. £
Fruit bowl	35.00	60.00	18.00

Shape 1975 Orbit fruit saucer

Designer:	Albert Hallam in 1964
Issued:	1964 - 1970
Size:	6 ½", 16.5 cm
Design:	1. Gilt edge
	2. Trend-setters

Description	U.S. $	Can. $	U.K. £
Fruit saucer	15.00	20.00	8.00

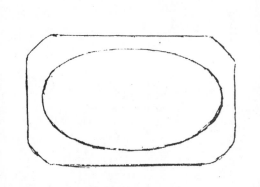

Shape 1976 Orbit meat dish

Designer:	Albert Hallam in 1964
Issued:	1964 - 1969
Size:	12 ¼" x 9 ¼", 31.1 x 23.5 cm
Design:	1. Plain colours
	2. Trend-setters

Description	U.S. $	Can. $	U.K. £
Meat dish	30.00	45.00	15.00

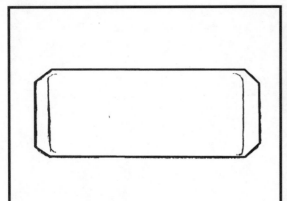

Shape 1977 Orbit sandwich tray

Designer:	Albert Hallam in 1964
Issued:	1964 - 1970
Size:	11″ x 5 ¼″, 27.0 x 13.3 cm
Design:	1. Gilt edge
	2. Trend-setters

Description	U.S. $	Can. $	U.K. £
Sandwich tray	30.00	45.00	15.00

Shape 1978 Orbit open sugar

Designer:	Albert Hallam in 1964
Issued:	1964 - 1969
Height:	2 ½″, 6.4 cm
Diameter:	3 ½″ 8.9 cm
Design:	1. Plain colours
	2. Trend-setters

Description	U.S. $	Can. $	U.K. £
Open sugar	10.00	15.00	6.00

Photograph not
available
at press time

Shape 2002 Orbit oatmeal dish

Designer:	Albert Hallam in 1964
Issued:	1965 - 1970
Diameter:	6 ½″, 16.5 cm
Design:	1. Gilt edge
	2. Nursery ware
	3. Trend-setters

Description	U.S. $	Can. $	U.K. £
Oatmeal dish	15.00	20.00	8.00

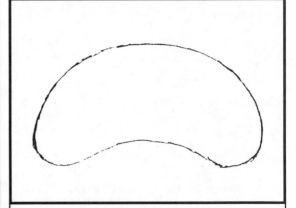

Shape 2004 Kidney dish

Designer:	Albert Hallam in 1965
Issued:	1965 - 1969
Length:	9 ½″, 24.0 cm
Deep:	3 ¼, 1.9 cm
Design:	1. Gilt edge
	2. Trend setters

Description	U.S. $	Can. $	U.K. £
Kidney dish	20.00	30.00	10.00

Shape 2027 Orbit soup jug

Designer:	Albert Hallam in 1964	
Issued:	1964 - 1969	
Height:	7 ¼", 18.4 cm	
Design:	Trend-setters	

Description	U.S. $	Can. $	U.K. £
Soup jug	30.00	45.00	15.00

Shape 2028 Soup cup and saucer

Designer:	Albert Hallam in 1965
Issued:	1965 - 1970
Height:	2 ¼", 5.7 cm
Design:	1. Gilt edge
	2. Plain colours
	3. Trend-setters

Description	U.S. $	Can. $	U.K. £
Soup cup/saucer	20.00	30.00	10.00

Note: Saucer not shown.

Shape 2039 TV tray with cup shape 1972

Designer:	Albert Hallam in 1965
Issued:	1965 - 1970
Length:	9", 22.9 cm
Design:	1. Gilt edge
	2. Plain colours
	3. Trend-setters

Description	U.S. $	Can. $	U.K. £
TV tray	30.00	45.00	15.00

Shape 2113-2116 Dish

Designer:	Albert Hallam in 1967
Issued:	1967 - 1969
Size:	Shape 2113 — 5 ½", 14.0 cm
	Shape 2116 — 6 ½", 16.5 cm
Design:	Gilt edge

Description	U.S. $	Can. $	U.K. £
Dish	20.00	30.00	10.00

Note: Set of four with shapes 2117 and 2120.

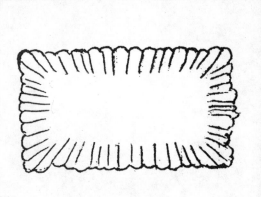

Shape 2117 Dish

Designer:	Albert Hallam in 1967
Issued:	1967 - 1969
Size:	7 ½" x 5", 19.1 x 12.7 cm
Design:	Gilt edge

Description	U.S. $	Can. $	U.K. £
Dish	30.00	45.00	15.00

Note: Set of four with shapes 2113, 2116 and 2120.

Shape 2120 Sandwich tray

Designer:	Albert Hallam in 1967
Issued:	1967 - 1969
Size:	11" x 5 ½", 27.9 x 14.0 cm
Design:	Gilt edge

Description	U.S. $	Can. $	U.K. £
Sandwich tray	35.00	50.00	18.00

Note: Set of four with shapes 2113, 2116 and 2117.

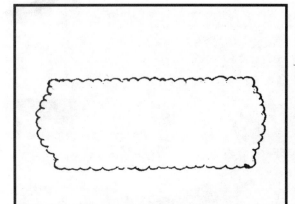

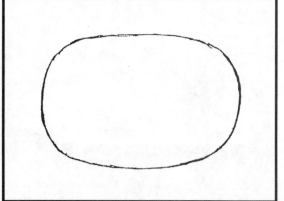

Shape 2164 Sandwich tray, large

Designer:	Albert Hallam in 1967
Issued:	1967 - 1969
Size:	12 ½" x 5 ½", 31.7 x 14.0 cm
Design:	Gilt edge

Description	U.S. $	Can. $	U.K. £
Sandwich tray	40.00	60.00	20.00

Shape 2244 Steak dish, no rim

Designer:	Graham Tongue in 1968
Issued:	1968 - 1969
Size:	10" x 8", 25.4 x 20.3 cm
Design:	Trend-setters (Verona only)

Description	U.S. $	Can. $	U.K. £
Steak dish	40.00	60.00	20.00

TROUGHS

This section lists fourteen pieces for holding flowers which because of their shape can not be included with the vases and bowls. Some of these were posy troughs, designed in a variety of shapes to hold short stemmed flowers, moss or heather in a well or trough of water. A special small-sized candle-holder (Shape 295) was modelled to slide into these (e.g. Shape 294), thus making it possible to combine flowers and candles in the one display. Other shapes of troughs are more in the nature of window boxes.

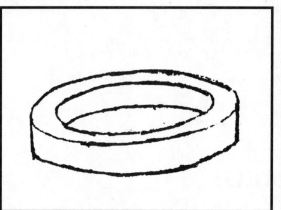

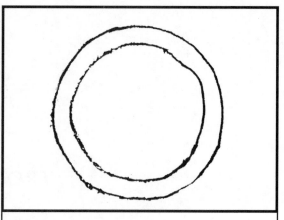

Shape 268   Round posy trough

Designer: Unknown
Issued: 1934 - by 1954
Diameter: 6, 15 cm
Colour: 1. Assorted decorations - satin matt
             2. White - matt

Market	Range
U.S.A.	$30.00 - 50.00
Canada	$45.00 - 75.00
U.K.	£15.00 - 25.00

Shape 294   Round posy trough

Designer: Mr. Symcox in 1935
Issued: 1935 - by 1963
Diameter: 10, 25.4 cm
Colour: 1. Assorted decorations - satin matt
             2. White - matt

Market	Range
U.S.A.	$30.00 - 50.00
Canada	$45.00 - 75.00
U.K.	£15.00 - 25.00

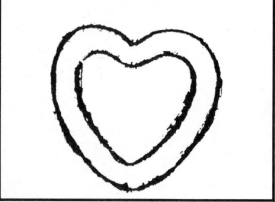

Shape 296   Horseshoe posy trough

Designer: Mr. Symcox in 1935
Issued: 1935 - by 1963
Width: 5 ½, 14 cm
Colour: 1. Assorted decorations - satin matt
             2. White - matt

Market	Range
U.S.A.	$30.00 - 50.00
Canada	$45.00 - 75.00
U.K.	£15.00 - 25.00

Shape 297   Heart shaped posy trough

Designer: Mr. Symcox in 1935
Issued: 1935 - by 1963
Width: 6, 15 cm
Colour: 1. Assorted decorations - satin matt
             2. White - matt

Market	Range
U.S.A.	$30.00 - 50.00
Canada	$45.00 - 75.00
U.K.	£15.00 - 25.00

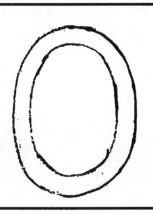

Shape 298   **Oval shaped posy trough**

Designer: Mr. Symcox in 1935
Issued: 1935 - by 1954
Size: 10 x 8, 25.4 x 20.3 cm
Colour: 1. Assorted decorations - satin matt
       2. White - matt

Market	Range
U.S.A.	$30.00 - 50.00
Canada	$45.00 - 75.00
U.K.	£15.00 - 25.00

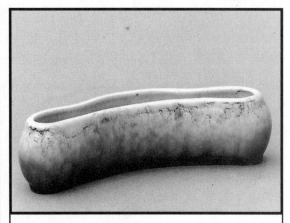

Shape 452/1/2 Posy trough

Designer: Mr. Symcox in 1936
Issued: 1936 - by 1963
Size: 1. Shape 452/1 — 9 ½ x 2, 24 x 5 cm
       2. Shape 452/2 — 7 ½ x 2, 19.1 x 5 cm
Colour: 1. Assorted decorations - satin matt
       2. White - matt

Market	Range
U.S.A.	$20.00 - 50.00
Canada	$30.00 - 75.00
U.K.	£10.00 - 25.00

Shape 459   **Posy trough**

Designer: James Hayward in 1936
Issued: 1937 - by 1954
Length: 10, 25.4 cm
Colour: 1. Assorted decorations - satin matt
       2. White - matt

Market	Range
U.S.A.	$40.00 - 75.00
Canada	$60.00 - 100.00
U.K.	£20.00 - 35.00

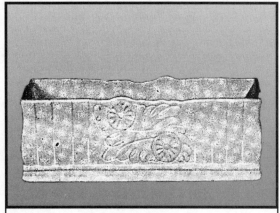

Shape 491   **Window box, trough**

Designer: Mr. Symcox in 1937
Issued: 1937 - by 1969
Size: 12 x 3 ½, 30.5 x 8.9 cm
Colour: 1. Assorted decorations - satin matt
       2. White or black - matt

Market	Range
U.S.A.	$40.00 - 75.00
Canada	$60.00 - 100.00
U.K.	£20.00 - 35.00

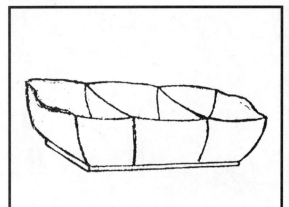

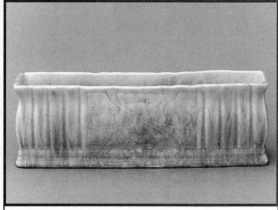

Shape 608   **Trough with three sections**

Designer:	Mr. Symcox in 1938
Issued:	1938 - by 1954
Size:	Unknown
Colour:	1. Assorted decorations - satin matt
	2. White - matt

Market	Range
U.S.A.	$40.00 - 75.00
Canada	$60.00 - 100.00
U.K.	£20.00 - 35.00

Shape 732   **Window box trough**

Designer:	James Hayward in 1939
Issued:	1939 - by 1968
Size:	12 x 3 ½, 30.5 x 8.9 cm
Colour:	1. Assorted decorations - satin matt
	2. White - matt

Market	Range
U.S.A.	$40.00 - 75.00
Canada	$60.00 - 100.00
U.K.	£20.00 - 35.00

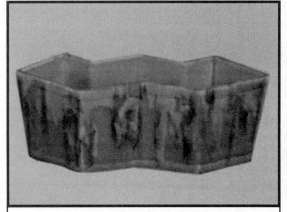

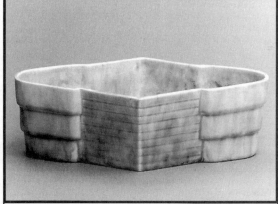

Shape 746   **Trough**

Designer:	Mr. Watkin in 1939
Issued:	1939 - by 1954
Size:	10 x 3 ½, 25.4 x 8.9 cm
Colour:	1. Assorted decorations - satin matt
	2. White - matt

Market	Range
U.S.A.	$40.00 - 75.00
Canada	$60.00 - 100.00
U.K.	£20.00 - 35.00

Shape 747   **Trough**

Designer:	Mr. Symcox in 1939
Issued:	1939 - by 1954
Size:	11 x 7 ¼ x 3 ½, 27.9 x 18.4 x 8.9 cm
Colour:	1. Assorted decorations - satin matt
	2. White - matt

Market	Range
U.S.A.	$40.00 - 75.00
Canada	$60.00 - 100.00
U.K.	£20.00 - 35.00

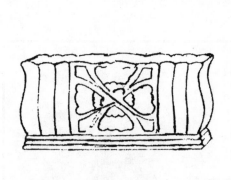

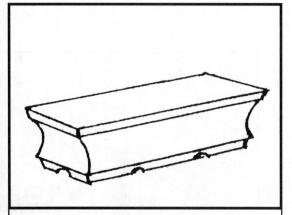

Shape 1356 Window box trough

Designer: Albert Hallam in 1954
Issued: 1955 - 1967
Length: 8, 20.3 cm
Colour: 1. Assorted decorations - satin matt
2. White or black - matt

Market	Range
U.S.A.	$40.00 - 75.00
Canada	$60.00 - 100.00
U.K.	£20.00 - 35.00

Shape 2279 Trough

Designer: Albert Hallam in 1969
Issued: 1969 - 1970
Size: 10 x 5 x 2 ½, 25.4 x 12.7 x 6.4 cm
Colour: 1. Assorted decorations - satin matt
2. White or black - matt
3. Copper - lustre

Market	Range
U.S.A.	$40.00 - 75.00
Canada	$60.00 - 100.00
U.K.	£20.00 - 35.00

Shape 2016, Shape 2014, Shape 2012

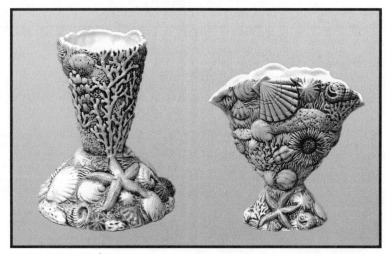

Shape 2020, Shape 2015

VASES AND PLANT POT HOLDERS

This section lists three hundred and sixteen shapes and is the largest single group.

Following the development of the matt glazes in 1933 there was an explosion in the number of vases modelled and by 1934 a hundred new shapes, which included jugs, in a multitude of different decorations, had been produced. Many of these were exhibited at The British Industries Fair in February of the same year.

Beswick continued to produce many vases over the years until 1972, when production of ornamental ware ceased.

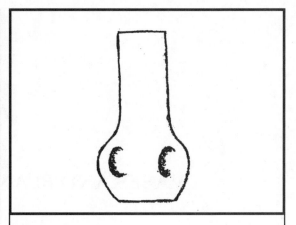

Shape 21   **Vase, two-handled**

Designer:	Mr. Symcox c.1933
Issued:	c.1933 - by 1940
Height:	12", 30.5 cm
Colour:	1. Assorted decorations - satin matt
	2. White - matt

Market	Range
U.S.A.	$30.00 - 150.00
Canada	$45.00 - 225.00
U.K.	£15.00 - 80.00

Shape 24   **Vase**

Designer:	Mr. Symcox c.1933
Issued:	c.1933 - by 1940
Size:	Unknown
Colour:	1. Assorted decorations - satin matt
	2. White - matt

Market	Range
U.S.A.	$30.00 - 150.00
Canada	$45.00 - 225.00
U.K.	£15.00 - 80.00

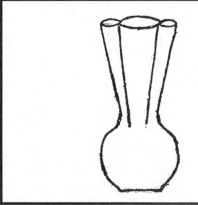

Shape 25   **Vase**

Designer:	Mr. Symcox c.1933
Issued:	c.1933 - by 1940
Height:	11", 27.9 cm
Colour:	1. Assorted decorations - satin matt
	2. White - matt

Market	Range
U.S.A.	$30.00 - 150.00
Canada	$45.00 - 225.00
U.K.	£15.00 - 80.00

Shape 27   **Fluted Vase**

Designer:	Mr. Symcox c.1933
Issued:	c.1933 - by 1940
Size:	Unknown
Colour:	1. Assorted decorations - satin matt
	2. White - matt

Market	Range
U.S.A.	$30.00 - 150.00
Canada	$45.00 - 225.00
U.K.	£15.00 - 80.00

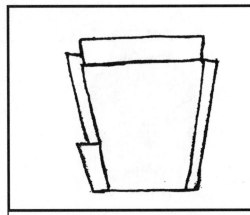

Shape 29   Vase

Designer: Mr. Symcox c.1933
Issued: c.1933 - by 1940
Size: Unknown
Colour: 1. Assorted decorations - satin matt
           2. White - matt

Market	Range
U.S.A.	$30.00 - 150.00
Canada	$45.00 - 225.00
U.K.	£15.00 - 80.00

Shape 30   Vase

Designer: Mr. Symcox c.1933
Issued: c.1933 - by 1940
Height: 9", 22.9 cm
Colour: 1. Assorted decorations - satin matt
           2. White - matt

Market	Range
U.S.A.	$30.00 - 150.00
Canada	$45.00 - 225.00
U.K.	£15.00 - 80.00

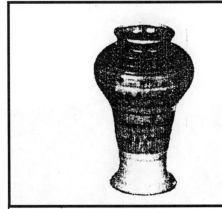

Shape 31   Vase

Designer: Mr. Symcox c.1933
Issued: c.1933 - by 1940
Size: 10", 25.4 cm
Colour: 1. Assorted decorations - satin matt
           2. White - matt

Market	Range
U.S.A.	$30.00 - 150.00
Canada	$45.00 - 225.00
U.K.	£15.00 - 80.00

Shape 32   Vase

Designer: Mr. Symcox c.1933
Issued: c.1933 - by 1940
Size: Unknown
Colour: 1. Assorted decorations - satin matt
           2. White - matt

Market	Range
U.S.A.	$30.00 - 150.00
Canada	$45.00 - 225.00
U.K.	£15.00 - 80.00

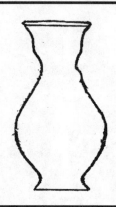

Shape 33   Vase

Designer:	Mr. Symcox c.1933
Issued:	c.1933 - by 1940
Size:	Unknown
Colour:	1. Assorted decorations - satin matt
	2. White - matt

Market	Range
U.S.A.	$30.00 - 150.00
Canada	$45.00 - 225.00
U.K.	£15.00 - 80.00

Shape 34   Vase

Designer:	Mr. Symcox c.1933
Issued:	c.1933 - by 1940
Size:	8 ¼", 21 cm
Colour:	1. Assorted decorations - satin matt
	2. White- matt

Market	Range
U.S.A.	$30.00 - 150.00
Canada	$45.00 - 225.00
U.K.	£15.00 - 80.00

Shape 35   Ribbed vase

Designer:	Mr. Symcox c.1933
Issued:	c.1933 - by 1940
Size:	8", 20.3 cm
Colour:	1. Assorted decorations - satin matt
	2. White- matt

Market	Range
U.S.A.	$30.00 - 150.00
Canada	$45.00 - 225.00
U.K.	£15.00 - 80.00

Shape 36   Vase, two-handled

Designer:	Mr. Symcox c.1933
Issued:	c.1933 - by 1940
Size:	7 ½", 19.1 cm
Colour:	1. Assorted decorations - satin matt
	2. White- matt

Market	Range
U.S.A.	$30.00 - 150.00
Canada	$45.00 - 225.00
U.K.	£15.00 - 80.00

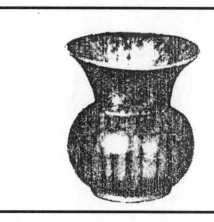

Shape 37   Vase, two-handled

Designer:	Mr. Symcox c.1933
Issued:	c.1933 - by 1954
Size:	7", 17.8 cm
Colour:	1. Assorted decorations - satin matt
	2. White - matt

Market	Range
U.S.A.	$30.00 - 150.00
Canada	$45.00 - 225.00
U.K.	£15.00 - 80.00

Shape 38   Vase

Designer:	Mr. Symcox c.1933
Issued:	c.1933 - by 1954
Size:	6 ½", 16.5 cm
Colour:	1. Assorted decorations - satin matt
	2. White - matt

Market	Range
U.S.A.	$30.00 - 150.00
Canada	$45.00 - 225.00
U.K.	£15.00 - 80.00

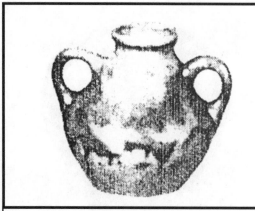

Shape 39   Vase

Designer:	Mr. Symcox c.1933
Issued:	c.1933 - by 1940
Size:	7", 17.8 cm
Colour:	1. Assorted decorations - satin matt
	2. White - matt

Market	Range
U.S.A.	$30.00 - 150.00
Canada	$45.00 - 225.00
U.K.	£15.00 - 80.00

Shape 40   Vase, two-handled

Designer:	Mr. Symcox c.1933
Issued:	c.1933 - by 1940
Size:	6", 15 cm
Colour:	1. Assorted decorations - satin matt
	2. White - matt

Market	Range
U.S.A.	$30.00 - 150.00
Canada	$45.00 - 225.00
U.K.	£15.00 - 80.00

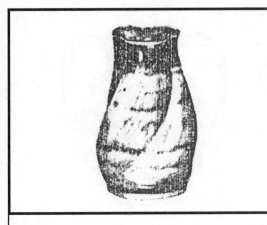

Shape 41   Vase, two-handled

Designer:	Mr. Symcox c.1933
Issued:	c.1933 - by 1940
Size:	5 ¾", 14.6 cm
Colour:	1. Assorted decorations - satin matt
	2. White - matt

Market	Range
U.S.A.	$30.00 - 150.00
Canada	$45.00 - 225.00
U.K.	£15.00 - 80.00

Shape 42   Vase

Designer:	Mr. Symcox c.1933
Issued:	c.1933 - by 1940
Size:	7", 17.8 cm
Colour:	1. Assorted decorations - satin matt
	2. White - matt

Market	Range
U.S.A.	$30.00 - 150.00
Canada	$45.00 - 225.00
U.K.	£15.00 - 80.00

Shape 43   Vase, two-handled

Designer:	Mr. Symcox c.1933
Issued:	c.1933 - by 1940
Size:	4", 10.1 cm
Colour:	1. Assorted decorations - satin matt
	2. White - matt

Market	Range
U.S.A.	$30.00 - 150.00
Canada	$45.00 - 225.00
U.K.	£15.00 - 80.00

Shape 44   Vase

Designer:	Mr. Symcox c.1933
Issued:	c.1933 - by 1940
Size:	6", 15 cm
Colour:	1. Assorted decorations - satin matt
	2. White - matt

Market	Range
U.S.A.	$30.00 - 150.00
Canada	$45.00 - 225.00
U.K.	£15.00 - 80.00

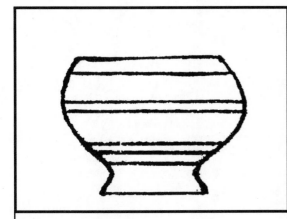

Shape 45	Ribbed vase
Designer:	Mr. Symcox c.1933
Issued:	c.1933 - by 1940
Size:	Unknown
Colour:	1. Assorted decorations - satin matt
	2. White - matt

Market	Range
U.S.A.	$30.00 - 150.00
Canada	$45.00 - 225.00
U.K.	£15.00 - 80.00

Shape 46	Vase
Designer:	Mr. Symcox c.1933
Issued:	c.1933 - by 1940
Size:	Unknown
Colour:	1. Assorted decorations - satin matt
	2. White - matt

Market	Range
U.S.A.	$30.00 - 150.00
Canada	$45.00 - 225.00
U.K.	£15.00 - 80.00

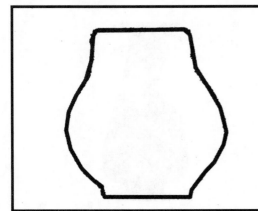

Shape 47	Vase/Lamp
Designer:	Mr. Symcox c.1933
Issued:	c.1933 - by 1940
Size:	Unknown
Colour:	1. Assorted decorations - satin matt
	2. White - matt

Market	Range
U.S.A.	$30.00 - 150.00
Canada	$45.00 - 225.00
U.K.	£15.00 - 80.00

Shape 50	Leyden, vase
Designer:	Unknown
Issued:	By 1930 - by 1937
Size:	11 ½", 29.2 cm
Colour:	Assorted decorations - gloss

Market	Range
U.S.A.	$30.00 - 150.00
Canada	$45.00 - 225.00
U.K.	£15.00 - 80.00

Photograph not
available
at press time

Shape 51   Opal, two-handled footed vase

Designer:	Unknown
Issued:	By 1930 - by 1937
Size:	12", 30.5 cm
Colour:	Assorted decorations - gloss

Market	Range
U.S.A.	$50.00 - 150.00
Canada	$75.00 - 225.00
U.K.	£25.00 - 80.00

Shape 52   Bude, vase

Designer:	Unknown
Issued:	By 1931 - by 1937
Size:	10", 25.4 cm
Colour:	Assorted decorations - gloss

Market	Range
U.S.A.	$50.00 - 150.00
Canada	$75.00 - 225.00
U.K.	£25.00 - 80.00

Shape 54   Roslin, vase

Designer:	Unknown
Issued:	By 1926 - by 1937
Size:	10 ½", 26.7 cm
Colour:	Assorted decorations - gloss

Market	Range
U.S.A.	$50.00 - 150.00
Canada	$75.00 - 225.00
U.K.	£25.00 - 80.00

Shape 55   Ryde, footed vase

Designer:	Unknown
Issued:	By 1930 - by 1937
Size:	10 ½", 26.7 cm
Colour:	Assorted decorations - gloss

Market	Range
U.S.A.	$50.00 - 150.00
Canada	$75.00 - 225.00
U.K.	£25.00 - 80.00

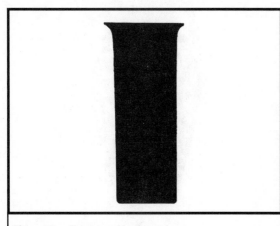

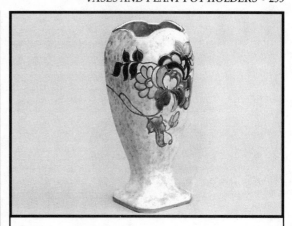

Shape 56	Rose, vase in three sizes
Designer:	Unknown
Issued:	By 1930 - by 1937
Sizes:	1. Large — 8 ½″, 21.6 cm
	2. Medium — 7 ½″, 19.1 cm
	3. Small — 6 ½″, 16.5 cm
Colour:	Assorted decorations - gloss

Market	Range
U.S.A.	$50.00 - 150.00
Canada	$75.00 - 225.00
U.K.	£25.00 - 80.00

Shape 57	Rhos, vase
Designer:	Unknown
Issued:	By 1929 - by 1937
Size:	9″, 22.9 cm
Colour:	Assorted decorations - gloss

Market	Range
U.S.A.	$50.00 - 150.00
Canada	$75.00 - 225.00
U.K.	£25.00 - 80.00

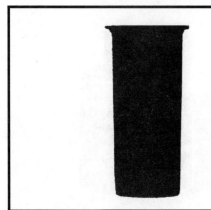

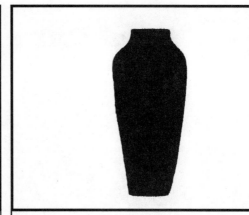

Shape 58	Flora, vase in three sizes
Designer:	Unknown
Issued:	By 1926 - by 1937
Sizes:	1. Large — 8 ½″, 21.6 cm
	2. Medium — 7 ½″, 19.1 cm
	3. Small — 6 ½″, 16.5 cm
Colour:	Assorted decorations - gloss

Market	Range
U.S.A.	$50.00 - 150.00
Canada	$75.00 - 225.00
U.K.	£25.00 - 80.00

Shape 59	Len, vase in three sizes
Designer:	Unknown
Issued:	By 1923 - by 1937
Sizes:	1. Large — 8 ½″, 21.6 cm
	2. Medium — 7 ½″, 19.1 cm
	3. Small — 5 ½″, 14 cm
Colour:	Assorted decorations - gloss

Market	Range
U.S.A.	$50.00 - 150.00
Canada	$75.00 - 225.00
U.K.	£25.00 - 80.00

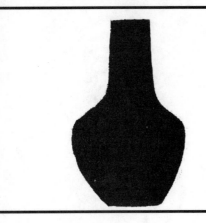

Shape 60   Windsor, vase

Designer: Unknown
Issued: By 1930 - by 1937
Size: 9", 22.9 cm
Colour: Assorted decorations - gloss

Market	Range
U.S.A.	$50.00 - 150.00
Canada	$75.00 - 225.00
U.K.	£25.00 - 80.00

Shape 61   Regal, vase

Designer: Unknown
Issued: By 1926 - by 1937
Size: 6 ½", 16.5 cm
Colour: Assorted decorations - gloss

Market	Range
U.S.A.	$50.00 - 150.00
Canada	$75.00 - 225.00
U.K.	£25.00 - 80.00

Shape 64   Alfa, vase

Designer: Unknown
Issued: c.1933 - by 1940
Size: 8 ½", 21.6 cm
Colour: 1. Assorted decorations - satin matt
             2. White - matt

Market	Range
U.S.A.	$30.00 - 150.00
Canada	$45.00 - 225.00
U.K.	£15.00 - 80.00

Shape 65   Cleo, vase

Designer: Unknown
Issued: c.1933 - by 1940
Size: 8", 20.3 cm
Colour: 1. Assorted decorations - satin matt
             2. White - matt

Market	Range
U.S.A.	$30.00 - 150.00
Canada	$45.00 - 225.00
U.K.	£15.00 - 80.00

Shape 66   **Crete, vase**

Designer: Unknown
Issued: c.1933 - by 1940
Size: 8", 20.3 cm
Colour: 1. Assorted decorations - satin matt
       2. White - matt

Market	Range
U.S.A.	$30.00 - 150.00
Canada	$45.00 - 225.00
U.K.	£15.00 - 80.00

Shape 68   **Arran, vase**

Designer: Unknown
Issued: c.1933 - by 1940
Size: 5", 12.7 cm
Colour: 1. Assorted decorations - satin matt
       2. White - matt

Market	Range
U.S.A.	$30.00 - 150.00
Canada	$45.00 - 225.00
U.K.	£15.00 - 80.00

Shape 69   **Eler , vase**

Designer: Unknown
Issued: c.1933 - by 1963
Size: 4 ¼", 10.8 cm
Colour: 1. Assorted decorations - satin matt
       2. White - matt

Market	Range
U.S.A.	$30.00 - 150.00
Canada	$45.00 - 225.00
U.K.	£15.00 - 80.00

Shape 70   **Ciro, vase**

Designer: Unknown
Issued: c.1933 - by 1940
Size: 7", 17.8 cm
Colour: 1. Assorted decorations - satin matt
       2. White - matt

Market	Range
U.S.A.	$30.00 - 150.00
Canada	$45.00 - 225.00
U.K.	£15.00 - 80.00

Shape 73   **Elite, vase**

Designer: Unknown
Issued: c.1934 - by 1940
Size: 8", 20.3 cm
Colour: 1. Assorted decorations - satin matt
                2. White - matt

Market	Range
U.S.A.	$30.00 - 150.00
Canada	$45.00 - 225.00
U.K.	£15.00 - 80.00

Shape 75   **Vase/Lamp base**

Designer: Mr. Symcox c.1933
Issued: c.1933 - by 1940
Size: 6 ½", 16.5 cm
Colour: 1. Assorted decorations - satin matt
                2. White - matt

Market	Range
U.S.A.	$30.00 - 150.00
Canada	$45.00 - 225.00
U.K.	£15.00 - 80.00

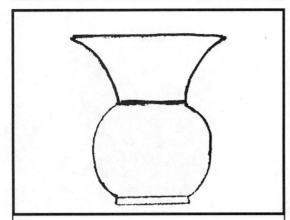

Shape 76   **Vase**

Designer: Mr. Symcox c.1933
Issued: c.1934 - by 1940
Size: Unknown
Colour: 1. Assorted decorations - satin matt
                2. White - matt

Market	Range
U.S.A.	$30.00 - 150.00
Canada	$45.00 - 225.00
U.K.	£15.00 - 80.00

Shape 77   **Vase**

Designer: Mr. Symcox c.1933
Issued: c.1934 - by 1940
Size: 9", 22.9 cm
Colour: 1. Assorted decorations - satin matt
                2. White - matt

Market	Range
U.S.A.	$30.00 - 150.00
Canada	$45.00 - 225.00
U.K.	£15.00 - 80.00

Shape 79   Vase

Designer:	Mr. Symcox c.1933
Issued:	c.1934 - by 1940
Size:	8″, 20.3 cm
Colour:	1. Assorted decorations - satin matt
	2. White - matt

Market	Range
U.S.A.	$30.00 - 150.00
Canada	$45.00 - 225.00
U.K.	£15.00 - 80.00

Shape 80/1/2   Vase, in two sizes

Designer:	Mr. Symcox c.1933
Issued:	c.1934 - by 1954
Size:	1. Shape 80/1 — 10 ½″, 26.7 cm
	2. Shape 80/2 — unknown
Colour:	1. Assorted decorations - satin matt
	2. White - matt

Market	Range
U.S.A.	$30.00 - 150.00
Canada	$45.00 - 225.00
U.K.	£15.00 - 80.00

Shape 90   Vase

Designer:	Mr. Symcox c.1933
Issued:	c.1934 - by 1940
Size:	9″, 22.9 cm
Colour:	1. Assorted decorations - satin matt
	2. White - matt

Market	Range
U.S.A.	$30.00 - 150.00
Canada	$45.00 - 225.00
U.K.	£15.00 - 80.00

Shape 93   Vase

Designer:	Mr. Symcox c.1933
Issued:	c.1934 - by 1954
Size:	7 ¾″, 19.7 cm
Colour:	1. Assorted decorations - satin matt
	2. White - matt

Market	Range
U.S.A.	$30.00 - 150.00
Canada	$45.00 - 225.00
U.K.	£15.00 - 80.00

Shape 95   **Vase, three-handled**

Designer: Mr. Symcox c.1933
Issued: c.1934 - by 1940
Size: 10", 25.4 cm
Colour: 1. Assorted decorations - satin matt
               2. White - matt

Market	Range
U.S.A.	$30.00 - 150.00
Canada	$45.00 - 225.00
U.K.	£15.00 - 80.00

Shape 96   **Vase**

Designer: Mr. Symcox c.1933
Issued: c.1934 - by 1940
Size: 8", 20.3 cm
Colour: 1. Assorted decorations - satin matt
               2. White - matt

Market	Range
U.S.A.	$30.00 - 150.00
Canada	$45.00 - 225.00
U.K.	£15.00 - 80.00

Shape 97   **Vase**

Designer: Mr. Symcox c.1933
Issued: c.1934 - by 1940
Size: 5 ½", 14 cm
Colour: 1. Assorted decorations - satin matt
               2. White - matt

Market	Range
U.S.A.	$30.00 - 150.00
Canada	$45.00 - 225.00
U.K.	£15.00 - 80.00

Shape 100   **Vase**

Designer: Mr. Symcox c.1933
Issued: c.1934 - by 1940
Size: 8", 20.3 cm
Colour: 1. Assorted decorations - satin matt
               2. White - matt

Market	Range
U.S.A.	$30.00 - 150.00
Canada	$45.00 - 225.00
U.K.	£15.00 - 80.00

Shape 101 Vase

Designer: Mr. Symcox c.1933
Issued: c.1934 - by 1966
Size: 6 ¼", 15.9 cm
Colours: 1. Various decorations - satin matt
2. White or black - matt

Market	Range
U.S.A.	$30.00 - 150.00
Canada	$45.00 - 225.00
U.K.	£15.00 - 80.00

Shape 102 Vase

Designer: Mr. Symcox c.1933
Issued: c.1934 - by 1940
Size: 9", 22.9 cm
Colour: 1. Assorted decorations - satin matt
2. White - matt

Market	Range
U.S.A.	$30.00 - 150.00
Canada	$45.00 - 225.00
U.K.	£15.00 - 80.00

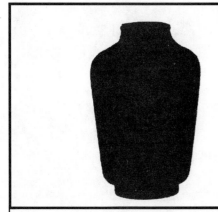

Shape 105/1/2/3 Lille, vase with cover in three sizes

Designer: Unknown
Issued: By 1929 - by 1937
Size: 1. Shape 105/1 — 10 ½", 26.7
2. Shape 105/2 — Unknown
3. Shape 105/3 — Unknown
Colour: Assorted decorations - gloss

Market	Range
U.S.A.	$30.00 - 150.00
Canada	$45.00 - 225.00
U.K.	£15.00 - 80.00

Shape 106 Blythe, vase

Designer: Unknown
Issued: By 1923 - by 1937
Size: 9", 22.9 cm
Colour: Assorted decorations - gloss

Market	Range
U.S.A.	$30.00 - 150.00
Canada	$45.00 - 225.00
U.K.	£15.00 - 80.00

Shape 107   Sparta, vase

Designer: Unknown
Issued: By 1930 - by 1937
Size: 9 ½", 24 cm
Colour: Assorted decorations - gloss

Market	Range
U.S.A.	$50.00 - 150.00
Canada	$75.00 - 225.00
U.K.	£25.00 - 80.00

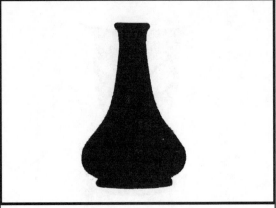

Shape 108   York, vase

Designer: Unknown
Issued: By 1930 - by 1937
Size: 9", 22.9 cm
Colour: Assorted decorations - gloss

Market	Range
U.S.A.	$50.00 - 150.00
Canada	$75.00 - 225.00
U.K.	£25.00 - 80.00

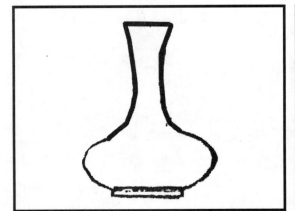

Shape 109   Lily, vase

Designer: Unknown
Issued: By 1923 - by 1937
Size: 5 ½", 14 cm
Colour: Assorted decorations - gloss

Market	Range
U.S.A.	$50.00 - 150.00
Canada	$75.00 - 225.00
U.K.	£25.00 - 80.00

Shape 110/1/2 Bell, vase

Designer: Unknown
Issued: By 1930 - by 1937
Size: 1. Shape 110/1 — 6 ¼", 15.9 cm
             2. Shape 110/2 — 7 ¼", 18.4 cm
Colour: Assorted decorations - gloss

Market	Range
U.S.A.	$50.00 - 150.00
Canada	$75.00 - 225.00
U.K.	£25.00 - 80.00

Shape 111   **Lynton, vase**

Designer: Unknown
Issued: By 1930 - by 1937
Size: 7 ½", 19.1 cm
Colour: Assorted decorations - gloss

Market	Range
U.S.A.	$50.00 - 150.00
Canada	$75.00 - 225.00
U.K.	£25.00 - 80.00

Shape 113   **Kew, vase**

Designer: Unknown
Issued: By 1923 - by 1937
Size: 12", 30.5 cm
Colour: Assorted decorations - gloss

Market	Range
U.S.A.	$50.00 - 150.00
Canada	$75.00 - 225.00
U.K.	£25.00 - 80.00

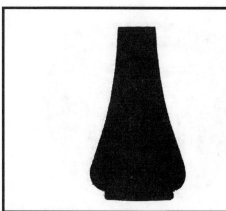

Shape 115   **Ruby, vase**

Designer: Unknown
Issued: By 1930 - by 1937
Size: 9", 22.9 cm
Colour: Assorted decorations - gloss

Market	Range
U.S.A.	$50.00 - 150.00
Canada	$75.00 - 225.00
U.K.	£25.00 - 80.00

Shape 116   **Vase/Lamp base**

Designer: Mr. Symcox c.1933
IssuedL: c.1934 - 1940
Size: Unknown
Colour: 1. Assorted decorations - satin matt
            2. White - matt

Market	Range
U.S.A.	$30.00 - 150.00
Canada	$45.00 - 225.00
U.K.	£15.00 - 80.00

Shape 117   Vase

Designer:	Mr. Symcox c.1933
Issued:	c.1934 - by 1940
Size:	5", 12.7 cm
Colour:	1. Assorted decorations - satin matt
	2. White - matt

Market	Range
U.S.A.	$30.00 - 150.00
Canada	$45.00 - 225.00
U.K.	£15.00 - 80.00

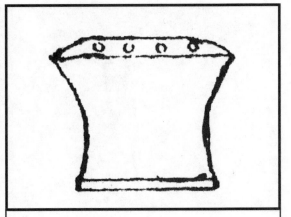

Shape 118   Vase with flower holder

Designer:	Mr. Symcox c.1933
Issued:	c.1934 - 1940
Size:	Unknown
Colour:	1. Assorted decorations - satin matt
	2. White - matt

Market	Range
U.S.A.	$30.00 - 150.00
Canada	$45.00 - 225.00
U.K.	£15.00 - 80.00

Shape 120   Vase

Designer:	Mr. Symcox c.1934
Issued:	c.1934 - by 1966
Size:	8 ½", 21.6 cm
Colour:	1. Assorted decorations - satin matt
	2. White or black - matt

Market	Range
U.S.A.	$30.00 - 150.00
Canada	$45.00 - 225.00
U.K.	£15.00 - 80.00

Shape 121   Vase

Designer:	Albert Hallam c.1934
Issued:	c.1934 - by 1940
Size:	7", 17.8 cm
Colour:	1. Assorted decorations - satin matt
	2. White - matt

Market	Range
U.S.A.	$30.00 - 150.00
Canada	$45.00 - 225.00
U.K.	£15.00 - 80.00

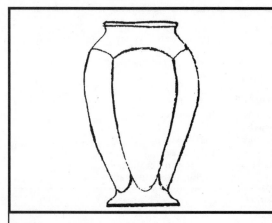

Shape 122   Dresden, vase

Designer: Albert Hallam c.1934
Issued: c.1934 - by 1940
Size: Unknown
Colour: 1. Assorted decorations - satin matt
                  2. White - matt

Market	Range
U.S.A.	$30.00 - 150.00
Canada	$45.00 - 225.00
U.K.	£15.00 - 80.00

Shape 124   Vase

Designer: Albert Hallam c.1934
Issued: c.1934 - by 1940
Size: 5 ½", 14 cm
Colour: 1. Assorted decorations - satin matt
                  2. White - matt

Market	Range
U.S.A.	$30.00 - 150.00
Canada	$45.00 - 225.00
U.K.	£15.00 - 80.00

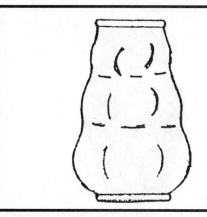

Shape 126   Vase

Designer: Mr. Owen c.1934
Issued: c.1934 - by 1940
Size: 9", 22.9 cm
Colour: 1. Assorted decorations - satin matt
                  2. White - matt

Market	Range
U.S.A.	$30.00 - 150.00
Canada	$45.00 - 225.00
U.K.	£15.00 - 80.00

Shape 127   Vase

Designer: Mr. Symcox c.1934
Issued: c.1934 - by 1940
Size: Unknown
Colour: 1. Assorted decorations - satin matt
                  2. White - matt

Market	Range
U.S.A.	$30.00 - 150.00
Canada	$45.00 - 225.00
U.K.	£15.00 - 80.00

Shape 128   Vase

Designer: Mr. Symcox c.1934
Issued: 1935 - by 1954
Reissued: 1962 - 1967
Size: 11 ½", 29.2 cm
Colour: 1. Various decorations - satin matt
                2. White or black - matt

Market	Range
U.S.A.	$30.00 - 150.00
Canada	$45.00 - 225.00
U.K.	£15.00 - 80.00

Note: Continued as "Caprice Series"
             Issued: 1968 - by 1972
             Colours: Orange, turquoise or yellow.

Shape 130   Vase

Designer: Mr. Symcox c.1934
Issued: c.1934 - by 1940
Size: 5 ½", 14 cm
Colour: 1. Assorted decorations - satin matt
               2. White - matt

Market	Range
U.S.A.	$30.00 - 150.00
Canada	$45.00 - 225.00
U.K.	£15.00 - 80.00

Shape 132   Vase

Designer: Mr. Symcox c.1934
Issued: c.1934 - by 1940
Size: 8", 20.3 cm
Colour: 1. Assorted decorations - satin matt
               2. White - matt

Market	Range
U.S.A.	$30.00 - 150.00
Canada	$45.00 - 225.00
U.K.	£15.00 - 80.00

Shape 133   Vase

Designer:	Albert Hallam and Mr. Owen c.1934
Issued:	c.1934 - by 1940
Height:	8 ½", 21.6 cm
Colour:	1. Assorted decorations - satin matt
	2. White - matt

Market	Range
U.S.A.	$30.00 - 150.00
Canada	$45.00 - 225.00
U.K.	£15.00 - 80.00

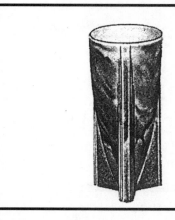

Shape 134   Vase

Designer:	Mr. Owen c.1934
Issued:	c.1934 - by 1940
Height:	10", 25.4 cm
Colour:	1. Assorted decorations - satin matt
	2. White - matt

Market	Range
U.S.A.	$30.00 - 150.00
Canada	$45.00 - 225.00
U.K.	£15.00 - 80.00

Shape 135   Vase/Lamp base

Designer:	Unknown c.1934
Issued:	c.1934 - by 1940
Height :	5 ½", 14 cm
Colour:	1. Assorted decorations - satin matt
	2. White - matt

Market	Range
U.S.A.	$30.00 - 150.00
Canada	$45.00 - 225.00
U.K.	£15.00 - 80.00

Shape 138   Vase, two-handled

Designer:	Mr. Symcox c.1934
Issued:	c.1934 - by 1940
Height:	3 ½", 8.9 cm
Colour:	1. Assorted decorations - satin matt
	2. White - matt

Market	Range
U.S.A.	$30.00 - 150.00
Canada	$45.00 - 225.00
U.K.	£15.00 - 80.00

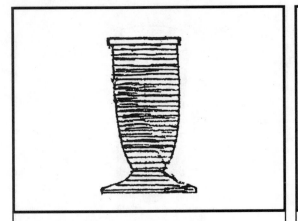

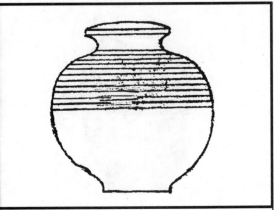

Shape 142   Vase

Designer:	Mr. Symcox c.1934
Issued:	c.1934 - by 1940
Height :	6", 15 cm
Colour:	1. Assorted decorations - satin matt
	2. White - matt

Market	Range
U.S.A.	$30.00 - 150.00
Canada	$45.00 - 225.00
U.K.	£15.00 - 80.00

Shape 143   Vase/Lamp

Designer:	Albert Hallam c.1934
Issued:	c.1934 - by 1940
Height:	9", 22.9 cm
Colour:	1. Assorted decorations - satin matt
	2. White - matt

Market	Range
U.S.A.	$30.00 - 150.00
Canada	$45.00 - 225.00
U.K.	£15.00 - 80.00

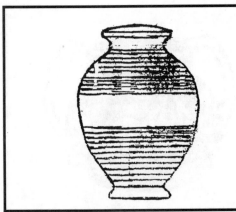

Shape 144   Vase/Lamp

Designer:	Albert Hallam c.1934
Issued:	c.1934 - by 1940
Height :	10 ½", 26.7 cm
Colour:	1. Assorted decorations - satin matt
	2. White - matt

Market	Range
U.S.A.	$30.00 - 150.00
Canada	$45.00 - 225.00
U.K.	£15.00 - 80.00

Shape 145   Vase

Designer:	Albert Hallam c.1934
Issued:	c.1934 - by 1940
Height:	6", 15 cm
Colour:	1. Assorted decorations - satin matt
	2. White - matt

Market	Range
U.S.A.	$30.00 - 150.00
Canada	$45.00 - 225.00
U.K.	£15.00 - 80.00

Shape 147   Vase

Designer: Mr. Symcox c.1934
Issued: c.1934 - by 1940
Height :   Unknown
Colour: 1. Assorted decorations - satin matt
             2. White - matt

Market	Range
U.S.A.	$30.00 - 150.00
Canada	$45.00 - 225.00
U.K.	£15.00 - 80.00

Shape 149   Vase, two-handled

Designer: Mr. Symcox c.1934
Issued: c.1934 - by 1940
Height: 6 ½", 16.5 cm
Colour: 1. Assorted decorations - satin matt
             2. White - matt

Market	Range
U.S.A.	$30.00 - 150.00
Canada	$45.00 - 225.00
U.K.	£15.00 - 80.00

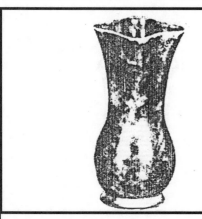

Shape 152   Vase

Designer: Mr. Symcox c.1934
Issued: c.1934 - by 1940
Height :   11 ½", 29.2 cm
Colour: 1. Assorted decorations - satin matt
             2. White - matt

Market	Range
U.S.A.	$30.00 - 150.00
Canada	$45.00 - 225.00
U.K.	£15.00 - 80.00

Shape 153   Vase

Designer: Mr. Symcox c.1934
Issued: c.1934 - by 1963
Height: 5 ¼", 13.3 cm
Colour: 1. Assorted decorations - satin matt
             2. White - matt

Market	Range
U.S.A.	$30.00 - 150.00
Canada	$45.00 - 225.00
U.K.	£15.00 - 80.00

Shape 154   Vase

Designer:	Mr. Symcox c.1934
Issued:	c.1934 - by 1940
Height:	5", 12.7 cm
Colour:	1. Assorted decorations - satin matt
	2. White - matt

Market	Range
U.S.A.	$30.00 - 150.00
Canada	$45.00 - 225.00
U.K.	£15.00 - 80.00

Shape 158   Vase, two-handled

Designer:	Mr. Symcox c.1933
Issued:	c.1934 - by 1940
Height:	5", 12.7 cm
Colour:	1. Assorted decorations - satin matt
	2. White - matt

Market	Range
U.S.A.	$30.00 - 150.00
Canada	$45.00 - 225.00
U.K.	£15.00 - 80.00

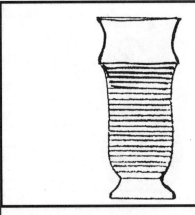

Shape 159   Vase, two-handled

Designer:	Mr. Symcox c.1934
Issued:	c.1934 - by 1940
Height:	5 ½", 14 cm
Colour:	1. Assorted decorations - satin matt
	2. White - matt

Market	Range
U.S.A.	$30.00 - 150.00
Canada	$45.00 - 225.00
U.K.	£15.00 - 80.00

Shape 161   Vase, two sizes

Designer:	Mr. Symcox c.1934
Issued:	c.1934 - by 1940
Heights:	Unknown
Colour:	1. Assorted decorations - satin matt
	2. White - matt

Market	Range
U.S.A.	$30.00 - 150.00
Canada	$45.00 - 225.00
U.K.	£15.00 - 80.00

Shape 164   Vase

Designer: Mr. Symcox c.1934
Issued: c.1934 - by 1940
Height :   Unknown
Colour: 1. Assorted decorations - satin matt
             2. White - matt

Market	Range
U.S.A.	$30.00 - 150.00
Canada	$45.00 - 225.00
U.K.	£15.00 - 80.00

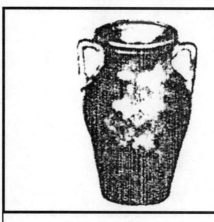

Shape 166   Vase, two-handled

Designer: Mr. Symcox c.1934
Issued: c.1934 - by 1940
Height: 6 ½", 16.5 cm
Colour: 1. Assorted decorations - satin matt
             2. White - matt

Market	Range
U.S.A.	$30.00 - 150.00
Canada	$45.00 - 225.00
U.K.	£15.00 - 80.00

Shape 167   Vase, two-handled

Designer: Mr. Symcox c.1934
Issued: c.1934 - by 1940
Height :   8 ½", 21.6 cm
Colour: 1. Assorted decorations - satin matt
             2. White - matt

Market	Range
U.S.A.	$30.00 - 150.00
Canada	$45.00 - 225.00
U.K.	£15.00 - 80.00

Shape 168   Vase, two-handled

Designer: Mr. Symcox c.1934
Issued: c.1934 - by 1940
Height: 7 ½", 19.1 cm
Colour: 1. Assorted decorations - satin matt
             2. White - matt

Market	Range
U.S.A.	$30.00 - 150.00
Canada	$45.00 - 225.00
U.K.	£15.00 - 80.00

Shape 169   Vase

Designer:	Mr. Owen c.1934
Issued:	c.1934 - by 1940
Height :	9", 22.9 cm
Colour:	1. Assorted decorations - satin matt
	2. White - matt

Market	Range
U.S.A.	$30.00 - 150.00
Canada	$45.00 - 225.00
U.K.	£15.00 - 80.00

Shape 180   Vase

Designer:	Mr. Symcox c.1934
Issued:	c.1934 - by 1954
Height:	8", 20.3 cm
Colour:	1 Assorted decorations - satin matt
	2. White - matt

Market	Range
U.S.A.	$30.00 - 150.00
Canada	$45.00 - 225.00
U.K.	£15.00 - 80.00

Shape 181   Vase

Designer:	Mr. Symcox c.1934
Issued:	c.1934 - by 1940
Height :	7 ¼", 18.4 cm
Colour:	1. Assorted decorations - satin matt
	2. White - matt

Market	Range
U.S.A.	$30.00 - 150.00
Canada	$45.00 - 225.00
U.K.	£15.00 - 80.00

Shape 182   Vase, two- handled

Designer:	Mr. Symcox c.1934
Issued:	c.1934 - by 1940
Height:	11 ¼", 28.5 cm
Colour:	1. Assorted decorations - satin matt
	2. White - matt

Market	Range
U.S.A.	$30.00 - 150.00
Canada	$45.00 - 225.00
U.K.	£15.00 - 80.00

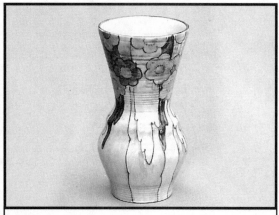

Shape 183	Vase, two-handled
Designer:	Mr. Symcox c.1934
Issued:	c.1934 - by 1940
Height :	7 ¾", 19.7 cm
Colour:	1. Assorted decorations - satin matt
	2. White - matt

Market	Range
U.S.A.	$30.00 - 150.00
Canada	$45.00 - 225.00
U.K.	£15.00 - 80.00

Shape 184	Vase
Designer:	Mr. Symcox c.1934
Issued:	c.1934 - by 1940
Height:	6 ½", 16.5 cm
Colour:	1. Assorted decorations - satin matt
	2. White - matt

Market	Range
U.S.A.	$30.00 - 150.00
Canada	$45.00 - 225.00
U.K.	£15.00 - 80.00

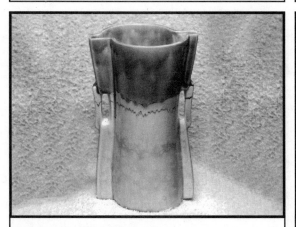

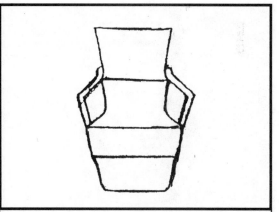

Shape 185	Vase, two-handled
Designer:	Mr. Symcox c.1934
Issued:	c.1934 - by 1940
Height :	8 ¼", 21 cm
Colour:	1. Assorted decorations - satin matt
	2. White - matt

Market	Range
U.S.A.	$30.00 - 150.00
Canada	$45.00 - 225.00
U.K.	£15.00 - 80.00

Shape 186	Vase, two-handled
Designer:	Mr. Symcox c.1934
Issued:	c.1934 - by 1940
Height:	Unknown
Colour:	1. Assorted decorations - satin matt
	2. White - matt

Market	Range
U.S.A.	$30.00 - 150.00
Canada	$45.00 - 225.00
U.K.	£15.00 - 80.00

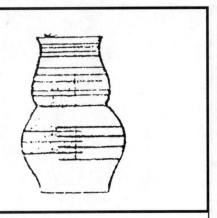

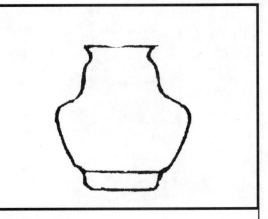

Shape 187   Vase

Designer:	Mr. Symcox c.1934
Issued:	c.1934 - by 1940
Height :	Unknown
Colour:	1. Assorted decorations - satin matt
	2. White - matt

Market	Range
U.S.A.	$30.00 - 150.00
Canada	$45.00 - 225.00
U.K.	£15.00 - 80.00

Shape 188   Vase

Designer:	Mr. Symcox c.1934
Issued:	c.1934 - by 1940
Height:	5", 12.7 cm
Colour:	1. Assorted decorations - satin matt
	2. White - matt

Market	Range
U.S.A.	$30.00 - 150.00
Canada	$45.00 - 225.00
U.K.	£15.00 - 80.00

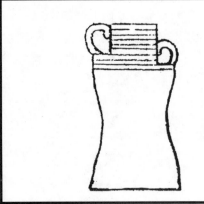

Shape 189   Vase

Designer:	Mr. Symcox c.1934
Issued:	c.1934 - by 1940
Height :	8 ¾", 22.2 cm
Colour:	1. Assorted decorations - satin matt
	2. White - matt

Market	Range
U.S.A.	$30.00 - 150.00
Canada	$45.00 - 225.00
U.K.	£15.00 - 80.00

Shape 190   Vase, two-handled

Designer:	Mr. Symcox c.1934
Issued:	c.1934 - by 1940
Height:	Unknown
Colour:	1. Assorted decorations - satin matt
	2. White - matt

Market	Range
U.S.A.	$30.00 - 150.00
Canada	$45.00 - 225.00
U.K.	£15.00 - 80.00

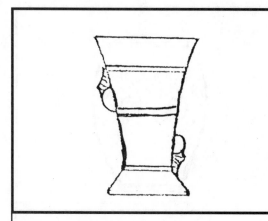

Shape 191   Vase

Designer:	Mr. Symcox c.1934
Issued:	c.1934 - by 1940
Height :	Unknown
Colour:	1. Assorted decorations - satin matt
	2. White - matt

Market	Range
U.S.A.	$30.00 - 150.00
Canada	$45.00 - 225.00
U.K.	£15.00 - 80.00

Shape 192   Vase

Designer:	Mr. Symcox c.1934
Issued:	c.1934 - by 1940
Height:	7", 17.8 cm
Colour:	1. Assorted decorations - satin matt
	2. White - matt

Market	Range
U.S.A.	$30.00 - 150.00
Canada	$45.00 - 225.00
U.K.	£15.00 - 80.00

Photograph not
available
at press time

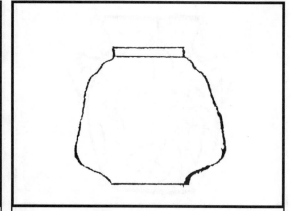

Shape 193   Vase

Designer:	Mr. Symcox c.1934
Issued:	c.1934 - by 1940
Height :	Unknown
Colour:	1. Assorted decorations - satin matt
	2. White - matt

Market	Range
U.S.A.	$30.00 - 150.00
Canada	$45.00 - 225.00
U.K.	£15.00 - 80.00

Shape 194   Vase

Designer:	Albert Hallam c.1934
Issued:	c.1934 - by 1940
Height:	Unknown
Colour:	1. Assorted decorations - satin matt
	2. White - matt

Market	Range
U.S.A.	$30.00 - 150.00
Canada	$45.00 - 225.00
U.K.	£15.00 - 80.00

Shape 195   Vase

Designer:	Albert Hallam c.1934
Issued:	c.1934 - by 1940
Height :	Unknown
Colour:	1. Assorted decorations - satin matt
	2. White - matt

Market	Range
U.S.A.	$30.00 - 150.00
Canada	$45.00 - 225.00
U.K.	£15.00 - 80.00

Shape 196   Vase

Designer:	Albert Hallam and Mr. Hayward c.1934
Issued:	c.1934 - by 1940
Height:	Unknown
Colour:	1. Assorted decorations - satin matt
	2. White - matt

Market	Range
U.S.A.	$30.00 - 150.00
Canada	$45.00 - 225.00
U.K.	£15.00 - 80.00

Shape 198   Vase, two-handled

Designer:	Mr. Symcox and Mr. Hayward c.1934
Issued:	c.1934 - by 1940
Height :	Unknown
Colour:	1. Assorted decorations - satin matt
	2. White - matt

Market	Range
U.S.A.	$30.00 - 150.00
Canada	$45.00 - 225.00
U.K.	£15.00 - 80.00

Shape 204   Vase

Designer:	Albert Hallam c.1934
Issued:	c.1934 - by 1940
Height:	Unknown
Colour:	1. Assorted decorations - satin matt
	2. White - matt

Market	Range
U.S.A.	$30.00 - 150.00
Canada	$45.00 - 225.00
U.K.	£15.00 - 80.00

Photograph not
available
at press time

Shape 208   Vase

Designer:	Unknown
Issued:	c.1934 - by 1940
Height:	Unknown
Colour:	1. Assorted decorations - satin matt
	2. White - matt

Market	Range
U.S.A.	$30.00 - 150.00
Canada	$45.00 - 225.00
U.K.	£15.00 - 80.00

Shape 267   Posy holder for vase

Designer	Unknown c.1934
Issued:	c.1934 - by 1940
Height:	Unknown
Colour:	1. Assorted decorations - satin matt
	2. White - matt

Market	Range
U.S.A.	$30.00 - 60.00
Canada	$45.00 - 90.00
U.K.	£15.00 - 30.00

Shape 289   Vase

Designer:	Mr. Symcox in 1934
Issued:	1934 - by 1963
Height :	4 ¼", 10.8 cm
Colour:	1. Assorted decorations - satin matt
	2. White - matt

Market	Range
U.S.A.	$30.00 - 150.00
Canada	$45.00 - 225.00
U.K.	£15.00 - 80.00

Shape 290   Vase

Designer:	Mr. Symcox in 1934
Issued:	1934 - by 1940
Height:	4", 10.1 cm
Colour:	1. Assorted decorations - satin matt
	2. White - matt

Market	Range
U.S.A.	$30.00 - 150.00
Canada	$45.00 - 225.00
U.K.	£15.00 - 80.00

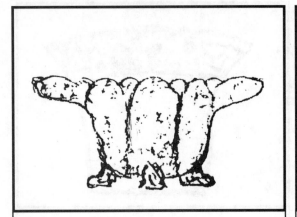

Shape 341   Vase

Designer:	Mr. Symcox in 1935
Issued:	1935 - by 1940
Height :	Unknown
Colour:	1. Assorted decorations -satin matt
	2. White - matt

Market	Range
U.S.A.	$30.00 - 150.00
Canada	$45.00 - 225.00
U.K.	£15.00 - 80.00

Shape 345   Vase

Designer:	Mr. Symcox in 1935
Issued:	1935 - by 1940
Height:	Unknown
Colour:	1. Assorted decorations - satin matt
	2. White - matt

Market	Range
U.S.A.	$30.00 - 150.00
Canada	$45.00 - 225.00
U.K.	£15.00 - 80.00

Shape 347   Vase

Designer:	Mr. Symcox in 1935
Issued:	1935 - by 1940
Height :	4 ½", 11.9 cm
Colour:	1. Assorted decorations -satin matt
	2. White - matt

Market	Range
U.S.A.	$30.00 - 150.00
Canada	$45.00 - 225.00
U.K.	£15.00 - 80.00

Shape 351   Vase

Designer:	Mr. Symcox in 1935
Issued:	1935 - by 1940
Height:	8 ½", 21.6 cm
Colour:	1. Assorted decorations - satin matt
	2. White - matt

Market	Range
U.S.A.	$30.00 - 150.00
Canada	$45.00 - 225.00
U.K.	£15.00 - 80.00

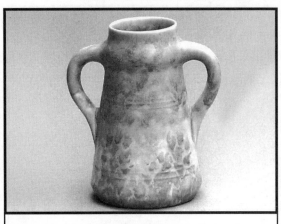

Shape 352   **Vase, two-handled**

Designer: Mr. Watkin in 1935
Issued: 1935 - by 1963
Height :   9 ¾", 24.7 cm
Colour: 1. Assorted decorations - satin matt
   2. White - matt

Market	Range
U.S.A.	$30.00 - 150.00
Canada	$45.00 - 225.00
U.K.	£15.00 - 80.00

Shape 353   **Vase, two-handled**

Designer: Mr. Symcox in 1935
Issued: 1935 - by 1940
Height: 6 ¼", 15.9 cm
Colour: 1. Assorted decorations - satin matt
   2. White - matt

Market	Range
U.S.A.	$30.00 - 150.00
Canada	$45.00 - 225.00
U.K.	£15.00 - 80.00

Shape 357   **Vase**

Designer: Mr. Symcox in 1935
Issued: 1935 - by 1940
Height :   4 ¾", 12.1 cm
Colour: 1. Assorted decorations - satin matt
   2. White - matt

Market	Range
U.S.A.	$30.00 - 150.00
Canada	$45.00 - 225.00
U.K.	£15.00 - 80.00

Shape 358   **Vase, two-handled**

Designer: Albert Hallam in 1935
Issued: 1935 - by 1954
Height: 7", 17.8 cm
Colour: 1. Assorted decorations - satin matt
   2. White - matt

Market	Range
U.S.A.	$30.00 - 150.00
Canada	$45.00 - 225.00
U.K.	£15.00 - 80.00

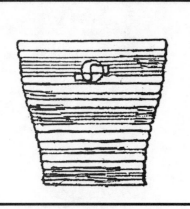

Photograph not
available
at press time

Shape 378/1/2 Plant pot holder, in two sizes

Designer:	Mr. Symcox in 1936
Issued:	1936 - by 1940
Height:	1. 8 ¼", 21 cm
	2. 7 ¼", 18.4 cm
Colour:	1. Assorted decorations - satin matt
	2. White - matt

Market	Range
U.S.A.	$30.00 - 150.00
Canada	$45.00 - 225.00
U.K.	£15.00 - 80.00

Shape 385 Vase

Designer:	Mr. Symcox in 1936
Issued:	1936 - by 1940
Height:	6", 15 cm
Colour	1. Assorted decorations - satin matt
	2. White - matt

Market	Range
U.S.A.	$30.00 - 150.00
Canada	$45.00 - 225.00
U.K.	£15.00 - 80.00

Shape 386 Vase

Designer:	Mr. Symcox in 1936
Issued:	1936 - by 1954
Height :	10", 25.4 cm
Colour:	1. Assorted decorations - satin matt
	2. White - matt

Market	Range
U.S.A.	$30.00 - 150.00
Canada	$45.00 - 225.00
U.K.	£15.00 - 80.00

Shape 395 Vase, two-handled

Designer:	Mr. Symcox in 1936
Issued:	1936 - by 1963
Height:	6", 15 cm
Colour:	1. Assorted decorations - satin matt
	2. White - matt

Market	Range
U.S.A.	$30.00 - 150.00
Canada	$45.00 - 225.00
U.K.	£15.00 - 80.00

Shape 396   Vase

Designer:	Mr. Symcox in 1936
Issued:	1936 - by 1940
Height :	4″, 10.1 cm
Colour:	1. Assorted decorations - satin matt
	2. White - matt

Market	Range
U.S.A.	$30.00 - 150.00
Canada	$45.00 - 225.00
U.K.	£15.00 - 80.00

Shape 418   Vase

Designer:	Mr. Symcox in 1936
Issued:	1936 - by 1940
Height:	6″, 15 cm
Colour:	1. Assorted decorations - satin matt
	2. White - matt

Market	Range
U.S.A.	$30.00 - 150.00
Canada	$45.00 - 225.00
U.K.	£15.00 - 80.00

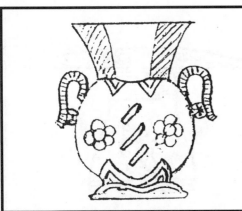

Shape 428   Vase, two-handled

Designer:	Mr. Symcox in 1936
Issued:	1936 - by 1940
Height :	Unknown
Colour:	1. Assorted decorations -satin matt
	2. White - matt

Market	Range
U.S.A.	$30.00 - 150.00
Canada	$45.00 - 225.00
U.K.	£15.00 - 80.00

Shape 429/1/2 Vase, two-handled

Designer:	Mr. Owen in 1936
Issued:	1936 - by 1940
Heights :	Unknown
Colour:	1. Assorted decorations - satin matt
	2. White - matt

Market	Range
U.S.A.	$30.00 - 150.00
Canada	$45.00 - 225.00
U.K.	£15.00 - 80.00

Shape 431   Vase

Designer:	Mr. Symcox in 1936
Issued:	1936 - by 1940
Height :	7 ½", 19.1 cm
Colour:	1. Assorted decorations - satin matt
	2. White - matt

Market	Range
U.S.A.	$30.00 - 150.00
Canada	$45.00 - 225.00
U.K.	£15.00 - 80.00

Shape 432   Vase, two-handled

Designer:	Mr. Owen in 1936
Issued:	1936 - by 1940
Height:	Unknown
Colour:	1. Assorted decorations - satin matt
	2. White - matt

Market	Range
U.S.A.	$30.00 - 150.00
Canada	$45.00 - 225.00
U.K.	£15.00 - 80.00

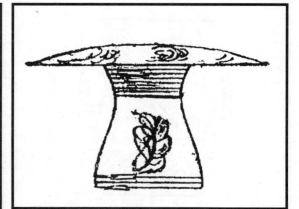

Shape 439   Vase, two-handled

Designer:	Mr. Symcox in 1936
Issued:	1936 - by 1940
Height :	5 ½", 14 cm
Colour:	1. Assorted decorations - satin matt
	2. White - matt

Market	Range
U.S.A.	$30.00 - 150.00
Canada	$45.00 - 225.00
U.K.	£15.00 - 80.00

Shape 466   Vase

Designer:	Mr. Symcox in1937
Issued:	1937 - by 1940
Height:	Unknown
Colour:	1. Assorted decorations - satin matt
	2. White - matt

Market	Range
U.S.A.	$30.00 - 150.00
Canada	$45.00 - 225.00
U.K.	£15.00 - 80.00

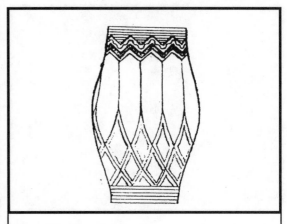

Shape 473 Vase, two-handled

Designer:	Mr. Symcox in 1937
Issued:	1937 - by 1940
Height :	Unknown
Colour:	1. Assorted decorations - satin matt
	2. White - matt

Market	Range
U.S.A.	$30.00 - 150.00
Canada	$45.00 - 225.00
U.K.	£15.00 - 80.00

Shape 479 Vase

Designer:	Mr. Symcox in 1937
Issued:	1937 - by 1940
Height:	Unknown
Colour:	1. Assorted decorations - satin matt
	2. White - matt

Market	Range
U.S.A.	$30.00 - 150.00
Canada	$45.00 - 225.00
U.K.	£15.00 - 80.00

Photograph not
available
at press time

Shape 481 Vase

Designer:	Mr. Symcox in 1937
Issued:	1937 - by 1940
Height :	5 ¼", 13.3 cm
Colour:	1. Assorted decorations - satin matt
	2. White - matt

Market	Range
U.S.A.	$30.00 - 150.00
Canada	$45.00 - 225.00
U.K.	£15.00 - 80.00

Shape 482 Vase

Designer:	Mr. Symcox in 1937
Issued:	1937 - by 1954
Height:	6", 15 cm
Colour:	1. Assorted decorations - satin matt
	2. White - matt

Market	Range
U.S.A.	$30.00 - 150.00
Canada	$45.00 - 225.00
U.K.	£15.00 - 80.00

Shape 484   Vase

Designer: Mr. Symcox in 1937
Issued: 1937 - by 1940
Height :   7", 17.8 cm
Colour: 1. Assorted decorations - satin matt
             2. White - matt

Market	Range
U.S.A.	$30.00 - 150.00
Canada	$45.00 - 225.00
U.K.	£15.00 - 80.00

Shape 485   Vase

Designer: Mr. Symcox in 1937
Issued: 1937 - by 1940
Height: Unknown
Colour: 1. Assorted decorations - satin matt
             2. White - matt

Market	Range
U.S.A.	$30.00 - 150.00
Canada	$45.00 - 225.00
U.K.	£15.00 - 80.00

Photograph not
available
at press time

Shape 486   Vase

Designer: Mr. Symcox in 1937
Issued: 1937 - by 1940
Height :   Unknown
Colour: 1. Assorted decorations - satin matt
             2. White - matt

Market	Range
U.S.A.	$30.00 - 150.00
Canada	$45.00 - 225.00
U.K.	£15.00 - 80.00

Shape 487   Vase

Designer: Mr. Symcox in 1937
Issued: 1937 - by 1940
Height: 7 ¾", 19.7 cm
Colour: 1. Assorted decorations - satin matt
             2. White - matt

Market	Range
U.S.A.	$30.00 - 150.00
Canada	$45.00 - 225.00
U.K.	£15.00 - 80.00

Shape 489	**Vase - two-handled (monkeys)**
Designer:	Mr. Symcox in 1937
Issued:	1937 - by 1940
Height :	9 ½", 24 cm
Colour:	1. Assorted decorations - satin matt
	2. White - matt

Market	Range
U.S.A.	$30.00 - 150.00
Canada	$45.00 - 225.00
U.K.	£15.00 - 80.00

Shape 494	**Vase**
Designer:	Mr. Watkin in 1937
Issued:	1937 - by 1940
Height:	11", 27.9 cm
Colour:	1. Assorted decorations -satin matt
	2. White - matt

Market	Range
U.S.A.	$30.00 - 150.00
Canada	$45.00 - 225.00
U.K.	£15.00 - 80.00

Shape 495	**Vase, two-handled**
Designer:	Mr. Symcox in 1937
Issued:	1937 - by 1940
Height :	5 ½", 14 cm
Colour:	1. Assorted decorations -satin matt
	2. White - matt

Market	Range
U.S.A.	$30.00 - 150.00
Canada	$45.00 - 225.00
U.K.	£15.00 - 80.00

Shape 496	**Vase**
Designer:	Mr. Watkin in 1937
Issued:	1937 - by 1940
Height:	8 ½", 21.6 cm
Colour:	1. Assorted decorations - satin matt
	2. White - matt

Market	Range
U.S.A.	$30.00 - 150.00
Canada	$45.00 - 225.00
U.K.	£15.00 - 80.00

Shape 499   Vase

Designer:	Mr. Symcox in 1937
Issued:	1937 - by 1940
Height :	6 ½", 16.5 cm
Colour:	1. Assorted decorations - satin matt
	2. White - matt

Market	Range
U.S.A.	$30.00 - 150.00
Canada	$45.00 - 225.00
U.K.	£15.00 - 80.00

Shape 500   Vase

Designer:	Mr. Watkin in 1937
Issued:	1937 - by 1940
Height:	8", 20.3 cm
Colour:	1. Assorted decorations - satin matt
	2. White - matt

Market	Range
U.S.A.	$30.00 - 150.00
Canada	$45.00 - 225.00
U.K.	£15.00 - 80.00

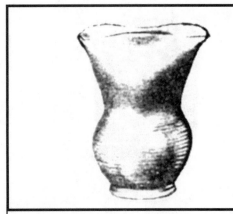

Shape 504   Vase

Designer:	Mr. Watkin in 1937
Issued:	1937 - 1954
Height :	7 ½", 19.1 cm
Colour:	1. Assorted decorations - satin matt
	2. White - matt

Market	Range
U.S.A.	$30.00 - 150.00
Canada	$45.00 - 225.00
U.K.	£15.00 - 80.00

Shape 509   Vase

Designer:	Mr. Symcox in 1937
Issued:	1938 - by 1940
Height:	Unknown
Colour:	1. Assorted decorations - satin matt
	2. White - matt

Market	Range
U.S.A.	$30.00 - 150.00
Canada	$45.00 - 225.00
U.K.	£15.00 - 80.00

Photograph not
available
at press time

Shape 529   Vase

Designer: Mr. Watkin in 1937
Issued: 1938 - by 1940
Height: Unknown
Colour: 1. Assorted decorations - satin matt
             2. White - matt

Market	Range
U.S.A.	$30.00 - 150.00
Canada	$50.00 - 225.00
U.K.	£15.00 - 80.00

Shape 543   Vase

Designer: Mr. Symcox in 1937
Issued: 1938 - by 1954
Height: 10", 25.4 cm
Colour: 1. Assorted decorations - satin matt
             2. White - matt

Market	Range
U.S.A.	$30.00 - 150.00
Canada	$50.00 - 225.00
U.K.	£15.00 - 80.00

Shape 545   Vase

Designer: Mr. Symcox in 1937
Issued: 1938 - by 1954
Height :   8", 20.3 cm
Colour: 1. Assorted decorations - satin matt
             2. White - matt

Market	Range
U.S.A.	$30.00 - 150.00
Canada	$50.00 - 225.00
U.K.	£15.00 - 80.00

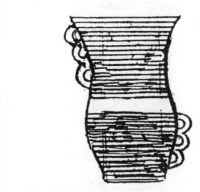

Shape 546   Handled vase

Designer: Mr. Symcox in 1937
Issued: 1938 - by 1963
Height: 8 ½", 21.6 cm
Colour: 1. Assorted decorations - satin matt
             2. White - matt

Market	Range
U.S.A.	$30.00 - 150.00
Canada	$50.00 - 225.00
U.K.	£15.00 - 80.00

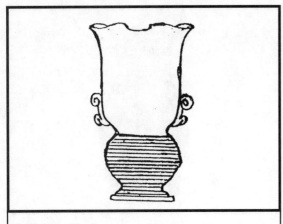

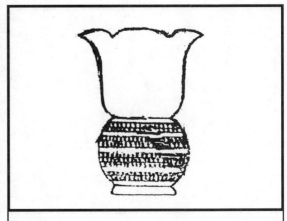

Shape 548   Vase

Designer:	Mr. Symcox in 1937
Issued:	1938 - by 1940
Height :	Unknown
Colour:	1. Assorted decorations - satin matt
	2. White - matt

Market	Range
U.S.A.	$30.00 - 150.00
Canada	$50.00 - 225.00
U.K.	£15.00 - 80.00

Shape 552   Vase

Designer:	Mr. Symcox in 1937
Issued:	1938 - by 1940
Height:	Unknown
Colour:	1. Assorted decorations - satin matt
	2. White - matt

Market	Range
U.S.A.	$30.00 - 150.00
Canada	$50.00 - 225.00
U.K.	£15.00 - 80.00

Photograph not
available
at press time

Shape 553   Vase

Designer:	Mr. Symcox in 1937
Issued:	1938 - by 1954
Height :	11", 27.9 cm
Colour:	1. Assorted decorations - satin matt
	2. White - matt

Market	Range
U.S.A.	$30.00 - 150.00
Canada	$50.00 - 225.00
U.K.	£15.00 - 80.00

Shape 558   Vase

Designer:	Mr. Symcox in 1937
Issued:	1938 - by 1940
Height:	Unknown
Colour:	1. Assorted decorations - satin matt
	2. White - matt

Market	Range
U.S.A.	$30.00 - 150.00
Canada	$50.00 - 225.00
U.K.	£15.00 - 80.00

Shape 560   Vase, two-handled

Designer:	Mr. Symcox in 1937
Issued:	1938 - by 1940
Height :	Unknown
Colour:	1. Assorted decorations - satin matt
	2. White - matt

Market	Range
U.S.A.	$30.00 - 150.00
Canada	$50.00 - 225.00
U.K.	£15.00 - 80.00

Shape 562   Vase, two-handled

Designer:	Mr. Symcox in 1937
Issued:	1938 - by 1940
Height:	Unknown
Colour:	1. Assorted decorations - satin matt
	2. White - matt

Market	Range
U.S.A.	$30.00 - 150.00
Canada	$50.00 - 225.00
U.K.	£15.00 - 80.00

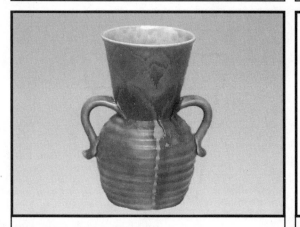

Shape 563   Vase, two-handled

Designer:	Mr. Symcox in 1937
Issued:	1938 - by 1940
Height :	Unknown
Colour:	1. Assorted decorations - satin matt
	2. White - matt

Market	Range
U.S.A.	$30.00 - 150.00
Canada	$50.00 - 225.00
U.K.	£15.00 - 80.00

Shape 566   Vase, two-handled

Designer:	Mr. Symcox in 1937
Issued:	1938 - by 1940
Height:	5 ½", 14 cm
Colour:	1. Assorted decorations - satin matt
	2. White - matt

Market	Range
U.S.A.	$30.00 - 150.00
Canada	$50.00 - 255.00
U.K.	£15.00 - 80.00

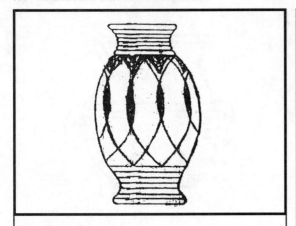

Shape 573	**Vase**
Designer:	Mr. Symcox in 1938
Issued:	1938 - by 1940
Height :	Unknown
Colour:	1. Assorted decorations - satin matt
	2. White - matt

Market	Range
U.S.A.	$30.00 - 150.00
Canada	$50.00 - 225.00
U.K.	£15.00 - 80.00

Shape 588	**Plant pot holder**
Designer:	Mr. Symcox in 1938
Issued:	1938 - by 1940
Height:	Unknown
Colour:	1. Assorted decorations - satin matt
	2. White - matt

Market	Range
U.S.A.	$30.00 - 125.00
Canada	$50.00 - 175.00
U.K.	£15.00 - 60.00

Photograph not
available
at press time

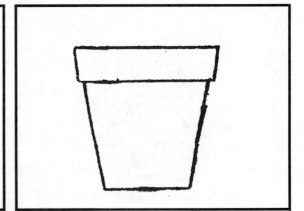

Shape 589	**Vase, two-handled**
Designer:	Mr. Symcox in 1938
Issued:	1938 - by 1940
Height :	Unknown
Colour:	1. Assorted decorations - satin matt
	2. White - matt

Market	Range
U.S.A.	$30.00 - 150.00
Canada	$50.00 - 225.00
U.K.	£15.00 - 80.00

Shape 597	**Plant pot holder**
Designer:	Albert Hallam in 1938
Issued:	1938 - by 1940
Height:	Unknown
Colour:	1. Assorted decorations - satin matt
	2. White - matt

Market	Range
U.S.A.	$30.00 - 125.00
Canada	$50.00 - 175.00
U.K.	£15.00 - 60.00

Shape 615   Vase

Designer:	Mr. Symcox in 1938
Issued:	1938 - by 1940
Height :	7", 17.8 cm
Colour:	1. Assorted decorations - satin matt
	2. White - matt

Market	Range
U.S.A.	$30.00 - 150.00
Canada	$50.00 - 225.00
U.K.	£15.00 - 80.00

Shape 620   Vase

Designer:	Mr. Symcox in 1938
Issued:	1939 - by 1940
Height:	Unknown
Colour:	1. Assorted decorations - satin matt
	2. White - matt

Market	Range
U.S.A.	$30.00 - 150.00
Canada	$50.00 - 225.00
U.K.	£15.00 - 80.00

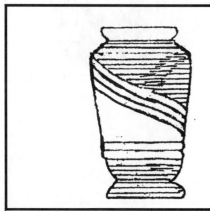

Shape 621   Vase

Designer:	Mr. Symcox in 1938
Issued:	1939 - by 1940
Height :	Unknown
Colour:	1. Assorted decorations - satin matt
	2. White - matt

Market	Range
U.S.A.	$30.00 - 150.00
Canada	$50.00 - 225.00
U.K.	£15.00 - 80.00

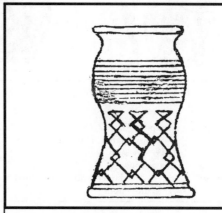

Shape 626   Vase

Designer:	Mr. Symcox in 1938
Issued:	1939 - by 1940
Height:	Unknown
Colour:	1. Assorted decorations - satin matt
	2. White - matt

Market	Range
U.S.A.	$30.00 - 150.00
Canada	$50.00 - 225.00
U.K.	£15.00 - 80.00

MODELLE SERIES

Vase Shape 656, Vase Shape 675 and Vase Shape 677

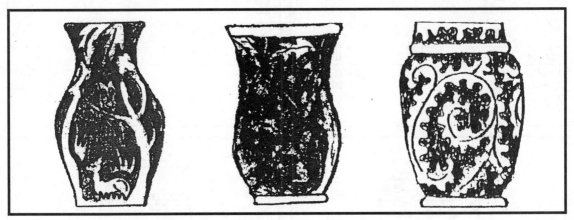

Vase Shape 678, Vase Shape 680 and Vase Shape 699

Designers: Shapes 655 - 677; 680 - 700 Mr. Watkin in 1938
              Shape 678 James Hayward in 1938
Issued: 1939 - by 1963
Height: See below
Colour: 1. Assorted decorations - satin matt
            2. White - matt

Shape	Height	U.S. $	Market Range Can. $	U.K. £
Shape 655	11", 27.9 cm	50.00 - 175.00	75.00 - 275.00	25.00 - 95.00
Shape 656	10 ½", 26.7 cm	50.00 - 175.00	75.00 - 275.00	25.00 - 95.00
Shape 675	9 ½", 24 cm	50.00 - 175.00	75.00 - 275.00	25.00 - 95.00
Shape 677	7 ½", 19.1 cm	50.00 - 175.00	75.00 - 275.00	25.00 - 95.00
Shape 678	10", 25.4 cm	50.00 - 175.00	75.00 - 275.00	25.00 - 95.00
Shape 680	8 ¼", 21 cm	50.00 - 175.00	75.00 - 275.00	25.00 - 95.00
Shape 699	8", 20.3 cm	50.00 - 175.00	75.00 - 275.00	25.00 - 95.00
Shape 700	9 ¼", 23.5 cm	50.00 - 175.00	75.00 - 275.00	25.00 - 95.00

Shape 702/1/2/3/4 Vase

Designer:	Mr. Symcox in 1939
Issued:	1939 - 1971
Height :	1. Shape 702/1 — 13", 33 cm
	2. Shape 702/2 — 11", 27.9 cm
	3. Shape 702/3 — 9", 22.9 cm
	4. Shape 702/4 — 7", 17.8 cm
Colour:	1. Various decorations - satin matt
	2. White or black - matt
	3. Copper - lustre

Market	Range
Shape 702/1	
U.S.A.	$30.00 - 100.00
Canada	$45.00 - 150.00
U.K.	£15.00 - 55.00
Shape 702/2	
U.S.A.	$30.00 - 100.00
Canada	$45.00 - 150.00
U.K.	£15.00 - 50.00
Shape 702/3	
U.S.A.	$30.00 - 75.00
Canada	$45.00 - 100.00
U.K.	£15.00 - 40.00
Shape 702/4	
U.S.A.	$30.00 - 60.00
Canada	$45.00 - 85.00
U.K.	£15.00 - 35.00

Shape 703   Vase/Lamp

Designer:	Albert Hallam in 1939
Issued:	1939 - by 1940
Height:	Unknown
Colour:	1. Assorted decorations - satin matt
	2. White - matt

Market	Range
U.S.A.	$30.00 - 125.00
Canada	$50.00 - 175.00
U.K.	£15.00 - 60.00

Shape 725   Vase, two-handled

Designer:	Mr. Symcox in 1939
Issued:	1939 - by 1954
Height :	8 ¾", 22.2 cm
Colour:	1. Assorted decorations - satin matt
	2. White - matt

Market	Range
U.S.A.	$30.00 - 150.00
Canada	$50.00 - 225.00
U.K.	£15.00 - 80.00

Shape 726   Vase

Designer: Mr. Symcox in 1939
Issued: 1939 - by 1954
Height: 8 ½", 21.6 cm
Colour: 1. Assorted decorations - satin matt
                    2. White - matt

Market	Range
U.S.A.	$30.00 - 150.00
Canada	$45.00 - 225.00
U.K.	£15.00 - 80.00

Shape 809/1/2/3 Vase

Designer: Mr. Symcox in 1940
Issued: 1940 - by 1954
Height :   12 ¼", 10 ¼", 9", 31.1, 26, 22.9 cm
Colour: 1 Assorted decorations - satin matt
                    2. White - matt

Market	Range
U.S.A.	$30.00 - 150.00
Canada	$45.00 - 225.00
U.K.	£15.00 - 80.00

Shape 829   Vase

Designer: Mr. Watkin in 1940
Issued: 1940 - by 1954
Height: Unknown
Colour: 1. Assorted decorations - satin matt
                    2. White - matt

Market	Range
U.S.A.	$30.00 - 150.00
Canada	$50.00 - 225.00
U.K.	£15.00 - 80.00

Shape 840/1/2/3 Vase

Designer: Unknown
Issued: 1940 - by 1954
Height :   1. Shape 840/1/3 — Unknown
                    2. Shape 840/2 — 9", 23.0 cm
Colour: 1. Assorted decorations - satin matt
                    2. White - matt

Market	Range
U.S.A.	$30.00 - 150.00
Canada	$50.00 - 225.00
U.K.	£15.00 - 80.00

TULIP VASES

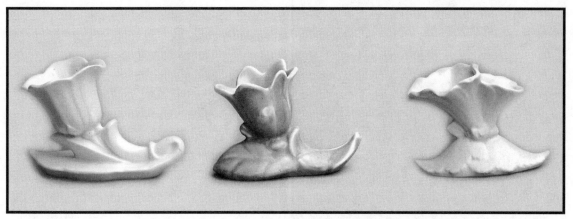

Shape 846,   Shape 848 and Shape 852

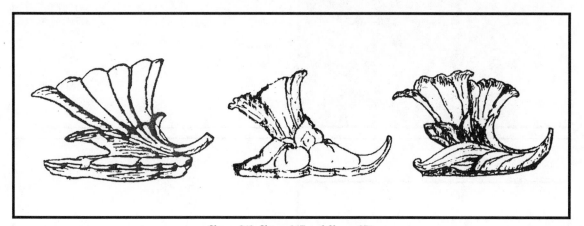

Shape 843, Shape 847 and Shape 851

Designer: Mr. Watkin in 1940
Issued: 1940 - by 1954
Size: 4", 10.1 cm
Colour: 1. Assorted decorations - satin matt
            2. White - matt

	Market Range		
Shape	**U.S. $**	**Can. $**	**U.K. £**
Shape 843	30.00 - 70.00	45.00 - 100.00	15.00 - 45.00
Shape 846	30.00 - 70.00	45.00 - 100.00	15.00 - 45.00
Shape 847	30.00 - 70.00	45.00 - 100.00	15.00 - 45.00
Shape 848	30.00 - 70.00	45.00 - 100.00	15.00 - 45.00
Shape 851	30.00 - 70.00	45.00 - 100.00	15.00 - 45.00
Shape 852	30.00 - 70.00	45.00 - 100.00	15.00 - 45.00

Shape 844/1/2/3 Vase

Designer:	Mr. Symcox in 1940
Issued:	1940 - 1972
Height :	1. Shape 844/1 — 11", 27.9 cm
	2. Shape 844/2 — 9", 22.9 cm
	3. Shape 844/3 — 7 ½", 19.1 cm
Colours:	1. Assorted decorations - satin matt
	2. White or black - matt
	3. Copper - lustre

Market	Range
Shape 844/1	
U.S.A.	$30.00 - 100.00
Canada	$45.00 - 150.00
U.K.	£15.00 - 55.00
Shape 844/2	
U.S.A.	$30.00 - 100.00
Canada	$45.00 - 150.00
U.K.	£15.00 - 50.00
Shape 844/3	
U.S.A.	$30.00 - 75.00
Canada	$45.00 - 100.00
U.K.	£15.00 - 40.00

Photograph not
available
at press time

Shape 923   Oval vase

Designer:	Unknown
Issued:	1941 - by 1954
Height :	Unknown
Colour:	1. Assorted decorations - satin matt
	2. White - matt

Market	Range
U.S.A.	$30.00 - 150.00
Canada	$50.00 - 225.00
U.K.	£15.00 - 80.00

Shape 1051 Deer vase

Designer: Albert Hallam, James Hayward in 1943
Issued: 1943 - by 1963
Height: 10″, 25.4 cm
Colour: 1. Assorted decorations - satin matt
             2. White - matt
Series: Festival

Market	Range
U.S.A.	$30.00 - 150.00
Canada	$45.00 - 225.00
U.K.	£15.00 - 80.00

Shape 1075 Primrose vase

Designer: Albert Hallam in 1946
Issued: 1947 - by 1954
Height   2 ½″, 6.4 cm
Colour: Assorted decorations - satin matt

Market	Range
U.S.A.	$10.00 - 40.00
Canada	$15.00 - 60.00
U.K.	£5.00 - 20.00

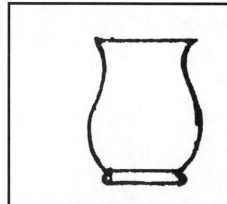

Shape 1076 Primrose vase

Designer: Albert Hallam in 1946
Issued: 1947 - by 1954
Height: Unknown
Colour: Assorted decorations - satin matt

Market	Range
U.S.A.	$10.00 - 40.00
Canada	$15.00 - 60.00
U.K.	£5.00 - 20.00

Shape 1077 Primrose vase

Designer: Albert Hallam in 1946
Issued: 1947 - by 1954
Height: Unknown
Colour: 1. Assorted decorations - satin matt
             2. White - matt

Market	Range
U.S.A.	$10.00 - 40.00
Canada	$15.00 - 60.00
U.K.	£5.00 - 20.00

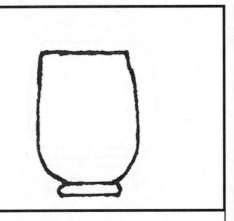

Shape 1078 Primrose vase

Designer:	Albert Hallam in 1946
Issued:	1947 - by 1954
Height:	Unknown
Colour:	1. Assorted decorations - satin matt
	2. White - matt

Market	Range
U.S.A.	$10.00 - 40.00
Canada	$15.00 - 60.00
U.K.	£5.00 - 20.00

Shape 1083 Galleon vase

Designer:	Albert Hallam, James Hayward in 1946
Issued:	1947 - by 1963
Height:	6 ¾", 17.2 cm
Colour:	Assorted colours - satin matt
Series:	Festival

Market	Range
U.S.A.	$30.00 - 150.00
Canada	$45.00 - 225.00
U.K.	£15.00 - 80.00

Shape 1095 Nymph Vase

Designer:	Albert Hallam, James Hayward in 1943
Issued:	1943 - by 1963
Height:	10 ½", 26.7 cm
Colour:	Assorted colours - satin matt
Series:	Festival

Market	Range
U.S.A.	$30.00 - 150.00
Canada	$45.00 - 225.00
U.K.	£15.00 - 80.00

Shape 1184 Column Vase

Designer:	Albert Hallam in 1949
Issued:	1949 - 1971
Height:	11 ½", 29.2 cm
Colour:	1. Assorted decorations - satin matt
	2. White or black - matt
	3. Copper - lustre
Series:	Festival

Market	Range
U.S.A.	$30.00 - 150.00
Canada	$45.00 - 225.00
U.K.	£15.00 - 80.00

Shape 1185 Flamingo vase

Designer:	James Hayward in 1950
Issued:	1950 - 1967
Height:	10 ½", 26.7 cm
Colour:	1. Assorted decorations - satin matt
	2. White or black - matt
	3. Copper - lustre
Series:	Festival

Market	Range
U.S.A.	$30.00 - 150.00
Canada	$45.00 - 225.00
U.K.	£15.00 - 80.00

Shape 1186 Shell vase

Designer:	Albert Hallam, James Hayward in 1950
Issued:	1950 - 1967
Height:	7 ½", 19.1 cm
Colour:	1. Assorted decorations - satin matt
	2. White or black - matt
	3. Copper - lustre
Series:	Festival

Market	Range
U.S.A.	$30.00 - 150.00
Canada	$45.00 - 225.00
U.K.	£15.00 - 80.00

Shape 1189 Square chequered vase

Designer:	Albert Hallam, James Hayward in 1950
Issued:	1950 - by 1959
Height:	6 ½", 16.5 cm
Colour:	Assorted decorations - satin matt
Series:	Festival

Market	Range
U.S.A.	$30.00 - 150.00
Canada	$45.00 - 225.00
U.K.	£15.00 - 80.00

Shape 1190 Urn vase

Designer:	Albert Hallam, James Hayward in 1950
Issued:	1950 - 1971
Height:	10", 25.4 cm
Colour:	1. Assorted decorations - satin matt
	2. White or black - matt
	3. Copper - lustre
Series:	Festival

Market	Range
U.S.A.	$30.00 - 150.00
Canada	$45.00 - 225.00
U.K.	£15.00 - 80.00

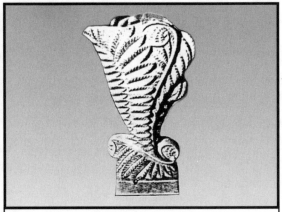

Shape 1191A   Fern vase

Designer:	James Hayward in 1950
Issued:	1950 - 1964
Height:	12", 30.5 cm
Colour:	1. Assorted decorations - satin matt
	2. White or black - matt
	3. Copper - lustre
Series:	Festival

Market	Range
U.S.A.	$30.00 - 150.00
Canada	$45.00 - 225.00
U.K.	£15.00 - 80.00

Shape 1191B   Fern vase

Designer:	James Hayward in 1950
Issued:	1950 - 1964
Height:	12", 30.5 cm
Colour:	1. Chartreuse
	2. Holly green
	3. Maroon
Series:	Elizabethan

Market	Range
U.S.A.	$30.00 - 150.00
Canada	$45.00 - 225.00
U.K.	£15.00 - 80.00

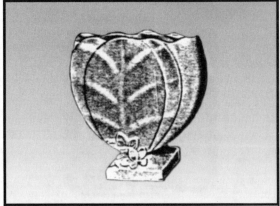

Shape 1193   Bell flower vase

Designer:	Albert Hallam, James Hayward in 1950
Issued:	1950 - 1968
Height:	9", 22.9 cm
Colour:	1. Assorted decorations - satin matt
	2. White or black - matt
	3. Copper - lustre
Series:	Festival

Market	Range
U.S.A.	$30.00 - 150.00
Canada	$45.00 - 225.00
U.K.	£15.00 - 80.00

Shape 1194   Magnolia Vase

Designer:	Albert Hallam, James Hayward in 1950
Issued:	1950 - 1964
Height:	7", 17.8 cm
Colour:	1. Assorted decorations - satin matt
	2. White or black - matt
	3. Copper - lustre
Series:	Festival

Market	Range
U.S.A.	$30.00 - 150.00
Canada	$45.00 - 225.00
U.K.	£15.00 - 80.00

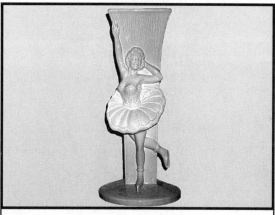

Shape 1284   Trout vase

Designer:	Albert Hallam, James Hayward in 1953
Isssued:	1953 - by 1959
Height:	8", 20.3 cm
Colour:	Chartreuse, holly green or maroon - gloss
Series:	Elizabethan

Market	Range
U.S.A.	$30.00 - 150.00
Canada	$45.00 - 225.00
U.K.	£15.00 - 80.00

Shape 1287   Skater vase

Designer:	Albert Hallam, James Hayward in 1953
Issued:	1953 - by 1959
Height:	11", 27.9 cm
Colour:	Chartreuse, holly green or maroon - gloss
Series:	Elizabethan

Market	Range
U.S.A.	$30.00 - 150.00
Canada	$45.00 - 225.00
U.K.	£15.00 - 80.00

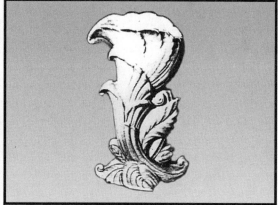

Shape 1293   Dove vase

Designer:	Albert Hallam, James Hayward in 1953
Issued:	1953 - by 1959
Height:	6 ½", 16.5 cm
Colour:	Chartreuse, holly green or maroon - gloss
Series:	Elizabethan

Market	Range
U.S.A.	$30.00 - 150.00
Canada	$45.00 - 225.00
U.K.	£15.00 - 80.00

Shape 1295   Maple bud vase

Designer:	Albert Hallam, James Hayward in 1953
Issued	1953 - by 1966
Height:	12", 30.5 cm
Colour:	1. Assorted decorations - satin matt
	2. White or black - matt
	3. Chartreuse, holly green or maroon - gloss
Series:	Elizabethan

Market	Range
U.S.A.	$30.00 - 150.00
Canada	$45.00 - 225.00
U.K.	£15.00 - 80.00

Shape 1298 Apple vase

Designer: Albert Hallam, James Hayward in 1953
Issued: 1953 - by 1962
Height: 9", 22.9 cm
Colour: Chartreuse, holly green or maroon - gloss
Series: Elizabethan

Market	Range
U.S.A.	$30.00 - 150.00
Canada	$45.00 - 225.00
U.K.	£15.00 - 80.00

Shape 1300 Stardust vase

Designer: Albert Hallam, James Hayward in 1953
Issued: 1953 - by 1959
Height: Unknown
Colour: Chartreuse, holly green or maroon - gloss
Series: Elizabethan

Market	Range
U.S.A.	$30.00 - 150.00
Canada	$45.00 - 225.00
U.K.	£15.00 - 80.00

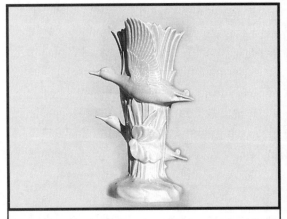

Shape 1305 Mallard vase

Designer: Albert Hallam, James Hayward in 1953
Issued 1953 - by 1959
Height: 11", 27.9 cm
Colour: Chartreuse, holly green or maroon - gloss
Series: Elizabethan

Market	Range
U.S.A.	$30.00 - 150.00
Canada	$45.00 - 225.00
U.K.	£15.00 - 80.00

Shape 1306 Pinewood vase

Designer: Albert Hallam, James Hayward in 1953
Issued: 1953 - by 1959
Height: 8 ½", 21.6 cm
Colour: Chartreuse, holly green or maroon - gloss
Series: Elizabethan

Market	Range
U.S.A.	$30.00 - 150.00
Canada	$45.00 - 225.00
U.K.	£15.00 - 80.00

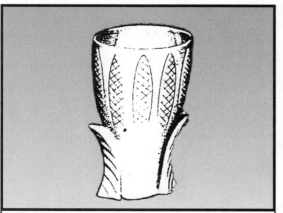

Shape 1342 Vase

Designer: Albert Hallam in 1954
Issued: 1954 - 1962
Height: 8 ½" , 21.6 cm
Colour: 1. Assorted decorations - satin matt
2. White - matt

Market	Range
U.S.A.	$30.00 - 150.00
Canada	$45.00 - 225.00
U.K.	£15.00 - 80.00

Shape 1343/1/2 Vase

Designer: Albert Hallam in 1954
Issued: 1954 - by 1962
Height : 1. Shape 1343/1 — 10", 25.4 cm
2. Shape 1343/2 — 6", 15 cm
Colour: 1. Assorted decorations - satin matt
2. White - matt

Market	Range
U.S.A.	$20.00 - 150.00
Canada	$30.00 - 225.00
U.K.	£10.00 - 70.00

Shape 1349 Vase

Designer: Albert Hallam in 1954
Issued: 1954 - 1962
Height: 5", 12.7 cm
Colour: 1. Assorted decorations - satin matt
2. White - matt

Market	Range
U.S.A.	$30.00 - 125.00
Canada	$45.00 - 175.00
U.K.	£15.00 - 60.00

Shape 1351 Vase

Designer: Albert Hallam in 1954
Issued: 1954 - by 1962
Height : 9 ½", 24 cm
Colour: 1. Assorted decorations - satin matt
2. White - matt

Market	Range
U.S.A.	$30.00 - 125.00
Canada	$45.00 - 175.00
U.K.	£15.00 - 60.00

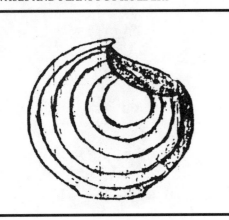

Shape 1352 Vase

Designer: Albert Hallam in 1954
Issued: 1954 - by 1962
Height: 4 ½", 11.9 cm
Colour: 1. Assorted decorations - satin matt
           2. White - matt

Market	Range
U.S.A.	$30.00 - 125.00
Canada	$45.00 - 175.00
U.K.	£15.00 - 60.00

Shape 1357 Vase

Designer: Albert Hallam in 1954
Issued: 1954 - by 1962
Height :   8", 20.3 cm
Colour: 1. Assorted decorations - satin matt
           2. White - matt

Market	Range
U.S.A.	$30.00 - 125.00
Canada	$45.00 - 175.00
U.K.	£15.00 - 60.00

Shape 1367 Vase

Designer: Albert Hallam in 1955
Issued: 1955 - by 1962
Height: 10 ½", 26.7 cm
Colour: 1. Assorted decorations - satin matt
           2. White - matt

Market	Range
U.S.A.	$30.00 - 125.00
Canada	$45.00 - 175.00
U.K.	£15.00 - 65.00

Shape 1370 Vase

Designer: Albert Hallam in 1955
Issued: 1955 - by 1962
Height :   12", 30.5 cm
Colour: 1. Assorted decorations - satin matt
           2. White - matt

Market	Range
U.S.A.	$30.00 - 125.00
Canada	$45.00 - 175.00
U.K.	£15.00 - 65.00

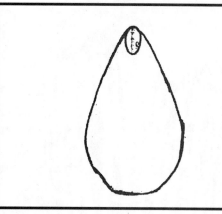

Shape 1371 Vase

Designer:	Albert Hallam in 1955
Issued:	1955 - 1962
Height:	6″, 15 cm
Colour:	1. Assorted decorations - satin matt
	2. White - matt

Market	Range
U.S.A.	$30.00 - 125.00
Canada	$45.00 - 175.00
U.K.	£15.00 - 60.00

Shape 1389 Vase

Designer:	Albert Hallam in 1955
Issued:	1955 - 1962
Height :	8 ¼″, 21 cm
Colour:	1. Assorted decorations - satin matt
	2. White - matt

Market	Range
U.S.A.	$30.00 - 75.00
Canada	$45.00 - 100.00
U.K.	£15.00 - 40.00

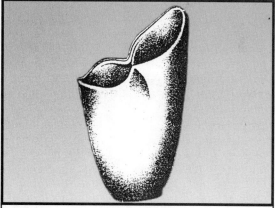

Shape 1455 Vase

Designer:	Albert Hallam in 1956
Issued:	1956 - 1962
Height:	10 ½″, 26.7 cm
Colour:	1. Assorted decorations - satin matt
	2. White - matt

Market	Range
U.S.A.	$30.00 - 125.00
Canada	$45.00 - 175.00
U.K.	£15.00 - 60.00

Shape 1456 Vase

Designer:	Albert Hallam in 1956
Issued:	1957 - 1965
Height :	9 ½″, 24 cm
Colour:	1. Assorted decorations - satin matt
	2. White or black - matt

Market	Range
U.S.A.	$30.00 - 125.00
Canada	$45.00 - 175.00
U.K.	£15.00 - 65.00

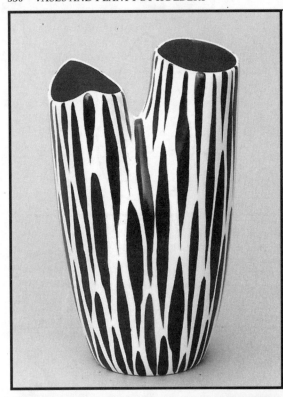

Shape 1457 Vase

Designer:	Albert Hallam in 1956
Issued:	1957 - by 1962
Height:	7", 17.8 cm
Colour:	1. Assorted decorations - satin matt
	2. White - matt

Market	Range
U.S.A.	$30.00 - 125.00
Canada	$45.00 - 175.00
U.K.	£15.00 - 60.00

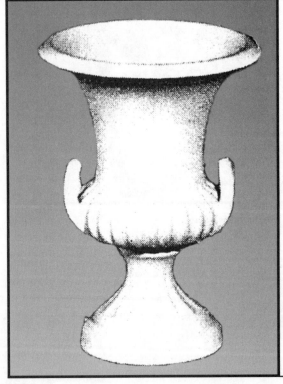

Shape No 1496 /1/2/3 Urn Vase

Designer:	Albert Hallam in 1957
Issued:	1957 - 1972
Height:	1. Shape 1496/1 — 10", 25.4 cm
	2. Shape 1496/2 — 8", 20.3 cm
	3. Shape 1496/3 — 6", 15 cm
Colour:	1. Assorted decorations - satin matt
	2. White or black - matt

Market	Range
Shape 1496/1	
U.S.A.	$30.00 - 125.00
Canada	$45.00 - 175.00
U.K.	£15.00 - 60.00
Shape 1496/2	
U.S.A.	$30.00 - 125.00
Canada	$45.00 - 175.00
U.K.	£15.00 - 60.00
Shape 1496/3	
U.S.A.	$30.00 - 125.00
Canada	$45.00 - 175.00
U.K.	£15.00 - 60.00

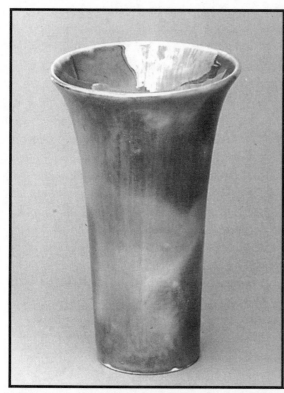

Shape 1502A/1/2/3 Vase

Designer: Albert Hallam in 1957
Issued: 1957 - 1967
Height: 1. Shape 1502/1 — 13", 33 cm
          2. Shape 1502/2 — 10 ¼",26 cm
          3. Shape 1502/3 — 8 ¼", 21 cm
Colour: 1. Various decorations - satin matt
          2. White or black - matt
          3. Copper - lustre

Market	Range
Shape 1502A/1	
U.S.A.	$30.00 - 150.00
Canada	$45.00 - 225.00
U.K.	£15.00 - 70.00
Shape 1502A/2	
U.S.A.	$30.00 - 125.00
Canada	$45.00 - 175.00
U.K.	£15.00 - 65.00
Shape 1502A/3	
U.S.A.	$30.00 - 125.00
Canada	$45.00 - 175.00
U.K.	£15.00 - 60.00

Note: Continued as Caprice Series, see shape 1502B/2/3.

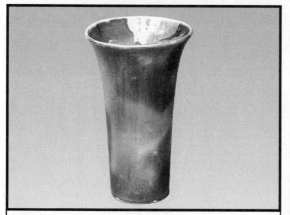

Shape 1502B/2/3 Vase, Caprice series

Designer: Albert Hallam in 1957
Issued: 1968 - by 1972
Height: 2. Shape 1502B/2 — 10 ¼",26 cm
          3. Shape 1502B/3 — 8 ¼", 21 cm
Colour: Orange, turquoise or yellow

Market	Range
U.S.A.	$30.00 - 125.00
Canada	$45.00 - 175.00
U.K.	£15.00 - 60.00

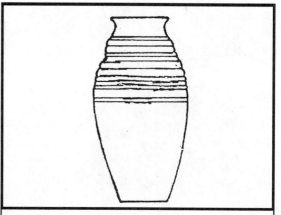

Shape 1552 Vase

Designer: Albert Hallam in 1958
Issued: 1958 - by 1966
Height: 8", 20.3 cm
Colour: 1. Various decorations - satin matt
          2. White or black - matt

Market	Range
U.S.A.	$30.00 - 150.00
Canada	$45.00 - 225.00
U.K.	£15.00 - 75.00

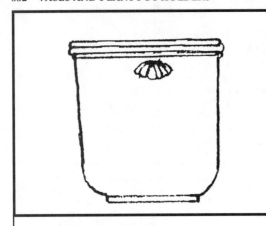

Shape 1554/1/2 Plant pot holder

Designer:	Albert Hallam in 1958
Issued:	1958 - 1966
Size:	1. Shape 1554/1 — 6 ¼", 15.9 cm
	2. Shape 1554/2 — 5", 12.7 cm
Colour:	1. Various decorations - satin matt
	2. White or black - matt

Market	Range
U.S.A.	$30.00 - 125.00
Canada	$45.00 - 175.00
U.K.	£15.00 - 60.00

Shape 1555   Vase in shape of swan

Designer:	Kathi Urbach
Modeller:	Albert Hallam in 1958
Issued:	1959 - by 1965
Size:	9 ¾" x 6 ¾", 24.7 x 17.2 cm
Colour:	Various colours - gloss

Market	Range
U.S.A.	$90.00 - 175.00
Canada	$125.00 - 275.00
U.K.	£45.00 - 90.00

Note: Pair with vase, shape no. 1556.

Shape 1556   Vase in shape of swan

Designer:	Kathi Urbach
Modeller:	Albert Hallam in 1958
Issued:	1959 - by 1965
Size:	9 ¾" x 6 ¾", 24.7 x 17.2 cm
Colour:	Various colours - gloss

Market	Range
U.S.A.	$90.00 - 175.00
Canada	$125.00 - 275.00
U.K.	£45.00 - 90.00

Note: Pair with vase, shape no. 1555.

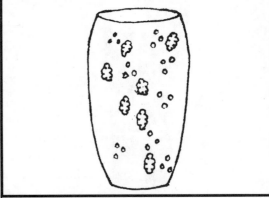

Shape 1590   Vase, oval

Designer:	Kathi Urbach
Modeller:	Albert Hallam in 1959
Issued:	1959 - by 1965
Height :	9", 22.9 cm
Colour:	Various colours - gloss

Market	Range
U.S.A.	$60.00 - 125.00
Canada	$90.00 - 175.00
U.K.	£30.00 - 65.00

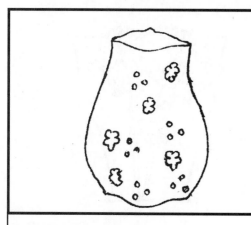

Shape 1591 Vase, triangular

Designer:	Kathi Urbach
Modeller:	Albert Hallam in 1959
Issued:	1959 - by 1965
Height:	7", 17.8 cm
Colour:	Various colours - gloss

Market	Range
U.S.A.	$60.00 - 125.00
Canada	$90.00 - 175.00
U.K.	£30.00 - 65.00

Shape 1592 Vase, square

Designer:	Kathi Urbach
Modeller:	Albert Hallam in 1959
Issued:	1959 - by 1965
Height :	11", 27.9 cm
Colour:	Various colours - gloss

Market	Range
U.S.A.	$60.00 - 125.00
Canada	$90.00 - 175.00
U.K.	£30.00 - 65.00

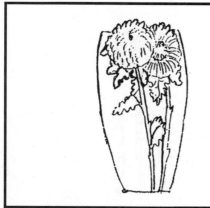

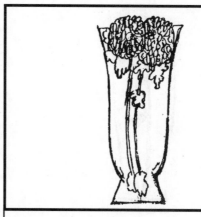

Shape 1602 Chrysanthemum vase

Designer:	Albert Hallam in 1959
Issued:	1959 - by 1963
Height:	11", 27.9 cm
Colour:	Coloured flowers on a white background
Series:	Chrysanthemum

Market	Range
U.S.A.	$90.00 - 175.00
Canada	$125.00 - 275.00
U.K.	£45.00 - 90.00

Shape 1604 Chrysanthemum vase

Designer:	Albert Hallam in 1959
Issued:	1959 - by 1963
Height:	12", 30.5 cm
Colour:	Coloured flowers on a white background
Series:	Chrysanthemum

Market	Range
U.S.A.	$90.00 - 175.00
Canada	$125.00 - 275.00
U.K.	£45.00 - 90.00

Shape 1605 **Chrysanthemum vase**

Designer: Albert Hallam in 1959
Issued: 1959 - by 1963
Height: Unknown
Colour: Bronze and pink flowers on a white background
Series: Chrysanthemum

Market	Range
U.S.A.	$90.00 - 175.00
Canada	$125.00 - 275.00
U.K.	£45.00 - 90.00

Shape 1606 **Chrysanthemum vase**

Designer: Albert Hallam in 1959
Issued: 1959 - by 1963
Height: 8", 20.3 cm
Colour: Coloured flowers on a white background
Series: Chrysanthemum

Market	Range
U.S.A.	$90.00 - 175.00
Canada	$125.00 - 275.00
U.K.	£45.00 - 90.00

Shape 1607 **Chrysanthemum vase**

Designer: Albert Hallam in 1959
Issued: 1959 - by 1963
Height: Unknown
Colour: Coloured flowers on a white background
Series: Chrysanthemum

Market	Range
U.S.A.	$90.00 - 175.00
Canada	$125.00 - 275.00
U.K.	£45.00 - 90.00

Shape 1608 **Chrysanthemum vase**

Designer: Albert Hallam in 1959
Issued: 1959 - by 1963
Height: Unknown
Colour: Coloured flowers on a white background
Series: Chrysanthemum

Market	Range
U.S.A.	$90.00 - 175.00
Canada	$125.00 - 275.00
U.K.	£45.00 - 90.00

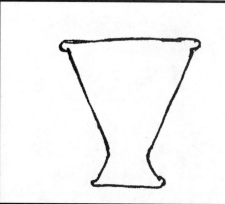

Shape 1611 Vase

Designer:	Albert Hallam in 1959
Issued:	1960 - 1968
Height:	10", 25.4 cm
Colour:	1. Various decorations - satin matt
	2. White or black - matt

Market	Range
U.S.A.	$30.00 - 125.00
Canada	$45.00 - 175.00
U.K.	£15.00 - 60.00

Shape 1612 Vase

Designer:	Albert Hallam in 1959
Issued:	1959 - by 1962
Height :	6", 15.0 cm
Colour:	1. Various decorations - satin matt
	2. White - matt

Market	Range
U.S.A.	$30.00 - 100.00
Canada	$45.00 - 150.00
U.K.	£15.00 - 50.00

Shape 1613A   Vase, Cornflower

Designer:	Albert Hallam in 1959
Issued:	1960 - 1967
Height:	9", 22.9 cm
Colour:	1. Various decorations - satin matt
	2. White or black - matt
	3. Copper- lustre

Market	Range
U.S.A.	$30.00 - 125.00
Canada	$45.00 - 175.00
U.K.	£15.00 - 60.00

Shape 1613B   Vase, Caprice Series

Designer:	Albert Hallam in 1959
Issued:	1968 - by 1972
Height:	9", 22.9 cm
Colour:	Orange, turquoise or yellow

Market	Range
U.S.A.	$30.00 - 125.00
Canada	$45.00 - 175.00
U.K.	£15.00 - 60.00

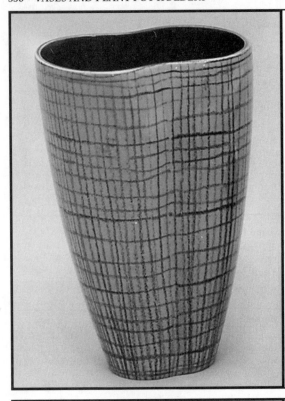

Shape 1649 Vase

Designer:	Albert Hallam in 1960
Issued:	1960 - by 1965
Height :	8", 20.3 cm
Colour:	1. Various decorations - satin matt
	2. White or black - matt

Market	Range
U.S.A.	$30.00 - 125.00
Canada	$45.00 - 175.00
U.K.	£15.00 - 60.00

Shape 1651A   Vase (pattern name unknown)

Designer:	Albert Hallam in 1959
Issued:	1959 - 1967
Height:	6", 15.0 cm
Colour:	1. Various decorations - satin matt
	2. White or black - matt
	3. Copper- lustre

Market	Range
U.S.A.	$30.00 - 125.00
Canada	$45.00 - 175.00
U.K.	£15.00 - 60.00

Shape 1651B   Vase, Caprice series

Designer:	Albert Hallam in 1959
Issued:	1968 - by 1972
Height:	6", 15.0 cm
Colour:	Orange, turquoise or yellow

Market	Range
U.S.A.	$30.00 - 125.00
Canada	$45.00 - 175.00
U.K.	£15.00 - 60.00

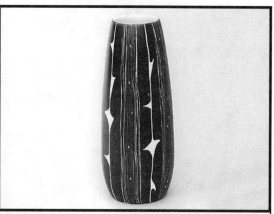

Shape 1652 Vase

Designer:	Albert Hallam in 1959
Issued:	1959 - by 1962
Height :	7″, 17.8 cm
Colour:	1. Various decorations - satin matt
	2. White - matt

Market	Range
U.S.A.	$30.00 - 125.00
Canada	$45.00 - 175.00
U.K.	£15.00 - 60.00

Shape 1653 Vase

Designer:	Albert Hallam in 1959
Issued:	1959 - by 1966
Height:	10 ½″, 26.7 cm
Colour:	1. Various decorations - satin matt
	2. White or black - matt

Market	Range
U.S.A.	$30.00 - 125.00
Canada	$45.00 - 175.00
U.K.	£15.00 - 60.00

Shape 1654A   Vase (pattern name unknown)

Designer:	Albert Hallam in 1959
Issued:	1959 - 1967
Height :	10″, 25.4 cm
Colour:	1. Various decorations - satin matt
	2. White or black - matt
	3. Copper - lustre

Market	Range
U.S.A.	$30.00 - 125.00
Canada	$45.00 - 175.00
U.K.	£15.00 - 60.00

Shape 1654B   Vase, Caprice series

Designer:	Albert Hallam in 1959
Issued:	1968 - by 1972
Height :	10″, 25.4 cm
Colour:	Orange, turquoise or yellow

Market	Range
U.S.A.	$30.00 - 125.00
Canada	$45.00 - 175.00
U.K.	£15.00 - 60.00

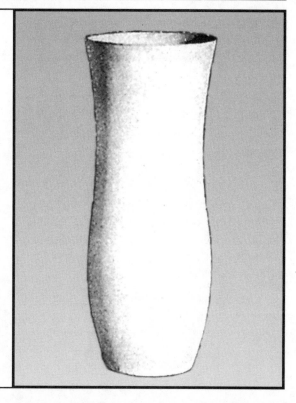

Shape 1655 Vase

Designer:	Albert Hallam in 1959
Issued:	1959 - by 1965
Height:	7", 17.8 cm
Colour:	1. Various decorations - satin matt
	2. White or black - matt

Market	Range
U.S.A.	$30.00 - 125.00
Canada	$45.00 - 175.00
U.K.	£15.00 - 60.00

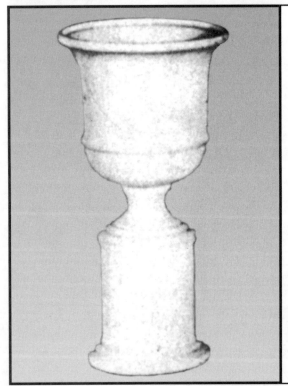

Shape 1656A Goblet vase (pattern name unknown)

Designer:	Albert Hallam in 1959
Issued:	1959 - 1967
Height :	8", 20.3 cm
Colour:	1. Various decorations - satin matt
	2. White or black - matt
	3. Copper - lustre

Market	Range
U.S.A.	$30.00 - 125.00
Canada	$45.00 - 175.00
U.K.	£15.00 - 60.00

Shape 1656B Goblet Vase, Caprice series

Designer:	Albert Hallam in 1959
Issued:	1968 - by 1972
Height :	8", 20.3 cm
Colour:	Orange, turquoise or yellow

Market	Range
U.S.A.	$30.00 - 100.00
Canada	$45.00 - 150.00
U.K.	£15.00 - 55.00

Shape 1657 Vase

Designer:	Albert Hallam in 1959
Issued:	1959 - by 1966
Height:	11", 27.9 cm
Colour:	1. Various decorations - satin matt
	2. White or black - matt

Market	Range
U.S.A.	$30.00 - 125.00
Canada	$45.00 - 175.00
U.K.	£15.00 - 60.00

Shape 1658 Rose vase, "Queen Elizabeth"

Designer:	Albert Hallam in 1959
Issued:	1960 - 1965
Height :	10", 25.4 cm
Colour:	Deep pink rose, green leaves on cream
	background - satin matt

Description	U.S. $	Can. $	U.K. £
"Queen Elizabeth"	150.00	200.00	75.00

Note: Set of six with no. 1659 (basket), 1660, 1661, 1662 and 1663.

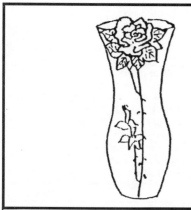

Shape 1660 Rose vase, "Peace"

Designer:	Albert Hallam in 1959
Issued:	1960 - 1965
Height:	11", 27.9 cm
Colour:	Yellow rose, green leaves on cream
	background - satin matt

Description	U.S. $	Can. $	U.K. £
"Peace"	150.00	200.00	75.00

Note: Set of six with no. 1658, 1659 (basket), 1661, 1662 and 1663.

Shape 1661 Rose vase, "Bayadere"

Designer:	Albert Hallam in 1959
Issued:	1960 - 1965
Height :	8", 20.3 cm
Colour:	Coloured rose, green leaves on cream
	background - satin matt

Description	U.S. $	Can. $	U.K. £
"Bayadere"	150.00	200.00	75.00

Note: Set of six with no. 1658, 1659 (basket), 1660, 1662 and 1663.

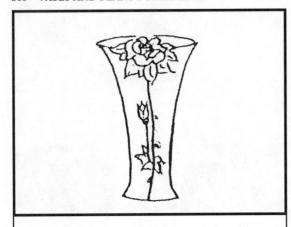

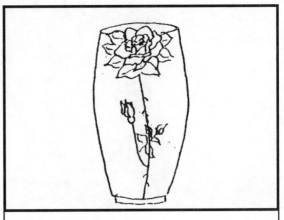

Shape 1662 Rose vase, "Cirius"

Designer:	Albert Hallam in 1959
Issued:	1960 - 1965
Height:	8", 20.3 cm
Colour:	Coloured rose, green leaves on cream background - satin matt

Description	U.S. $	Can. $	U.K. £
"Cirius"	150.00	200.00	75.00

Note: Set of six with no. 1658, 1659 (basket), 1660, 1661 and 1663.

Shape 1663 Rose vase, "Soraya"

Designer:	Albert Hallam in 1959
Issued:	1960 - 1965
Height :	10", 25.4 cm
Colour:	Coloured rose, green leaves on cream background - satin matt

Colour	U.S. $	Can. $	U.K. £
"Soraya"	150.00	200.00	75.00

Note: Set of six with no. 1658, 1659 (basket), 1660, 1661 and 1662.

Shape 1664/0/1/2 Vase

Designer:	Albert Hallam in 1959
Issued:	Shape 1664/0 — 1963 - 1969
	Shape 1664/1/2 — 1960 - 1969
Height:	1. Shape 1664/0 — 12 ½", 31.7 cm
	2. Shape 1664/1 — 9", 22.9 cm
	3. Shape 1664/2 — 7", 17.8 cm
Colour:	1. Various decorations - satin matt
	2. White or black - matt
	3. Copper - lustre

Market	Range
U.S.A.	$30.00 - 125.00
Canada	$45.00 - 175.00
U.K.	£15.00 - 60.00

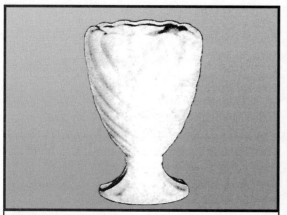

Shape 1682 Goblet vase

Designer:	Albert Hallam in 1960
Issued:	1960 - 1969
Height :	8", 20.3 cm
Colour:	1. Various decorations - satin matt
	2. White or black - matt
	3. Copper - lustre

Market	Range
U.S.A.	$30.00 - 150.00
Canada	$45.00 - 200.00
U.K.	£15.00 - 70.00

Shape 1719 Vase mustard pot without the lid

Designer:	Albert Hallam in 1960
Issued:	1960 - 1970
Height:	2 ¾", 7.0 cm
Colour:	1. Various decorations - satin matt
	2. White or black - matt
	3. Copper - lustre

Market	Range
U.S.A.	$8.00 - 35.00
Canada	$15.00 - 50.00
U.K.	£5.00 - 20.00

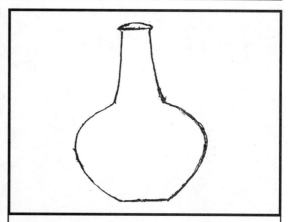

Shape 1723 Bongo flower holder

Designer:	Albert Hallam in 1960
Issued:	c.1960
Height :	Unknown
Colour:	1. Various decorations - satin matt
	2. White or black - matt
	3. Copper - lustre

Market	Range
U.S.A.	$20.00 - 125.00
Canada	$30.00 - 175.00
U.K.	£10.00 - 60.00

Shape 1724 Vase in shape of a bottle

Designer:	Mr. Garbet in 1960
Issued:	c.1960
Height:	13 ¾", 34.9 cm
Colour:	1. Various decorations - satin matt
	2. White or black - matt
	3. Copper - lustre

Market	Range
U.S.A.	$20.00 - 125.00
Canada	$30.00 - 175.00
U.K.	£10.00 - 60.00

Shape 1749A   Vase (pattern name unknown)

Designer: Albert Hallam in 1961
Issued: 1961 - 1967
Height : 9″, 22.9 cm
Colour: 1. Various decorations - satin matt
2. White or black - matt

Market	Range
U.S.A.	$30.00 - 150.00
Canada	$45.00 - 225.00
U.K.	£15.00 - 80.00

Shape 1749B   Vase, Caprice series

Designer: Albert Hallam in 1961
Issued: 1968 - by 1972
Height: 9″, 22.9 cm
Colour: Orange, turquoise or yellow

Market	Range
U.S.A.	$30.00 - 150.00
Canada	$45.00 - 225.00
U.K.	£15.00 - 80.00

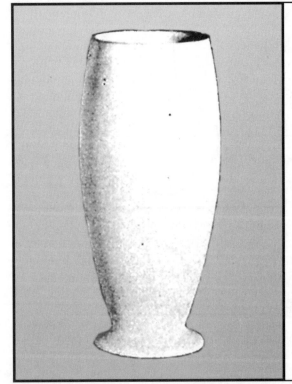

Shape 1750A   Vase (pattern name unknown)

Designer: Albert Hallam in 1961
Issued: 1961 - 1967
Height: 9″, 22.9 cm
Colour: 1. Various decorations - satin matt
2. White or black - matt

Market	Range
U.S.A.	$30.00 - 175.00
Canada	$45.00 - 225.00
U.K.	£15.00 - 80.00

Shape 1750B   Vase, Caprice Series

Designer: Albert Hallam in 1961
Issued 1968 - by 1972
Height: 9″, 22.9 cm
Colour: Orange, turquoise or yellow

Market	Range
U.S.A.	$30.00 - 175.00
Canada	$45.00 - 225.00
U.K.	£10.00 - 80.00

Shape 1751A   Vase (pattern name unknown)

Designer:	Albert Hallam in 1961
Issued:	1961 - 1967
Height :	7", 17.8 cm
Colour:	1. Various decorations - satin matt
	2. White or black - matt

Market	Range
U.S.A.	$30.00 - 150.00
Canada	$45.00 - 225.00
U.K.	£15.00 - 80.00

Shape 1751B   Vase, Caprice series

Designer:	Albert Hallam in 1961
Issued:	1968 - by 1972
Height :	7", 17.8 cm
Colour:	Orange, turquoise or yellow

Market	Range
U.S.A.	$30.00 - 150.00
Canada	$45.00 - 225.00
U.K.	£15.00 - 80.00

Shape 1752A   Vase (pattern name unknown)

Designer:	Albert Hallam in 1961
Issued:	1961 - 1967
Height:	6", 15.0 cm
Colour:	1. Various decorations - satin matt
	2. White or black - matt
	3. Copper - lustre

Market	Range
U.S.A.	$30.00 - 175.00
Canada	$45.00 - 225.00
U.K.	£15.00 - 80.00

Shape 1752B   Vase, Caprice Series

Designer:	Albert Hallam in 1961
Issued:	1968 - by 1972
Height:	6", 15.0 cm
Colour:	Orange, turquoise or yellow

Market	Range
U.S.A.	$30.00 - 150.00
Canada	$45.00 - 200.00
U.K.	£15.00 - 70.00

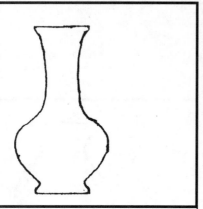

Shape 1773 Vase

Designer:	Albert Hallam in 1961
Issued:	1961 - by 1965
Height :	8", 20.3 cm
Colour:	1. Various decorations - satin matt
	2. White or black - matt

Market	Range
U.S.A.	$20.00 - 125.00
Canada	$30.00 - 175.00
U.K.	£10.00 - 60.00

Shape 1799 Chalice vase

Designer:	Albert Hallam in 1962
Issued:	1962 - 1969
Height:	12", 30.5 cm
Colour:	1. Various decorations - satin matt
	2. White or black - matt
	3. Copper - lustre

Market	Range
U.S.A.	$20.00 - 125.00
Canada	$30.00 - 175.00
U.K.	£10.00 - 60.00

Note: This vase is a pair with shape 2070.

Shape 1858 Vase

Designer:	Albert Hallam in 1962
Issued:	1963 - 1968
Height :	8", 20.3 cm
Colour:	1. Various decorations - satin matt
	2. White or black - matt
	3. Copper - lustre

Market	Range
U.S.A.	$20.00 - 125.00
Canada	$30.00 - 175.00
U.K.	£10.00 - 60.00

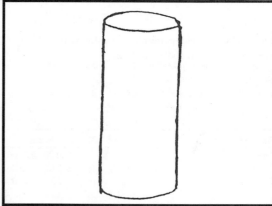

Shape 1873 Vase

Designer:	Albert Hallam in 1963
Issued:	1963 - by 1965
Height:	8 ¾", 22.2 cm
Colour:	1. Various decorations - satin matt
	2. White or black - matt

Market	Range
U.S.A.	$20.00 - 125.00
Canada	$30.00 - 175.00
U.K.	£10.00 - 60.00

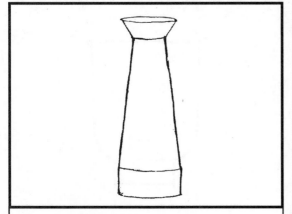

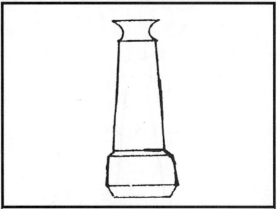

Shape 1879 Vase

Designer:	Albert Hallam in 1963
Issued:	1963 - by 1965
Height :	10 ½", 26.7 cm
Colour:	1. Various decorations - satin matt
	2. White or black - matt

Market	Range
U.S.A.	$20.00 - 125.00
Canada	$30.00 - 175.00
U.K.	£10.00 - 60.00

Shape 1881 Vase

Designer:	Albert Hallam in 1963
Issued:	1963 - by 1965
Height:	8", 20.3 cm
Colour:	1. Various decorations - satin matt
	2. White or black - matt

Market	Range
U.S.A.	$20.00 - 125.00
Canada	$30.00 - 175.00
U.K.	£10.00 - 60.00

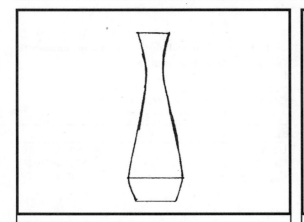

Shape 1884 Vase

Designer:	Albert Hallam in 1963
Issued:	1963 - by 1965
Height :	9", 22.9 cm
Colour:	1. Various decorations - satin matt
	2. White or black - matt

Market	Range
U.S.A.	$20.00 - 125.00
Canada	$30.00 - 175.00
U.K.	£10.00 - 60.00

Shape 1888 Vase

Designer:	Albert Hallam in 1963
Issued:	1963 - by 1965
Height:	5 ¾", 14.6 cm
Colour:	1. Various decorations - satin matt
	2. White or black - matt

Market	Range
U.S.A.	$20.00 - 125.00
Canada	$30.00 - 175.00
U.K.	£10.00 - 60.00

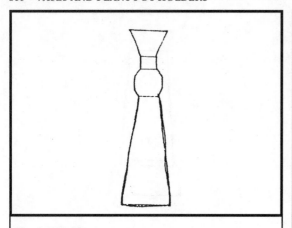

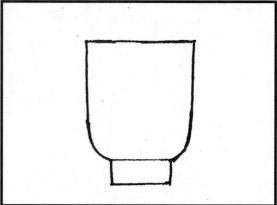

Shape 1890 Vase

Designer:	Albert Hallam in 1963
Issued:	1963 - by 1967
Height :	11 ½", 29.2 cm
Colour:	1. Various decorations - satin matt
	2. White or black - matt

Market	Range
U.S.A.	$20.00 - 125.00
Canada	$30.00 - 175.00
U.K.	£10.00 - 60.00

Shape 1891 Vase

Designer:	Albert Hallam in 1963
Issued:	1963 - by 1967
Height:	5 ½", 14.0 cm
Colour:	1. Various decorations - satin matt
	2. White or black - matt

Market	Range
U.S.A.	$20.00 - 125.00
Canada	$30.00 - 175.00
U.K.	£10.00 - 60.00

Shape 1896A   Plant pot holder (pattern name unknown)

Designer:	Albert Hallam in 1963
Issued:	1963 - 1967
Size :	5 ½" x 6 ½", 14 x 16.5 cm
Colour:	1. Various decorations - satin matt
	2. White or black - matt

Market Range	
U.S.A.	$20.00 - 75.00
Canada	$30.00 - 100.00
U.K.	£10.00 - 40.00

Shape 1896B   Vase, Caprice series

Designer:	Albert Hallam in 1963
Issued:	1968 - by 1972
Height:	5 ½" x 6 ½", 14 x 16.5 cm
Colour:	Orange, turquoise or yellow

Market	Range
U.S.A.	$20.00 - 75.00
Canada	$30.00 - 100.00
U.K.	£10.00 - 40.00

Shape 1935 Vase two-handled

Designer:	Albert Hallam in 1964
Issued:	1964 - 1967
Height:	5 ½″, 14.0 cm
Colour:	1. Various decorations - satin matt
	2. White or black - matt
	3. Copper - lustre

Market	Range
U.S.A.	$20.00 - 125.00
Canada	$30.00 - 175.00
U.K.	£10.00 - 60.00

Shape 1936 Goblet vase

Designer:	Albert Hallam in 1964
Issued:	1964 - 1971
Height :	7 ¾″, 19.7 cm
Colour:	1. Various decorations - satin matt
	2. White or black - matt
	3. Copper - lustre

Market	Range
U.S.A.	$20.00 - 100.00
Canada	$30.00 - 150.00
U.K.	£10.00 - 50.00

Shape 2003 Plant pot holder

Designer:	Albert Hallam in 1965
Issued:	1965 - by 1972
Height:	6 ¼", 15.9 cm
Colour:	Soft variegated pastel colours - gloss
Series:	Sea Shell

Market	Range
U.S.A.	$50.00 - 100.00
Canada	$75.00 - 150.00
U.K.	£25.00 - 50.00

Shape 2006 Vase

Designer:	Albert Hallam in 1965
Issued:	1965 - by 1972
Height :	7 ½", 19.1 cm
Colour:	1. Various decorations - satin matt
	2. White or black - matt

Market	Range
U.S.A.	$30.00 - 150.00
Canada	$45.00 - 200.00
U.K.	£15.00 - 80.00

Shape 2012 Shell vase

Designer:	Albert Hallam in 1965
Issued:	1965 - by 1972
Height:	4 ½", 11.9 cm
Colour:	Soft variegated pastel colours - gloss
Series:	Sea Shell

Market	Range
U.S.A.	$50.00 - 100.00
Canada	$75.00 - 150.00
U.K.	£25.00 - 50.00

Shape 2014 Shell vase

Designer:	Albert Hallam in 1965
Issued:	1965 - by 1972
Size:	6" x 12 ½", 15 x 32.7 cm
Colour:	Soft variegated pastel colours - gloss
Series:	Sea Shell

Market	Range
U.S.A.	$50.00 - 100.00
Canada	$75.00 - 150.00
U.K.	£25.00 - 50.00

Shape 2015 Shell vase

Designer: Albert Hallam in 1965
Issued: 1965 - by 1972
Height: 8", 20.3 cm
Colour: Soft variegated pastel colours - gloss
Series: Sea Shell

Market	Range
U.S.A.	$50.00 - 100.00
Canada	$75.00 - 150.00
U.K.	£25.00 - 50.00

Shape 2016 Shell plant pot holder

Designer: Albert Hallam in 1965
Issued: 1965 - by 1972
Height: 4 ¾", 12.1 cm
Colour: Soft variegated pastel colours - gloss
Series: Sea Shell

Market	Range
U.S.A.	$50.00 - 100.00
Canada	$75.00 - 150.00
U.K.	£25.00 - 50.00

Shape 2017 Vase

Designer: Albert Hallam in 1965
Issued: 1965 - by 1972
Height: 5 ¼", 13.3 cm
Colour: 1. Various decorations - satin matt
            2. White or black - matt

Market	Range
U.S.A.	$30.00 - 150.00
Canada	$45.00 - 200.00
U.K.	£15.00 - 80.00

Shape 2020 Shell vase

Designer: Albert Hallam in 1965
Issued: 1965 - by 1972
Height: 6 ½", 16.5 cm
Colour: Soft variegated pastel colours - gloss
Series: Sea Shell

Market	Range
U.S.A.	$50.00 - 100.00
Canada	$75.00 - 150.00
U.K.	£25.00 - 50.00

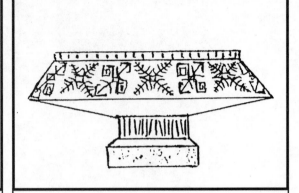

Shape 2021 Shell vase

Designer:	Albert Hallam in 1965
Issued:	1965 - by 1972
Height:	9 ¾", 24.7 cm
Colour:	Soft variegated pastel colours - gloss
Series:	Sea Shell

Market	Range
U.S.A.	$50.00 - 100.00
Canada	$75.00 - 150.00
U.K.	£25.00 - 50.00

Shape 2022 Vase on pedestal

Designer:	Albert Hallam in 1965
Issued:	1965 - by 1972
Size:	5 ½" x 11 ¾", 14 x 29.8 cm
Colour:	1. Various decorations - satin matt
	2. White or black - matt

Market	Range
U.S.A.	$30.00 - 150.00
Canada	$45.00 - 200.00
U.K.	£15.00 - 80.00

Shape 2025 Goblet vase

Designer:	Albert Hallam in 1965
Issued:	1965 - by 1972
Height:	8 ¾", 22.2 cm
Colour:	1. Various decorations - satin matt
	2. White or black - matt

Market	Range
U.S.A.	$30.00 - 150.00
Canada	$45.00 - 200.00
U.K.	£15.00 - 80.00

Shape 2046 Vase

Designer:	Albert Hallam in 1965
Issued:	1965 - by 1972
Height :	8", 20.3 cm
Colour:	1. Various decorations - satin matt
	2. White or black - matt

Market	Range
U.S.A.	$30.00 - 150.00
Canada	$45.00 - 200.00
U.K.	£15.00 - 80.00

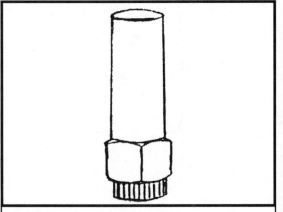

Shape 2049 Vase

Designer: Albert Hallam in 1965
Issued: 1965 - by 1972
Height: 10″, 25.4 cm
Colour: 1. Various decorations - satin matt
             2. White or black - matt

Market	Range
U.S.A.	$20.00 - 125.00
Canada	$30.00 - 175.00
U.K.	£10.00 - 60.00

Shape 2070 Chalice vase

Designer: Albert Hallam in 1962
Issued: 1962 - 1969
Height :   9 ½″, 24 cm
Colour: 1. Various decorations - satin matt
             2. White or black - matt
             3. Copper - lustre

Market	Range
U.S.A.	$30.00 - 100.00
Canada	$45.00 - 150.00
U.K.	£15.00 - 50.00

Note: Pair with shape 1799.

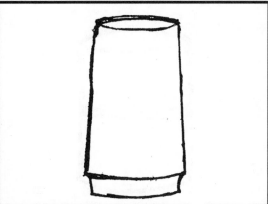

Shape 2081 Vase, round

Designer: Graham Tongue in 1966
Issued: 1967 - 1972
Height: Unknown
Colour: 1. Various decorations - satin matt
             2. White or black - matt

Market	Range
U.S.A.	$20.00 - 100.00
Canada	$30.00 - 150.00
U.K.	£10.00 - 50.00

Shape 2111 Vase

Designer: Albert Hallam in 1967
Issued: 1967 - by 1972
Height :   7″, 17.8 cm
Colour: 1. Various decorations - satin matt
             2. White or black - matt
             3. Copper - lustre

Market	Range
U.S.A.	$20.00 - 125.00
Canada	$30.00 - 175.00
U.K.	£10.00 - 60.00

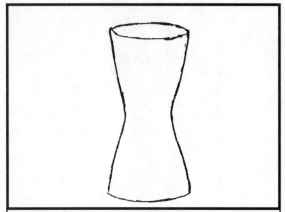

Shape 2121 Vase

Designer:	Graham Tongue in 1967
Issued:	1967 - by 1972
Height:	8 ½″, 21.6 cm
Colour:	1. Various decorations - satin matt
	2. White or black - matt
	3. Copper - lustre

Range	Market
U.S.A.	$30.00 - 125.00
Canada	$45.00 - 175.00
U.K.	£15.00 - 60.00

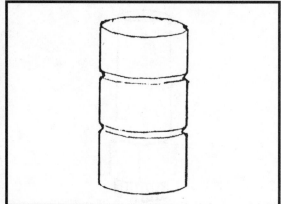

Shape 2122 Vase

Designer:	Graham Tongue in 1967
Issued:	1967 - by 1972
Height :	8″, 20.3 cm
Colour:	1. Various decorations - satin matt
	2. White or black - matt
	3. Copper - lustre

Range	Market
U.S.A.	$20.00 - 125.00
Canada	$30.00 - 175.00
U.K.	£10.00 - 60.00

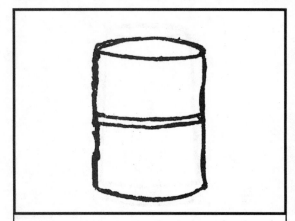

Shape 2123 Vase

Designer:	Graham Tongue in 1967
Issued:	1967 - by 1972
Height:	5 ½″, 14.0 cm
Colour:	1. Various decorations - satin matt
	2. White or black - matt
	3. Copper - lustre

Market	Range
U.S.A.	$20.00 - 100.00
Canada	$30.00 - 150.00
U.K.	£10.00 - 50.00

Shape 2124 Vase

Designer:	Graham Tongue in 1967
Issued:	1967 - by 1972
Height :	6 ½″, 16.5 cm
Colour:	1. Various decorations - satin matt
	2. White or black - matt
	3. Copper - lustre

Market	Range
U.S.A.	$20.00 - 100.00
Canada	$30.00 - 150.00
U.K.	£10.00 - 50.00

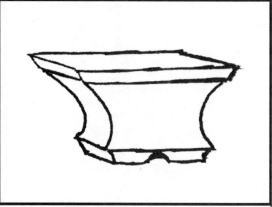

Shape 2134 Vase, oval top

Designer:	Graham Tongue in 1967
Issued:	1967 - by 1972
Height:	11", 27.9 cm
Colour:	1. Various decorations - satin matt
	2. White or black - matt
	3. Copper - lustre

Market	Range
U.S.A.	$20.00 - 125.00
Canada	$30.00 - 165.00
U.K.	£10.00 - 60.00

Shape 2140 Vase

Designer:	Albert Hallam in 1967
Issued:	1968 - 1970
Height:	2 ½", 6.4 cm
Colour:	1. Various decorations - satin matt
	2. White or black - matt
	3. Copper - lustre

Market	Range
U.S.A.	$20.00 - 75.00
Canada	$30.00 - 100.00
U.K.	£10.00 - 40.00

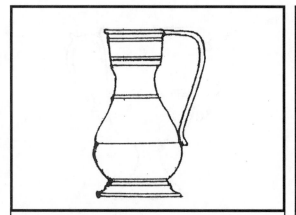

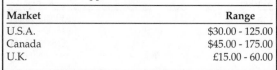

Shape 2172/2173/2174 Vase

Designer:	Mr. Garbet in 1967
Issued:	1967 - 1972
Height :	9 ¾", 5 ½", 4 ½", 24.7, 14.0, 11.9 cm
Colour:	1. Various decorations - satin matt
	2. White or black - matt
	3 Copper - lustre

Market	Range
U.S.A.	$30.00 - 125.00
Canada	$45.00 - 175.00
U.K.	£15.00 - 60.00

Shape 2288 Cherub vase

Designer:	Graham Tongue in 1969
Issued:	1969 - 1972
Height:	10", 25.4 cm
Colour:	1. Various decorations - satin matt
	2. White or black - matt
	3. Copper - lustre

Market	Range
U.S.A.	$30.00 - 150.00
Canada	$45.00 - 200.00
U.K.	£15.00 - 80.00

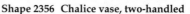

Photograph not
available
at press time

Shape 2297 Goblet vase

Designer:	Unknown
Issued:	1969 - by 1972
Height :	9", 22.9 cm
Colour:	1. Various decorations - satin matt
	2. White or black - matt
	3. Copper - lustre

Market	Range
U.S.A.	$20.00 - 125.00
Canada	$30.00 - 175.00
U.K.	£10.00 - 60.00

Shape 2356 Chalice vase, two-handled

Designer:	Graham Tongue in 1971
Issued:	1972 only
Height:	10 ½", 26.7 cm
Colour:	1. Pewteramic
	2. White - matt

Market	Range
U.S.A.	$30.00 - 100.00
Canada	$45.00 - 150.00
U.K.	£15.00 - 50.00

Shape 2378 Goblet vase

Designer:	Graham Tongue in 1971
Issued:	1972 only
Height :	8 ½", 21.6 cm
Colour:	1. Pewteramic
	2. White - matt

Market	Range
U.S.A.	$30.00 - 100.00
Canada	$45.00 - 150.00
U.K.	£15.00 - 50.00

Shape 2379 Goblet vase

Designer:	Graham Tongue in 1971
Issued:	1972 only
Height:	6", 15 cm
Colour:	1. Pewteramic
	2. White - matt

Market	Range
U.S.A.	$30.00 - 100.00
Canada	$45.00 - 150.00
U.K.	£15.00 - 50.00

WALL ORNAMENTS/MASKS/PLAQUES/VASES

There are eighty-eight wall ornaments listed here. These do not include character ware or the animal, bird, butterfly and horse plaques. Details for this latter group can be found in *The Charlton Standard Catalogue of Beswick Animals*.

Here we have eighteen face masks, mostly of thirties style girls, also two plaques in the Shakespearian Series, three Beatrix Potter, seven of Christmas Around The World and various wall vases, advertising wares and four plaques featuring animals.

In 1940, a freelance modeller, Miss Joachim, modelled eleven plaques for Beswick. Four featured scenes from the book *Alice In Wonderland*, they were No. 857 - Alice with the White Rabbit, No. 858 - After the Caucus Race, No. 859 - The Duchess with the Baby and No. 860 - A Game of Croquet. Five featured scenes from *Cinderella*, these were No. 861 - Cinderella with the Birds, No. 863 - The Ugly Sisters getting ready for the Ball, No. 865 Cinderella with the Prince, No. 866 - The Herald with the Slipper and No. 867 - The Slipper Fits Cinderella. In addition to these there were two floral plaques (No. 856 a single rose and No. 864 a floral spray). No further information is available and although samples must have been made up at the time and possibly even some were marketed, it is quite likely that these plaques were never put into full commercial production.

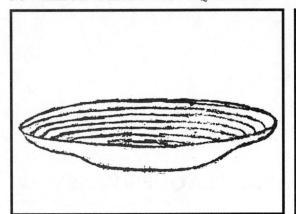

Shape 139   Plaque

Designer: Albert Hallam c.1933
Issued: c.1933 - by 1940
Diameter: 12", 30.5 cm
Colour: 1. Assorted decos - satin matt
             2. White - matt

Market	Range
U.S.A.	$30.00 - 75.00
Canada	$45.00 - 100.00
U.K.	£15.00 - 40.00

Shape 197   Girl with hat, wall mask

Designer: Unknown
Issued: c.1933 - by 1954
Height: 6 ½", 16.5 cm
Colour: 1. Hat in various colours, hair blonde - gloss
             2. White - matt

Colour	U.S. $	Can. $	U.K. £
1. Coloured hat - gloss	400.00	600.00	200.00
2. White - matt		Rare	

Shape 263   Galleon, plaque

Designer: Mr. Fletcher
Issued: c.1934 - by 1954
Height: 9 ½", 24.0 cm
Colour: 1. Blue sea, galleon in grey and brown, on
                a cream background - gloss
             2. Stone - satin matt

Market	Range
U.S.A.	$70.00 - 175.00
Canada	$100.00 - 225.00
U.K.	£35.00 - 85.00

Shape 277   Girl with hat, wall mask

Designer: Unknown
Issued: c.1934 - by 1940
Height: 4 ½" 11.9 cm
Colour: Blonde hair, hat black and green - gloss

Description	U.S. $	Can. $	U.K. £
Girl with hat	400.00	600.00	200.00

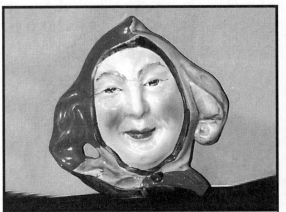

Shape 279   Jester, wall mask

Designer: Mr. Dean c.1933
Issued: c.1934 - by 1954
Height: 6", 15 cm
Colour: Orange and green motley with
             brown trim - gloss

Description	U.S. $	Can. $	U.K. £
Jester	200.00	300.00	100.00

Shape 282   Red Indian, wall mask

Designer: Mr. Dean c.1933
Issued: c.1934 - by 1954
Height: 7 ½", 19.1 cm
Colour: 1. Blue, green, cream, and dark brown - gloss
             2. White - matt

Colour	U.S. $	Can. $	U.K. £
1. Blue, green, cream, brown	200.00	300.00	100.00
2. White		Rare	

Shape 314   Girl with black beret, wall mask

Designer: Miss Greaves c.1934
Issued: c.1935 - by 1940
Height: 9 ¼", 23.5 cm
Colour: Blonde hair, black beret - gloss

Description	U.S. $	Can. $	U.K. £
Girl with black beret	400.00	600.00	200.00

Shape 362   Girl with orange beret, wall mask

Designer: Unknown
Issued: c.1935 - by 1940
Height: 3 ¾", 9.5 cm
Colour: Orange beret, black hair and
             orange bow - gloss

Description	U.S. $	Can. $	U.K. £
Girl with orange beret	400.00	600.00	200.00

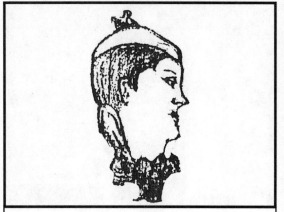

Shape 363   Girl with hat (facing right), wall mask

Designer:	Unknown
Issued:	c.1935 - by 1940
Size:	Unknown
Colour:	Unknown - gloss

Description	U.S. $	Can. $	U.K. £
Girl with hat	400.00	600.00	200.00

Shape 364   Girl with beret, wall mask

Designer:	Unknown
Issued:	c.1935 - by 1940
Size:	Unknown
Colour:	Unknown - gloss

Description	U.S. $	Can. $	U.K. £
Girl with beret	400.00	600.00	200.00

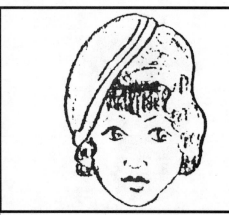

Photograph not
available
at press time

Shape 365   Girl with beret, wall mask

Designer:	Unknown
Issued:	c.1935 - by 1940
Size:	Unknown
Colour:	Unknown - gloss

Description	U.S. $	Can. $	U.K. £
Girl with beret	400.00	600.00	200.00

Shape 366   Girl with hat, wall mask

Designer:	Unknown
Issued:	c.1935 - by 1940
Size:	Unknown
Colour:	Unknown - gloss

Description	U.S. $	Can. $	U.K. £
Girl with hat	400.00	600.00	200.00

Shape 367   Girl with hat (facing left), wall mask

Designer:	Unknown
Issued:	c.1935 - by 1940
Size:	Unknown
Colour:	Unknown - gloss

Description	U.S. $	Can. $	U.K. £
Girl with hat	400.00	600.00	200.00

Shape 380   Young girl with bonnet, wall mask

Designer:	Mr. Owen in 1936
Issued:	1936 - by 1940
Height:	9", 22.9 cm
Colour:	Blonde hair, pink bonnet with green bow - gloss

Description	U.S. $	Can. $	U.K. £
Young girl with bonnet	400.00	600.00	200.00

Shape 393   Girl with plaits, wall mask

Designer:	Miss Greaves in 1936
Issued:	1936 - by 1940
Size:	8 ½", 21.6 cm
Colour:	Unknown - gloss

Description	U.S. $	Can. $	U.K. £
Girl with plaits	400.00	600.00	200.00

Shape 433   Wall vase

Designer:	Mr. Symcox in 1936
Issued:	1936 - by 1940
Size:	8 ½", 21.6 cm
Colour:	1. Assorted decorations - satin matt
	2. White - matt

Market	Range
U.S.A.	$30.00 - 75.00
Canada	$45.00 - 100.00
U.K.	£15.00 - 40.00

Shape 436   Hyacinth lady, wall mask

Designer:	Miss Greaves in 1936
Issued:	1936 - by 1954
Height:	12", 30.5 cm
Colour:	1. Fair or dark hair, blue flowers, red beads - satin matt
	2. Stone - satin matt 3. White - matt

Market	Range
U.S.A.	$200.00 - 500.00
Canada	$300.00 - 750.00
U.K.	£100.00 - 250.00

Shape 449   Lady with hat and scarf, wall mask

Designer:	Mr. Owen in 1936
Issued:	1936 - by 1940
Height:	12 ½", 31.7 cm
Colour:	Unknown - gloss

Description	U.S. $	Can. $	U.K. £
Lady with hat and scarf	600.00	900.00	300.00

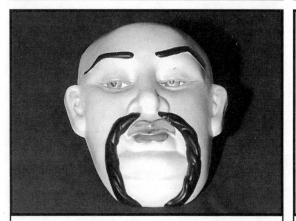

Shape 457   Genie, wall mask

Designer:	Miss Greaves in 1936
Issued:	1936 - by 1940
Size:	9 ¼", 23.5 cm
Colour:	Black hat and moustache - gloss

Description	U.S. $	Can. $	U.K. £
Genie	350.00	500.00	175.00

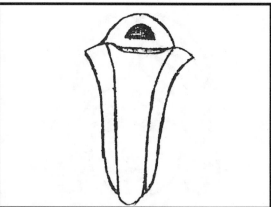

Shape 467   Wall vase

Designer:	Mr. Symcox in 1937
Issued:	1937 - by 1959
Size:	9", 22.9 cm
Colour:	1. Assorted decorations - satin matt
	2. White - matt

Market	Range
U.S.A.	$30.00 - 75.00
Canada	$45.00 - 100.00
U.K.	£15.00 - 40.00

Shape 470   George VI, coronation plaque

Designer: Mr. Weiss in 1937
Issued: 1937 - 1937
Size: Unknown
Colour: Ivory - satin matt

Colour	U.S. $	Can. $	U.K. £
Coronation plaque		Rare	

Shape 483   Girl with headdress, wall mask

Designer: Miss Greaves in 1937
Issued: 1937 - by 1940
Length: 9", 22.9 cm
Colour: Light brown hair, light grey-blue headdress; beige with yellow flowers

Description	U.S. $	Can. $	U.K. £
Girl with headdress	500.00	750.00	250.00

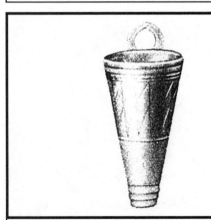

Shape 490   Wall vase, in two sizes

Designer: Mr. Owen in 1937
Issued: 1937 - by 1940
Sizes: 1. 8 ½", 21.6 cm
             2. 10", 25.4 cm
Colour: 1. Assorted decorations - satin matt
             2. White - matt

Market	Range
U.S.A.	$30.00 - 75.00
Canada	$45.00 - 100.00
U.K.	£15.00 - 40.00

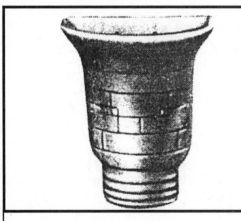

Shape 492   Wall vase

Designer: Mr. Owen in 1937
Issued: 1937 - by 1940
Height: 7 ½", 19.1 cm
Colour: 1. Assorted decorations - satin matt
             2. White - matt

Market	Range
U.S.A.	$30.00 - 75.00
Canada	$45.00 - 100.00
U.K.	£15.00 - 40.00

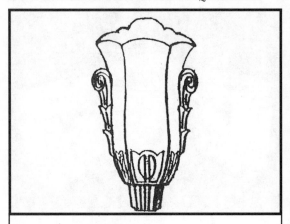

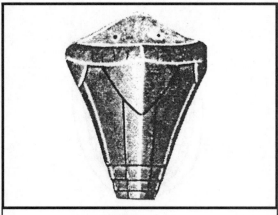

Shape 498   Wall vase

Designer: Mr. Owen in 1937
Issued: 1937 - by 1940
Height: 11 ½", 29.2 cm
Colour: 1. Assorted decorations - satin matt
             2. White - matt

Market	Range
U.S.A.	$30.00 - 75.00
Canada	$45.00 - 100.00
U.K.	£15.00 - 40.00

Shape 503   Wall vase

Designer: Mr. Owen in 1937
Issued: 1937 - by 1940
Height: 9", 22.9 cm
Colour: 1. Assorted decorations - satin matt
             2. White - matt

Market	Range
U.S.A.	$30.00 - 75.00
Canada	$45.00 - 100.00
U.K.	£15.00 - 40.00

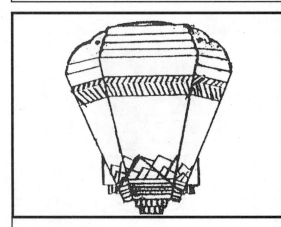

Shape 506   Wall vase

Designer: Mr. Owen in 1937
Issued: 1937 - by 1940
Size: Unknown
Colour: 1. Assorted decorations - satin matt
             2. White - matt

Market	Range
U.S.A.	$30.00 - 100.00
Canada	$45.00 - 150.00
U.K.	£15.00 - 50.00

Shape 507   The Gleaners

Designer: Mr. Watkin in 1937
Issued: 1937 - 1940
Size: 11", 27.9 cm
Colour: Green rim with scene in various shades of
             brown - satin matt

Description	U.S. $	Can. $	U.K. £
The Gleaners	300.00	450.00	150.00

Note: This plaque is a pair with shape 508.

Shape 508   **The Angelus**

Designer: Mr. Watkin in 1937
Issued: 1937 - 1940
Size: 11", 27.9 cm
Colour: Green rim with scene in various shades of brown - satin matt

Description	U.S. $	Can. $	U.K. £
The Angelus	300.00	450.00	150.00

Note: This plaque is a pair with shape 507.

Shape 551   **Flowers in basket, plaque**

Designer: Mr. Hayward in 1937
Issued: 1938 - by 1954
Height: 10", 25.4 cm
Colour: Flowers in various colours, basket in beige and light brown - satin matt

Description	U.S. $	Can. $	U.K. £
Flowers in basket	150.00	225.00	75.00

Shape 556   **Flowers in basket plaque**

Designer: Mr. Watkin in 1937
Issued: 1938 - by 1954
Height: 10 ½", 26.7 cm
Colour: Flowers in various colours, basket in beige and light brown - satin matt

Description	U.S. $	Can. $	U.K. £
Flowers in basket	150.00	225.00	75.00

Shape 557   **Spray of flowers, plaque**

Designer: Miss Greaves in 1937
Issued: 1938 - by 1954
Size: 6 ½", 16.5 cm
Colour: Flowers in various colours, yellow bowl - satin matt

Description	U.S. $	Can. $	U.K. £
Spray of flowers	150.00	225.00	75.00

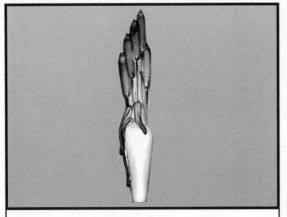

Shape 564   **Bulrushes, plaque**

Designer: Miss Greaves in 1937
Issued: 1938 - by 1954
Height: 14", 35.5 cm
Colour: Brown bulrushes in blue or white holder - satin matt

Description	U.S. $	Can. $	U.K. £
Bulrushes	90.00	125.00	50.00

Shape 565   **Anemones, plaque**

Designer: Unknown
Issued: 1938 - by 1954
Size: 5 ½", 14.0 cm
Colour: Flowers in various colours, holder in yellow - satin matt

Description	U.S. $	Can. $	U.K. £
Anemones	150.00	225.00	75.00

Shape 571   **Bowl of roses, plaque**

Designer: Miss Greaves in 1938
Issued: 1938 - by 1954
Height: 4 ½", 11.9 cm
Colour: Pink and yellow flowers with green leaves - satin matt

Description	U.S. $	Can. $	U.K. £
Bowl of roses	150.00	225.00	75.00

Shape 572   **Robin on bough, plaque**

Designer: Miss Greaves in 1938
Issued: 1938 - by 1954
Size: Unknown
Colour: Bird natural colour, brown bough, foliage green - satin matt

Description	U.S. $	Can. $	U.K. £
Bird on bough	150.00	225.00	85.00

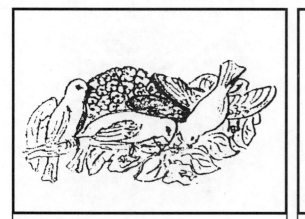

Shape 574   **Three blue tits, plaque**

Designer: Miss Greaves in 1938
Issued: 1938 - by 1954
Size: Unknown
Colour: Unknown - satin matt

Description	U.S. $	Can. $	U.K. £
Three blue tits	150.00	225.00	75.00

Shape 583   **Wall vase**

Designer: Mr. Symcox in 1938
Issued: 1938 - by 1940
Size: Unknown
Colour: 1. Assorted decorations - satin matt
       2. White - matt

Market	Range
U.S.A.	$30.00 - 75.00
Canada	$45.00 - 100.00
U.K.	£15.00 - 40.00

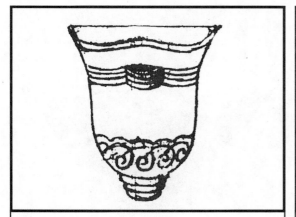

Shape 584   **Wall vase**

Designer: Mr. Symcox in 1938
Issued: 1938 - by 1940
Size: Unknown
Colour: 1. Assorted decorations - satin matt
       2. White - matt

Market	Range
U.S.A.	$30.00 - 75.00
Canada	$45.00 - 100.00
U.K.	£15.00 - 40.00

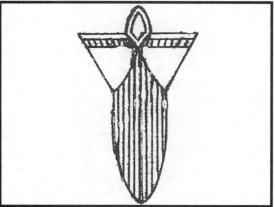

Shape 585   **Wall vase**

Designer: Mr. Symcox in 1938
Issued: 1938 - by 1940
Size: 9", 22.9 cm
Colour: 1. Assorted decorations - satin matt
       2. White - matt

Market	Range
U.S.A.	$30.00 - 75.00
Canada	$45.00 - 100.00
U.K.	£15.00 - 40.00

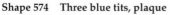

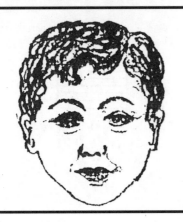

Shape 612   Young boy's head, wall mask

Designer: Mr. Owen in 1938
Issued: 1938 - by 1954
Size: 7 ¼", 18.4 cm
Colour: Brown hair, face in natural colour - satin matt

Descripton	U.S. $	Can. $	U.K. £
Young boy's head	500.00	750.00	250.00

Shape 614   Butterfly, wall vase

Designer: Mr. Watkin in 1938
Issued: 1938 - by 1954
Size: Unknown
Colour: Blue, green, yellow, brown
             and cream - satin matt

Description	U.S. $	Can. $	U.K. £
Butterfly	150.00	225.00	75.00

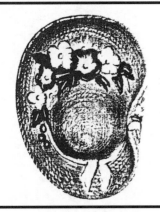

Shape 651   Hat with flowers, wall vase

Designer: Mr. Watkin in 1938
Issued: 1938 - by 1965
Size: 9 ¼", 23.5 cm
Colour: Stone or straw coloured hat with flowers in
             various colours - gloss or matt

Description	U.S. $	Can. $	U.K. £
Hat with flowers	150.00	225.00	75.00

Shape 693   Modelle, wall vase

Designer: Unknown
Issued: 1939 - by 1963
Length: 13", 33 cm
Colour: 1. Assorted decorations - satin matt
             2. White - matt

Market	Range
U.S.A.	$50.00 - 75.00
Canada	$75.00 - 100.00
U.K.	£30.00 - 50.00

Shape 708   Cupid, wall vase

Designer:	Arthur Gredington in 1939
Issued:	1939 - by 1954
Size:	6 ¾, 17.2 cm
Colour:	Natural coloured body with pale green wings and blonde hair - satin matt

Description	U.S. $	Can. $	U.K. £
Cupid, wall vase		Rare	

Shape 710   Courting couple, plaque

Designer:	Arthur Gredington in 1939
Issued:	1939 - by 1954
Size:	8", 20.3 cm
Colour:	Green background, white dress with pink and yellow flowers, man in red jacket, yellow, waistcoat, green breeches and white hose - gloss

Description	U.S. $	Can. $	U.K. £
Courting couple	200.00	300.00	125.00

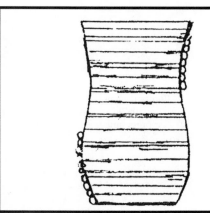

Shape 713   Wall vase

Designer:	Albert Hallam in 1939
Issued:	1939 - by 1954
Size:	Unknown
Colour:	1. Assorted decorations - satin matt
	2. White - matt

Market	Range
U.S.A.	$30.00 - 75.00
Canada	$45.00 - 100.00
U.K.	£15.00 - 40.00

Shape 714   "Hear no evil, say no evil, see no evil," motto plaque or letter rack

Designer:	Arthur Gredington in 1939
Issued:	1939 - by 1954
Size:	6 x 4 ½, 15 cm x 11.9 cm
Colour:	Grey/blue, green and brown on light background - gloss

Description	U.S. $	Can. $	U.K. £
"Hear no evil....."	200.00	300.00	125.00

Shape 715   "A world without friends would be like a garden without flowers," motto plaque

Designer:	Mr. Owen in 1939
Issued:	1939 - by 1954
Size:	9 ½" x 7 ½", 24.0 x 19.1 cm
Colour:	1. Multi-coloured border - satin matt
	2. White - matt

Colour	U.S. $	Can. $	U.K. £
1. Multi-coloured border	150.00	225.00	75.00
2. White	100.00	150.00	50.00

Photograph not
available
at press time

Shape 719   "One of the best things to have up your sleeve is a funny bone," motto plaque

Designer:	Mr. Owen in 1939
Issued:	1939 - by 1954
Size:	9 ½" x 7 ½", 24.0 x 19.1 cm
Colour:	1. Multi-coloured border - satin matt
	2. White - matt

Colour	U.S. $	Can. $	U.K. £
1. Multi-coloured border	150.00	225.00	75.00
2. White	100.00	150.00	50.00

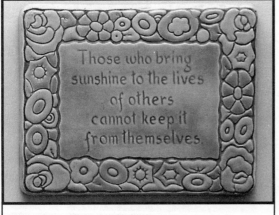

Shape 723   "Those who bring sunshine to the lives of others cannot keep it from themselves," motto plaque

Designer:	Mr. Owen in 1939
Issued:	1939 - by 1954
Size:	9 ¼" x 7 ¼", 23.5 x 18.4 cm
Colour:	1. Multi-coloured border - satin matt
	2. White - matt

Colour	U.S. $	Can. $	U.K. £
1. Multi-coloured border	150.00	225.00	75.00
2. White	100.00	150.00	50.00

Photograph not
available
at press time

Shape 724   "Don't worry it may never happen," motto plaque

Designer:	Mr. Owen in 1939
Issued:	1939 - by 1954
Size:	8" x 8 ¾", 20.3 x 22.0 cm
Colour:	1. Multi-coloured border - satin matt
	2. White - matt

Colour	U.S. $	Can. $	U.K. £
1. Multi-coloured border	150.00	225.00	75.00
2. White	100.00	150.00	50.00

Photograph not
available
at press time

Shape 733   **Cupid, wall vase**

Designer: Arthur Gredington in 1939
Issued: 1939 - by 1954
Size: 6 ¾", 17.2 cm
Colour: Natural coloured body with pale green wings
            and blonde hair - satin matt

Description	U.S. $	Can. $	U.K. £
Cupid		Rare	

Shape 739   **"Lifes a melody if youll only hum the tune,"**
              motto plaque

Designer: Mr. Owen in 1939
Issued: 1939 - by 1954
Size: 8" x 8 ¾", 20.3 x 22.0 cm
Colour: 1. Multi-coloured border - satin matt
            2. White - matt

Colour	U.S. $	Can. $	U.K. £
1. Multi-coloured border	150.00	225.00	75.00
2. White	100.00	150.00	50.00

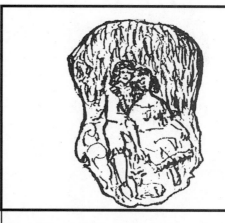

Shape 740   **"When you are up to your neck in hot water,**
              think of the kettle and sing," motto plaque

Designer: Mr. Owen in 1939
Issued: 1939 - by 1954
Size: 8" x 8 ¾", 20.3 x 22.0 cm
Colour: 1. Multi-coloured border - satin matt
            2. White - matt

Colour	U.S. $	Can. $	U.K. £
1. Multi-coloured border	150.00	225.00	75.00
2. White	100.00	150.00	50.00

Shape 741   **Courting couple, plaque**

Designer: Arthur Gredington in 1939
Issued: 1939 - by 1954
Size: 8", 20.3 cm
Colour: Unknown

Description	U.S. $	Can. $	U.K. £
Courting couple	250.00	375.00	125.00

Shape 806	Horse head, tie rack, wall ornament
Designer:	Mr. Owen in 1938
Issued:	1939 - 1968
Size:	7 ¼", 18.4 cm
Height:	6", 15 cm
Colour:	Brown - gloss

Description	U.S. $	Can. $	U.K. £
Horse head, tie rack	150.00	225.00	75.00

Note: Modelled from no. 686 (flat back) but with raised back.

Shape 807	Horse head, tie rack, wall ornament
Designer:	Mr. Owen in 1938
Issued:	1939 - 1968
Size:	7 ¼," 18.4 cm
Height:	6", 15 cm
Colour:	Brown - gloss

Description	U.S. $	Can. $	U.K. £
Horse head, tie rack	150.00	225.00	75.00

Note: Modelled from no. 687 (flat back) but with raised back.

Photograph not
available
at press time

Shape 837	Plain plaque
Designer:	Albert Hallam in 1940
Issued:	1940 - by 1954
Diameter:	16", 40.5 cm
Colour:	Unknown

Description	U.S. $	Can. $	U.K. £
Plain plaque	Possibly not put into production		

Shape 842	Gargoyle/cat, plaque
Designer:	Miss Joachim in 1940
Issued:	1940 - by 1954
Size:	4 ½" x 4 ½", 11.5 x 11.5 cm
Colour:	Dark grey/black - gloss

Description	U.S. $	Can. $	U.K. £
Gargoyle/cat		Rare	

Shape 1209 **"As You Like It," Shakespeare, plaque**

Designer:	Arthur Gredington in 1950
Issued:	1951 - 1968
Diameter:	12", 30.5 cm
Colour:	Multi-coloured scene - gloss

Description	U.S. $	Can. $	U.K. £
"As You Like It", plaque	250.00	375.00	125.00

Note: This plaque is a pair with shape 1210.

Shape 1210 **"Romeo and Juliet," Shakespeare plaque**

Designer:	Arthur Gredington in 1950
Issued:	1951 - 1968
Diameter:	12", 30.5 cm
Colour:	Multi-coloured scene - gloss

Description	U.S. $	Can. $	U.K. £
'Romeo and Juliet", plaque	250.00	375.00	125.00

Note: This plaque is a pair with shape 1209.

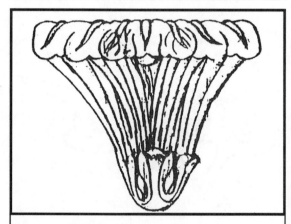

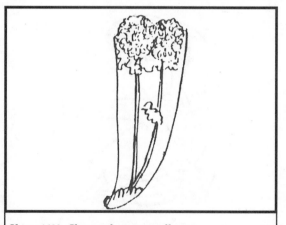

Shape 1322 **Corner wall vase**

Designer:	Albert Hallam and Mr. Hayward in 1953
Issued:	1954 - by 1956
Size:	Unknown
Colour:	Unknown

Description	U.S. $	Can. $	U.K. £
Corner wall vase	75.00	100.00	30.00

Shape 1609 **Chrysanthemum, wall vase**

Designer:	Albert Hallam in 1959
Issued:	1959 - by 1963
Size:	Unknown
Colour:	Coloured flowers on a white background - satin matt

Description	U.S. $	Can. $	U.K. £
Chrysanthemum, wall vase	100.00	150.00	50.00

Note: Set of nine with vases nos. 1602, 1604,1605, 1606, 1607, 1608, bowl 1603 and basket 1668

Shape 1632 Yacht GP14, plaque

Designer:	Albert Hallam in 1959
Issued:	1960 - by 1963
Height:	7 ¾", 19.7 cm
Colour:	White sails, blue boat on shaded blue-green sea - satin matt

Description	U.S. $	Can. $	U.K. £
Yacht GP14	175.00	250.00	90.00

Note: Set of four with ornaments 1610, 1633 and 1634.

Shape 1679 Double Diamond pub, plaque

Designer:	Albert Hallam in 1960
Issued:	Unknown
Size:	Unknown
Colour:	Pub - brown roof, stone coloured walls and blue sills; green leaves on tree - gloss

Description	U.S. $	Can. $	U.K. £
Double Diamond pub	350.00	500.00	200.00

Note: Special Commission.

Shape 1680 Double Diamond man, plaque

Designer:	Albert Hallam in 1960
Issued:	Unknown
Height:	7", 17.8 cm
Colour:	Black hat and jacket, black and white striped trousers with white shirt - gloss

Description	U.S. $	Can. $	U.K. £
Double Diamond man	200.00	300.00	110.00

Note: Special Commission.

Shape 1681 Double Diamond dog, plaque

Designer:	Albert Hallam in 1960
Issued:	Unknown
Size:	Unknown
Colour:	Unknown - gloss

Description	U.S. $	Can. $	U.K. £
Double Diamond dog	200.00	300.00	110.00

Note: Special Commission.

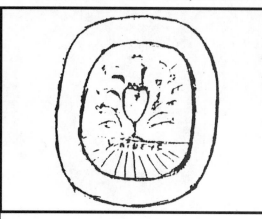

Shape 2060   Hunts plaque

Designer:	Albert Hallam in 1966
Issued:	Unknown
Height:	7 ½", 19.1 cm
Colour:	Grey horse, green tree and grass with brown fence - gloss

Description	U.S. $	Can. $	U.K. £
Hunts plaque	300.00	450.00	175.00

Note: Special Commission.

Shape 2079   Watneys plaque

Designer:	Graham Tongue in 1966
Issued:	Unknown
Size:	6 ¼", 15.9 cm
Colour:	Unknown - gloss

Description	U.S. $	Can. $	U.K. £
Watneys plaque	100.00	150.00	50.00

Note: Special Commission.

Shape 2233   Cat and dog plaque

Designer:	Graham Tongue in 1968
Issued:	1968 - unknown
Size:	9" x 6 ¼", 22.9 x 15.9 cm
Colour:	Unknown - gloss

Description	U.S. $	Can. $	U.K. £
Cat and dog plaque	150.00	225.00	75.00

Shape 2235   Basset dog plaque, concave

Designer:	Graham Tongue in 1968
Issued:	1968 - unknown
Size:	4 ½" x 6 ¼", 11.9 x 15.9 cm
Colour:	Tan and white dog with black background - gloss

Description	U.S. $	Can. $	U.K. £
Basset dog plaque	130.00	175.00	75.00

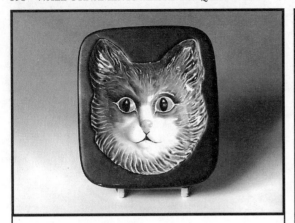

Shape 2236 Cat plaque

Designer: Graham Tongue in 1968
Issued: 1968 - unknown
Size: 6 ¼″ x 9″, 15.9 x 22.9 cm
Colour: Ginger cat, with yellow eyes, on a dark
             pewter background - gloss

Description	U.S. $	Can. $	U.K. £
Cat plaque	125.00	175.00	75.00

Shape 2237 Babycham plaque

Designer: Graham Tongue in 1968
Issued: c.1970 - c.1975
Size: 3″ x 6 ¼″, 7.6 x 15.9 cm
Colour: Unknown - gloss

Description	U.S. $	Can. $	U.K. £
Babycham plaque	175.00	225.00	100.00

Note: Special Commission.

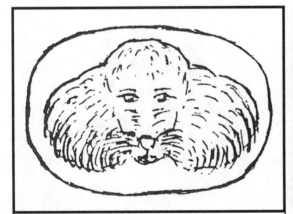

Shape 2268 Poodle plaque

Designer: Graham Tongue in 1969
Issued: 1969 - unknown
Size: 6″ x 4 ½″, 15 x 11.9 cm
Colour: Unknown - gloss

Description	U.S. $	Can. $	U.K. £
Poodle plaque	175.00	250.00	95.00

Shape 2376 Christmas 1972, Latama plaque

Designer: Albert Hallam in 1971
Issued: 1972 only
Size: 11 ¼″ x 5 ½″, 28.5 x 14 cm
Colour: Multi-coloured scene - gloss

Description	U.S. $	Can. $	U.K. £
Christmas 1972	300.00	400.00	175.00

Note: Developed from shape 2375 Christmas 1972
Tankard "The Carol Singers."

Shape 2393 Christmas Plaque, England 1972

Designer:	Albert Hallam in 1971
Issued:	1972 - 1972
Size:	8" x 8", 20.3 x 20.3 cm
Colour:	Multi-coloured scene

Description	U.S. $	Can. $	U.K. £
England 1972	75.00	100.00	50.00

Shape 2419 Christmas Plaque, Mexico 1973

Designer:	Albert Hallam in 1972
Issued:	1973 - 1973
Size:	8" x 8", 20.3 x 20.3 cm
Colour:	Multi-coloured scene

Description	U.S. $	Can. $	U.K. £
Mexico 1973	70.00	85.00	40.00

Shape 2430 Christmas 1973, Latama plaque

Designer:	Albert Hallam in 1972
Issued:	1973 only
Size:	11 ¼" x 5 ½", 28.5 x 14 cm
Colour:	Multi-coloured scene - gloss

Description	U.S. $	Can. $	U.K. £
Christmas 1973	250.00	375.00	150.00

Note: Developed from Shape 2423 Christmas
1973 Tankard "A Christmas Carol."

Shape 2443 Regent Street, Latama plaque

Designer:	Albert Hallam in 1972
Issued:	1973 - unknown
Length:	11 x 7", 27.9" x 17.8 cm
Colour:	Multi-coloured scene - gloss

Description	U.S. $	Can. $	U.K. £
Regent Street	200.00	300.00	125.00

Shape 2462 Christmas Plaque, Bulgaria 1974

Designer:	Albert Hallam in 1973
Issued:	1974 - 1974
Size:	8″ x 8″, 20.3 x 20.3 cm
Colour:	Multi-coloured scene

Description	U.S. $	Can. $	U.K. £
Bulgaria 1974	70.00	85.00	40.00

Shape 2522 Christmas Plaque, Norway 1974

Designer:	Graham Tongue in 1974
Issued:	1975 - 1975
Size:	8″ x 8″, 20.3 x 20.3 cm
Colour:	Multi-coloured scene

Description	U.S. $	Can. $	U.K. £
Norway 1974	70.00	85.00	40.00

Shape 2538 Christmas Plaque, Holland 1976

Designer:	Mr. Lyttleton, Graham Tongue in 1976
Issued:	1976 - 1976
Size:	8″ x 8″, 20.3 x 20.3 cm
Colour:	Multi-coloured scene

Description	U.S. $	Can. $	U.K. £
Holland 1976	70.00	85.00	40.00

Shape 2567 Christmas Plaque, Poland 1977

Designer:	Mr. Plant, Graham Tongue in 1977
Issued:	1977 - 1977
Size:	8″ x 8″, 20.3 x 20.3 cm
Colour:	Multi-coloured scene

Description	U.S. $	Can. $	U.K. £
Poland 1977	70.00	85.00	40.00

Shape 2594 Jemima Puddleduck and Foxy Whiskered Gentleman Plaque, Beatrix Potter plaque

Designer:	David Lyttleton, Harry Sales in 1977
Issued:	1978 - 1982
Size:	7 ½" x 7 ½", 19.1 x 19.1 cm
Colour:	White duck, brown fox in woodland scene of greens and browns - gloss

Description	U.S. $	Can. $	U.K. £
Jemima/Foxy	200.00	275.00	110.00

Note: Set of three with shape nos. 2650 and 2685.

Shape 2598 Christmas Plaque, America 1978

Designer:	Albert Hallam in 1978
Issued:	1978 - 1978
Size:	8" x 8", 20.3 x 20.3 cm
Colour:	Multi-coloured scene

Description	U.S. $	Can. $	U.K. £
America 1978	75.00	100.00	50.00

Shape 2650 Peter Rabbit in Vegetable Patch, Beatrix Potter plaque

Designer:	David Lyttleton, Harry Sales in 1979
Issued:	1980 - 1982
Size:	7 ½" x 7 ½", 19.1 x 19.1 cm
Colour:	Blue jacket; orange carrots; background greens and browns - gloss

Description	U.S. $	Can. $	U.K. £
Peter Rabbit	200.00	275.00	100.00

Note: Set of three with shape nos. 2594 and 2685.

Shape 2685 Mrs. Tiggywinkle at the Door, Beatrix Potter plaque

Designer:	Harry Sales in 1981
Issued:	1982 - 1982
Size:	7 ½" x 7 ½", 19.1 x 19.1 cm
Colour:	White and pink striped dress with white apron; background greens and browns - gloss

Description	U.S. $	Can. $	U.K. £
Mrs. Tiggywinkle	250.00	350.00	150.00

Note: Set of three with shape nos. 2594 and 2650.

Shape 2393 Christmas Plaque England 1972

NOVELTIES

Bookends, serviette holders, cruet sets, teapots, toothbrush holders, lemon squeezers, money boxes and hen baskets are some of the items to be found in this "fun" section. Here we find animals featuring in the majority of the shapes and some pieces actually modelled in the shapes of animals, eg. teapots.

It is hardly surprising that animals feature so prominently, as the House of Beswick was internationally known for its realistic and true to life modelling of a wide variety of animals (see *The Charlton Standard Catalogue of Beswick Animals*).

As with the Miscellaneous Section most of the items listed here are individuals, there is a good variety and some are very imaginative, such as the mirror featuring a polar bear (shape 287) a delightful piece, which is also very rare.

Although numbers were allocated to the shapes listed below, there is no indication that these items were ever put into commercial production: No 2346 Cat sellotape holder, 2354 and 2355 Mushroom salt and pepper, 2812 and 2813 Cat's Fun cups and 2818 Cat's Fun teapot.

Shape 87   **Dog bookends**

Designer: Unknown c.1933
Issued: 1934 - by 1963
Height: 6 ¼", 15.9 cm
Colour: 1. Assorted decorations - satin matt
              2. White - matt

Market	Range
U.S.A.	$75.00 - 175.00
Canada	$125.00 - 275.00
U.K.	£40.00 - 90.00

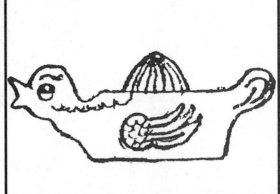

Shape 283   **Duck lemon squeezer**

Designer: Mr. Symcox c.1934
Issued: 1935 - by 1954
Height :   Unknown
Colour: 1. Assorted decorations - satin matt
              2. White - matt

Description	U.S. $	Can. $	U.K. £
Duck lemon squeezer		Rare	

Shape 284   **Lady with beret, serviette holder**

Designer: Mr. Watkin c.1934
Issued: 1935 - by 1940
Height: Unknown
Colour: Blonde hair with either a black or blue
              beret - gloss

Description	U.S. $	Can. $	U.K. £
Serviette holder	175.00	250.00	90.00

Shape 287   **Stand with mirror and polar bear**

Designer: Mr. Watkin in 1934
Issued: 1935 - by 1954
Height: 6 ¾", 17.2 cm
Colour: White bear on blue ice - gloss

Description	U.S. $	Can. $	U.K. £
Stand with mirror and polar bear	200.00	300.00	100.00

Photograph not
available
at press time

Shape 311   Duck serviette holder

Designer:	Miss Greaves in 1934
Issued:	1935 - by 1940
Height:	2 ½", 6.4 cm
Colour:	1. Assorted decorations - satin matt
	2. White - matt

Market	Range
U.S.A.	$40.00 - 150.00
Canada	$60.00 - 200.00
U.K.	£20.00 - 70.00

Photograph not
available
at press time

Shape 312   Rabbit serviette holder

Designer:	Miss Greaves in 1934
Issued:	1935 - by 1940
Height:	2 ½", 6.4 cm
Colour:	1. Assorted decorations - satin matt
	2. White - matt

Market	Range
U.S.A.	$40.00 - 150.00
Canada	$60.00 - 200.00
U.K.	£20.00 - 70.00

Photograph not
available
at press time

Shape 313   Rabbit serviette holder

Designer:	Miss Greaves in 1934
Issued:	1935 - by 1940
Size:	2 ½", 6.4 cm
Colour:	1. Assorted decorations - satin matt
	2. White - matt

Market	Range
U.S.A.	$40.00 - 150.00
Canada	$60.00 - 200.00
U.K.	£20.00 - 70.00

Shape 376   Rabbit place card holder

Designer:	Unknown
Issued:	1936 - by 1954
Height:	2 ¼", 5.7 cm
Colour:	1. Assorted decorations - satin matt
	2. White - matt

Description	U.S. $	Can. $	U.K. £
Rabbit place card holder		Rare	

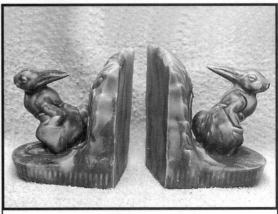

Shape 401   Lemon squeezer, two pieces

Designer: Unknown
Issued: 1936 - 1970
Height: 3 ½", 8.9 cm
Colour: Lemon, red or orange base, white top - gloss

Description	U.S. $	Can. $	U.K. £
Lemon squeezer	25.00	35.00	15.00

Shape 455   Rabbit bookends

Designer: Mr. Hayward in 1936
Issued: 1937 - by 1954
Size: 6 3/4", 17.2 cm
Colour: 1. Assorted decorations - satin matt
             2. White - matt

Market	Range
U.S.A.	$75.00 - 175.00
Canada	$125.00 - 275.00
U.K.	£40.00 - 90.00

Photograph not
available
at press time

**Shape 460   Cruet, Dutch boy and girl (salt and pepper)
                in boat with capstan (mustard)**

Designer: Mr. Symcox in 1936
Issued: 1937 - by 1940
Size: Unknown
Colour: 1. Assorted decorations - satin matt
             2. White - matt

Description	U.S. $	Can. $	U.K. £
Cruet		Rare	

Shape 472   George VI bookends

Designer: Mr. Weiss in 1937
Issued: 1937 - 1937
Size: Unknown
Colour: 1. Assorted decorations - satin matt
             2. White - matt

Market	Range
U.S.A.	$60.00 - 125.00
Canada	$90.00 - 175.00
U.K.	£30.00 - 60.00

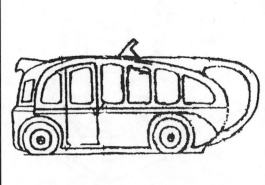

Shape 575   Laurel and Hardy cruet

Designer: Mr. Watkin in 1938
Issued: 1938 - 1968
Height: 4 ¼", 10.8 cm
Colour: Black, white, brown, with flesh coloured
             faces - gloss

Description	U.S. $	Can. $	U.K. £
Laurel and Hardy cruet	125.00	175.00	65.00

Shape 576   Bus teapot

Designer: Mr. Watkin in 1938
Issued: 1938 - by 1954
Size: Unknown
Colour: Unknown - gloss

Description	U.S. $	Can. $	U.K. £
Bus teapot		Rare	

Photograph not
available
at press time

Shape 577   Caravan preserve

Designer: Mr. Watkin in 1938
Issued: 1938 - by 1954
Size: 4 ½" x 3 ¾, 11.9 x 9.5 cm incl. knob
Colour: Green, black and silver - gloss

Description	U.S. $	Can. $	U.K. £
Caravan preserve		Rare	

Shape 590/610 Speedboat preserve

Designer: Mr. Watkin in 1938
Issued: 1938 - by 1954
Size: Unknown
Colour: Unknown

Description	U.S. $	Can. $	U.K. £
Speedboat preserve		Rare	

Shape 609   Chess cruet — salt, pepper, mustard, base

Designer: Mr. White in 1938
Issued: 1938 - by 1954
Size: Unknown
Colour: 1. Assorted decorations
          2. White - matt

Description	U.S. $	Can. $	U.K. £
Chess cruet		Rare	

Photograph not
available
at press time

Shape 613   Soldier cruet

Designer: Mr. White in 1938
Issued: 1938 - by 1954
Size: Unknown
Colour: Unknown

Description	U.S. $	Can. $	U.K. £
Soldier cruet		Rare	

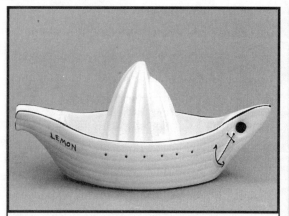

Shape 619   Yacht lemon squeezer

Designer: Mr. Hayward in 1938
Issued: 1938 - 1970
Height: 2 ¼", 5.7 cm
Colour: Orange, red, yellow or white - gloss

Market	Range
U.S.A.	$20.00 - 60.00
Canada	$30.00 - 90.00
U.K.	£10.00 - 30.00

Shape 624   Dog toothbrush holder

Designer: Miss Catford in 1938
Issued: 1938 - by 1954
Size: 4", 10.1 cm
Colour: 1. Brown and green - satin matt
          2. Blue - gloss

Colour	U.S. $	Can. $	U.K. £
1. Brown and green	300.00	350.00	150.00
2. Blue	300.00	350.00	150.00

Shape 625   Rabbit cruet

Designer:	Miss Catford in 1938
Issued:	1938 - by 1954
Size:	Unknown
Colour:	1. Assorted decorations - satin matt
	2. White - matt

Description	U.S. $	Can. $	U.K. £
Rabbit cruet		Rare	

Shape 663   Elephant toothbrush holder

Designer:	Miss Catford in 1938
Issued:	1938 - by 1954
Size:	4 ½", 11.9 cm
Colour:	1. Assorted decorations - satin matt
	2. White - matt
	3. Blue - gloss

Description	U.S. $	Can. $	U.K. £
Elephant toothbrush holder	325.00	425.00	175.00

Shape 664   Fox toothbrush holder

Designer:	Miss Catford in 1938
Issued:	1938 - by 1954
Size:	4 ¾", 12.1 cm
Colour:	1. Assorted decorations - satin matt
	2. White - matt
	3. Blue - gloss

Description	U.S. $	Can. $	U.K. £
Fox toothbrush holder	325.00	425.00	175.00

Shape 665   Rabbit toothbrush holder

Designer:	Miss Catford in 1938
Issued:	1938 - by 1954
Size:	4 ¾", 12.1 cm
Colour:	1. Assorted decorations - satin matt
	2. White - matt
	3. Blue - gloss

Description	U.S. $	Can. $	U.K. £
Rabbit toothbrush holder	325.00	425.00	175.00

Shape 742   Panda teapot (First version)

Designer: Mr. Watkin in 1939
Issued: 1939 - by 1954
Size: 6", 12.7 cm
Colour: Black and white panda with beige/yellow
             bamboo shoot - gloss

Description	U.S. $	Can. $	U.K. £
Panda teapot	125.00	175.00	65.00

Shape 751   Guard in sentry box bookend

Designer: Mr. Watkin in 1939
Issued: 1939 - by 1954
Size: 6", 15.0 cm
Colour: Black busby, red jacket and black
             trousers - gloss

Description	U.S. $	Can. $	U.K. £
Guard in sentry box	150.00	225.00	100.00

Shape 769   Duck night light holder

Designer: Mr. Watkin in 1939
Issued: 1939 - by 1954
Size: 6", 15 cm
Colour: White and yellow duck, orange beak - gloss

Description	U.S. $	Can. $	U.K. £
Duck night light holder	Rare		

Shape 940   Anderson Shelter bookends (pair)
Family (left), Warden (right)

Designer: Unknown
Issued: 1941 - by 1954
Size: Unknown
Colour: Ivory - gloss

Description	U.S. $	Can. $	U.K. £
Bookends	300.00	450.00	200.00

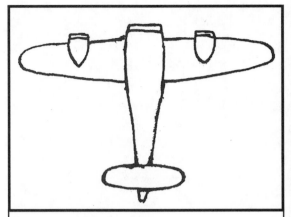

Shape 945   Aeroplane

Designer:	Mr. White in 1941
Issued:	1941 - by 1954
Size:	Unknown
Colour:	Unknown

Description	U.S. $	Can. $	U.K. £
Aeroplane		Rare	

Shape 952   Army co-operation bookends (pair)

Designer:	Unknown
Issued:	1941 - by 1954
Size:	Unknown
Colour:	Unknown

Description	U.S. $	Can. $	U.K. £
Bookends	300.00	450.00	200.00

Shape 1099   Cock and hen, salt and pepper

Designer:	Unknown
Issued:	1947 - 1959
Height:	2″, 5.0 cm
Colour:	Teal green, brown, yellow and red - gloss

Description	U.S. $	Can. $	U.K. £
Salt and pepper	65.00	90.00	40.00

Shape 1201   Friar liqueur set
              Monk, tray and six measures

Designer:	Arthur Gredington, Albert Hallam in 1950
Issued:	1950 - 1950
Size:	8 ¼″, 21.0 cm
Colour:	Brown with cream inners to measures - gloss

Description	U.S. $	Can. $	U.K. £
Friar liqueur set	150.00	225.00	75.00

Note: Special Commission for Heatmaster.

Shape 1760 Piggy bank

Designer:	Albert Hallam in 1961
Issued:	1961 - 1967
Height:	8 ½", 21.6 cm
Colour:	White, grey and pink - gloss

Description	U.S. $	Can. $	U.K. £
Piggy bank	125.00	165.00	75.00

Shape 1761 Foxy bank

Designer:	Albert Hallam in 1961
Issued:	1961 - 1967
Height:	8 ½", 21.6 cm
Colour:	Tan, brown and black on white - gloss

Description	U.S. $	Can. $	U.K. £
Foxy bank	125.00	165.00	75.00

Shape 1869 Dubonnet stand

Designer:	Albert Hallam in 1963
Issued:	Unknown
Size:	Unknown
Colour:	Blue with red lettering - gloss

Description	U.S. $	Can. $	U.K. £
Dubonnet stand	30.00	40.00	20.00

Shape 1870 Dubonnet bottle

Designer:	Albert Hallam in 1963
Issued:	Unknown
Height:	5 ½", 14.0 cm
Colour:	Unknown

Description	U.S. $	Can. $	U.K. £
Dubonnet bottle	30.00	40.00	20.00

Shape 1871 Dubonnet poodle

Designer:	Albert Hallam in 1963
Issued:	Unknown
Height:	4", 10.1 cm
Colour:	White - gloss

Description	U.S. $	Can. $	U.K. £
Dubonnet poodle	135.00	175.00	85.00

Shape 1872 Dubonnet bulldog

Designer:	Albert Hallam in 1963
Issued:	Unknown
Height:	3 ¾", 9.5 cm
Colour:	White - gloss

Description	U.S. $	Can. $	U.K. £
Dubonnet bulldog	135.00	135.00	85.00

Note: The four items (1869 to 1872) create one display. Special Commission. The dogs were available separately until 1967.

Shape 2135 Loaf, butter dish

Designer:	Albert Hallam in 1967
Issued:	1968 - 1970
Size:	5 ½" x 3 ¾", 14 x 9.5 cm
Colour:	Brown with dark brown top - gloss

Description	U.S. $	Can. $	U.K. £
Loaf, butter dish	35.00	50.00	20.00

Shape 2156-2157 Cat pepper and salt

Designer:	Harry Sales, Graham Tongue in 1967
Issued:	1968 - 1969
Height:	5 ½", 14 cm
Colour:	1. Shape — 2156 black - gloss
	2. Shape — 2157 white - gloss

Description	U.S. $	Can. $	U.K. £
1. Shape 2156 — black cat	75.00	100.00	50.00
2. Shape 2157 — white cat	75.00	100.00	50.00

Shape 2298 Hen basket

Designer:	Graham Tongue in 1969
Issued:	1970 - 1974
Height:	4 ½", 11.9 cm
Colour:	Brown with light brown basket - gloss

Description	U.S. $	Can. $	U.K. £
Hen basket	30.00	40.00	20.00

Shape 2306 Hen basket

Designer:	Graham Tongue in 1970
Issued:	1970 - 1980
Height:	8", 20.3 cm
Colour:	Brown with light brown basket - gloss

Description	U.S. $	Can. $	U.K. £
Hen basket	75.00	100.00	40.00

Photograph not
available
at press time

Photograph not
available
at press time

Shape 2346 Cat sellotape holder

Designer:	Unknown
Issued:	Unknown
Size:	Unknown
Colour:	Unknown - gloss

Description	U.S. $	Can. $	U.K. £
Cat sellotape holder		Rare	

Note: Possibly not issued.

Shape 2354-2355 Mushroom pepper and salt (pair)

Designer:	Graham Tongue in 1971
Issued:	Unknown
Height:	3 ½", 8.9 cm
Colour:	Unknown - gloss

Colour	U.S. $	Can. $	U.K. £
1. Shape 2354 — Pepper		Possibly	
2. Shape 2355 — Salt		not issued	

Shape 2397 Hen basket

Designer:	Albert Hallam, Graham Tongue in 1972
Issued:	1972 - 1972
Size:	8" x 8 ½", 20.3 x 21.6 cm
Colour:	Brown with light brown basket - gloss

Description	U.S. $	Can. $	U.K. £
Hen basket	125.00	175.00	70.00

Shape 2761 Cat on chimney pot, salt and pepper

Designer:	Unknown
Issued:	1982 - 1985
Size:	4", 20.1 cm
Colour:	White and gold - gloss
Series:	Fun ceramics

Description	U.S. $	Can. $	U.K. £
Salt and pepper	150.00	175.00	90.00

Shape 2792 Daisy the cow creamer

Designer:	Graham Tongue in 1982
Issued:	1982 - 1989
Height:	5 ¾", 14.6 cm
Colour:	Floral decorations, blue or yellow being the most common, on a white background - gloss
Series:	Fun ceramics

Description	U.S. $	Can. $	U.K. £
Daisy the cow creamer	125.00	150.00	50.00

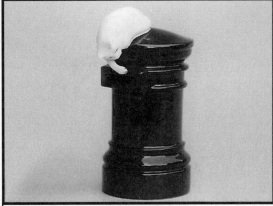

Shape 2805 Cat on post box, money box

Designer:	Unknown
Issued:	1983 - 1986
Height:	6 ¼", 15.9 cm
Colour:	White cat on red post box
Series:	Fun ceramics

Description	U.S. $	Can. $	U.K. £
Money box	100.00	125.00	75.00

Shape 2808 Money box — Saving for a rainy day

Designer:	Unknown
Issued:	1983 - 1986
Height:	5 ¼", 13.3 cm
Colour:	Shaded browns with red umbrella - gloss
Series:	Fun ceramics

Description	U.S. $	Can. $	U.K. £
Money box	100.00	125.00	75.00

Shape 2810 Cat egg cup

Designer:	Unknown
Issued:	1983 - 1986
Height:	2 ½", 6.4 cm
Colour:	Ginger kitten with white egg cup - gloss
Series:	Fun ceramics

Description	U.S. $	Can. $	U.K. £
Cat egg cup	75.00	100.00	50.00

Shape 3015-3105 Panda teapot

Designer:	Mr. Platt and Mr. Alcock in 1987
Issued:	1989 - 1990
Height:	6", 15 cm
Colour:	Black and white panda - gloss

Description	U.S. $	Can. $	U.K. £
Panda teapot	125.00	175.00	65.00

Note: Set of four with nos. 3138, 3139 and 3142.

Shape 3138 Cat teapot

Designer:	Mr. Alcock in 1988
Issued:	1989 - 1990
Size:	7 ¼", 18.4 cm
Colour:	White cat - gloss

Desription	U.S. $	Can. $	U.K. £
Cat teapot	125.00	175.00	65.00

Note: Set of four with nos. 3105, 3139 and 3142.

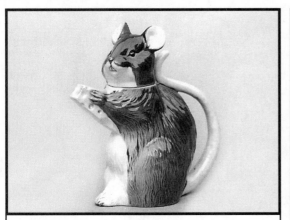

Shape 3139 Mouse teapot

Designer:	Mr. Platt in 1988
Issued:	1989 - 1990
Height:	7″, 17.8 cm
Colour:	White and brown mouse - gloss

Description	U.S. $	Can. $	U.K. £
Mouse teapot	125.00	175.00	65.00

Note: Set of four with nos. 3105, 3138 and 3142.

Shape 3142 Squirrel teapot

Designer:	Amanda Hughes in 1988
Issued:	1989 - 1990
Height:	7 ¼″, 18.4 cm
Colour:	Red squirrel, with white - gloss

Description	U.S. $	Can. $	U.K. £
Squirrel teapot	125.00	175.00	65.00

Note: Set of four with nos. 3105, 3138 and 3139.

MISCELLANEOUS

The shapes listed here do not fit into any of the other chapters in this book. Included are some items of tableware, preserve pots, honey pots, biscuit containers, cruets and ornaments. Most of these shapes are individual pieces and are not members of larger groups and sets.

For ornamental figures please see *The Charlton Standard Catalogue of Royal Doulton Beswick Figurines*.

Shape 377, an Edward VIII motif for use on other items, Shape 451 a Bust of Edward VIII and Shape 458 an Edward VIII jar were designed in anticipation of his coronation, and although a few were made, they were not put into full commercial production.

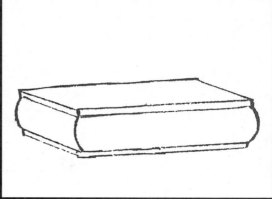

Shape 53   Rome preserve

Designer:	Unknown
Issued:	1931 - by 1940
Height:	3 ½", 8.9 cm
Colour:	1. Assorted decorations - gloss
	2. White

Market	Range
U.S.A.	$30.00 - 75.00
Canada	$45.00 - 100.00
U.K.	£15.00 - 35.00

Shape 89   Cigarette box

Designer:	Unknown
Issued:	1933 - by 1940
Size:	Unknown
Colour:	1. Assorted decorations - satin matt
	2. White

Market	Range
U.S.A.	$30.00 - 75.00
Canada	$45.00 - 100.00
U.K.	£15.00 - 35.00

Shape 170   Biscuit container

Designer:	Mr. Owen in 1933
Issued:	1933 - by 1954
Size:	4 ¾" x 5", 12.0 x 12.7 cm
Colour:	1. Assorted decorations - satin matt
	2. White

Market	Range
U.S.A.	$40.00 - 90.00
Canada	$60.00 - 125.00
U.K.	£20.00 - 45.00

Shape 202/2 Globe teapot

Designer:	Unknown
Issued:	1933 - by 1940
Size:	Unknown
Colour:	1. Assorted decorations - satin matt
	2. White

Market	Range
U.S.A.	$60.00 - 200.00
Canada	$90.00 - 300.00
U.K.	£30.00 - 100.00

Shape 206	**Apple shaped preserve with stand, (stalk used as a knob)**
Designer:	Mr. Symcox 1933
Issued:	1933 - 1940
Height:	5", 12.7 cm incl. stand
Colour:	1. Assorted decorations - gloss
	2. White

Market	Range
U.S.A.	$20.00 - 75.00
Canada	$30.00 - 100.00
U.K.	£10.00 - 40.00

Shape 207/1/2	**Preserve (available with or without stand)**
Designer:	1. Shape 207/1 — Mr. Symcox in 1933
	2. Shape 207/2 — Albert Hallam in 1950
Issued:	1. Shape 207/1 — 1933 - 1950
	2. Shape 207/2 — 1950 - 1970
Diameter:	3 ¾", 9.5 cm
Colour:	Lime green, orange, red or yellow - gloss

Market	Range
U.S.A.	$30.00 - 75.00
Canada	$45.00 - 100.00
U.K.	£15.00 - 35.00

Photograph not
available
at press time

Photograph not
available
at press time

Shape 209	**Baby plate**
Designer:	Albert Hallam in 1933
Issued:	1933 - by 1954
Size:	Unknown
Colour:	Unknown - gloss

Description	U.S. $	Can. $	U.K. £
Baby plate		Rare	

Shape 264	**Baby plate**
Designer:	Albert Hallam in 1933
Issued:	1933 - by 1954
Size:	Unknown
Colour:	Unknown - gloss

Description	U.S. $	Can. $	U.K. £
Baby plate		Rare	

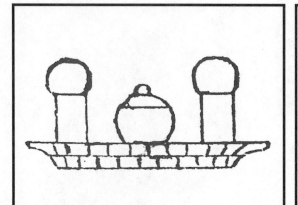

Shape 278   Cruet, three pieces on a stand

Designer:	Mr. Symcox in 1933
Issued:	1934 - by 1940
Size:	Unknown
Colour:	1. Assorted decorations - gloss
	2. White

Description	U.S. $	Can. $	U.K. £
Cruet		Rare	

Shape 318   Preserve with lid

Designer:	Mr. Symcox in 1933
Issued:	1934 - by 1940
Size:	Unknown
Colour:	1. Assorted decorations - gloss
	2. White

Market	Range
U.S.A.	$20.00 - 75.00
Canada	$30.00 - 100.00
U.K.	£10.00 - 40.00

Shape 319   Cruet

Designer:	Mr. Symcox in 1933
Issued:	1934 - by 1954
Size:	Unknown
Colour:	Green, blue, yellow, pink on cream
	background - gloss

Description	U.S. $	Can. $	U.K. £
Cruet	100.00	150.00	50.00

Photograph not
available
at press time

Shape 400   Teapot

Designer:	Mr. White in 1936
Issued:	1936 - by 1954
Size:	Unknown
Colour:	1. Assorted decorations - gloss
	2. White

Market	Range
U.S.A.	$60.00 - 200.00
Canada	$90.00 - 300.00
U.K.	£30.00 - 100.00

Shape 402   Beehive honey pot

Designer:	Unknown
Issued:	1936 - by 1962
Height:	4 ¾", 12.1 cm
Colour:	1. Brown or white - gloss
	2. White with coloured bees - gloss

Market	Range
U.S.A.	$40.00 - 75.00
Canada	$60.00 - 100.00
U.K.	£20.00 - 40.00

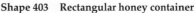

Photograph not
available
at press time

Shape 403   Rectangular honey container

Designer:	Unknown
Issued:	1936 - by 1954
Height:	4 ½", 11.9 cm
Colour:	Brown, white or white and gold - gloss

Description	U.S. $	Can. $	U.K. £
Honey container		Rare	

Shape 456   Biscuit container

Designer:	Mr. Symcox in 1936
Issued:	1936 - by 1954
Length:	7 ½", 19.1 cm
Colour:	1. Assorted decorations - satin matt
	2. White - matt

Market	Range
U.S.A.	$40.00 - 90.00
Canada	$60.00 - 125.00
U.K.	£20.00 - 45.00

Shape 468   Bust of George VI

Designer:	Mr. Weiss in 1937
Issued:	1937 - 1937
Size:	Unknown
Colour:	Ivory - satin matt

Description	U.S. $	Can. $	U.K. £
Bust of George VI	150.00	175.00	50.00

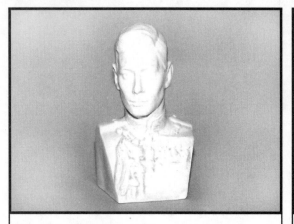

Shape 469   Bust of George VI

Designer: Mr. Weiss in 1937
Issued: 1937 - 1937
Size: Unknown
Colour: Ivory - satin matt

Colour	U.S. $	Can. $	U.K. £
Ivory	100.00	150.00	50.00

Photograph not
available
at press time

Shape 471   Head of George VI

Designer: Mr. Weiss in 1937
Issued: 1937 - 1937
Size: Unknown
Colour: Ivory - satin matt

Colour	U.S. $	Can. $	U.K. £
Ivory	100.00	150.00	50.00

Shape 474   Clock case

Designer: Mr. Symcox in 1937
Issued: 1937 - by 1954
Size: Unknown
Colour: 1. Assorted decorations - satin matt
             2. White - matt

Market	Range
U.S.A.	$40.00 - 125.00
Canada	$60.00 - 175.00
U.K.	£20.00 - 60.00

Shape 559   Biscuit container

Designer: Mr. Owen in 1937
Issued: 1937 - by 1954
Height: 5 ¼″, 13.3 cm
Colour: 1. Assorted decorations - satin matt
             2. White - matt

Market	Range
U.S.A.	$40.00 - 100.00
Canada	$60.00 - 150.00
U.K.	£20.00 - 50.00

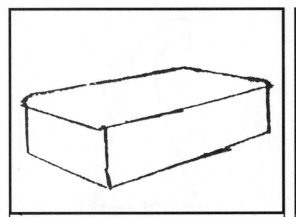

Shape 587 **Cigarette box**

Designer: Mr. Symcox in 1938
Issued: 1938 - by 1954
Size: Unknown
Colour: 1. Assorted decorations - satin matt
             2. White - matt

Market	Range
U.S.A.	$30.00 - 75.00
Canada	$45.00 - 100.00
U.K.	£15.00 - 35.00

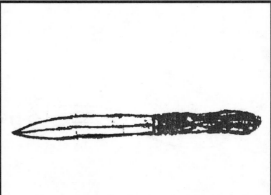

Shape 598 **Butter knife**

Designer: Mr. White in 1938
Issued: 1938 - by 1954
Size: Unknown
Colour: 1. Assorted decorations - satin matt
             2. White - matt

Market	Range
U.S.A.	$30.00 - 75.00
Canada	$45.00 - 100.00
U.K.	£15.00 - 35.00

Shape 599 **Spoon**

Designer: Mr. White in 1938
Issued: 1938 - by 1954
Size: Unknown
Colour: Assorted decorations - satin matt

Market	Range
U.S.A.	$30.00 - 40.00
Canada	$45.00 - 60.00
U.K.	£15.00 - 20.00

Photograph not
available
at press time

Shape 622 **Bust of Mr. Chamberlain**

Designer: Mr. Owen in 1938
Issued: 1938 - 1938
Size: Unknown
Colour: Ivory - satin matt

Description	U.S. $	Can. $	U.K. £
Bust of Chamberlain	100.00	150.00	50.00

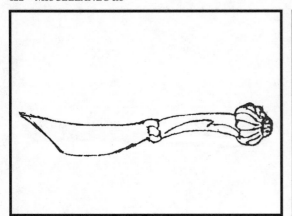

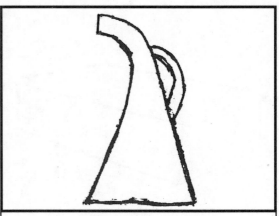

Shape 650   Butter knife

Designer: Mr. Watkin in 1938
Issued: 1938 - by 1954
Size: Unknown
Colour: Assorted decorations - satin matt

Market	Range
U.S.A.	$30.00 - 40.00
Canada	$45.00 - 60.00
U.K.	£15.00 - 20.00

Shape 684   Bath salts container

Designer: Mr. Owen in 1939
Issued: 1939 - by 1954
Size: Unknown
Colour: 1. Assorted decorations - satin matt
             2. White - matt

Market	Range
U.S.A.	$20.00 - 50.00
Canada	$30.00 - 75.00
U.K.	£10.00 - 30.00

Photograph not
available
at press time

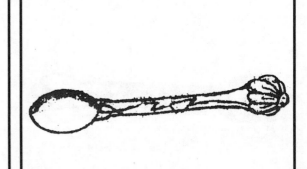

Shape 695/1/2   Butter dish in two sizes

Designer: Unknown
Issued: 1939 - by 1954
Size: Unknown
Colour: 1. Assorted decorations - satin matt
             2. White - matt

Market	Range
U.S.A.	$30.00 - 75.00
Canada	$45.00 - 100.00
U.K.	£15.00 - 35.00

Shape 730   Spoon

Designer: Mr. Watkin in 1939
Issued: 1939 - by 1954
Size: Unknown
Colour: Assorted decorations - gloss

Market	Range
U.S.A.	$30.00 - 75.00
Canada	$45.00 - 100.00
U.K.	£15.00 - 35.00

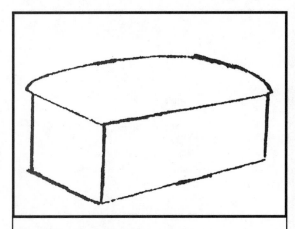

Shape 744   Cigarette box

Designer: Mr. Owen in 1939
Issued: 1939 - by 1954
Size: Unknown
Colour: 1. Assorted decorations - satin matt
             2. White - matt

Market	Range
U.S.A.	$30.00 - 75.00
Canada	$45.00 - 100.00
U.K.	£15.00 - 35.00

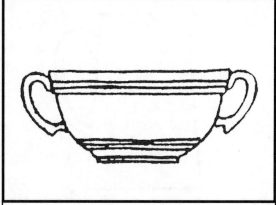

Shape 958/959 Soup bowl and soup saucer

Designer: Albert Hallam in 1941
Issued: 1941 - by 1954
Size: Unknown
Colour: White

Description	U.S. $	Can. $	U.K. £
Soup bowl and soup saucer	30.00	45.00	15.00

Shape 960   Tea caddy

Designer: Albert Hallam in 1941
Issued: 1941 - 1954
Size: Unknown
Colour: White

Description	U.S. $	Can. $	U.K. £
Tea caddy	30.00	45.00	15.00

Shape 983   R.A.F. Teapot

Designer: Unknown
Issued: 1942
Size: Unknown
Colour: Unknown

Description	U.S. $	Can. $	U.K. £
R.A.F. Teapot	40.00	60.00	20.00

Note: Special Commission in 1942.
Set of four with shapes 984, 985 and 986.

Shape 984   R.A.F. Jug

Designer: Unknown
Issued: 1942
Size: Unknown
Colour: Unknown - gloss

Description	U.S. $	Can. $	U.K. £
R.A.F. Jug	30.00	45.00	15.00

Note: Special commission in 1942.
Set of four with shapes 983, 985 and 986.

Photograph not
available
at press time

Shape 985   R.A.F. Cup and saucer

Designer: Unknown
Issued: 1942
Size: Unknown
Colour: Unknown - gloss

Description	U.S. $	Can. $	U.K. £
R.A.F. Cup and saucer	30.00	45.00	15.00

Note: Special commission in 1942.
Set of four with shapes 983, 984 and 986.

Shape 986   R.A.F. Jam dish

Designer: Unknown
Issued: 1942
Size: Unknown
Colour: Unknown - gloss

Description	U.S. $	Can. $	U.K. £
R.A.F. Jam dish	30.00	45.00	15.00

Note: Special commission in 1942.
Set of four with shapes 983, 984 and 985.

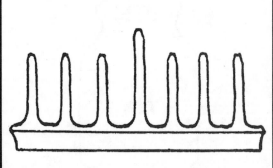

Shape 989   Toast rack, six slices

Designer: Mr. Watkin in 1942
Issued: 1942 - by 1954
Size: Unknown
Colour: Unknown - gloss

Colour	U.S. $	Can. $	U.K. £
Unknown	30.00	45.00	15.00

Shape 1339 Goblet

Designer:	Albert Hallam in 1954
Issued:	1954 - by 1963
Size:	Unknown
Colour:	1. Assorted decorations - satin matt
	2. White - matt

Market	Range
U.S.A.	$20.00 - 75.00
Canada	$30.00 - 100.00
U.K.	£10.00 - 35.00

Shape 1341 Minton tea cup

Designer:	Albert Hallam in 1954
Issued:	1954 - by 1965
Size:	Unknown
Colour:	Assorted decorations - gloss

Market	Range
U.S.A.	$10.00 - 20.00
Canada	$15.00 - 30.00
U.K.	£5.00 - 10.00

Photograph not
available
at press time

Photograph not
available
at press time

Shape 1376 Muffin

Designer:	Albert Hallam in 1955
Issued:	1955 - by 1959
Size:	8″, 20.3 cm
Colour:	1. Assorted decorations - gloss
	2. White

Description	U.S. $	Can. $	U.K. £
Muffin	Possibly not put into production		

Shape 1600/1601 Minton breakfast cup and saucer

Designer:	Albert Hallam in 1959
Issued:	1959 - by 1962
Size:	Unknown
Colour:	Assorted decorations - gloss

Market	Range
U.S.A.	$20.00 - 40.00
Canada	$30.00 - 60.00
U.K.	£10.00 - 20.00

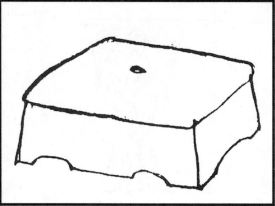

Shape 1610 Firefly dinghy

Designer:	Albert Hallam in 1959
Issued:	1959 - by 1963
Size:	5 ½″, 14 cm
Colour:	1. Blue boat with F261 on the sail - gloss
	2. Red boat with F126 on the sail - gloss

Description	U.S. $	Can. $	U.K. £
1. Blue boat	200.00	300.00	100.00
2. Red boat	200.00	300.00	100.00

Note: Set of four with no. 1633, 1634 and
1632 (wall plaque).

Shape 1619 Covered square butter

Designer:	Mr. Garbet in 1959
Issued:	Unknown
Size:	Unknown
Colour:	Unknown - gloss

Colour	U.S. $	Can. $	U.K. £
Unknown	25.00	35.00	15.00

Photograph not
available
at press time

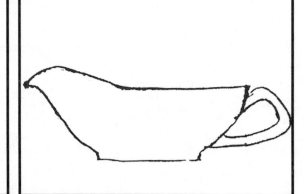

Shape 1621 Covered scallop

Designer:	Albert Hallam in 1959
Issued:	Unknown
Size:	Unknown
Colour:	Unknown - gloss

Colour	U.S. $	Can. $	U.K. £
Unknown	40.00	60.00	20.00

Shape 1622 Gravy boat

Designer:	Albert Hallam in 1959
Issued:	Unknown
Size:	Unknown
Colour:	Unknown - gloss

Colour	U.S. $	Can. $	U.K. £
Unknown	20.00	30.00	10.00

Shape 1630/1/2/3 Urn, three sizes

Designer: Albert Hallam in 1959
Issued: 1959 - 1971
Sizes: 1. Shape 1630/1 — 10", 25.4 cm
2. Shape 1630/2 — 8", 20.3 cm
3. Shape 1630/3 — 6", 12.7 cm
Colour: 1. Various decorations - satin matt
2. White or black - matt
3. Copper - lustre

Market	Range
Shape 1630/1	
U.S.A.	$40.00 - 100.00
Canada	$60.00 - 125.00
U.K.	£20.00 - 45.00
Shape 1630/2	
U.S.A.	$30.00 - 75.00
Canada	$45.00 - 100.00
U.K.	£15.00 - 40.00
Shape 1630/3	
U.S.A.	$20.00 - 90.00
Canada	$30.00 - 60.00
U.K.	£10.00 - 30.00

Shape 1633 Yacht GP 14

Designer: Albert Hallam in 1959
Issued: 1959 - by 1963
Height: 11 ¾", 29.8 cm
Colour: Red boat with 2242 on the sail - satin matt

Colour	U.S. $	Can. $	U.K. £
Red	300.00	450.00	150.00

Note: Set of four with nos. 1610, 1634 and 1632 (wall plaque)

Shape 1634 Yacht Heron

Designer:	Albert Hallam in 1959		
Issued:	1959 - by 1963		
Height:	9″, 22.9 cm		
Colour:	Red or blue boat with 1575 on the sail - satin matt		

Colour	U.S. $	Can. $	U.K. £
1. Red	250.00	375.00	125.00
2. Blue	250.00	375.00	125.00

Note: Set of four with nos. 1610, 1633 and 1632 (wall plaque).

Shape 1697 Mustard

Designer:	Albert Hallam in 1960
Issued:	Unknown
Size:	Unknown
Colour:	Unknown - gloss

Description	U.S. $	Can. $	U.K. £
Mustard	Possibly not put into production		

Note: Replaced by shape 1719 in 1960.

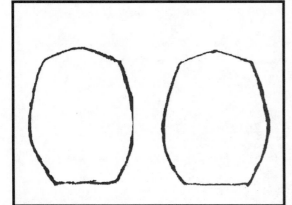

Shape 1698/1699 Salt and pepper

Designer:	Albert Hallam in 1960
Issued:	Unknown
Size:	Unknown
Colour:	Unknown - gloss

Description	U.S. $	Can. $	U.K. £
Salt and pepper	Possibly not put into production		

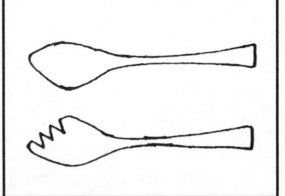

Shape 1700 Servers

Designer:	Albert Hallam in 1960
Issued:	Unknown
Size:	Unknown
Colour:	Various decorations - gloss

Description	U.S. $	Can. $	U.K. £
Servers	Possibly not put into production		

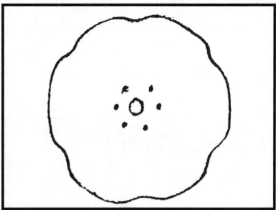

Shape 1739 Shave lotion container, replica of an 18th century gunpowder flask

Designer:	Albert Hallam in 1961
Issued:	Unknown
Size:	Unknown
Colour:	Ivory background with decoration in blues and greys - gloss

Description	U.S. $	Can. $	U.K. £
Shave lotion container	75.00	100.00	40.00

Note: Special commission for Royal Stag by Kosler.

Shape 1764 Cress drainer for fruit bowl

Designer:	Albert Hallam in 1961
Issued:	1961 - Unknown
Size:	Unknown
Colour:	Assorted decorations - gloss

Description	U.S. $	Can. $	U.K. £
Cress drainer	30.00	45.00	15.00

Shape 1797 Urn on pedestal with cover

Designer:	Albert Hallam in 1962
Issued:	1962 - 1968
Height:	1. 9 ½″, 22.9 with cover
	2. 7 ½″, 19.1 cm without cover
Colour:	1. Various decorations - satin matt
	2. White or black - matt
	3. Copper - lustre

Market	Range
U.S.A.	$30.00 - 90.00
Canada	$45.00 - 125.00
U.K.	£15.00 - 45.00

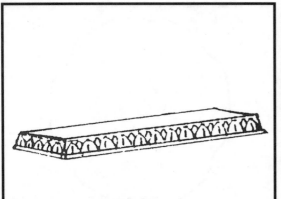

Shape 1809 Stand for horse

Designer:	Albert Hallam in 1962
Issued:	1962 - Unknown
Size:	Unknown
Colour:	1. Brown - gloss
	2. Copper - lustre

Colour	U.S. $	Can. $	U.K. £
1. Brown	20.00	30.00	10.00
2. Copper	20.00	30.00	10.00

Shape 1810 Urn with cover

Designer:	Albert Hallam in 1962
Issued:	1962 - 1969
Height:	1. 6 ½", 16.5 cm with cover
	2. 4 ½", 11.9 cm without cover
Colour:	1. Various decorations - satin matt
	2. White or black - matt
	3. Copper - lustre

Market	Range
U.S.A.	$20.00 - 75.00
Canada	$30.00 - 100.00
U.K.	£10.00 - 40.00

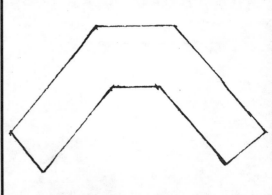

Shape 1819 Beehive honey pot

Designer:	Albert Hallam in 1962
Issued:	1962 - 1972
Height:	3 ¾", 9.5 cm
Colour:	1. Brown or white - gloss
	2. White with coloured bees and flowers - gloss

Colour	U.S. $	Can. $	U.K. £
1. Brown or white	30.00	45.00	15.00
2. White with coloured bees	30.00	45.00	15.00

Shape 1863 Stand for bull and cow or pigs

Designer:	Albert Hallam in 1963
Issued:	c.1963
Height:	1", 2.54 cm
Colour:	Unknown - gloss

Colour	U.S. $	Can. $	U.K. £
Unknown	18.00	25.00	10.00

Shape 1893/1894 Sugar and creamer

Designer: Albert Hallam in 1963
Issued: 1964 - 1971
Size: Sugar — 6" x 3", 15 x 7.6 cm
       Creamer - 4 ½", 11.9 cm
Colour: 1. Various decorations - satin matt
       2. White or black - matt
       3. Copper - lustre

Market	Range
Shape1893 — Sugar	
U.S.A.	$10.00 - 30.00
Canada	$15.00 - 45.00
U.K.	£5.00 - 15.00
Shape 1894 — Creamer	
U.S.A.	$10.00 - 30.00
Canada	$15.00 - 45.00
U.K.	£5.00 - 15.00

Shape 1893 — Sugar bowl

Shape 1894 — Creamer

Shape 1895 Grapefruit bowl

Designer: Albert Hallam in 1963
Issued: 1964 - 1972
Height: 3 ¼", 8.3 cm
Colour: Blue, mauve, maroon, mauve, pink
       or yellow - lustre

Description	U.S. $	Can. $	U.K. £
Grapefruit bowl	15.00	25.00	7.50

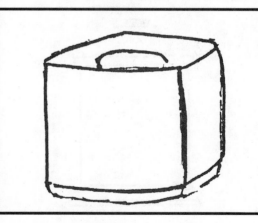

Shape 1914 Table lighter

Designer: Albert Hallam in 1963
Issued: 1963 - unknown
Height: 8 ½", 21.6 cm
Colour: Unknown - gloss

Description	U.S. $	Can. $	U.K. £
Table lighter	35.00	50.00	20.00

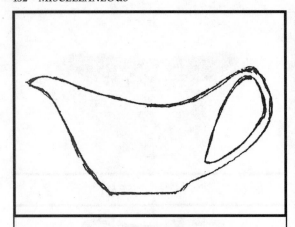

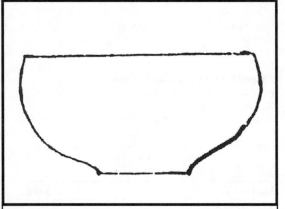

Shape 1920 Gravy boat and stand

Designer: Albert Hallam in 1963
Issued: 1963 - unknown
Size: Unknown
Colour: Unknown - gloss

Description	U.S. $	Can. $	U.K. £
Gravy boat and stand	30.00	45.00	15.00

Shape 1921 Sugar

Designer: Albert Hallam in 1964
Issued: Unknown
Size: Unknown
Colour: Unknown - gloss

Description	U.S. $	Can. $	U.K. £
Sugar	20.00	30.00	10.00

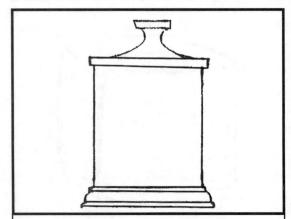

Shape 1931 Apothecary jar

Designer: Albert Hallam in 1964
Issued: 1964 - unknown
Height: 6 ½", 16.5 cm
Colour: Unknown - gloss

Description	U.S. $	Can. $	U.K. £
Apothecary jar	50.00	75.00	25.00

Shape 1945 Jar with lid

Designer: Albert Hallam in 1964
Issued: 1964 - unknown
Size: Unknown
Colour: Unknown - gloss

Description	U.S. $	Can. $	U.K. £
Jar with lid	30.00	45.00	15.00

Shape 1999 Bath oil bottle (pair with shape 2000)

Designer:	Albert Hallam in 1965
Issued:	c.1965
Size:	Unknown
Colour:	Very light lime green, light yellow or pink pearl - satin matt

Market	Range
U.S.A.	$30.00 - 50.00
Canada	$45.00 - 75.00
U.K.	£15.00 - 25.00

Note: Special commission for Cussons.

Shape 2000 Bath salts container (pair with shape 1999)

Designer:	Albert Hallam in 1965
Issued:	c.1965
Height:	6 ¼″, 15.9 cm incl. lid
Colour:	Very light lime green, light yellow or pink pearl - satin matt

Market	Range
U.S.A.	$30.00 - 50.00
Canada	$45.00 - 75.00
U.K.	£15.00 - 25.00

Note: Special commission for Cussons.

Shape 2040-2041-2042 Vinegar, Salt and Pepper

Designer:	Albert Hallam in 1965
Issued:	c.1965
Size:	1. Shape 2040 — 5 ¼″, 13.3 cm
	2. Shape 2041 — 5 ½″, 14.0 cm
	3. Shape 2042 — 5 ½″, 14.0 cm
Colour:	1. Various decorations - satin matt
	2. White or black - matt

Market	Range
U.S.A.	$10.00 - 30.00
Canada	$15.00 - 45.00
U.K.	£5.00 - 15.00

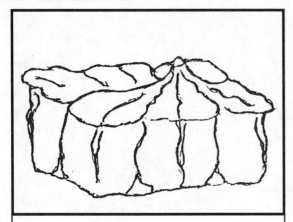

Shape 2043 Butter dish

Designer:	Albert Hallam in 1965
Issued:	c.1965
Size:	5 ¾″ x 3 ½″, 14.6 x 8.9 cm
Colour:	1. Various decorations - satin matt
	2. White or black - matt

Market	Range
U.S.A.	$20.00 - 50.00
Canada	$30.00 - 75.00
U.K.	£10.00 - 25.00

Shape 2054 Double egg cup

Designer:	Albert Hallam in 1966
Issued:	1966 - 1969
Height:	4″, 10.1 cm
Colour:	1. Various decorations - satin matt
	2. White or black - matt
	3. Copper - lustre

Market	Range
U.S.A.	$10.00 - 30.00
Canada	$15.00 - 45.00
U.K.	£5.00 - 15.00

Shape 2074 Porringer

Designer:	Graham Tongue in 1966
Issued:	1967 - 1971
Diameter:	5 ½″, 14 cm
Colour:	1. Various decorations - satin matt
	2. White or black - matt
	3. Copper - lustre

Market	Range
U.S.A.	$20.00 - 40.00
Canada	$30.00 - 60.00
U.K.	£10.00 - 20.00

Shape 2091 Double egg cup

Designer:	Graham Tongue in 1967
Issued:	1967 - 1969
Height:	3 ¾″, 9.5 cm
Colour:	Blue or yellow - gloss

Description	U.S. $	Can. $	U.K. £
Double egg cup	20.00	30.00	10.00

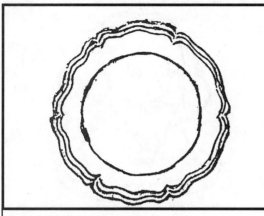

Shape 2136/1/2/3 Chippendale plates

Designer:	Albert Hallam, shape 2136/3 in 1967 and 2136/1/2 in 1968
Issued:	Shape 2136/1/2 — c.1968
	Shape 2136/3 — 1968 - 1971
Size:	Shape 2136/1 — 5", 12.7 cm
	Shape 2136/2 — 7", 17.8 cm
	Shape 2136/3 — 10", 25.4 cm

Market	Range
U.S.A.	$20.00 - 75.00
Canada	$30.00 - 100.00
U.K.	£10.00 - 35.00

Shape 2138 Wine taster

Designer:	Albert Hallam in 1967
Issued:	1968 - 1970
Height:	5 ½", 14.0 cm
Colour:	1. Black - matt
	2. Copper lustre with black gloss inner
	3. Pewter - satin matt

Market	Range
U.S.A.	$20.00 - 40.00
Canada	$30.00 - 60.00
U.K.	£10.00 - 20.00

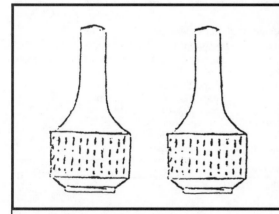

Shape 2151-2152 Salt and pepper

Designer:	Shape 2151 — G. Tongue, H. Sales in 1967
	Shape 2152 — G. Tongue
Issued:	1967 - unknown
Height:	5", 12.7 cm
Colour:	Unknown - gloss

Market	Range
U.S.A.	$20.00 - 30.00
Canada	$30.00 - 45.00
U.K.	£10.00 - 15.00

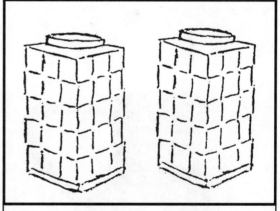

Shape 2154 -2155 Chimney - Pepper and salt

Designer:	Graham Tongue in 1967
Issued:	1967 - unknown
Height:	4", 10.1 cm
Colour:	Unknown - gloss

Market	Range
U.S.A.	$20.00 - 30.00
Canada	$30.00 - 45.00
U.K.	£10.00 - 15.00

Shape No 2179 - Honey pot

Designer:	Albert Hallam in 1968
Issued:	1968 - unknown
Height:	3 ¼", 8.3 cm
Colour:	Brown - gloss

Description	U.S. $	Can. $	U.K. £
Honey pot	50.00	75.00	25.00

Shape 2213 Bust of Shakespeare

Designer:	Graham Tongue in 1968
Issued:	1968 - unknown
Height:	3", 7.6 cm
Colour:	Unknown - satin matt

Description	U.S. $	Can. $	U.K. £
Bust of Shakespeare	75.00	100.00	35.00

Shape 2220/1/2/3 Measures

Designer:	Shape 2220/1 — Albert Hallam in 1968
	Shape 2220/2/3/ — Graham Tongue in 1968
Issued:	1969 - 1972
Height:	Shape 2220/1 — 5", 12.7 cm
	Shape 2220/2 — 4", 10.1 cm
	Shape 2220/3 — 3", 7.6 cm
Colour:	1. Pewteramic - satin matt
	2. White or black - matt
	3. Copper - lustre

Market	Range
Shape 2220/1	
U.S.A.	$10.00 - 40.00
Canada	$15.00 - 60.00
U.K.	£5.00 - 20.00
Shape 2220/2	
U.S.A.	$10.00 - 40.00
Canada	$15.00 - 60.00
U.K.	£5.00 - 20.00
Shape 2220/3	
U.S.A.	$10.00 - 40.00
Canada	$15.00 - 60.00
U.K.	£5.00 - 20.00

Shape 2227   **Shakespeare book**

Designer:	Graham Tongue in 1968
Issued:	1968 - unknown
Length:	6″, 15.0 cm
Colour:	Unknown - satin matt

Description	U.S. $	Can. $	U.K. £
Shakespeare book	60.00	90.00	30.00

Shape 2243   **Shakespeare bust on pedestal**

Designer:	Graham Tongue in 1968
Issued:	1968 - unknown
Height:	5″, 12.7 cm
Colour:	Ivory - satin matt

Description	U.S. $	Can. $	U.K. £
Bust on pedestal	100.00	150.00	50.00

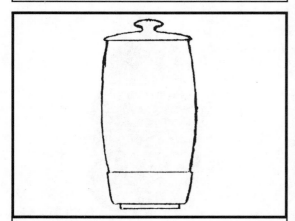

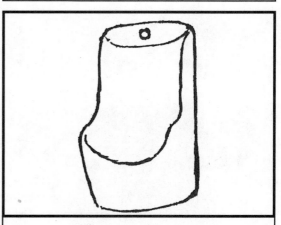

Shape 2260   **Bemax jar**

Designer:	Albert Hallam in 1969
Issued:	c.1969
Size:	Unknown
Colour:	Unknown - gloss

Description	U.S. $	Can. $	U.K. £
Bemax jar	20.00	30.00	10.00

Note: Special Commission.

Shape 2270   **Shaving brush stand**

Designer:	Graham Tongue in 1969
Issued:	c.1969
Height:	4 ½″, 11.9 cm
Colour:	Unknown - gloss

Description	U.S. $	Can. $	U.K. £
Shaving brush stand	20.00	30.00	10.00

Note: Special Commission. Pair with shape 2313.

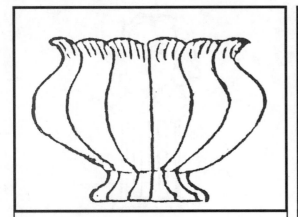

Shape 2289 Sugar (pair with shape 2290)

Designer:	Graham Tongue in 1969
Issued:	1969 - 1970
Height:	2 ¼", 5.7 cm
Colour:	1. Various decorations - satin matt
	2. White or black - matt
	3. Copper - lustre

Market	Range
U.S.A.	$10.00 - 30.00
Canada	$15.00 - 45.00
U.K.	£5.00 - 15.00

Shape 2290 Cream Jug (pair with shape 2289)

Designer:	Graham Tongue in 1969
Issued:	1969 - 1970
Height:	3 ½", 8.9 cm
Colour:	1. Various decorations - satin matt
	2. White or black - matt
	3. Copper - lustre

Market	Range
U.S.A.	$10.00 - 30.00
Canada	$15.00 - 45.00
U.K.	£5.00 - 15.00

Shape 2295 Display Stand for Beatrix Potter Figures

Designer:	A. Brindley in 1969
Issued:	1969 - 1989
Size:	12 ½" X 2 ½", 31.7 x 6.4 cm
Colour:	Shaded browns and greens - gloss

Description	U.S. $	Can. $	U.K. £
Display stand	75.00	100.00	40.00

Note: Transferred to Royal Albert backstamp.

Shape 2304 Honey Jar Container

Designer:	Albert Hallam in 1970
Issued:	1970 - 1972
Size:	Unknown
Colour:	Brown - gloss

Description	U.S. $	Can. $	U.K. £
Honey jar container	75.00	100.00	35.00

Shape 2313 Shaving brush handle (pair with 2270)

Designer: Graham Tongue in 1969
Issued: c.1969
Size: Unknown
Colour: Unknown - gloss

Description	U.S. $	Can. $	U.K. £
Shaving brush handle	15.00	25.00	8.00

Note: Special Commission

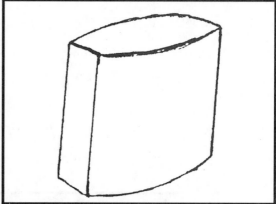

Shape 2347 Napkin holder

Designer: Unknown
Issued: Unknown
Size: 4″, 10.1 cm
Colour: Unknown - gloss

Description	U.S. $	Can. $	U.K. £
Napkin holder	30.00	45.00	15.00

Shape 3017-3028-3029-3044-3068 Ceramic plinths

Designer: Graham Tongue 1986-1987
Issued: c.1987
Length: Shape 3017 — 11″
           Shape 3028 — 5 ½″
           Shape 3029 — 13″
           Shape 3044 — 9 ½″
           Shape 3068 — unknown (circular)
Colour: Green top, brown sides - gloss

Market	Range
U.S.A.	$10.00 - 30.00
Canada	$15.00 - 45.00
U.K.	£5.00 - 15.00

Note: These ceramic plinths were used for mounting animal models for Special Commissions (see *The Charlton Standard Catalogue of Beswick Animals*.)

Warning: Surplus plinths were made available to the public and have since been found mounted with other makes of animals not produced by Beswick.

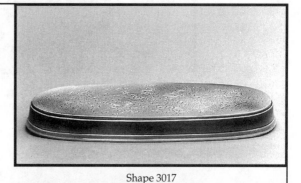

Shape 3017

Shape 3044

"Douglas" Plant Pot

INDEX

Turquoise Cathay